JZ
1254
.F73
2002

D0930114

LAUNCHING INTO CYBERSPACE

iPolitics: Global Challenges in the Information Age

Renée Marlin-Bennett, series editor

LAUNCHING INTO CYBERSPACE

Internet Development and Politics in Five World Regions

MARCUS FRANDA

LYNNE
RIENNER
PUBLISHERS

BOULDER
LONDON

Published in the United States of America in 2002 by
Lynne Rienner Publishers, Inc.
1800 30th Street, Boulder, Colorado 80301
www.rienner.com

and in the United Kingdom by
Lynne Rienner Publishers, Inc.
3 Henrietta Street, Covent Garden, London WC2E 8LU

© 2002 by Lynne Rienner Publishers, Inc. All rights reserved

Library of Congress Cataloging-in-Publication Data
Franda, Marcus F.
    Launching into cyberspace : Internet development and politics in five world
      regions / Marcus Franda.
      p. cm. — (iPolitics)
    Includes bibliographical references and index.
    ISBN 1-58826-012-7 (alk. paper) — ISBN 1-58826-037-2 (pbk. : alk. paper)
    1. International relations. 2. Technological innovations. 3. Internet.
4. International relations—Case studies. I. Title. II. iPolitics
JZ1254.F73 2001
327'.0285'4678—dc21   2001031627

British Cataloguing in Publication Data
A Cataloguing in Publication record for this book
is available from the British Library.

Printed and bound in the United States of America

       The paper used in this publication meets the requirements
   ⊗ of the American National Standard for Permanence of
       Paper for Printed Library Materials Z39.48-1984.

5 4 3 2 1

To seven grandchildren—Emily and Jaimee,
Jeffory and Timothy, Nicholas (nació el Cinco de Mayo),
Andrew Emerson, and Laura Vonetta—
With the hope that they all become true world
citizens and leaders of the first generation to
grow to adulthood in the twenty-first century

May they advance humankind's search for
knowledge and the quest for world order

Contents

Acknowledgments

An appreciation of the complexities of the relationship between technology and political and economic development first became possible for me in the 1960s and 1970s, during a period when I was offering seminars at centers of advanced technology in the United States and Europe while conducting research in Asia, Africa, and the Middle East—often from a research residence maintained over a sixteen-year period in India. As a senior associate of the American Universities Field Staff (AUFS), which later became Universities Field Staff International, and a research associate at the Center for International Studies at the Massachusetts Institute of Technology (MIT), I would offer seminars at MIT, Dartmouth, Cal Tech, and other Field Staff campuses in the United States, as well as at Cambridge University in England, the Sorbonne in France, the AUFS Center in Rome, and other European sites. The degree of familiarity with the latest technological inventions at these meetings, and especially the enthusiasm for computer technology among seminar participants, contrasted sharply with research interviews and studies out in "third world" research situations—there I found myself interacting with peasants, clerics, policymakers, business people, scientists, students, and faculty who were much more skeptical than their Western counterparts about the efficacy of advanced technology and far more cautious about its adoption into their societies.

Ideas for a research project specifically focusing on the diffusion of computer (and eventually Internet) technology across several world regions first occurred to me during the summer seminars I offered as director of the Institute of World Affairs (founded with substantial support from Thomas Watson of IBM) in Salisbury, Connecticut, in the early 1980s. These initial ideas were nurtured during my years with the Asia Foundation in the mid-1980s and began to take on greater clarity once I joined the University of Maryland as professor and director of international affairs in 1989. I am particularly grateful to William E. Kirwan, with whom I had the opportunity to work closely during his ten years as president of the University of Maryland, for the many professional and research doors he opened for my colleagues and me before he left in 1999 to become president of Ohio State University. The happy arrangement under which I have worked at College Park—with research time and funding to balance administrative and teaching commitments—was put together by Irving Goldstein, currently dean of behavioral and social sciences, and George Quester, currently professor of government and politics, when they were provost and department chair, respectively, during my first year on the faculty in 1989. Support from the current department chair, Jonathan Wilkenfeld, as well as from colleagues in the department generally, has been important in easing my transition back into a research and teaching mode in political science after ten years of intense concentration on building Maryland's interdisciplinary international affairs capabilities.

Most of the intellectual debts incurred in writing this book are detailed in the notes and bibliography, but I would particularly like to thank the many colleagues at Maryland not otherwise mentioned who contributed to the completion of the project. Much of my education in and exposure to the politics and diplomacy of Central/Eastern Europe and Eurasia have been provided over the past dozen years by Karen Dawisha (now Walter E. Havighurst Professor of Political Science and director of the Havighurst Center for Russian and Post-Soviet Societies at Miami University of Ohio) and the team she put together at College Park as part of the large-scale "Russian Littoral" project with which I was fortunate enough to be involved from its inception. The opportunities to travel through portions of Central Asia with Karen and with Janine Ludlam (then executive director of the Russian Littoral project), to team teach a course on Central Asia with Karen, to meet and work with the many Russian Littoral project fellows, and to sit in on the seminars planned by Karen and the codirector of the Russian Littoral project—Bruce Parrott of the Johns Hopkins School of Advanced International Studies—were rare privileges, much appreciated for helping me understand this complex geographic expanse.

A second major influence on my understanding of Central/Eastern Europe and Eurasia has been the IRIS (Institutional Reform and the

Informal Sector) project at Maryland, creatively established by Mancur Olson in 1990 and carried on by Charles Cadwell and his associates after Mancur's death in 1999. It was my good fortune to be invited by Mancur to help develop the IRIS project when I came to Maryland in 1989, and IRIS repaid incalculable dividends by providing innumerable opportunities to learn from the project's many activities over the next decade. My education in Central and Eastern Europe was also enhanced by involvement as project leader of a study team focusing on Hungary, the Czech Republic, and Poland for the American Council for International Leadership in the early 1990s; as an initial board member and, later, participant in the activities of the Center for the Study of Post-Communist Societies in the mid-1990s; and as leader of a series of Fulbright International Center seminars on Central and Eastern Europe in the late 1990s, organized within the Office of International Affairs and culminating in a semester-long for-credit seminar in spring 2000.

Faculty colleagues in the Department of Government and Politics at Maryland who have read portions of this book in manuscript form and offered helpful comments include Shibley Telhami, incumbent of the Sadat Chair for Population, Development, and Peace; Suheil Bushrui, incumbent of the Baha'i Chair for World Peace; Vlad Tismaneanu, director of the Center for the Study of Post-Communist Societies; and Virginia Haufler, Bart Kaminski, Margaret Pearson, and Karol Soltan. Ernest Wilson III, director of the Center for International Development and Conflict Management (CIDCM), has not only given me a congenial physical home at the center but has also familiarized me with some of the literature on information technology that he knows so well and has introduced me to a number of institutions and people who made valuable contributions to various aspects of this study. I have depended on many of the projects on Africa that Ernie has brought to College Park for my education on information technology in that important part of the world. Colleagues Charles Butterworth and Edy Kaufman put me in touch with readings on and people in the Middle East who were particularly helpful in exploring some of the more complex and otherwise unreachable aspects of the study.

Jayanta Sircar, longtime director of information technologies at Maryland's Clark School of Engineering and now at Harvard, deepened my understanding of Internet development in India, as did Kalyani Chadha, who in 1999 received a Ph.D. for a first-rate dissertation on telecommunications in India from Maryland's Philip Merrill College of Journalism. Lee Preston, professor emeritus in the Robert H. Smith School of Business at Maryland, has been a constant source of support and encouragement for many research activities related to this study, as well as a mentor in international regime theory.

The people who keep CIDCM functioning—particularly Executive Director Carola Weil and Program Coordinator Barbara Bartsch-Allen—were invaluable in providing logistical backup, as was the support staff in the department: Cissy Abu Rumman, Karen Bond, To Anh Chang, Szilvia Rohoska, and David Del Marr. Graduate students Michael Dravis, John Watson, and Sepedeh Hooshidari were far more patient and responsive to my pleas for help than one could expect, always making me feel as though I were part of the "family" that Suheil Bushrui and the Baha'i Chair supporters have so thoughtfully put together at Maryland. Adedayo Adekson, a graduate student in the department, was a constant resource on Africa and shared many ideas extremely useful to this book and to some of my other research projects.

Many of the conclusions reached about China were developed during innumerable visits to universities, research institutes, and other organizations in the People's Republic of China, Hong Kong, and Taiwan over the past two decades. I particularly want to thank faculty and administrators, many of them University of Maryland alumni, with whom I interacted regularly in the 1990s—from Peking and Tsinghua Universities in Beijing, Fudan University in Shanghai, Nanjing and Southeast Universities in Nanjing, the University of Science and Technology in Hefei, Hong Kong University of Science and Technology, and in Taiwan, Academia Sinica, National Taiwan University, the Institute of International Relations, and computer science–related organizations at National Chengchi University.

Working with the many wonderful people Lynne Rienner has assembled at her publishing company has been a special experience. Lynne was involved in an earlier book that I wrote on the Seychelles, and I never thought I would find her equal as an editorial expert, but Shena Redmond and her colleagues were very much up to the challenge—for this book and a previous book in this series. I learned a great deal from Shena's editorial interactions, and especially appreciated the spirit and enthusiasm that she, Sally Glover, and Renée Marlin-Bennett—editor of the iPolitics series—brought to these two book projects.

None of the above would agree with everything in this book, nor should they, but all of them played roles in making it possible. Responsibility for content is solely mine.

— *Marcus Franda*

Introduction:
The Internet and World Politics

When one sets out to explore the impact of the Internet on international relations, two rather extreme positions stand as outposts that circumscribe the literature. One is the argument—what the *Economist* once called the "founding myth" of the Internet—that it was created by people acting outside the control of governments and international order and would in the future *not* be subject to the old laws of nation-states and previous rules of trade and diplomacy.[1] In an article that describes many elements of this position, Neil Munro summarized the argument as follows:

> In cyberspace, borders and national sovereignty lose meaning, and the individual reigns. The sovereign power of nation-states and national governments rose in lockstep with artillery and the Industrial Revolution—and will probably shrink as the age of mass production is supplanted by the information-powered age of catalogued, customized, cross-border consumerism. For decades, nation-states have been losing autonomy on the big issues of war and wealth because democracy, international trade, global financial markets, and the spread of conventional and nuclear weapons have all eroded their power. Over the next few years, the Internet will restrict their sovereignty in the not-so-big things—taxes, regulation, and public expectations.[2]

Perhaps the most extreme assertions of this position have come from technology and business leaders at the intersection of activities where the Internet becomes enmeshed with international affairs. Richard L. Brandt, a senior editor at the Internet-driven business magazine *Upside,*

1

for example, argued in September 1998 that the Internet has made "local laws . . . unenforceable globally," with the result that "the lowest common denominator—in other words, the weakest laws—will win." In Brandt's view, lack of enforcement of law internationally will so weaken the control of governments throughout the world that he predicted: "I expect to see the overthrow of the U.S. government in my lifetime."[3]

At the opposite extreme of what one might call the libertarian position of Internet activists are the writings of Lawrence Lessig, a law professor at Harvard University, and Andrew Shapiro, a former student of Lessig's.[4] Although Lessig and Shapiro focus on different aspects of Internet impacts, both argue that the revolutionary potential of the Internet for liberating people from previous forms of government control might well result in its architecture being used to "re-enable" whomever is responsible for writing Internet "code" to assume positions of power and influence over the lives of individuals—on a worldwide basis—to a degree unimaginable under nineteenth- and twentieth-century international systems. Lessig believes that "change is possible. I don't doubt that revolutions remain in our future; the open code movement is just such a revolution. But I fear that it is too easy for the government to dislodge these revolutions, and that too much will be at stake for it to allow the revolutionaries to succeed."[5] In contrast to predictions that computer code will be written by computer experts acting as individuals to promote libertarian values, Lessig and Shapiro argue that code is already under the authority of large companies and governments—"corporate in a commercial sense"—and that a number of network architectures have been developed that "would enable sovereigns to reclaim some of their authority." In Lessig's view, "Sovereigns will get this. They will come to understand that there is a different architecture for the Net that would re-enable their own control."[6]

The conclusion of this book is that, at least thus far, the relationship between the Internet and international relations has not developed on a worldwide basis toward either of the extremes described here. To be sure, for short periods of time in specific countries, individuals could feel a sense of exhilaration about the unprecedented freedom that accompanied the global spread of the Internet, particularly in its early stages. This was the case, for example, in the United States in the early to mid-1990s, when e-mail became possible for a fairly substantial number of people and the wonders of the World Wide Web were first evident and imaginable. It was the case in China in the mid-1990s, immediately following the 1994 decision by the People's Republic of China's (PRC) leadership that development of the Internet by Chinese computer experts and engineers would be encouraged but before State Council Order No. 195 was promulgated on February 1, 1996, leading to governmental organization and regulations that have since limited—with varying degrees of effectiveness—Internet content available within the PRC.[7]

In almost all countries, governments have stepped in to regulate and develop rules and laws for administering Internet behavior, both within nations and between nations. In doing so, in many instances autocratic rulers, companies seeking unfair advantage, and meddling bureaucrats or legislators have tried to either exploit or curb the growing power of the Internet, often in nontransparent ways. But they have at least been counterbalanced by a vast array of judicial challenges, intellectual discussion, and creative policymaking—at both the national and international levels in different parts of the world—that have provided considerable evidence that the Internet can (but will not necessarily) promote the values of open democratic societies. The goal of this volume is to gain some sense of the complex interaction taking place between Internet development and the changing nature of international relations in the early twenty-first century in five large and important specific regions of the world: Africa, the Middle East, Asia, Eurasia, and Central/Eastern Europe.

Because of its unprecedented global dimension, reach, and pervasiveness, the Internet has offered major challenges to existing law—at the local, national, and international levels—and is creating new dilemmas for governance, particularly in relationships between nations. The goal of this book is to understand empirically some of the complexities of the impact of the Internet on international relations in these early years of the Internet's existence, not with the overt intention of predicting inevitable changes into the future but rather by simply trying to determine what has actually happened to the Internet at the international level thus far. An assumption of this work is that the Internet has been received rather differently and has had differing impacts in the various regions and countries of the world and that an understanding of the relationship between the Internet and international relations will require familiarity with these differences. It is hoped that an empirical analysis of the Internet, based on this approach, will not only enable us to eventually gain more reliable predictive capabilities about the future of the Internet and information technology (IT) but will also shed light on some of the more important aspects of the discipline of international relations where the impact of the new information technology has been significant.

This volume is part of a larger long-term study I am organizing to understand the role of international regimes in the development of modern information technology. The first volume in this larger research project attempted to relate the existing theoretical literature on international regimes to the embryonic regime developing for the global Internet, necessarily emphasizing developments taking place primarily in the advanced IT societies of North America, Europe, and Japan.[8] The present book seeks to extend this analysis to five additional world regions—Africa, the Middle East, the former Soviet portions of Eurasia, Central and Eastern Europe, and the two largest nations in Asia (China and India)—each of which has been much less involved with the international regime for the Internet than those parts of the world discussed in detail in the first volume. Taken together, the portions of the world covered in these first two volumes contain more than 80 percent of the global population. A third volume, comparing the development of Internet use and IT in China and India in the context of their great power rivalry, should be available in 2002.[9] It is hoped that as part of the larger research project, future studies can be devoted to those remaining regions of the world—Latin America and Central America, Southeast Asia and the remaining sections of East Asia, Australia and New Zealand—not explored in the first three volumes.

Chapter 1 of the present volume examines various ways the Internet has affected and has been affected by international relations in the early years of its existence, particularly in Africa and other less developed countries (LDCs), and provides a basic outline of the rationale for this book in the context of the emerging international regime for the Internet. Chapters 2 and 3 focus on the Middle East; Chapters 4, 5, and 6 focus on Central/Eastern Europe and Eurasia. These chapters detail ways each region has reacted differently to the spread of the global Internet, with equally diverse consequences for their international relationships. Because of the size and dimensions of the world's two largest nations, it was necessary to include detailed analyses of Internet development in China and India in a separate volume, but Chapter 7 in the current volume compares Internet development in these two Asian giants in a manner relevant to the current volume while summarizing conclusions reached in the more detailed study.

The five geographic areas discussed in this volume were selected for initial intensive analysis primarily because they have responded in such distinctly different ways to the development of the Internet and because each is likely to play a key role in shaping discrete aspects of the Internet's development into the future. An additional factor was the opportunity I had over the past few decades to gain access in these geographic regions to the kinds of data and research facilities necessary to conduct meaningful research. This was more than anything a result of serendipitous factors, such as teaching and administrative responsibilities that directed or made possible travel for research to one area rather than another. Choice of world regions for more intensive study was not the result of any structural impediment imposed by any country in any part of the world. The three major parts of the world that are not dealt with in the first three volumes—Central and Latin America, Southeast Asia and portions of East Asia, and Australia/New Zealand—would each present a wealth of additional material on Internet development and international Internet regime formation, some of which is briefly alluded to in various parts of the present book.

■ **NOTES**

1. The term *founding myth* appears in "The Internet: Founding Myths," p. 4.
2. Munro, "Governments Off-Line," p. 3380.
3. Brandt, "It's the Internet, Damn It!" p. 18.
4. See Lessig, *Code,* and Shapiro, *The Control Revolution.*
5. Lessig, *Code,* p. 8.
6. All quotes in this subparagraph are from ibid., p. 207.
7. For an analysis of the early years of the Internet in China see Tan, Foster, and Goodman, "China's State-Coordinated Internet Infrastructure," pp. 44–52.
8. See Franda, *Governing the Internet.*
9. Franda, "China and India Online."

1

Thin Cyberspace
in Africa and the LDCs

The major difference the Internet has brought to international relations at the beginning of the twenty-first century is a vast reduction in the cost of communicating and sending data across great distances in the most developed parts of the world. Whereas all forms of interactive transcontinental communication prior to the Internet were too expensive to be used except by the wealthy and very sparingly by others, the purchase of a computer and access to the Internet make frequent global communication affordable to many more people than would previously have thought of using an international telephone line or sending a cable. For many people, banks, corporations, and other organizations in the developed world, this reduction in the cost of international communications transactions has amounted to a paradigm shift. As the keynote speaker at the 1999 annual meeting of the National Association for Business Economics pointed out, a firm that spent $300,000 per year gathering international market information in the early 1990s needed to spend only $2,000 in 1999 to get 80 percent of that information over the Internet, with the added benefit that the Internet allows much greater possibilities for instant interaction because of the vastly reduced cost of two-way communication.[1]

Even before the Internet became a worldwide phenomenon in the 1990s, the cost of storing, transmitting, and processing information had been dropping in the economically developed parts of the world during the previous two decades, on average, *by 25 to 35 percent per year*— producing a megatrend unprecedented in history for the cost of so important an economic factor to drop so rapidly for such an extended period of time over such a large geographic area. In the United States, where this reduction in cost was almost immediately passed on to the consumer through competition among private companies, the speed of evolution for information technology escalated rapidly during the last thirty years of the twentieth century. By 1996 four companies (AT&T, MCI, World-Com, and Sprint) had installed capacities in long-distance telephone lines of one terabit per second—in other words, the capability of handling 15 million simultaneous phone conversations—capacity that has continued to grow, has been extended to many parts of the world and to other companies, and has made possible unimagined use of the Internet since 1996.[2] This massive increase in the capacity to communicate, combined with an increase in the competition to handle it, has reduced the cost of sending information in some societies to points approaching zero and has set in motion the revolution in information technology (IT) that has fueled financial markets in the developed economies.

The Information Society Index (ISI) for the year 2001, assembled by International Data Corporation (IDC) and the World Times, identified 55 countries (accounting for 97 percent of global gross national product [GNP] and 99 percent of IT expenditures) as among those with the basic infrastructures needed to take advantage of the information age. This leaves 131 independent states without such infrastructures at the onset of the twenty-first century.[3] Among the 55 leaders, only 16 (the United States, Canada, and Australia; the Scandinavian countries; Japan, Singapore, and Hong Kong; and six other countries of Western Europe) ranked among the leading countries in three successive annual IDC/World Times indexes (1999, 2000, 2001), identified as the countries "in a strong position to take full advantage of the Information Revolution because of advanced information, computer, Internet and social infrastructures."[4] A second tier of 12 countries (New Zealand, Taiwan, South Korea, Israel, the Czech Republic, and seven other countries of Western Europe) were identified in the index as having "much of the necessary infrastructure in place." A third tier of 15 countries (primarily from Central and Eastern Europe, Latin America, and Southeast Asia but including South Africa, the United Arab Emirates, Russia, Mexico, and Turkey) were described in the 2001 index as "moving forward in spurts" but being held back somewhat by shifts in priorities as a result of domestic "economic, social, and political pressures." The last 12 of the 55 countries on the ISI2001 list (including Saudia Arabia, Jordan, Egypt, China, Indonesia, Peru, India, and Pakistan, plus three countries in Latin America and three in Southeast Asia) were analyzed as "moving ahead, but inconsistently, often because of limited financial resources in relation to their vast populations."

▪ GLOBALIZATION AND INTERDEPENDENCE

Although many aspects of the information revolution have been responsible for lowering the cost of storing, processing, and transmitting data since the early 1970s, the twin inventions of the Internet and the World Wide Web more than anything else spread or, more accurately, seem destined to spread the information revolution throughout the world.[5] Significant internationalization of the information revolution has given rise to a vast literature on globalization that has become part of everyday speech, with the word *globalization* meaning many different things to many different people.[6] Robert Keohane and Joseph Nye were among the first to systematically identify and define increasing interdependence among nations as a significant phenomenon in international relations in the 1970s and 1980s. They have recently tried to trace the evolution of the concept of *interdependence* to the concept of *globalization,* which became something of a buzzword in the 1990s as the Internet and the Web dramatically interjected the new variable of reduced communication costs for a significant portion of the world's population.[7] Keohane and Nye point out that globalization, defined as increases involving networks of interdependence at multicontinental distances, has been going on for a long time, and that spurts of military, economic, environmental, social, and cultural globalization in the nineteenth and twentieth centuries produced increasing global interdependence well before the onset of the information revolution in the last quarter of the twentieth century. For Keohane and Nye,

> The issue is not how old globalism is, but rather how "thin" or "thick" it is at any given time. As an example of "thin globalization," the Silk Road provided an economic and cultural link between ancient Europe and Asia, but the route was plied by a small group of hardy traders, and the goods that were traded back and forth had a direct impact primarily on a small (and relatively elite) stratum of consumers along the road. In contrast, "thick" relations of globalization . . . involve many relationships that are intensive as well as extensive: long-distance flows that are large and continuous, affecting the lives of many people.

The operations of global financial markets today, for instance, affect people from Peoria to Penang. Globalization is the process by which globalism becomes increasingly thick.[8]

If globalization is the process by which globalism becomes "increasingly thick," the Internet can be viewed as essential to the development of the thickest forms of globalism. But the need to gain access to the Internet on a regular basis to share in the process of globalization has thus far been the catch for the vast majority of people in the world who have either no or very tenuous access to the wired world. In those parts of the globe that lack sufficient telecommunications infrastructures, it is either impossible or remains extremely costly for an individual or a business firm to become connected to the Internet and the Web. The result is that only 23 of the world's 190 independent countries had Internet-connected computers (hosts) for more than 1 percent of the population, according to the 1999 *Human Development Report* of the United Nations Development Programme (UNDP). In 131 countries in 1999, connections to the Internet stood at *less than 0.1 percent.* Although Internet-related business firms often like to present figures indicating that Internet use is doubling every few years, these figures usually refer to use only in developed parts of the world or, in the less developed nations, to a doubling of use from an extremely low base (e.g., from 0.1 percent of the population to 0.2 percent). For most people and countries of the world, becoming a significant player in the information technology revolution remains far in the future.[9]

It is often argued that increasingly new technologies—for example, wireless, mobile, or satellites—will eventually bring the Internet to almost everyone, but there is no guarantee that this will happen rapidly. The costs involved in building infrastructures to spread the new technologies are equal to, or often more than, those of installing older telecommunications infrastructures. Moreover, getting a country into the position to be able to build new infrastructures involves much more than money, as the case studies in this book attest. It requires human resources, cultures conducive to the spread of modern technology and communications, a willingness and ability to tap into the resources of global private capital, and much more. In many societies investment in Internet-related technology has to compete with other possible uses of investment funds often considered more essential. Spreading the Internet around the globe, therefore, is likely to take several decades, just as the spread of radio and television has taken several decades, with neither available on a regular basis—even at the dawn of the twenty-first century—to billions of the earth's residents.

Because Internet diffusion has been highly variable in different countries and regions of the globe, it has had dissimilar impacts on international relations in diverse political, economic, cultural, and security settings. The remainder of this chapter is an attempt to understand its impact in three major areas of international affairs undergoing substantial change: (1) the distribution of wealth and degrees of globalization thickness in different parts of the world, (2) the role and operational capabilities of the nongovernmental sector in international affairs, and (3) the development of world public opinion and a global civil society. The focus here and in the rest of the book will be on large portions of the world outside the United States and Europe where the development of Internet-related technology has been less advanced and where the Internet has encountered resistance from cultures, nondemocratic governments, and poorer societies that do not view it in the same way Western nations do.

▪ THE INTERNET AND THE GAP BETWEEN RICH AND POOR

The introduction of the Internet has not made any part of the world poorer. One cannot, for example, trace lowered productivity or interruption of food supplies in any part of the world to Internet-related variables. But the Internet is contributing to a widening of the gap between the better-off and worse-off parts of the world because it has enabled some nations to create new sources of wealth and of international diplomatic and political power relative to others.[10] The dynamics involved in Internet-related creation of wealth and the Internet's role in helping to widen the gap between rich and poor will be explored in several ways in Chapters 2 through 6 and in the remainder of this chapter. First, however, it might be useful to look at the diffusion of the Internet to the world's poorest region in some detail in an effort to better understand the major forces preventing the many poor people in the world from being full participants in global Internet culture and activities.

If one excludes South Africa, in January 2000 about 25,000 computers were permanently connected to the Internet in Africa (counting personal computers as well as computers in businesses, universities, and elsewhere). This meant the entire continent of Africa, excluding South Africa—with a population of 734 million people in fifty-three countries—had about as many Internet-connected computers (hosts) as

Latvia, which in 2000 had a population of only 2.5 million. Put even more dramatically, the entire continent of Africa, excluding South Africa, had far fewer computers connected to the Internet in January 2000 than did New York City.[11] These figures place the entire African continent, with the exception of South Africa, at the bottom of the list of world regions with connectivity to the Internet.

The entire continent of Africa, *including* South Africa, had just over 500,000 subscribers with dial-up accounts with Internet service providers (ISPs) in 2000, and the UN Economic Commission for Africa estimated that each of these connections was being used by an average of three people. This put estimates of the total number of Internet users in all of Africa at the time at 1.5 million, with approximately 1 million located in South Africa (population 46 million) and the remainder in the rest of Africa (population 734 million). In other words, approximately 2 percent of the population of South Africa had some form of access to the Internet in 2000, whereas *less than 0.1 percent* of those in the rest of Africa had access. In South Africa there was one Internet user for every 46 people in 2000. For the rest of Africa there was one user for every 1,468 people, compared with an average of approximately 1 of every 2 people in North America and 1 of every 4 people in Europe. In 2000 only twenty-six of Africa's fifty-four countries had 1,000 or more dial-up Internet subscribers; only nine African countries (Egypt, Morocco, Kenya, Ghana, Mozambique, South Africa, Tunisia, Uganda, and Zimbabwe) had 5,000 or more.[12]

The countries of northern and southern Africa were among those that predominated in first introducing the Internet to Africa, and they have continued to predominate among countries with increasing numbers of Internet users.[13] The major reasons the vast populations of Africa have been unable to gain access to the Internet include the lack of basic telecommunications and other Internet-related infrastructures, the extremely high costs of using those facilities that do exist, and the lack of skills, resources, and awareness necessary to enable people to use the Internet for any purpose. In southern Africa, for example, which is more advanced than other parts of Africa, in 1999 only 20 percent of households had electricity.[14] In East Africa in 2000, where 49 percent of the population was below the poverty line established by the United Nations, there was only one telephone line for every 1,000 persons.[15] The average cost of using a local dial-up Internet account for only five hours a month in African countries in 2000 averaged about $60 (including usage fees and telephone time but not telephone line rental), compared with an average of $29 per month for all charges for twenty hours of Internet access in the United States. In a country with lower incomes and fewer assets than any other world region except South Asia, the Organization for Economic Cooperation and Development (OECD) estimated in 2000 that the average *hourly* cost of Internet access in Africa was $14.00, compared with $1.45 in the United States, $3.70 in Germany, $3.25 in the United Kingdom, and less than $3.00 in the rest of Europe.

Aside from sheer lack of Internet facilities, the high cost of Internet access throughout Africa, as in most parts of the world, can be traced to previous patterns of international telecommunications development, which were led by large government-run telecommunications monopolies. In every African country, government-run companies continue to monopolize telecommunications service, including the provision of phone lines to computers and even of Internet access as ISPs. The government-run companies have remained small because their emphasis has been on serving particular governments, and governments in Africa have traditionally had little or no interest in mass communications. In South Africa under apartheid, for example, the government extended telephone service to "white areas," particularly in the cities, and allowed "white" capital to be spent only in "white" areas, which meant "nonwhite" people living in urban or rural areas seldom had telephones. In postcolonial Africa, authoritarian rulers were sometimes able to eliminate racist aspects of telecommunications distribution patterns but often ended up disproportionately constructing highly coveted new telecommunications infrastructures for their supporters or in parts of the country crucial to their remaining in office.[16]

As a result of this pattern of development, the African Telecommunications Union (ATU) estimated in mid-2000 that Africa, with 2 percent of the world's population, has only 2 percent of the telephone lines and less than 0.1 percent of Internet connections (500,000 connections for 780 million people, a figure lower than the OECD estimate earlier), even including South Africa. Of those who have telephone connections in Africa, according to PricewaterhouseCoopers of Botswana, 73 percent are connected to the four largest networks (in South Africa, Morocco, Algeria, and Egypt).[17] Although mobile and satellite telecommunications services are expected to overtake fixed land access to telephones and the Internet in much of Africa during the first decade of the twenty-first century, this transition is likely to intensify the "digital divide" within Africa itself, with the better-off segments of the population—particularly in urban areas—being able to adopt the new technologies long in advance of poorer and more rural inhabitants. This is true primarily because the costs involved in building or leasing infrastructures that connect mobile phones within Africa to global networks are prohibitively expensive by African standards, with global satellite and mobile networks being dominated by large private-sector multinational and transnational companies that are less interested in investing in Africa than elsewhere.[18] In mid-2000 there were 5 million mobile cellular telephones in South Africa and 400,000 in the rest of Africa, but none of these were connected to the Internet, and no international roaming agreements or facilities for data communication were provided by any mobile telephone companies.[19]

The difficulties involved in trying to escape from the pattern of telecommunications development described here is well illustrated by the case of South Africa, where the new democratic government that replaced the apartheid regime is trying to make up for decades of neglect by providing telephone networks to poor and rural households. What the new government has found is that, among many other intractable problems, rural South African homes are three times as expensive to wire as urban homes, poor people are unable to pay for service, copper wire phone lines are stolen because the copper is considered more valuable than the phone service, and telephone repairs are almost impossible to maintain on a regular basis in rural areas that have few paved roads or other modern amenities. Despite these difficulties, by 2000 South Africa's monopoly telecommunications company (Telkom) had added almost 1.6 million lines to the 4.3 million lines that existed before 1997, with over a million of the new lines being located in poor areas. Around 86,000 public telephones had been installed, the widespread introduction of prepayment cards eliminated the risk that poor customers would not pay their bills, international charges had been reduced by 50 percent in real terms, and South Africa had started to lay a massive undersea optical fiber cable to carry data between Africa and Europe.

What Telkom has not been able to do in South Africa is to raise the massive amounts of capital necessary to more rapidly spread telecommunications and Internet access throughout the country. Indeed, Telkom fought an extended court case in the late 1990s to prevent other firms (private or public) from offering Internet access services and had an understanding with the government that its monopoly would be extended if it met specific targets for installing new lines, converting analog lines to digital, training staff, and fixing faults quickly. A privatization program, mooted in 1995, was supported by the senior partner in the government coalition (the African National Congress) but stiffly opposed by others in the coalition (e.g., the South African Communist Party and the Congress of South African Trade Unions), which were able to postpone considerably implementation of privatization measures.[20] Finally, in mid-2000, 20 percent of Telkom was sold to a consortium of companies led by Southern Bell in the United States, a Malaysian group led by Telekom Malaysia, and South African Airlines (SAA), which is 20 percent owned by Swissair. Later in the year Telkom raised Euro 500 million (U.S.$450 million) with the largest South African bond issue ever in European markets, and in February 2001 the South African government announced a public offering to sell an additional 30 percent share of Telkom.[21] Once it completes the sale of half of Telkom (which is estimated to be worth at least $15 billion in 2001), the government will have to decide whether it will use the proceeds for capital investment in IT and the Internet, to pay down the national debt, or for other significant national needs in other sectors. The government will also have to decide how many competitors—public and private—will eventually be licensed to provide telecommunications and Internet services in South Africa.

One option for the South African government would be to license the telephone networks of other state-owned firms, such as Eskom (the state electricity firm) and Transnet (the state transport group), so there would be limited competition among those firms to provide better telecommunications and Internet services while leaving ownership in government hands. A second option would be to sell the government's Telkom holdings to large international private firms and require that those firms bring in large amounts of capital and meet government social service targets. South Africa's business community is solidly in favor of the latter solution, arguing that Telkom's monopoly is retarding economic growth by maintaining high prices for the use of bandwidth while restricting access to it, thus making South African banks and businesses less competitive internationally than would be the case otherwise. Their position with regard to social services was summarized by the *Economist:*

> Potential competitors to Telkom could be obliged, as part of their licence agreements, to hire more black employees than South Africa's stringent positive-discrimination laws require. . . . Potential competitors could also be obliged to install telephones in poor areas. Such strings would reduce the revenue that the government could raise from selling licences. But competition would bring lower prices, better service and perhaps more creative ways of connecting the poor.[22]

At a postcabinet briefing in March 2001, South African Communications Minister Ivy Matsepe-Casaburri suggested that the government had decided to allow at least two additional telecommunications operators to function as competitors to Telkom, but "the second of these would only be considered after the first had been in operation for at least five years."[23] She indicated that the first Telkom competitor would most likely be introduced by the granting of a license in May 2002, when Telkom's exclusive license expires, although some Telkom backers argue that Telkom could postpone the introduction of competition by invoking an option in its license for an extra year of "exclusivity."[24] A number of financial and political leaders are concerned that the chief regulatory body governing telecommunications—the Communications Authority of South Africa—is not being supported by the current government, which could make it impossible to develop competition even were two additional companies to be created in the near future.[25]

Whatever decisions the South African government makes regarding future Internet development, it is clear that the relationships it establishes internationally will clearly be the key variables in either narrowing or widening the digital divide between South Africans and people in the wealthier parts of the world. The same is the case for other African nations. It is one of the great ironies of the Internet age that the costs of becoming involved are initially so high that most poor nations have been unable to gain the advantage of having the bottom fall out of their international communications costs because they lack the capital to enter into the initial revolutionary phase of the information era. In a seminal article on why Africa has grown so slowly, Paul Collier and Jan Willem Gunning suggest that economic failures may be the result of what they call "a low productivity trap":

> Because African firms are oriented to small domestic markets, they are not able to exploit economies of scale, nor are they exposed to significant competition, and their technology gap with the rest of the world is unusually wide. . . . This suggests that African manufacturing might have atypically large potential to raise productivity through exporting. However, most African firms fail to step into this productivity escalator [because] . . . transactions costs are unusually high. With transport unreliable, firms typically need to carry very large stocks of inputs to maintain continuity of production, despite higher interest rates than elsewhere. Telecommunications are much worse than other regions. Malfunctioning of the courts makes contract enforcement

unreliable, so that firms are reluctant to enter into deals with new partners, in turn making markets less competitive.[26]

If Collier and Gunning's analysis is correct, a continued emphasis on infrastructural, legal, and financial reforms is essential to ensure better delivery of public services and attract the kind of international investment needed to move African economies up the "productivity escalator." This will not be easy, because global financial rating services list Africa as "the riskiest region in the world to invest," a rating some economists consider unwarranted in terms of Africa's fundamentals.[27] To gain greater confidence from international investors and correct any ratings misperceptions, Collier and Gunning suggest that African governments become more involved with the World Trade Organization, shift their relations with the European Union (EU) from unreciprocated trade preferences to a wider range of reciprocated commitments, make policy decisions more transparent by promoting greater openness and democracy (including freedom of the press), and create "independent centers of authority in central banks and revenue authorities."[28] Adoption of any of these suggestions entails significant risks for African politicians.[29]

In an atmosphere in which international factors have become crucial for economic development and for the growth of thicker globalization streams, the impact of the Internet in Africa at the turn of the twenty-first century does not stem from any accomplishments related to speeding up global transactions or from any dramatic reduction of communications costs, as is the case in the more developed world. There is little e-commerce in the entire continent, although the tourism industry and foreign investment firms are beginning to lead the way with informational websites and contact numbers.[30] Attempts have been made to create websites providing medical information to assist doctors in poor and rural areas, but the number of such sites does not compare with the numbers in Asia and Latin America.[31] Even at universities, which in most other regions of the world were substantially connected by the late 1990s, Africa has lagged far behind in Internet development. A survey by the Association of African Universities in 1998 found that 52 of the 232 responding academic and research institutions had full Internet connectivity, and 180 had access considered "inadequate."[32] Mike Jensen's 2000 figures suggest that the 1998 survey may have overstated the extent to which universities are wired to the Internet; Jensen found that only twenty countries in Africa had universities with "full Internet connectivity" in 2000 and that "full connectivity" in these cases usually meant restrictive use for faculty, staff, and graduate students with no access provided to the general student population.[33]

▪ NEW INTERNET COMMUNICATORS
AND NONGOVERNMENTAL ORGANIZATIONS

Despite its shallow penetration, something is happening in Africa as a result of the Internet that is likely to have a significant impact on international affairs in the future: the growth of a new group of Internet communicators more readily able to converse with one another across international boundaries and even within nations and cities with frequencies and in ways not previously possible. These new communicators constitute more a "class" than a "community," since they do share elite characteristics not previously discernible but identify with a heterogeneous diversity of organizations and groups.[34] In a survey carried out by the UN Economic Commission for Africa (ECA) in early 2000, the largest number of Africa's 1.5 million Internet users were young (25–35 was the majority age category), were predominantly male, were well educated (e.g., 87 percent in Zambia and 98 percent in Ethiopia had university degrees), had above-average incomes, were English-speaking, and belonged to nongovernmental organizations, the news media, private companies (especially IT and computer businesses), and universities. The average level of Internet use among respondents to the ECA survey was three to four pages of e-mail daily, with interaction most frequent with Internet sites outside the continent. Surfing the World Wide Web or downloading data are relatively minor activities for this new elite when compared to sending and receiving e-mail, primarily because the online time necessary for non-e-mail activities escalates costs to prohibitive levels.[35]

Although much of the e-mail activity among African "netizens" is for personal or family use—for example, to stay in touch with relatives abroad or apply for admission to universities in the West—the ECA survey identifies a number of broader online interests that have implications for organizational behavior, both within Africa and in the international arena. What the ECA survey profiles, in addition to those who are online strictly for personal or family reasons, is a group of young elites interested in international affairs and taking advantage of unprecedented opportunities to use Internet technology to become more meaningfully involved with a wide variety of people from other countries. Prominent among these young elites, for example, are journalists and aspiring journalists who use the Internet to research and send stories, either as employees of an African news service or as freelancers.[36]

Use of the Internet by young African elites is particularly impressive because few have full-time access to their own computer, either at home or at the office. They use whatever access is available, often spending hours a day waiting for their turn to get online. Because of the high cost of full Internet-based services and slow access speeds, many African ISPs offer lower-cost "e-mail-only" services, and a large proportion of Africans gain Internet access through free services such as Hotmail, Yahoo! or Excite—most of which are based in the United States. Use of public facilities for getting online is rapidly increasing throughout Africa, including use of privately run kiosks (small, stand-alone Internet access units found in markets or public places), cybercafés, and community Internet units located in schools, police stations, and clinics. This pattern of Internet development—using public rather than private facilities—is consistent with the way radio and television were previously introduced and continue to be used in Africa.[37]

Perhaps the most salient organizational aspect of Internet use in Africa has been the way the new technology has helped accelerate the proliferation and strengthening of nongovernmental organizations (NGOs) and other private associations.[38] This is a worldwide phenomenon that Jessica Matthews has described as the central factor in an unprecedented worldwide redistribution of power among states, markets, and what she calls "global civil society." In Matthews's words,

> The most powerful engine of change in the relative decline of states and the rise of nonstate actors is the computer and telecommunications revolution. . . . By drastically reducing the importance of proximity, the new technologies change people's perceptions of community. Fax machines, satellite hookups, and the Internet connect people across borders with exponentially growing ease while separating them from natural and historical associations within nations. In this sense a globalizing force, they can also have the opposite effect, amplifying political and social fragmentation by enabling more and more identities and interests scattered around the globe to coalesce and thrive.[39]

Although many of the generalizations Matthews summarizes or develops have had a significant impact on the way intellectuals in the West think about NGOs and the Internet, her assertion that the proliferation and influence of NGOs and other nonstate international organizations have substantially diminished the power of states is open to question. The most successful campaigns of NGOs in the 1990s resulted from well-organized movements across national boundaries (in most cases joined by some governments and businesses) that had a major impact on specific international issues, in much the same way that pressure groups within domestic constituencies can influence the governments of nation-states. The most successful NGO campaigns in the 1990s have been summarized by the *Economist:*

> The watershed was the Earth Summit in Rio de Janeiro in 1992, when the NGOs roused enough public pressure to push through agreements on controlling greenhouse gases. In 1994, protesters dominated the World Bank's anniversary meeting with a "Fifty Years is Enough" campaign, and forced a rethink of the Bank's goals and methods. In 1998, an ad hoc coalition of consumer-rights activists and environmentalists helped to sink the Multilateral Agreement on Investment (MAI), a draft treaty to harmonise rules on foreign investment under the aegis of the OECD. In the past couple of years another global coalition of NGOs, Jubilee 2000, has pushed successfully for a dramatic reduction in the debts of the poorest countries. . . . One of the biggest successes of the 1990s was the campaign to outlaw landmines, where hundreds of NGOs, in concert with the Canadian government, pushed through a ban in a year. . . . In a case in 1995 that particularly shocked business, Royal Dutch/Shell, although it was technically in the right, was prevented by Greenpeace, the most media-savvy of all NGOs, from disposing of its Brent Spar oil rig in the North Sea.[40]

Anne-Marie Slaughter does not dispute that nonstate actors are increasingly developing multiple allegiances and a more global reach as a result of the Internet and the information revolution, but she argues that Matthews and other "new medievalists" miss two central points: (1) that "private power is still no substitute for state power" and (2) that "a gain in power by nonstate actors does not necessarily translate into a loss of power for the state."[41] In the context of Africa and other poorer regions of the world, Slaughter's observations are important. Although the Internet and other aspects of IT have enabled a small elite class of Africans, Asians, and Latin Americans to organize somewhat more effectively than had been the case previously, they have not been able to overwhelm or supplant state power, and their ability to pressure governments and international organizations on specific issues has been dependent on considerable support—especially funding—from organizations (often including government organizations) in the developed world.

Rather than supplanting state power, NGOs and private voluntary organizations (PVOs) worked in the poorer regions of the world throughout the twentieth century and are continuing to do so in the twenty-first century in rather close cooperation with governments and international organizations. The usual assumption of these joint activities is that NGOs and PVOs are not competitors with state power but instead are working cooperatively with national governments and international organizations to implement common programs. In some cases one group of NGOs will be aligned with one government or perhaps a factional group within a government, pitted against an alliance of other NGOs and governments or factional government groupings on the other side of the issue. A prominent global example pitting some governments and NGOs against specific NGOs was the attempt in May 2001 within the UN Human Rights Commission to try to ban several private human rights organizations (including Freedom House, the Baptist World Alliance, the Simon Weisenthal Center, and the Family Research Council) from participation in UN activities.[42]

For NGOs of long standing, as well as for most newly created NGOs and PVOs, the Internet has proven extremely useful in monitoring membership and mobilizing members behind programs, but in this context Matthews's assertion that "increasingly, NGOs are able to push around even the largest governments" is somewhat misleading. Although in many dramatic cases in recent years NGOs and PVOs have been able to effectively mobilize against and change policies proposed by national governments or international organizations, such impacts have been marginal rather than central to the purposes and dominance of the governments of most nations. More representative of modern nation-state relationships with NGOs and PVOs in Africa, for example, was a week-long meeting in Bamako, Mali, in February 2000, where more than 500 representatives from NGOs, PVOs, the business community, the media, academia, and government met to discuss ways they could use the Internet cooperatively to promote development.[43]

It would be impossible to determine with any accuracy the number of NGOs and PVOs that exist in the world, but some countries have traditions of nongovernmental associational life that date back more than a century. Such a tradition in India has produced several hundred thousand organizations if one includes cooperatives and credit societies as well as development-oriented organizations, advocacy and protest groups, and legal, scientific, technical, and policy associations.[44] If caste, religious, educational, linguistic, regional, and communal organizations count, there might be as many as a million or more, the vast majority of which were in existence long before the Internet was invented.[45] Although the Internet has clearly enhanced the ability of some nonstate organizations to mobilize followers behind their positions on particular issues—especially in democratic countries like India—the extent to which this has diminished the power of the state, as indicated in the case study of India in a companion volume to this one, is minimal.[46] In Africa and the rest of the developing world, one can also conclude that the Internet has been responsible for a proliferation of the number of NGOs and PVOs with international interests, often enhancing their effectiveness on international issues vis-à-vis governments, but that it has not seriously diminished the power and authority of nation-states.

Perhaps more than for NGOs and PVOs, the Internet has enhanced the ability and willingness of national governments to communicate with one another. Slaughter pointed out that the Internet has contributed substantially to a process of "transgovernmentalism," first identified by Keohane and Nye in the 1970s as "the most widespread and effective mode of international governance."[47] The Internet, for example, prompted widespread adoption of the principle of *positive comity,* a concept that has enabled judiciaries and justice departments from different countries to work more closely with one another to ensure that conflicts among the laws of different nation-states are handled amicably and that infringements of state sovereignty are either avoided entirely or satisfactorily resolved.[48] The U.S. Department of Justice and the EU's European Commission worked out an arrangement in the mid-1990s whereby regulatory authorities in countries on both sides of the Atlantic (e.g., in securities regulation, banking and insurance supervision, or criminal law enforcement) alert one another to violations within their jurisdictions and decide which national or local authority is responsible for taking action. Study of the international regime for the Internet that has been developing over the past few decades also makes clear that it is increasingly being developed by a process of transgovernmentalism, working in conjunction with nongovernmental actors.[49]

As Slaughter has pointed out, transgovernmental regulatory and enforcement networks often develop their own rules for networking, but both the rules and the networking itself are designed to enhance the enforcement of *national* law. The burgeoning growth of such networks reflects the need to develop coordinated responses among national governments on issues beyond the reach of any one country, often because the Internet has complicated an issue that cannot be dealt with by existing international organizations. In this sense, transgovernmentalism is an alternative to the ineffectiveness of existing international organizations and to the temptation by some to want to build an ever increasing number of international institutions or enlarge bureaucracies within existing institutions. In Slaughter's words,

> [Transgovernmentalism] is fast, flexible, and effective . . . it provides a powerful alternative to a liberal internationalism that has reached its limits and to a new medievalism that, like the old Marxism, sees the state slowly fading away. The new medievalists are right to emphasize the dawn of a new era, in which information technology will transform the globe. But government networks are government for the information age. They offer the world a blueprint for the international architecture of the twenty-first century.[50]

■ THE ROLE OF INTERNATIONAL BUSINESS

In addition to those who see the primary influence of the Internet as the internationalization of NGOs and the growth of transgovernmental mechanisms, others have suggested that the growing mastery over certain aspects of Internet-related technology by some companies has given international business the wherewithal to overwhelm sovereign states and national governments almost at will. Matthews has outlined the argument as follows:

> Amid shifting alliances and joint ventures, made possible by computers and advanced communications, nationalities blur. Offshore banking encourages widespread evasion of national taxes. Whereas the fear in the 1970s was that multinationals would become an arm of government, the concern now is that they are disconnecting from their home countries' national interests, moving jobs, evading taxes, and eroding economic sovereignty in the process. . . .
>   The even more rapid globalization of financial markets has left governments far behind. Where governments once set foreign exchange rates, private currency traders, accountable only to their bottom line, now trade $1.3 trillion a day, 100 times the volume of world trade. . . . Again, technology has been a driving force, shifting financial clout from states to the market with its offer of unprecedented

speed in transactions—states cannot match market reaction times measured in seconds—and its dissemination of financial information to a broad range of players.[51]

Matthews's argument, like so much of the literature on globalization, rests on assertions that the world is becoming increasingly economically integrated and that this process is likely to continue in a unilinear fashion into the future. Although such arguments are common in the international relations literature in political science, international economists tend to view the world's markets for goods, services, and factors of production in a more hardheaded manner as less integrated than the political science literature assumes. In a summary study of the economics literature, for example, Dani Rodrik of Harvard University concluded that "contrary to conventional wisdom and much punditry, international economic integration remains remarkably limited."[52] Rodrik pointed out, for example, that despite a significant increase in international transactions because of the Internet, national borders—even those as porous as the one between the United States and Canada—"have a significantly depressing effect on commerce." He also found substantial agreement among economists that investment portfolios in the advanced industrial countries typically reflect a "home bias," with people investing "a higher proportion of assets in their own countries than the principles of asset diversification would seem to suggest." Even in periods of investor exuberance, Rodrik concluded, capital flows between rich and poor nations "fall considerably short of what theoretical models would predict," and "severe restrictions on the international mobility of labor are the rule rather than the exception."

Rodrik and other international economists account for the continued limitations on international economic integration by pointing to the persistence of the rules and bureaucracies of the nation-state, despite the spread of the Internet, as a means for conducting global business. This finding is confirmed in the case studies in this volume. It is also confirmed by independent data gathered from other sources, indicating that the growth of e-commerce alone has prompted a literal flood of new legislation to control the Internet in almost all countries of the world. In the United States, where the government tends to be somewhat less intrusive on Internet activities than is true in other nations, *more than 2,000 laws* designed to regulate Internet behavior were put on the legislative agendas of the fifty U.S. states in 1999 alone. Rodrik points to such phenomena as perhaps the major factor in preventing a thicker degree of globalization:

While formal barriers to trade and capital flows have been substantially reduced over the last three decades, international markets for goods, services, and capital are not nearly as "thick" as they would be under complete integration. Why so much trade in goods and capital has gone missing is the subject of an active research agenda in international economics. The answers are not yet entirely clear.

But at some level there is no mystery. National borders demarcate political and legal jurisdictions. Such demarcations serve to segment markets in much the same way that transport costs or border taxes do. Exchanges that cross national jurisdictions are subject to a wide array of transaction costs introduced by discontinuities in political and legal systems.[53]

Rodrik suggests that only two alternatives exist for eliminating the negative impact of political and legal jurisdictions on the integration of markets in the information age: either (1) bring about a degree of world integration—perhaps in a world federation patterned after U.S. federalism—such that "a world government would take care of a world market," or (2) "maintain the nation-state system largely as is, but ensure that national jurisdictions—and the differences among them—do not get in the way of economic transactions."[54]

If Rodrik and other international economists are correct, the mere addition of the Internet and information technology to the world mix of international economics and sovereign states has not been enough to bring about the significant economic integration that the globalization literature would suggest.[55] At best, the Internet can be viewed as a contributing factor to a much larger evolution of the global economy toward increasing interdependence, which has been going on at an accelerating rate since World War II. Lee Preston and Duane Windsor have perhaps put this in the most balanced perspective by identifying three interrelated types of linkages as the key variables in the integration of the world economy: trade and investment flows, multinational enterprises, and international policy regimes. From this perspective, information technology generally can be viewed as a significant factor that has helped propel economic integration forward, particularly with the spread of the Internet in the 1990s, but the Internet and information technology themselves are not viewed as the primary cause or causes of increasing interdependence or thicker degrees of globalization. Preston and Windsor summarize their argument as follows:

These three strong forms of international economic and policy linkage [trade and investment linkages, international policy regimes, and multinational enterprises] rest, of course, on underlying foundations of history, language, and culture, geographic proximity, economic complementarity, and so forth. In addition, these functional links are supported by a continuously expanding global web of communication and information that is itself a major source of increased international interdependence.[56]

Conclusions reached by Rodrik, Preston and Windsor, and other scholars were reinforced by a January 2001 survey of international business managers whose firms pursued globalization strategies in the 1990s based on concepts of convergence and standardization—that is, the idea that the Internet and other factors were producing a worldwide convergence of individual and cultural tastes and preferences across regions, countries, and economies of the world, with the result that companies could cut their costs and expand the scope and scale of their marketing reach as geographic differences disappeared in the global village. Based on his analysis of the 2001 survey, the Eli Lilly Chair Professor of Innovation, Business and Society at Insead, Philip M. Parker, concluded, "If you are still thinking this way, it is time to reconsider. The data are in and standardisation is out. . . . [Assumptions that] emerging markets were ready to take major products from developed markets and [that] the demand would be explosive [were] bad assumptions that produced bad results. . . . Companies that planned for convergence paid the price in excess capacity and devalued assets."[57]

■ THE INTERNET AND WORLD GOVERNMENT

Several proposals have been made for the development of a world government built around the Internet, variously labeled cyberfederalism, cyberdemocracy, or simply cybergovernment. Many of these proposals suggest that the existing UN organization be substantially strengthened by enabling it to collect a "world tax" on the Internet, initially to improve world revenue streams to third world governments or create an international fund that might be used for Internet development in those parts of the world on the downside of the digital divide. One of the largest and most ambitious of these schemes, devised by the UNDP in October 1999, calls for a tax equivalent to one U.S. cent on every 100 e-mails sent by individuals anywhere in the world, which the UNDP estimates would have generated U.S.$70 billion in development assistance for the UN in the four-year period 1996–2000.[58] Perhaps the most widely read cyberfederalism proposal was published in 1996 by David Post, codirector of the Cyberspace Law Institute at Georgetown University Law Center.[59]

As Timothy Wu has pointed out, proposals to create world governments built around the Internet, or imaginative suggestions that cyberspace is itself a sovereign territory in some sense, run against the acknowledged principle of sovereignty among nation-states, which have increasingly asserted their power to regulate all aspects of information technology. Based on several years of research on this topic, Wu concludes that the metaphor of "cyberspace" as a legal place or a location for a legitimate government is "a model so far from the technology that it was useful only as a publicity tool . . . its limits, especially for legal purposes, have become all too apparent. It's time to move on."[60] Instead of conceptualizing cyberspace as sovereign, Wu prefers to think of the Internet as

> a regime of transnational norms and rules (a logical counterpart to transnational law) that regulates international interactions between individuals. These norms and rules may be formally constituted, such as the Internet standards promulgated by the Internet Engineering Task Force, or informal, such as the discourse norms on the Usenet. Such preexisting norms and rules may in themselves generate state behavior that would respect cyberspace sovereignty. Thus cyberspace sovereignty may spring from a consensus among individuals in different states that these rules and norms are reasonable and deserve respect. At the second stage, domestic institutions may transmit this consensus to the state, and a respect for these norms and rules may become a state preference.[61]

Wu goes on to argue that the creation of a robust "regime" for the Internet might at some distant "third stage" result in modification of the behavior of states and that the result of this process could be "a minimally sovereign cyberspace, where the extent of sovereignty corresponds precisely to what the consensus holds to be the proper breadth of freedom from state regulation."[62]

One of the most significant uses of the Internet in international relations, which is consistent with Wu's advanced third stage of an international regime, has been the unparalleled growth of human rights organization websites and the attention that human rights activists have given to cyberspace. A number of NGOs have adopted Internet freedom as a human rights norm and use international computer networks in a variety of ways to press for respect of that position. The basis of the argument for the norm is Article 19 of the Universal Declaration of Human Rights, which states that "everyone has the right to freedom of opinion and expression; this right includes freedom to hold opinions without interference and to seek, receive and impart information and ideas through any media and regardless of frontiers." Some human rights organizations have supported selective judicial actions in the courts of various nation-states in defense of the norm, whereas others have developed literature, assisted human rights leaders with the acquisition and installation of encryption technology to protect their privacy, and pursued many other ways of incorporating the Internet as a key component in twenty-first-century human rights work.[63]

Based on the work of human rights organizations and the development of regularized interaction over the Internet among academics, businesspeople, policymakers, and professionals—particularly in Europe—the Norwegian scholar Torbjorn L. Knutsen has suggested that a *publicum* of "informed and concerned citizens who confer about matters of general interest" is emerging at the global level.[64] In Knutsen's words, "The growth of cyberspace and the rapid spread of interconnecting microcomputers have created a public sphere of unprecedented cosmopolitan scope." Knutsen derives the notion of a *publicum*—a public sphere of civil society—from Kant, Hegel, Weber, and Schmitt, all of whom associate it with the ascendancy of the modern state, modern capitalist markets, and rational state bureaucracies. To quote Knutsen's understanding of the concept as derived from earlier philosophers, "At the core of their discussion lies the notion of the rise of the modern bourgeoisie—a distinct stratum of literate and knowledgeable citizens who constitute a *publicum* through their informed discussion of social and economic issues. When informed citizens confer in an unrestricted fashion—that is, with the guarantee of freedom of assembly and association and the liberty to express and publish their opinions—about matters of general interest, they prepare the basis of the public sphere."[65]

Knutsen's conception of the *publicum* is similar to that of the leadership of the Internet Society (ISOC), the Internet Corporation for Assigned Names and Numbers (ICANN), and other Internet-based organizations that are trying to develop various forms of online democracy, with decisions being made on the basis of input or even votes from Internet users around the world.[66] For Knutsen and these organizations, the Internet *publicum* includes the small number of elites in Africa, Asia, and Latin America who are presently logging on to the Internet or at least those portions of these elites who use the Internet for purposes beyond entertainment. The difficulties in operationalizing these attempts at cyberdemocracy result from the massive gaps in Internet access among various nations and peoples, with the result that participants "voting" in Internet "cyberdemocracies" tend to be overwhelmingly from the wealthier and better-educated communities in the developed world.[67]

▪ THE INTERNET REGIME
AND INTERNATIONAL RELATIONS

The case studies in this volume are an attempt to examine in some detail the ways in which the Internet has impacted international relations in specific world regions. The cases in Chapters 2 through 6 are analyses of the extent to which the Internet has promoted thicker degrees of globalism and interdependence, assisted nongovernmental organizations and transgovernmental processes for mobilizing people across international borders, and developed a class of new Internet communicators in three vast world regions. The case studies also attempt to link Internet-related developments in the various regions to the evolution of an international regime for the Internet, which has begun to take on more than embryonic form in those more developed parts of the world with the highest Internet penetration rates. Since the concept of *international regimes* is often used rather loosely, with so many different referents, it might be useful to outline its definitional meaning in this volume before trying to draw conclusions about its relevance for this study.

The overall conception of international regimes used in this book and in my previous, more comprehensive book, *Governing the Internet,* follows the pathbreaking work of Stephen Krasner and associates, who define international regimes as "principles, norms, rules, and decision-making procedures around which actor expectations converge in a given issue-area."[68] This does not mean international regimes constitute *all* of the activities in a given issue area, such as Internet-related behavior. International regimes are simply those selected principles, norms, rules, and decisionmaking procedures on which key actors can agree so they might build cooperation across international borders. There may be and usually are many other principles, norms, rules, and decisionmaking procedures proposed in the same issue area on which the relevant actors cannot agree, but the areas on which agreement can be reached are significant enough to constitute an international regime. In some cases international regimes are so robust that they are able to circumscribe the behavior of nation-states and the citizens within them, thereby shaping international behavior in a way that would not be possible without the existence of the international regime.[69]

One could define the international regime for the Internet so broadly as to consist of any and all interactions that involve the Internet at the international level. In this case the concept of a *regime* would have little or no conceptual meaning because the regime would in no way circumscribe or define patterns of international behavior. At the other extreme, regimes are sometimes identified with international institutions or organizations, such as (in the case of the Internet) the International Telecommunications Union, the World Trade Organization (WTO), or ICANN. If one conceives of regime theory in this way, the study of regimes becomes indistinguishable from traditional studies of international organizations, none of which alone circumscribes or defines patterns of international behavior to the extent that takes place within international regimes.

The conceptualization of regimes used in this book is based on the classic international relations paradigm in which nation-states are assumed to be "sovereign entities dedicated to their own self-preservation, ultimately able to depend only on themselves, and prepared to resort to force."[70] As long as states are unconstrained and able to engage in independent decisionmaking, international regimes do not exist. An international regime comes into being when states decide not to engage in independent decisionmaking but instead accede to certain principles, norms, rules, and decisionmaking procedures to deal with either common interests or common aversions. This gives rise to two different kinds of international regimes, each with its own required behavior; regimes established to deal with dilemmas involved in trying to develop common interests require *collaboration,* and those established to deal with dilemmas resulting from common aversions require *coordination.*[71]

The international regime forming around the Internet is being established to deal with dilemmas resulting from attempts to maximize common interests that result from this new technology among nation-states that jealously guard their national sovereignty in an anarchic international political order. As detailed elsewhere, the international regime for the Internet can be viewed as a "spontaneous order," brought into being with little or no coordinated direction since 1990 or so largely because of the nature of the technology.[72] Because of its rapid worldwide diffusion and potential for effecting dramatic change in global communications networks, the Internet has caught the attention of states and other organizations interested in transforming it into a "negotiated order."[73] The recent attempt by the United States to turn a major portion of the technical infrastructure of the Internet over to an international private organization (ICANN) is one indication among many that U.S. leadership conceives of an "imposed order" for the Internet as undesirable or impossible (or both), preferring to support a private organization outside the framework of states—and to a considerable extent outside of U.S. control—that could develop agreements for procedures relating to Internet governance while eliciting the consent of actors for negotiated resolution of problems.[74] Another indication that the international regime for the Internet is moving from a spontaneous order to a negotiated order is, among many others, the inclusion of Internet-related issues in the negotiations of major international organizations and in bilateral and multilateral negotiations, particularly in the economic sphere.

In summary, the principles and norms of the nascent international regime for the Internet can be outlined as follows:[75]

1. With regard to the technical aspects of the global Internet, the two principles that have been substantially agreed on worldwide are
   a. that authority for operationalizing the Internet be decentralized internationally
   b. that the process for developing international technical standards be inclusive rather than proprietary or government directed.
2. Two norms originally hammered out among all major Internet providers and users in the 1970s and that have since gained global acceptance as the Internet has spread internationally are
   a. that operation of the Internet be designed to handle diversity at all network levels
   b. that the Internet be characterized by interoperability and heterogeneity, both within and between networks.
3. International regime principles and norms successfully negotiated for management and governance of the Internet are
   a. the *principle* that the private sector should take the lead in the development of Internet governance and management and the concomitant *norm* that governments will avoid placing undue restrictions on the Internet while facilitating its development

by enforcing a predictable, minimalist, consistent, and simple legal environment

b. the *principle* of openness in the organization of the Internet's governance and management functions, with the concomitant *norms* that some form of at-large membership, functional and geographic representation of international stakeholders and users, and international participation in decisionmaking be built into the structure of the Internet's governing and management mechanisms.

4. In the late 1990s and the early twenty-first century, basic regime principles and norms for the operationalization of the commercial aspects of the Internet gained widespread acceptance among all major world actors and interests involved substantially in e-commerce and e-business. The two working principles of the Internet in the commercial area are

a. that the private sector shall play a lead role in the development of electronic commerce on a global basis

b. that regulatory and other government activities should avoid undue restrictions on Internet commercial activities while facilitating the development of international electronic commerce by the private sector.

5. The two working regime norms that grow out of these principles are

a. that diverse sets of national rules and procedures governing Internet commerce will be accommodated at the international level by "soft law" arrangements designed to promote global cooperation and expand commercial activities

b. that regional and international organizations (e.g., WIPO [World Intellectual Property Organization], OECD, WTO) will play a major role in facilitating the growth of the regime for the commercial aspects of the Internet on a global basis.

These principles and norms have resulted from a number of compromises that have been hammered out during a series of negotiations in the last two decades of the twentieth century and the first years of the twenty-first century.[76] They have given rise to rules and procedures for conducting day-to-day business among those who manage the global Internet—rules and procedures that can be expected to undergo many alterations in the coming years as the Internet matures and technology changes. Identification of emergent international regime principles and norms for operationalizing the Internet does not mean a robust regime has emerged full-blown. In a number of areas—related primarily to international legal and security matters—it has been impossible even to develop a workable agenda for negotiating rudimentary Internet-related principles and norms among internationally sovereign states. The existence of international regime principles and norms in technical and commercial areas, however, has served as the basis for negotiations between nations and other actors involved with the global Internet and will be essential in the future if the kind of cooperative functioning that has characterized Internet activity is to continue.

Since most of the initial inventions that made international computer networking possible were products of the United States and Europe, it is not surprising that these two parts of the world have been in the forefront of the international regime's formation and growth in its early years. But other parts of the world have been catching up at various speeds, and some have started to play key roles in either accepting or challenging regime principles and norms or participating in the development of regime rules and procedures. The People's Republic of China (PRC) has been perhaps the key world actor in this respect, in part because of the sheer size of its population and the enthusiasm of its leadership in promoting Internet growth but also because of the massive investments it has attracted—from all over the world and primarily from the private sector—in Internet-related information technology ventures.

China and India are singled out for special study in Chapter 7 because accommodation of these two Asian giants—the two largest nations in the world in population size—can be conceived as test cases for the global Internet regime for at least three reasons. First, China and India are not only larger and more powerful than other less developed countries (LDCs), they are also pacesetters in various aspects of computer networking and the production of computer hardware and software. This means they are both capable of playing major roles in shaping the operation of the global Internet and will expect to do so. Second, their business and political leaders, as well as computer professionals, have been more involved than comparable leadership groups from other developing countries in establishing rules and procedures for the Internet's international operations. Third, India and the PRC represent the aspirations of a large number of LDCs that would like to control the Internet within their national boundaries by either finding ways to establish and enforce their own rules, independent of other nations, or changing consensual and globally negotiated Internet rules to enhance

GARDNER HARVEY LIBRARY
Miami University-Middletown
Middletown, Ohio 45042

possibilities for government control of computer networking within national borders.[77]

Aspirations by LDCs to be relatively independent of the global Internet regime are not very different from LDC aspirations in support of sovereignty and autonomy in other issue areas. But their aspirations seem especially significant in Internet-related areas for two reasons: (1) because of the nature of Internet technology, which poses special challenges to the independence of communications across national borders; and (2) because IT is such a crucial factor in world economic development and global power equations. The studies in this volume seek to provide empirical data that might help assess the extent to which the Internet is being adapted and integrated into political cultures in five world regions where IT capabilities are not yet at the same level as those of advanced IT societies. In this sense, accommodation of all of the countries in all five of these regions will challenge the potential weakness or robustness of emerging regime norms.

▪ NOTES

1. Guldimann, "How Technology Is Reshaping Finance and Risks," pp. 41–42. All figures in the first two paragraphs are from this source.

2. Quoted in ibid., p. 41.

3. The U.S. State Department listed 190 "independent states" in the world in mid-2000 (see www.state.gov/www/regions/independent_states.html), of which 174 are detailed in the statistical tables (pp. 51–56) of the UNDP's *Human Development Report 1999* for Internet hosts, personal computers, and other aspects of information technology that contribute to the ISI. Subtracting the 55 countries listed in the ISI2001 count from the UNDP's 1999 list would leave 119 countries without IT infrastructures, but the UNDP's list does not include 12 additional countries not on the ISI list significantly lacking in IT infrastructures as well (Afghanistan, Bosnia, Kiribati, North Korea, Liberia, Marshall Islands, Micronesia, Nauru, Palau, Somalia, Tonga, and Tuvalu). These are countries for which UNDP was unable to obtain reliable data for its 1999 report. In addition, four countries (Andorra, the Holy See, Liechtenstein, and San Marino) not on the UNDP list did have IT infrastructures comparable to those on the ISI list but were too small to be included in the ISI2001 count.

4. Quoted from *ISI2001 Information Society Index,* pp. 1–2. The index is based on twenty-three indicators clustered under four categories: computer infrastructure, Internet infrastructure, information infrastructure (telecommunications, television, radio, fax, and the like), and social infrastructure (education, newspaper readership, press freedom, civil liberties). For more information

contact wwelch@worldtimes.com or mtoolan@idc.com. The six other countries of Western Europe were the United Kingdom, Germany, the Netherlands, Switzerland, Belgium, and Austria.

5. For definitions, conceptual development, and an analysis of the role of the Internet and the World Wide Web in the evolution of the Internet internationally, see Franda, *Governing the Internet.*

6. A comprehensive survey of the globalization literature is available in Held et al., *Global Transformations.*

7. Keohane and Nye, "Globalization," pp. 104–130.

8. Ibid., p. 108.

9. An early study that recognized the looming digital divide is Wresch, *Disconnected.*

10. An Organization for Economic Cooperation and Development (OECD) report *(Understanding the Digital Divide)* estimated that there were 94 million Internet hosts in the world in early 2001, of which 95.6 percent were in the developed world (82 hosts per 1,000 people), whereas there was only *1* host per 1,000 people in the LDCs. Africa had only 0.25 percent of the world's Internet hosts at the time, most of them in South Africa. For an analysis of the OECD report, see Mcrae, "Only Deregulation," p. 20.

11. Most of the figures in this and the following two paragraphs are from Jensen, "Making the Connection," pp. 215–221. Jensen is an independent consultant based in Port St. Johns, South Africa, who draws on databases from a variety of sources to maintain a data bank that constantly updates figures on African Internet use.

12. A Business Marketing Intelligence–Tech Knowledge (BMI-T) report estimated that there were almost 2 million Internet users in South Africa in late 2000, but the report departed from most Internet usage studies that count only those people online. The BMI-T study estimated the number of Internet devices being used in South Africa, estimated the number of multiple users for those devices, and included all of these figures in its "user" totals. See *South African Internet Access,* reported in "South African Web Presence Is Growing."

13. A summary of northern Africa's Internet development appears in Jensen, "North African Internet." See also Drummond, "North Africa's Mobile Connections," p. 32.

14. "In Southern Africa, Only 20 Percent Have Electricity."

15. Karanja, "Expanding the East African Internet Market," p. 22.

16. For an overview of telecommunications development in Africa, see Noam, *Telecommunications in Africa.*

17. Figures quoted in Beresford, "South Africa."

18. A major factor in Western reluctance to invest in Africa is its staggering debt to the rest of the world (more than three-quarters of its gross domestic product [GDP] and nearly four times its annual exports in 2000), which was the subject of the first European/African "summit" in Cairo in April 2000. For an analysis of the results of the summit, see "African Debt, European Doubt," pp. 46–51.

19. Jensen, "Making the Connection," p. 219. See also Marsden, "Enterprise."
20. For an analysis of the politics, see Nevin, "South Africa," pp. 35–36.
21. The bond offering is analyzed in "Telkom Sets Out Its Stall," pp. 30–32. See also "Comment and Analysis: South Africa," and Hazelhurst, "Will Privatisations Hit Sweet Spot?" p. 36.
22. "Wiring the Wilderness: South African Telecoms," p. 68.
23. "DA [Democratic Alliance] Disappointed at Government Telkom Decision," p. 1.
24. "Telkom Welcomes Competition," p. 1.
25. For discussions of the politics and diplomacy of the relevant issues, see "Telecoms: ANC Government Must Underwrite Competition," p. 14; see also Commey, "Let the Telkom Games Begin!" pp. 37–39, and "USTR [U.S. Trade Representative] Says Mexico, Colombia, Taiwan, South Africa Must Open Telecom Markets," pp. 1–2.
26. Collier and Gunning, "Why Has Africa Grown Slowly?" pp. 18–19.
27. See Huque, Mark, and Mathieson, "Risk in Africa," p. 270. International investment in Africa as a share of GDP was only 18 percent in 1999 but if recalculated at international relative prices would have been approximately 9–10 percent. This compares with 23 percent in South Asia and 29 percent on average in lower-middle-income countries. See Collier and Gunning, "Why Has Africa Grown Slowly?" p. 19.
28. Collier and Gunning, "Why Has Africa Grown Slowly?" p. 20. Collier is director of the Development Research Group at the World Bank in Washington, D.C., and Gunning is director of the Centre for the Study of African Economies at Oxford University in England.
29. A major research project at the University of Maryland, called the Africa Telematics Initiative, reached the tentative conclusion in mid-2001 that African "institutional and leadership commitments to advancing ICT [information and communications technologies] are still modest" and that "weak institutions, half-hearted leadership and slowly changing policies" are not a recipe for revolutionary changes. Quoted with permission from an unpublished project paper by Ernest Wilson III and Kelvin Wong, "African Information Revolution: A Balance Sheet," Center for International Development and Conflict Management, June 2001, p. 28.
30. See Currie, "E-Lack-of-Commerce," pp. 7–15, and Mbogo, "Can Africa Exploit the Internet?" pp. 127–130. See also "South Africa Gets Heavy on the Internet," p. 7, reporting that the South African Revenue Service is preparing plans to tax e-commerce in South Africa before it has even started.
31. Surprisingly, the president of South Africa, Thabo Mbeki, picked up information through the Internet in 1999 about the toxic side effects of AZT, the anti-AIDS drug, as well as reports of lawsuits pending against the drug in the United States, Britain, and elsewhere. He used that information to effectively oppose the sale of AZT within South Africa. See "Mbeki's Words," p. 46, and "Thabo Mbeki, Micro-Manager," p. 44.

32. The survey is detailed in Useem, "Wiring African Universities," p. A51. Useem points out that some African academic institutions—for example, Eduardo Mondlane University in Mozambique, the University of Zambia, and the Kigali Institute of Science, Technology, and Management in Rwanda—have up-to-date facilities and outstanding human resources, but even at some of Africa's most advanced universities dial-up access to the Internet can be found "only in the president's office or the library of the offices of a handful of academics involved in international projects financed by outside donor organizations."

33. Jensen, "Making the Connection," p. 217.

34. A delightful analysis of Africa's new Internet communicators is an unpublished 16-page paper titled "Writing Up African News," delivered to the Commonwealth Editors Conference in Durban by Irwin Manoim, publisher of the *Daily Mail and Guardian* (Johannesburg), February 22, 2000. Manoim begins the paper as follows: "Africa has the world's worst phone systems, the world's worst postal systems, the world's worst roads. That's in the dry months. In the wet months, bad roads become impassable, phone lines are blown down and post disappears in the mud. Bad phones, bad roads and bad postal deliveries are three good reasons for confidence about the future of the Internet in Africa. The Internet is going to succeed in Africa, because it has to. There is no alternative" (p. 1).

35. A summary of the ECA survey appears in Mutume, *Africa-Development.* Jensen, in "Making the Connection" (pp. 216 ff.), analyzes the ECA data and points out that the profile of Internet users in the survey is consistent with other surveys conducted in individual African countries.

36. The African Studies Department at Columbia University in New York has identified 120 African newspapers and news magazines available on the Internet, many hosted by Africa's largest ISP, AfricaOnline, which has offices in six countries. Two continent-wide African news agencies—Inter Press Service and the Panafrican News Agency—use electronic media extensively. For more information, see Accone, "Digital Dividends," pp. 67–70. See also Joe S.M. Kadhi, "Internet Plays Increasing Role in Africa's Free Press," an unpublished paper delivered at a conference in Johannesburg, September 3, 1999, available at www.freedomforum.org.

37. A comprehensive 1995 United Nations Educational, Scientific, and Cultural Organization survey detailed the extent to which radio is the dominant mass medium in Africa, with radio ownership estimated at close to 180 per 1,000 inhabitants, compared with 35 per 1,000 inhabitants for television and 3 per 1,000 inhabitants for computers. As Jensen points out, both radios and television sets are commonly shared, and "it is not uncommon to find most of a small village crowded around the only television set, often powered by a car battery or small generator." See Jensen, "Making the Connection," p. 217.

38. For an analysis of the global significance of the proliferation of NGOs within the context of international Internet politics, including Africa, see Warkentin, *Reshaping World Politics,* especially pp. 27–38.

39. Matthews, "Power Shift," p. 51.

40. "After Seattle," p. 21.

41. Slaughter, "The Real New World Order," p. 184.

42. Pisik, "U.N. Panel Now Aims," p. A1.

43. For a description of the meeting, see Beale, "Developing Under the Net," p. 44.

44. For an analysis of India's associational life, see Wirsing, *Socialist Society.*

45. These are estimates I made long before the Internet was introduced to India. See Franda, *Voluntary Associations,* pp. 12 ff. A discussion of linguistic, religious, and regional group formation appears in Brass, *Language, Religion, and Politics,* pp. 32 ff. See also Ramphele, "India: Networking," and Sarin, "A Caring System," p. 37.

46. See Franda, "China and India Online," chaps. 3 and 4.

47. Quoted in Slaughter, "The Real New World Order," p. 184. For a detailed explication of the relationship between transgovernmentalism and interdependence, see Keohane and Nye, *Power and Interdependence.*

48. "Comity among nations" is a phrase that has been used for centuries by diplomats and international lawyers, signifying rather loosely the deference a given state grants to another state in recognition of their mutual sovereignty. For an analysis of its use in resolving Internet-related conflicts between nations, see Rothchild, "Protecting the Digital Consumer," pp. 985–986.

49. See Franda, *Governing the Internet,* pp. 378 ff.

50. Slaughter, "The Real New World Order," pp. 196, 198.

51. Matthews, "Power Shift," p. 54.

52. Rodrik, "How Far?" p. 178. All quotations in this paragraph are from this source. Rodrik based his conclusions on a wide range of studies, including Helliwell, *How Much?*

53. Rodrik, "How Far?" p. 179.

54. Ibid., p. 182.

55. Similar conclusions for EU integration are reached by Holman, "Integrating Eastern Europe," pp. 12–43. See also Burwell and Daalder, *The United States and Europe.*

56. Preston and Windsor, *The Rules of the Game,* p. 7.

57. The survey was conducted by the *Financial Times* (London) and is reported in Parker, "Survey—Mastering Management," p. 12.

58. Dean, "UN Proposes Global Email Tax." See also Carter, "Critics," p. A4.

59. Post, "The New Electronic Federalism," pp. 93–94. See also Best, "Federalism and International Democracy," pp. 17–21, and Chatfield, "The Federalism Papers," pp. 373–379.

60. Wu, "When Law and the Internet First Met," p. 177.

61. Wu, "Cyberspace Sovereignty?" p. 663.

62. Ibid., pp. 663–664. This perspective is consistent with my approach, based on the international regime literature of political science. See Franda, *Governing the Internet,* pp. 1–12.

63. For more information, see Hansen, *Getting Online,* and Hansen, *AAAS Directory.*

64. Knutsen, *The Rise and Fall of World Orders,* pp. 130, 158, 267. Quotations in this paragraph are from this source.

65. Ibid., p. 130.

66. For an analysis of ICANN's worldwide election for its at-large council, see McNatt and Yang, "Democratic Rule," pp. 8–9. For the role of the American Library Association and the Markle Foundation in supporting the ICANN council election through the Internet, see "ALA to Play a Role," pp. 12–13.

67. An early study relating computer networking to civil societies is Fortier, "Civil Society." Two thoughtful later studies of cyberdemocracy are Hurwitz, "Who Needs Politics?" pp. 655–662, and Netanel, "Cyberspace Self-Governance," pp. 395–499. See also the analysis of the 2000 ICANN elections in Franda, *Governing the Internet.*

68. Krasner, *International Regimes,* p. 1.

69. This conception is heavily dependent on the work of Stein, "Coordination and Collaboration," pp. 115 ff.

70. Ibid., p. 116.

71. Ibid., p. 128. Examples of international regimes designed to deal with the dilemma of aversions are traffic conventions, such as those in the airline industry that recognize English as the lingua franca of air traffic control. All pilots who fly between nations must speak enough English to communicate with traffic control towers, and all flight control centers must keep a sufficient number of English speakers on duty to direct all pilots who do not speak the language of the country into which they are flying. As a result, in Stein's words, "the mutual aversion, an air disaster, is avoided and a safe equilibrium is assured" (p. 129).

72. For an expanded discussion of theories of international regimes, see Franda, *Governing the Internet,* pp. 1–3, 19–21. See also Hasenclever, Mayer, and Rittberger, *Theories of International Regimes,* and Rittberger, *Regime Theory.*

73. The concepts *spontaneous order, negotiated order,* and *imposed order,* as used to discuss international regime theory, have been developed by Young, "Regime Dynamics," pp. 93–113.

74. The thinking of the U.S. government at the time of the creation of ICANN in 1998 is discussed in Harmon, "U.S. Gives Up." In fact, the U.S. did not relinquish its authority over the global Internet's governing structure but instead has entered into agreements with two private organizations (ICANN and Network Solutions, Inc.) to manage the structure for the period 1998–2006. Professor Lawrence Lessig of Harvard University expressed his concern with this approach in 1999: "We are creating the most significant new jurisdiction since the Louisiana Purchase, yet we are building it just outside the Constitution's review. Indeed, we are building it just so that the Constitution will not govern—as if we want to be free of the constraints of value embedded by that tradition." See Lessig, *Code and Other Laws,* p. 217. See also Kleinwachter, "ICANN."

75. This summary is taken from the conclusions in Franda, *Governing the Internet;* see especially pp. 203ff.

76. These negotiations and compromises are the subject of a substantial portion of ibid.

77. An analysis of some of the manifestations of LDC aspirations to gain greater independence from the global Internet regime appears in Glater, "Hemming in the World Wide Web."

2

Internet Cultures
in Israel and the Arab World

In the Middle East the Internet is viewed alternatively by those in positions of power as politically intrusive, culturally threatening, and an opportunity to reshape Middle Eastern relationships with the rest of the world. With widely varying degrees of understanding of the new technology in leadership circles, the Middle Eastern nations are hoping to settle on coherent strategies to both accommodate and control the Internet, which has come to be accepted as potentially a major factor in the organization and reorganization of Middle Eastern societies and polities in the twenty-first century. Because leaders in this part of the world have been extremely wary of the possible consequences of immediate connectivity to cyberspace, the pace of Internet development was originally as slow as or slower than in any global region other than Africa, with the result that meaningful links between the Middle East and the nascent international regime for the Internet are still minimal. At the dawn of the millennium, however, many Middle Eastern leaders are beginning to work together rather aggressively and purposefully to involve their nations more closely with worldwide Internet developments.[1]

The Middle Eastern nations have not yet formed a regional association of Internet service providers (ISPs), as has been the case in other regions of the world—in part because there are a limited number of ISPs and relatively few Internet users in the region, in part because Internet growth and usage are supervised at higher levels of government.[2] As is clear from Table 2.1, the Arab states constitute a minor blip on the screen of Internet users worldwide, with less than 1 percent (0.7 percent) of their 280 million people having some access to the Internet in

41

Table 2.1   Internet Users in the Middle East, March 2000

Country	Number of Subscribers	Users per Account	Total Number of Users	Users per 1,000 Population
UAE	160,000	2.5	400,000	150.0
Israel	Not available	Not available	700,000	112.0
Qatar	18,000	2.5	45,000	61.0
Bahrain	15,000	2.5	37,500	60.0
Lebanon	65,000	3.5	227,500	57.0
Kuwait	40,000	2.5	100,000	50.0
Oman	20,000	2.5	50,000	20.0
Jordan	25,000	3.5	87,500	19.0
Saudi Arabia	100,000	3.0	300,000	14.0
Tunisia	22,000	5.0	110,000	12.0
Egypt	55,000	8.0	440,000	6.5
Morocco	15,000	3.5	52,500	1.7
Libya	1,500	5.0	7,500	1.6
Syria	4,000	5.0	20,000	1.0
Yemen	3,000	4.0	12,000	0.7
Sudan	2,000	5.0	10,000	0.3
Totals	545,500	3.8 (average)	2,599,500	7.1

Source: NUA Internet Surveys, March 2000, at www.nua.ie/surveys/how_many_online/. Although later figures are available from diverse sources, the March 2000 figures are used here because they capture a snapshot of relative Internet development among Middle Eastern countries. Later figures, when available, indicate that the relative positions of countries vis-à-vis one another (the purpose of the table) had been altered within a maximum of two rankings in March 2001.

March 2000. Although Israel is a major manufacturer of hardware and software for the Internet, a surprisingly small portion of the Israeli population (somewhere between 12 percent and 20 percent, depending on definitions) has logged on to use this new technology. Middle Easterners are also notably absent from leadership positions in the major organizations concerned with overall operation of the Internet's technical infrastructure, including those associated with the organization that controls Internet domain names and the global Internet root server, the Internet Corporation for Assigned Names and Numbers (ICANN).

Middle Eastern nations are active members of a number of international organizations that have played a lead role in developing various facets of the international regime for the Internet—such as the World Trade Organization (WTO), the World Intellectual Property Organization (WIPO), the Internet Trademark Organization (ITO), and the International Telecommunications Union (ITU)—but Middle Eastern representatives to these organizations have thus far been concerned with more general matters (e.g., trade, telecommunications, intellectual property) and are just beginning to become involved in activities within these organizations relating specifically to the Internet. This situation could begin to change significantly in the years ahead following the decision to locate the November 5–9, 2001, worldwide WTO meeting in Doha, Qatar.[3] The percentage of Middle Easterners participating in organizations concerned with Internet standards—such as the Internet Society (ISOC), the Internet Engineering Task Force (IETF), the ATM Forum, the Frame Relay Forum, and the Network Management Forum—is far less than 1 percent, reflecting both the minuscule numbers of Internet users depicted in Table 2.1 and the tentative approach of Middle Eastern governments to modern information technology. Arab leaders are generally convinced that the legal frameworks governing the Internet in Europe and the United States cannot be adopted in their entirety by Middle Eastern nations, but the construction of a more appropriate indigenous Internet regime has proceeded rather haltingly because of a lack of consensus among diverse interests in the Arab world.[4]

▪ ISRAEL AS A HIGH-TECH ENCLAVE

One of the surprises in the Middle East's lackadaisical Internet development is Israel's ambiguous position as a major producer of Internet-related equipment and software while its citizenry has not been nearly as intensely involved with the Internet as might be expected (in this sense, Israel reflects more a European than a U.S. pattern of development). Israel's leadership in global Internet-related products is the result of a series of decisions over the past few decades to reinvent itself to become a high-tech enclave of world-class dimension and quality. The "father of Israeli high tech" is often said to be Uzia Galil, a Romanian-born electrical engineer who was trained by the Israeli navy in the late 1940s, graduated from the Technion in Haifa, earned a master's degree in electrical engineering from Purdue University in the early 1950s, and worked at Motorola on the development of its first colored television set.[5] Galil returned to the Israeli navy in 1954 while he taught at the Technion. In 1962 he persuaded the Rockefeller Fund to give him $160,000 for a start-up medical electronics company called Elron, operated out of a garage in Haifa. Under Galil's chairmanship, Elron gradually became a company devoted to identifying entrepreneurial teams, incubating them in-house, and spinning them off as start-up high-tech companies in many other fields. Galil estimated in 1999 that companies originally under Elron's umbrella accounted for 20 percent of the Israeli electronics industry.[6]

High-tech development in Israel is also related to the country's involvement in several wars with its neighbors and its constant quest for greater security. For example, Israel turned dramatically to the United States for technological assistance following the Six Day War in 1967, when President Charles de Gaulle imposed an embargo on the sale of French weaponry (Israel had fought the 1967 war primarily with arms from France). In the 1973 Yom Kippur War, Israel was caught off-guard by the technological advances of its enemies and the difficulty it had procuring vital matériel from foreign suppliers. This spurred a drive for technological self-sufficiency, including an attempt to develop an indigenous combat aircraft (the Lavi). Although the Lavi experiment failed, it resulted in hundreds of top-flight engineers being trained and released into the market in the mid-1980s. A leading Israeli business journal has described the Lavi project's demise as "one of the greatest ever boosts to Israeli high-tech industry."[7] Finally, during the 1991 Gulf War, Israel proved vulnerable to long-range missile attacks by Iraq, prompting the development of considerable advances in radar, ballistics, and weapons but also in high-tech fields related to intelligence gathering, command and control, and other areas in which information technology is crucial.

The major push for Israel to seriously restructure its economy toward high-tech development occurred under the Labor government in 1986, in part a result of military-strategic considerations but also in an effort to bring hyperinflation under control. The original policies were similar to those of Reaganomics in the United States, with severe cutbacks in government spending accompanied by a freeze on the value of the shekel and relaxation of regulations on entrepreneurial enterprises. In succeeding years Israel's economic emphasis has shifted from agricultural and military employment to information technology companies (early areas of expertise were often defense related—e.g., electro-optics, semiconductor design and communications, networking—but this vastly expanded to fields of wider societal and commercial interest in the 1990s, including many areas of central importance to the Internet). Israeli companies are now at the cutting edge of development in such fields as data compression, Internet security and encryption, antivirus software, printing and prepress equipment, software, and multimedia.

This is the third time in its short history that Israel has effected a major reorientation of its economy, having first built a solid agricultural base and, later, an industrial economy known for exceptional defense industry products. With a population about the size of greater Philadelphia (6.2 million people in 2000) occupying a total land area less than the size of New Jersey, Israel became a world player in information technology at some point in the mid-1990s. By 1997 a leading publisher estimated that Israelis accounted for about a thousand high-tech start-up companies, primarily in the information technology sector, with eighty of them—more than for all of Europe—listed on the Nasdaq Exchange.[8] A November 1998 *Newsweek* survey identified Tel Aviv as one of the world's "top ten" centers for high-tech development.[9] By mid-2000 *Wired* magazine ranked Israel as the fourth most influential "hi-tech hub" in the world, trailing only Silicon Valley, Boston, Massachusetts, and the Stockholm-Kista area of Sweden.[10] Israel was also ranked fairly high among "global leaders" in the Emerging Markets Focus (EMFocus) technology permeation index (TPI) for emerging market economies.[11]

Israel has attained its position among high-tech leaders as a result of a number of factors in addition to its entrepreneurs (as represented by Galil), including conscious government policies to develop the necessary human and financial resources and physical infrastructure. Beginning in the 1950s, fellowships and scholarships were made available to Israeli students (like Galil) studying abroad in high-technology fields, including especially information technology, semiconductors, biotechnology, and medical instrumentation. At the same time, significant computer-based and advanced technology programs were initiated in Israeli schools, colleges, and universities.[12] Israelis wishing to become high-tech entrepreneurs could take advantage of government-approved incentive programs such as those that waived income taxes for ten years for companies located in Jerusalem and for four years for companies in Tel Aviv. Starting in the 1990s particularly, aspiring entrepreneurs have been offered a full range of incentives and amenities in new facilities like those in the new Hi-Tech Park in Haifa. Since the late 1970s the Office of the Chief Scientist in Israel has supported and promoted the Binational Industrial Research and Development (BIRD) Foundation, jointly organized and funded by an initial $110 million endowment provided in equal parts by the U.S. and Israeli governments to bring about matches between Israeli and U.S. high-tech companies. BIRD provides funding for up to 50 percent of project development and product commercialization costs and has built a significant record for seeding Israeli high-tech start-ups.[13] A number of other venture capital funds for high-tech development were initiated by the Israeli government in the 1990s.

The major breeding ground for Israel's high-tech development has been the country's defense forces. In Barbara Tuck's words, "The seeds of nearly every hi-tech startup are sown in the military, where Israeli youths bond with their fellows and learn to innovate and improvise. . . . Israelis often get crash courses in hi-tech in the military, preparing them to hit the ground running in the technology business. Most often . . . startups are begun by people who [have] been in the military together and developed loyalty to one another."[14] An additional factor speeding along Israel's high-tech growth is the in-country presence of almost a million well-educated and motivated Russian, Eastern European, and other recent immigrants—most of whom had scientific and engineering backgrounds when they entered the country, making them amenable to retrain in high-tech fields.[15] Israelis' facility with English (the dominant language of high tech) and Israel's many links with the United States have also been important in the rapid expansion of the country's high-tech capabilities, as have cultural factors and historical circumstances.[16]

High-tech linkages to the United States begin for most Israelis with education experiences, which have been extensive at every level. Many, if not most, Israeli professionals have secured their education—even at the elementary and secondary school levels—at least in part in the United States, and both U.S. higher education and U.S. work experience are common for Israeli high-tech leaders. In the words of Dr. Yoav Nissan-Cohen, co–chief executive officer (CEO) of Tower Semiconductor in Migdal Haemek, Israel's high-tech leaders constitute a "network" based largely on common experiences in, and linkages to, the United States: "We Israelis all spent time in America, working for GE, Bell Labs, IBM, or in Silicon Valley, and we made our Ph.D.s together."[17]

The Israeli-U.S. high-tech network has been strengthened since the 1960s by the location in Israel of dozens of U.S. high-tech firms—led by such powerhouses as Motorola (which established its first non-U.S. subsidiary in Tel Aviv in 1964), Intel (which built its first design and development center outside the United States in Haifa in 1974), Microsoft, and many others—and by the formal linkages or mergers of Israeli and U.S. companies. In March 1999 alone, U.S. companies (including America Online, ADC, BMC, Lucent, Platinum, and SunGard) paid nearly $1.2 billion to purchase Israeli software firms, compared with $1.5 billion for all of 1998.[18] In 1999 the *Venture Capital Journal* estimated that Israel captured 7.7 percent of U.S. venture dollars—more than the United Kingdom (4–5 percent), all of Asia (4.1 percent), and all of Eastern Europe (3.6 percent).[19] During the first quarter of 2000, more than $590 million poured into Israel's venture capital market.[20] Whether merged or otherwise linked, the common pattern is to locate high-tech research and development (R&D) in Israel, with management, sales, and marketing based in the United States.[21]

■ INTERNET DEVELOPMENT IN ISRAEL

Given Israel's considerable success in high-tech (including directly Internet-related) development, it is surprising that Israelis are not (by world standards) more frequent Internet users. In January 2000 the number of Internet Web surfers in Israel was estimated at 700,000, only 12 percent of the Israeli population (compared, for example, with the United States, which had at the time more than 100 million Web surfers and a penetration rate of more than 50 percent).[22] Moreover, Israel has much less online banking, online trading, and use of the Internet for e-commerce than one finds in the United States and Europe—a surprising phenomenon, particularly in light of Israel's world leadership in developing Internet technology.[23] The Israeli legislature (the Knesset) became so agitated over this anomaly in late 1999 that Knesset chairman Avraham Burg acceded to a suggestion by Knesset member Michael Eitan to cosponsor an "Internet Day" in the Knesset during the first week of the new millennium. A survey of global venture capitalism by the Internet marketing firm Kesselman and Kesselman in mid-2000 revealed the astounding finding that "there were no Israeli-based business-to-business or business-to-consumer e-commerce companies funded [in the previous year]."[24]

The major reasons Israelis have been reluctant to integrate an Internet culture into their daily lives have largely to do with (1) the technological shortcomings of the Internet's operation on computers in Israel, which in turn stem from (2) the unwillingness of the Israeli government in the 1990s to allow privatization of the telecommunications infrastructure to the degree necessary for high-speed, efficient operation, and (3) an accompanying unwillingness to allow freedom of operation and competition among local telecommunications providers and

ISPs. The result is an Internet backbone and infrastructure not readily available to the consumer and, when available, often slow and cumbersome to access. As Efi Landau observed, "Anyone who has not had the frustrating experience of facing his computer, cursing and waiting for the site to materialise on the display screen, and then continuing to fume and rage with every repeated try, every new page, has no notion of what surfing in Israel means."[25]

Recent governments have pledged to improve Israel's inferior Internet backbone facilities, beginning with campaign promises in the mid-1990s. These promises were pushed forward substantively for the first time in a November 1997 interministerial recommendation that competition be introduced into the telecommunications sector of the Israeli economy by "not later than January 1999."[26] Pressure to open telecommunications to competition since that time has come primarily from the multilateral agreement on basic telecommunications Israel signed with the WTO in 1997, committing Israel to policies that allowed foreign investment in telecommunications in Israel on more favorable terms while allowing for more open and unregulated competition. The WTO agreement is considered essential if Israel is to continue to share in the benefits of world trade and the international Internet regime. But Israel's monopoly telecommunications provider, Bezeq, successfully stalled or prevented implementation of the agreement over the second half of the 1990s, despite pressure from several government ministries, while it positioned itself to cement and preserve advantages derived from its past monopoly position once competition is allowed.[27]

In fall 2000, in moves designed to diminish the monopoly of Bezeq, the Israeli Ministry of Communications finally announced a series of measures that promised substantial eventual privatization of the telecommunications sector and greater degrees of competition and deregulation as required by Israel's 1997 agreement with the WTO. Communications Minister Binyamin (Fuad) Ben-Eliezer announced in September 2000 that the government intended to sell all of its holdings in Bezeq within the next year and at the same time to establish a new independent regulatory authority for the telecoms sector charged with diminishing government regulation while increasing transparency in decisionmaking and pricing. Bezeq was instructed to shed 2,000 members of its 6,500 workforce before September 2001 in preparation for the day it would become a completely private company.

Under new deregulation measures, also announced in September 2000, the government indicated that it would immediately begin selling

3.6 percent of its stake in Bezeq over the next year, diminishing its share of company stock from 54.6 percent to 51.0 percent in order to raise funds to finance the pensions and severance payments for dismissed employees. Under this plan, after September 2001 foreign investors would be allowed to own 80 percent of the shares of Bezeq, providing none of the companies was linked to any government (including the Israeli government) or was associated with a hostile country. The remainder of the shares (20 percent) would be held by an Israeli company, yet to be determined. Minister Ben-Eliezer insisted in that the Israeli "strategic partner" would not hold a disproportionate share of voting rights.[28]

Immediately following the September 2000 announcement, Bezeq employees stopped work in protest of the proposed deregulation plan and launched a series of labor-led actions against the government. The protests coincided with the increased bloodshed and violence between Israelis and Palestinians that accompanied the breakdown of the Bill Clinton–led attempt to bring peace to the Middle East. Both manifestations of unrest were accompanied by a severe downturn in the Israeli economy in fall and early winter 2000, brought about in part by a dramatic decline in the U.S. economy and stock markets. When Prime Minister Ehud Barak resigned in December 2000 and scheduled new elections for the Knesset for February 2001, plans for Bezeq's privatization were put on hold. Yaron Jacobs, director-general of the Israel Government Companies Authority, announced in January 2001 that "recent local and global developments . . . have rendered irrelevant . . . the schedule . . . for the core control of *Bezeq*."[29] In May 2001, Jacobs and a new communications minister, Reuven Rivlin, recommended that the question of Bezeq's privatization be referred to a ministerial committee, headed by Prime Minister Ariel Sharon, with the admonition that the "problematic" world markets of 2001 might make it impossible to attract a satisfactory price and terms of sale.[30]

Bezeq's monopoly position was at least temporarily buttressed in November 2000 when the Ministry of Communications agreed to license Bezeq as a "fast" Internet service provider, using broadband asymmetric digital subscriber line (ADSL) technology, while denying broadband licenses to cable companies that were potentially formidable competitors. Minister Ben-Eliezer was in favor of granting licenses to cable companies as well as Bezeq, but he was overruled by Attorney General Elyakim Rubinstein, who demanded that the legal status of Bezeq as a privatized company be finalized before legal agreements were drawn up with the cable companies. In November 2000 Ben-Eliezer expressed regret at his inability to grant licenses for high-speed Internet service to Israeli cable companies and warned that Bezeq's head start in providing high-speed broadband services would most likely perpetuate its monopoly even after it was privatized. "This is not what I wanted," he said. "I was not given the authority, so that, contrary to my wishes, *Bezeq* is becoming a monopoly that will be hard to shake."[31]

Most analysts agree with the Ministry of Communications that the way in which privatization and increased competition are being allowed into the telecommunications sector in Israel will, at the very least, allow Bezeq to maintain a competitive advantage over potential rivals for several years into the future and could result in the telecommunications giant maintaining a monopoly position as a private company for an even longer period. A market analyst at Logtel Telecommunications, an international consulting firm, has argued publicly that Israeli leadership "does not totally support a free and competitive market [because] . . . as the owner of Bezeq, the government does not want to see the company fail."[32] It is clear, however, that some conservative and pro–free enterprise Israeli leaders genuinely favor privatization and increased competition and could, if given power in a future election, accelerate free market reforms already in motion. In the meantime, current policies are expected to gradually improve the speed and services of Internet access, although not at a pace fast enough to satisfy the most demanding Internet users.[33]

In other societies, both privatization and enforcement of an orderly regulatory regime in the telecommunications sector have been crucial to the development of information technology and the Internet.[34] Whether Israel will be able to move significantly in these directions is sometimes questioned because of the country's past history with heavy government involvement in key sectors of the economy, particularly in those sectors (like communications) that are also defense related. If significant progress toward privatization and deregulation is not made, most observers suggest the full potential for rapid development of Internet use in Israel is unlikely to be realized.

Since 1999 the Ministry of Communications and Bezeq have tried to reduce the cost of Internet-related telephone services, but reductions have not been drastic enough to make a dramatic difference in the cost of cyberspace access over telephone lines. In August 1999, when some Internet surfers tried to organize a strike against prices being charged for Internet-related telecommunications services provided by Bezeq, the Ministry of Commerce reiterated its goal of expanding competition and reducing rates in some parts of the telecommunications sector but refused to accede to the argument that privatization and competition alone would significantly reduce costs to consumers. As Tami Sheinkman, spokesperson for the ministry, said, "The Ministry's policy is to encourage the use of [the] Internet by expanding competition, yet one must realize that, by lowering these particular rates, other call rates will unjustly increase as cross subsidies."[35] Once Bezeq was granted the only license for providing broadband services in Israel in November 2000, its charges to customers for those services tended to reflect its monopoly position.[36]

Perhaps because of the lack of a solid Internet infrastructure and backbone, Israel's governmental, corporate, and advertising leadership has been reluctant to invest in Internet use. The first Israeli newspaper to create an Internet edition was *Ha'aretz* in 1997, the same year the prime minister's office initiated a public Internet presence for much of the government. Most Israeli banks now offer "passive services" over the Internet, including verification of account balances and portfolio management advice, but many are still reluctant to allow money to be moved from one place to another online. Companies (including high-tech companies) only began investing meaningfully in Internet sites in 1997 and 1998, and very few have instituted corporate advertising on the Web. As Doron Avigad observed in late 1999, "An advertisement and/or site on the 'Net is still regarded in Israel as a doubtful venture. The aim of advertisers who do go on the 'Net is still to show a presence, and not, it is believed, to break through to a new market segment."[37]

Lack of Internet-related investment in Israel by Israelis has been primarily the result of high capital-gains taxes in connection with initial public offerings—varying from 35 to 50 percent (compared with 20 percent in the United States)—with the result that Israel's premier companies have flocked to the U.S. stock market, where since 1993 they have raised more shares on the Nasdaq than companies from any other country. The Internet boom, therefore, has not helped the Israeli economy as much as one might expect. In a March 2000 article in the *Wall Street Journal*, Stephen Glain described what he called "an economic Hydra" in Israel, resulting from "high taxes, red tape, resilient unions and stultifying monopolies," to account for Israel's slow overall economic growth during the period 1997–2000: "Only a small, high-tech elite is getting rich. Unemployment remains at double-digit levels. Economic growth is slowing and is barely keeping up with population growth.

Gross domestic product advanced just 2.2 percent last year, even with 1998 and down from 2.9 percent the year before."[38]

One factor likely to enhance Internet use in the first few years of the twenty-first century—in Israel and other parts of the Middle East—is wireless Internet technology. Mobile telephones are already widely used in Israel (28 per 100 population), Lebanon (16), the United Arab Emirates (13), and Kuwait (11). Cell phones are popular in the Middle East because they tend to work better than most of the phones connected to the old and more expensive fixed-line networks (or in the case of Lebanon, a fixed-line network destroyed by war[39]). They are also suited to an environment subject to traffic jams and other hassles and forms of delay, where conservative sexual and social mores create many situations in which people prefer to talk in private over a phone line rather than be seen talking to one another in public.[40] On the basis primarily of mobile telephone use in the Middle East, the Internet analyst company Ovum is projecting that 30,000 people in Africa and the Middle East will be using wireless Internet devices in 2001, 2.1 million in 2002, and 23.1 million (2 percent of the population) by 2005.[41] Although mobile Internet devices will allow only a limited number of websites to be visited, with fewer options and a much smaller viewing screen than a desktop computer, the great benefit of the technology will be its convenience and capabilities for quickly identifying location-specific data. For these reasons, mobile technology could be more suitable for a larger number of people in the Middle East than the traditional Internet devices of previous years.[42]

▪ INFORMATION TECHNOLOGY IN THE ARAB MIDDLE EAST

In contrast to Israel, the Arab Middle East has not developed a thriving information technology (IT) manufacturing industry and in most countries has enacted regulations consciously designed to limit and restrict use of the Internet by citizens. Reluctance to embrace a new technology is consistent with long-standing historical patterns, evident since the sixteenth century, of unsuccessful adaptation by most Middle Eastern nations to the challenges of European technological and scientific advances. Prior to the sixteenth century the Arab-Islamic world was connected by a widespread system of trade and transport that extended into Africa and eastward into Asia at a time when the Arab world and Europe were at relative technological parity.[43] All of that began to change drastically in 1498 when Vasco da Gama reached the waters of the Gulf by circumnavigating the Cape of Good Hope, initiating an extended period of European colonization and dominance based on technological innovation.[44] In subsequent centuries Arab shipbuilders failed to construct the increasingly sophisticated oceangoing vessels built by European and East Asian shipbuilders, the extensive Arab international trading network that had extended into Africa and western, and southern Asia dramatically lost market share and profits to larger-scale and more effective European-based trading organizations and companies (beginning with the East India Company in the seventeenth century); and Arab-dominated regional and local overland trade and transport systems were dismantled and replaced by the construction of railway systems and the Suez Canal in the nineteenth century.

In the last few centuries the Arab world has lost its dominant position in regional coffee and textile trades because of an inability to keep up with technological advances in these two areas.[45] Most Middle Eastern nations have become highly dependent on the importation of products in almost all aspects of modern life, including steam power, machinery, chemical sciences, electrification, petroleum production and refining, communications technologies, radio and television, electric power and engineering, satellite development, advances in medical science and pharmaceuticals, construction technologies, defense equipment and armaments, city planning, management systems, and much else. With very few exceptions the Arab states have procured technology through turnkey modes of contracting that have left most Middle Eastern nations with meager human resources to develop their own technological capabilities. The historical process that led to this denouement has been summarized by Antoine Zahlan:

> New technology was imported in a dependent mode and packaged with its consultants, contractors, operators, and financiers. The cost of all of this dependent luxury was enormous; the resulting Egyptian and Ottoman debts had well known economic and political consequences. . . . The net result was the further divorce of the elites, the culture, and the economy from technical matters. . . . When independence was finally achieved, the rulers and elites of the new states who came forward had little knowledge of contemporary developments in science and technology. Foreign control of the political life and economies of the Arab countries was less complete than the foreign control of government operations and of technological activity. Not only did all equipment, industrial supplies, and maintenance services have to be

imported but also the Arab countries depended completely on foreign consulting and contracting services when they sought to alter their economic circumstances.[46]

Even during the period of high world oil prices and expanded petroleum exports in the 1970s and 1980s, the wealthy oil-producing countries of the Middle East found it impossible to develop effective indigenous science and technology policies but instead, in most cases, stepped up importation of lavish technological marvels under traditional turnkey arrangements. This new level of imports was often repackaged under high-sounding government programs variously labeled "client-in-hand" (Gulf Cooperation Council), "explosive development" (Iraq), or "technologie-de-pointe" (Algeria). The consequences of this splurge of investment in new technologies by Middle Eastern nations has again been summarized by Zahlan:

> Truly wondrous things were built: power and desalination plants, hospitals which could boast the best and latest in medical sciences, irrigation schemes, enormous dams, transport systems, airports, airlines, military installations, radar stations, remote sensing facilities, solar stations, communications systems, super-guns, [and] . . . Liquid Natural Gas technology. . . . The Arab countries total GFCF [gross fixed capital formation] during the past two decades was in excess of $2,000 billion (in current prices). If this sum were to be converted into 1991 dollars, these investments would probably total between $4,000 and $5,000 billion. The 1993 combined GNP [gross national product] of the Arab countries resulting from this enormous GFCF was barely $380 billion. The gap between the Arab world and industrial countries has continued to grow, and the Arab economies suffer from chronic stagnation and low productivity.[47]

▪ INERTIA AND RESTRAINT IN INTERNET AND IT DEVELOPMENT

As part of the pattern outlined here, governments in most of the Middle East did not begin to import the world's most advanced information and communications technologies, particularly for consumer use, until the twenty-first century. In this respect the experience of Middle Eastern nations, with perhaps the exception of Israel, is in sharp contrast to those countries (e.g., the United States, most of Europe, Singapore) where the Internet has been enthusiastically accepted and promoted.

Outside the Middle East, the governments of nations significantly wired to cyberspace (even including China and India, both of which have been somewhat wary of Internet development) have provided substantial initial funding to build backbone telecommunications networks; enacted standards, laws, and regulations designed to stimulate private investment; created training and human resource programs to support the various facets of the Internet enterprise; and in other ways encouraged use of the new technology. Prior to 2000 little of this had been done in the Arab Middle East.

Instead of enthusiastically welcoming the Internet, Arab leaders were initially cautious, and their attitudes and actions in support of its development can best be described as ones of inertia and restraint. This was largely a result of the widespread and long-standing fear in Arab government circles that loss of control over basic information networks might result in revolutionary political change. Jon Alterman has identified four major grounds for censorship in the Arab world that grow out of this fear:[48]

1. The bounds of political debate, with established "red lines" that cannot be crossed. Alterman points out that the nature and restrictions inherent in these red lines vary from country to country (e.g., promotion of any political opposition in Saudi Arabia, discussions of terrorism in Egypt, Shi'a opposition movements in Bahrain).
2. Criticism of a country's rulers or their families. Throughout the Middle East, rulers cannot be criticized by name, and cartoons can depict only secondary or anonymous political figures.
3. Writing of a religious nature that might cause dissension. What is generally allowed are debates over the nature of Islamic finance, cultural conflict with Western secularism, and the role of women in the family and workplace. Not allowed are "discussions that seek to delegitimize Muslim groups or that incite violence against religious minorities."
4. Social and sexual mores. These vary from country to country, but "the most common denominator is a regional ban on pornography" and "materials that are likely to cause (or have caused) offense among the domestic clergy or political opposition figures."

These four grounds for censorship have been present in the Middle East for more than a century, but they take on added significance for the

Internet because of the personal, instantaneous, and more randomly accessible nature of the new technology. Although government leaders in the Middle East—almost without exception—realize the potential value of the Internet to business and research competitiveness, as well as its appeal to elite classes, they also understand the threat the Internet might pose in the hands of opposition forces, terrorists, or hostile countries. Most Arab governments will mention Muslim sensibilities (e.g., pornography) as the main reason for go-slow approaches to Internet development, but as Eric Goldstein points out, "almost without exception, their restrictions also target political or human-rights criticism."[49]

The desire to control information is not the only factor responsible for cautious Arab predispositions toward new information technologies. Both national and local religious leaders, as well as conservative sectors of society, are concerned that the Internet will open the Islamic world to outside ideas and create opportunities for freedom of expression in ways deleterious for the existing social and political order. In addition, most governments in the Middle East have been unwilling to commit to the huge financial investments necessary to become a significant actor in cyberspace. In some cases, including Israel as well as the Arab nations, the growth of the Internet has suffered because state telecommunications monopolies concerned with short-run profits have been unable to build modern infrastructural facilities and provide services at prices low enough for the rapid growth of information technology use.[50]

Although some Arab governments have gained the reputation of being "enemies of the Internet," none has come out explicitly in opposition to its presence in their countries.[51] Only Iraq (for a short period in 1997–1998) has actually banned use of the Internet by making it illegal for anyone to log on within its territorial boundaries. By mid-1999 every country in the Middle East and northern Africa except Iraq and Libya had some form of international connectivity, and only Syria had connectivity but refused to allow ordinary citizens to log on to local ISPs.[52] After the death of Hafez-al-Assad in June 2000, Syria reversed its policy and may well begin to encourage Internet development at a fairly brisk pace (discussed later). All recent Middle Eastern governments have acknowledged the importance of the new information technologies to their futures. Moreover, there are a number of indications—from all Middle Eastern and Arab nations—that the Internet is already empowering citizens and helping nongovernmental forces to mobilize in ways not previously possible.

▪ BUILDING INTERNET INFRASTRUCTURES AND BACKBONE

The major breakthrough in linking the Arab Middle East to the Internet came in January 1999 when forty-one firms in Saudi Arabia were allowed to become ISPs, acting as a "middle tier" between the monopoly provider (the Saudi Telecommunications Company [STC]) and the consumer. The forty-one new ISPs were selected by the STC from a list of seventy-one companies that had applied for the privilege. Several of the original applicants had dropped out of the contest after King Abdul Aziz City for Science and Technology (the government organization in charge of the initial development of the Internet for Saudi Arabia) imposed a legal ceiling of 4.5 Saudi rials (U.S.$1.22) per hour on the amount ISPs could charge consumers, thereby reducing potential profit margins to minimal levels.[53] Prior to the 1999 Saudi initiative, the United Arab Emirates (UAE) monopoly telecommunications company Etisalat had been the first Internet service provider in the Middle East, establishing its service in 1996. Several other Arab countries had initiated modest Internet services following Etisalat's lead.

The 1999 Saudi initiative is especially significant, in part because of the size and importance of Saudi Arabia in the Middle East but also because of the nature of the leadership behind the initiative and the dimensions of Saudi plans for the future.[54] The key figure in bringing direct Internet access to Saudi Arabia in 1999 was Prince Alwaleed bin Talal, a nephew of King Fahd, who in 2000 was ranked by *Forbes* magazine as the eighth wealthiest person in the world. Prince Alwaleed controls a fortune he estimates at $20 billion, much of it gained from his leadership of an organization called Kingdom Holding Company that has specialized since 1990 or earlier in acquiring large stakes in telecommunications and information technology companies, including Netscape Communications, AOL, Teledesic, Apple Computer, and Motorola.[55] Beginning in early 1998, the telecommunications arm of Kingdom Holding, Silki La Silki, signed a partnership agreement with the Kuwait-based satellite communications firm ZakSat to provide satellite Internet services throughout Saudi Arabia, the Middle East, and North Africa.[56] The first stage is expected to see the buildout of ZakNet, the satellite Internet delivery platform owned by ZakSat, with SilkiNet extending ZakNet's reach into Saudi Arabia and Bahrain by establishing local franchises throughout the two countries.[57] Planning for the second stage includes a regional multimedia platform providing digital television, high-speed Internet, and broadcast ("push technology") services, all available online through a Network Operating Center (NOC) expected to become the building block for a full Internet backbone in the region.[58]

SilkiNet and ZakSat are negotiating with both Arab and foreign companies to procure investment capital for new initiatives and to bring world-class technology to their various projects. Much of this activity is being coordinated by Kuwait Investment Projects Company (KIPCO), the parent company of ZakSat. ZakNet has partnered with three major information technology companies—Fantastic Corporation, Lotus Development, and Microsoft—to establish a distance learning capability (including a major open university for the Arab Gulf region and for other aspects of Internet development). One of KIPCO's principal holdings is partial ownership of United Broadcasting Company, a joint venture with Viacom International for the Showtime network in the Middle East region.

Saudi Arabia's initiatives in planning an information and communications technology infrastructure have come very late, although in the Middle East they lag behind only Israel and the UAE. In the *World Paper*'s Information Society Index for the year 2000, Saudi Arabia ranked 41st of 55 major countries included in the index (up from 45th the year before), with Israel (20th) and the UAE (25th) the only Middle Eastern nations to rank higher (Jordan and Egypt were ranked 49th and 50th respectively). No other Middle Eastern nation was included in the index.[59] Prior to the Saudi initiatives, the UAE had stood out as the one Arab nation to seriously attempt to build a modern information technology capability, beginning with the Gulf War in 1991.[60] At the onset of the Gulf War, UAE authorities launched an intensive appraisal of Arab information services and immediately decided to allow CNN to transmit into the Emirates on an uncensored basis twenty-four hours a day. Although initially designed to facilitate the spread of accurate information about the war, this dramatic opening of communications to the outside world has had a more lasting effect. CNN transmissions led to the purchase of television sets and satellite receivers by families and organizations throughout the UAE, which in turn has made possible relatively up-to-date transmission to computers and the transition to Internet technology.[61]

The UAE has several cybercafés and the largest number of corporate websites of all Arab countries. In 1999 it lagged behind only tiny Qatar in the percentage of Arab national populations online (2.9 percent in UAE, 3.1 percent in Qatar) and has since been engaged in a race with Qatar to lead the Arab world in the number of Internet users.[62] The UAE government leads the Arab states in the maintenance of sophisticated government websites and in its support for a government think tank—the Emirates Center for Strategic Studies and Research—which maintains considerable expertise, data, and other resources on information technology (with a focus on the Middle East). In June 2000, UAE's Emirates Internet and Multimedia (EIM) introduced a subscriber facility designed to reduce the time involved in registering for Internet service to five minutes, eliminating bureaucratic forms and procedures that previously took days to complete.[63] EIM had earlier launched Arab-Vista, a pioneering search engine in Arabic designed to facilitate the ability of Arab users to surf the Web.

Despite some progress in building an infrastructure for Internet participation by Arabs in the Middle East, industry sources and knowledgeable observers do not expect a dramatic jump in Internet use until far more substantial investments in consistent planned policies have produced more reliable services than are presently available. More than a year after the introduction of the Internet in Saudi Arabia, for example, Saudis complain that service is unreliable, with users suffering from slow connections and frequent disconnects. The STC is blamed for delays in developing its infrastructure and telephone lines, resulting in disruptions to service, with users frequently cut off from the Net when a link is lost between the STC and ISPs or between ISPs and users. ISPs complain that an insufficient number of modem ports have been made available by the STC, with the result that the ISPs are now taking on an average of twenty subscribers per modem—four times as many as the STC has recommended for "quality service." The resulting congestion on networks has added to the deterioration of Internet performance and is widely resented by those subscribing to the Saudi ISPs when they discover they are paying user rates estimated to be as much as five times those in the United States.[64]

Perhaps the most balanced assessment of the progress of Middle Eastern nations in getting online was provided in an editorial by Abdul Kader Kamli, editor-in-chief of *PC Magazine* for the Arabic and Internet Arab world, in April 2000. Kamli contrasted the massive international investments in Israel with the relative lack of investment in the Arab Middle East and asked whether the impressive list of current IT activities taking place in the Middle East was sufficient to attract international investment that would begin to approach levels for Israel and other highly successful IT environments. The conclusion, in his words, was "for the most part, 'no.'" Kamli pointed to the absence of advanced IT research centers in Middle Eastern universities and the scarcity of

Arab companies specializing in IT development as key factors curtailing the extent to which human resources indigenous to the Middle East exist to work with international companies to bring Internet-related development to the region. His overall assessment could be the starting point for a number of the plans and projects that abound in the Middle East:

> Investment in research, development and manufacture necessitates a number of conditions, several of which are missing in the Arab world. A weak IT infrastructure in the majority of the Arab countries acts as a great hindrance to investment. Infrastructure in this sense does not refer only to the quality of communication lines but extends to databases, modern financial services, flexible administrative systems and laws regulating investment and intellectual copyrights, etc. A few Arab countries such as the United Arab Emirates, Egypt and Morocco have begun to realize the importance of [a] strong infrastructure for the attraction of investment and have taken steps to provide for one, which we hope will occur at an increasingly fast pace.[65]

▪ NOTES

1. For an overall perspective on diverse leadership approaches to the Internet in the Middle East, see Amin and Gher, "Digital Communications," pp. 109–140.

2. For an analysis of various attempts to establish a regional Arabic data communications network, see Kirchner, "Internet in the Arab World," pp. 146 ff.

3. Cooper, "Far Cry from Seattle," p. A8.

4. For a discussion of the issues, see the extended comments by Jameel Al Alawi, legal adviser to the government of Bahrain, in "Bahrain Cannot Adopt." See also the discussions at a seminar on the subject held in Bahrain, November 6–8, 2000, reported in "Seminar to Focus on IT," "Over-Abundance of Rules," and "Call for Expert-led Internet Laws."

5. One could put forth many other candidates as founders of high-tech development in Israel. For example, the Advisory Committee of the Applied Mathematics Department of the Weizmann Institute (Albert Einstein, Hans Kramer, Robert Oppenheimer, John von Neumann, and Abram Pais) recommended in July 1947 that the institute build an electronic digital computer, thus placing Israel (not yet a nation) first in the world to commit itself to computing. Estrin, "The WEIZAC Years," pp. 317–339.

6. Galil's contributions are described in Gerstenfeld, "Hi-Tech Pioneer," p. 17.

7. "How Israeli High-Tech Happened." See also Ein-dor, Myers, and Raman, "Information Technology," pp. 61–90.

8. Tuck, "Israel," p. 16.

9. See Rees, "Where Wired Is a Way of Life," pp. 23–33.

10. Berger, "Israel Fourth," pp. 1–3. The ranking was based on the assessments of local leaders in government, industry, and the media in the forty-six locations that were ranked.

11. The EMFocus index is based on such quantitative factors as personal computer penetration, Internet usage, and cost of Internet usage, as well as nonquantitative parameters like government funding, global presence of companies, and quality of ISP service. See www.emfocus.com.

12. For information on the role of universities in building Israel as a "scientific society," see Sachar, *A History of Israel,* pp. 943 ff. See also home page websites of the leading high-tech universities in Israel, including the Technion, Jerusalem College of Technology, and the Weizmann Institute of Science.

13. BIRD is headquartered in Tel Aviv and Santa Clara, California, and has eight regional offices in the United States. BIRD does not take equity or get involved in project management but is legally entitled to repayment of between 100 and 150 percent of its investments, based on product sales. By 2000, BIRD had invested in more than 500 projects, with an additional 40 projects projected for approval each year (more than 50 percent of all new projects involve companies that were introduced to one another by BIRD). For more information, see the BIRD Foundation Web pages at www.birdf.com.

14. Tuck, "Israel," p. 17. Dan Avida, CEO of Electronics for Imaging, Inc. (of Israel and San Mateo, California), told Karen Southwick, "A lot of companies are started by people who graduated from the Army as engineers. When I was 22 [in the Israeli army], I was managing 15 engineers and a million-dollar budget" (Southwick, "Beating Swords," p. 4). Tuck and others have noted that former jet pilots and soldiers trained in military intelligence tend to dominate Israeli high-tech management. See, for example, Bagnall, "Israel's High-Tech Revolution," pp. C3–4.

15. An estimated 700,000 people emigrated to Israel in just the seven-year period 1988 to 1994, including 200,000 from the former Soviet Union (other major countries/regions of origin included Central and Eastern Europe, Asia, North America, Iraq, Egypt, and Ethiopia). Nearly 70 percent of the immigrants, according to Israeli figures, had been trained in scientific, professional, and technical fields. An example of the use of these human resources is Vishay Israel of Holon—a start-up manufacturer of resistors and capacitors for the chip industry, located in a desolate part of southern Israel—where 80 percent of the original 1,800 workers were Russian; plant notices were posted in Russian, Hebrew, and English; and the plant manager was a Russian female engineer. The presence in Israel of these highly educated recent immigrants is the major reason for Israel's advantage over other nations in intellectual capital (e.g., 130 of every 10,000 employees in Israel are engineers, compared with 70 in the United States and 65 in Japan). See Southwick, "Beating Swords," p. 4.

16. An excellent article that attempts to understand the contributions of cultural and historical factors in the development of the software industry in Israel is Ariav and Goodman, "Israel," pp. 17–21.

17. Quoted in Tuck, "Israel," p. 19.

18. Sandler and McNatt, "Israeli High Tech's New Promised Land," p. 8.

19. The figures are based on information provided by VentureOne and Evergreen Canada Israel Investments. See Leibowitz, "Cover Story: Strong Technology," pp. 1–2.

20. Kalman, "Investors Cash In," p. C14.

21. One of the less obvious reasons for this pattern was identified by a QualComm senior vice president: "It's not just a ten-hour difference in time. . . . It's really a 34-hour difference because the Israeli work week starts on Sunday. By the time U.S. engineers come to work Monday morning, the Israelis have already worked two days." Quoted in Tuck, "Israel," p. 20.

22. Figures are from Landau, "Internet Later." Gallup Israel placed Internet use in Israel in March 2000 at 21 percent of the population, but Gallup's definition includes anyone who has logged on to the Internet, for even a brief time and for any purpose during the year.

23. For example, the first of Israel's five large banks to create a mechanism for customers to conduct online foreign currency trading and trading in securities listed on the Tel Aviv Stock Exchange on the Internet was First International, but this did not happened until January 2000. Prior to that only Investec General had facilities for online foreign currency trading, but the daily volume of such trading was only a few hundred thousand dollars per day. Reported in Maltz, "First of Large Banks."

24. Leibowitz, "Cover Story: Strong Technology," p. 1.

25. Landau, "Internet Later."

26. The government of Prime Minister Benjamin Netanyahu was particularly active in IT development in support of Netanyahu's vision of Israel as "the Silicon Valley of the Eastern Hemisphere" (quoted in CNN Interactive, November 11, 1998). Netanyahu's interministerial committee announced its recommendations for privatization and liberalization of the telecom sector on November 3, 1997, arguing that implementation of the recommendations would "eliminate much of the prevailing uncertainty [and] enable every citizen throughout the country to obtain a better service, have a choice of a larger assortment, and pay a lower price." See Ministry of Communication Press Release, November 3, 1997, available at www.moc.gov.il.

27. For example, when competition was introduced into the local Israeli telephone market in June 2000 by allowing alternative companies to be formed to handle domestic telephone service, the effect of the measure was blunted by the fact that any potential competitor to Bezeq still had to negotiate with Bezeq for use of Israel's only countrywide fiber-optic network. With this in mind, the country manager of IDC (formerly International Data Corporation), Nisso Cohen, argued that "not one thing has changed." See Gordon, "Experts," p. 11.

28. For details see Dempsey, "Israel Opens Telecoms Market," p. 13.

29. Quoted in Ackerman, "Bezeq's Tender Schedule," p. 12A.

30. Ackerman, "Latest Debate."

31. Ackerman, "Ben-Eliezer," p. 11.

32. Agassi, "Bezeq Deliberately Holds Up Progress," p. 12A. See also Peled, "First-Class Technology," pp. 45–58.

33. Agassi, "Bezeq's Internet Monopoly," p. 12A.

34. For a brief analysis, see Vogel, *Freer Markets,* especially pp. 1–64.

35. Ministry of Communications Press Release, August 5, 1999, available at www.moc.gov.il.

36. See Agassi, "Bezeq's Internet Monopoly," p. 12A.

37. Avigad, "Internet Conquers Israel."

38. Glain, "New Economy Hits Snag," p. A1.

39. For a discussion of the effects of the war in Lebanon on the Internet and IT development, see Jalloul, "Computing in Lebanon," pp. 25–26.

40. These aspects of mobile phone use in the Middle East are explored in "A Toy," p. 45.

41. Lake, "Wireless Net," p. 202.

42. The appropriateness of mobile Internet technology for the Middle East is explored in "The Value of Mobile," pp. 50–53. See also Gordon, "The New Wireless," p. 9.

43. For a historical study, see Emergy, Graham, and Oppenheimer, *Technology Trade.* See also King, "Some Illustrations," pp. 149–178.

44. An analysis of the role of technology in Europe's relationship with the Middle East appears in Headrick, *The Tools of Empire.*

45. See Zahlan, "The Impact of Technology Change," pp. 143–187.

46. Zahlan, "Technology: A Disintegrative Factor," pp. 267–268.

47. Ibid., p. 269.

48. These points are outlined in greater detail in Alterman, *New Media, New Politics?* pp. 45–47. Quotations in this paragraph are from this source.

49. Goldstein, "Cyber-Censorship," p. 53.

50. Chakib Lahrichi, president of the independent Internet Association in Morocco, for example, told Human Rights Watch in 1998 and 1999 that the growth of the Internet in Morocco had been stunted by unfair advantages granted to the state-controlled telecommunications company Itissalat al-Maghrib in its competition with private ISPs, even thought the Moroccan government had no explicit policy of censoring or restricting access to the Internet. See *The Internet in the Mideast and North Africa,* available at http://www. hrw.org.

51. The term *enemies of the Internet* was coined by the Paris-based organization Reporters Sans Frontieres (RSF), which has identified forty-five countries that restrict their citizens' access to the Internet, among which twenty are described by RSF as "real enemies of this new means of communication" because they have enacted extreme measures to control access, censor websites, and prosecute users. Among the RSF's twenty enemies of the Internet, seven (Iran, Iraq, Libya, Saudi Arabia, Sudan, Syria, and Tunisia) are in the Middle East and northern Africa. See "The Twenty Enemies of the Internet," August 9, 1999, press release of RSF, available at http://www.rsf.fr/uk/alaune/ennemisweb.html.

52. *The Internet in the Mideast and North Africa,* p. 12.

53. "Saudi Goes Live! Saudi Arabia Lets the Internet in on Its Own Terms," *DITnet News Online* (December 1998), available at www.ditnet.co. ae/html.

54. Thomas Friedman ("The Fast Eat the Slow") has pointed out that most Internet-related innovation in the Arab world—politically, economically, and technologically—has taken place in the small peripheral Arab states, whereas the large traditional Arab powers—Iraq, Egypt, Syria, and Saudi Arabia—have been slower to globalize and adopt new technologies. Friedman accounts for this by contrasting rule by "kings who are progressive and relatively close to their people" in the small states with "the big central states . . . led by army officers who are autocrats and afraid of their people" (p. A19). The analysis in these two case study chapters and in the concluding chapter suggests more complex reasons for the cautious approach of leaders in the larger Middle East nations.

55. An extensive biography of Prince Alwaleed appears in Jehl, "Buffett of Arabia?" pp. 1ff. See also Silver, "Saudi Prince," p. C2, and Frank, "A 'Desert Man.'"

56. See "ZakSat and Silkinet Enter Agreement to Provide Satellite Internet Services," *DITnet News Online* (April 30, 1998), available at www.ditnet. co.ae.

57. ZakNet is a satellite Internet delivery platform that uses the AsiaSat2 satellite to provide services over a sixty-three-country footprint stretching from Turkey to Australia, with its uplink facilities located in Subic Bay, Philippines. SilkiNet was formed in 1996 as an offshore spinoff of Silki La Silki to implement the latter's expansion programs in the IT industry. SilkiNet intends to become a major ISP provider in Saudi Arabia and, through VSAT satellite networks, in the entire Middle East and northern Africa, as well as a content provider with specialties in distance learning, e-commerce, e-mail, and other electronic services. For more information, see www.zak-sat.net, www.zakshack. com., and www.silkinet.com.

58. "Push" technology—sometimes called Internet broadcasting, content delivery, or Web casting—is often likened to television and radio because signals are broadcast constantly, enabling users to tune in at will. By way of contrast, traditional "pull" technology requires that Web surfers first locate the specific information they want, wait for Web pages to load, and retrieve information by giving instructions to their Web browsers. For more detail, see Moschovitis et al., *History of the Internet,* pp. 220–221.

59. Variables in the Information Society Index, which is updated every six months, include computer infrastructure, Internet infrastructure, information infrastructure (telephone, TV, radio, fax), and social infrastructure (school enrollment, newspaper readership, press freedom, and the like). The fifty-five countries included in the index account for 97 percent of world gross domestic product and 99 percent of expenditures on information technology. The index is prepared for *World Paper* by the *World Times* and the International Data

Corporation. Scores quoted here are for January 2000. For details see www.worldpaper.com.

60. The result is that the UAE quickly jumped out in front of other Middle Eastern nations in Internet use. Figures for 1998 compiled by the Dabbagh Information Technology Group estimated that 88,552 people in the UAE were online, compared with 46,538 in Bahrain and Saudi Arabia combined, 43,828 in Lebanon, and 42,350 in Kuwait. For more information, see *The Internet in the Mideast and North Africa,* pp. 52–53.

61. This is pointed to as a major factor in the UAE's political, economic, and social development in the 1990s by Heard-Bey, "The United Arab Emirates"; see especially pp. 146–147.

62. Qatar's enthusiasm for the Internet is a direct result of the interest of its leader, Shaikh Hamad, in modern communications, including the Internet. In addition to providing Internet infrastructure and allowing substantial Internet access, Shaikh Hamad founded by decree al-Jezira ("the Peninsula"), one of the two major Arabic satellite television channels in the Gulf (the other is MBC out of Saudi Arabia). Al-Jezira is staffed substantially by recruits from the British Broadcasting Company (BBC) after the BBC gave up its Arabic television service. Although Shaikh Hamad appoints the board of governors of al-Jezira, he leaves day-to-day operations and choices to the staff, and the station has become prominent (and popular) for its willingness to criticize leaders of other Arab states and to interview opposition politicians on-camera. The Qatar-based channel is so profitable that it is expected to be self-sufficient when Shaikh Hamad's original five-year start-up grant expires in 2001. See "Telling the News," p. 39, and Feuilherade, "Qatar's Al-Jazeera Livens Up Arab TV Scene," pp. 1–2.

63. "Emirates Internet and Multimedia," pp. 1–2.

64. For an analysis of the Saudi case, see Jarrah, "Saudi Telecom Criticized," available at www.ditnet.co. A 20 percent reduction in Internet charges to ISPs in June 2000 is expected to provide some reduction in costs to consumers, but many ISPs will likely keep most of the savings to make up for past deficits and pass only a 3–4 percent reduction in costs on to the consumer. See Jarrah, "Saudi Telecom Abolishes Extra Charge."

65. Kamli, "Attracting Foreign Investment," p. 3.

3

The Middle East
and the Global Internet Regime

lthough the Internet clearly has enormous potential for changing
the relationships of Middle Eastern nations with the rest of the
world and with each other, thus far its impact in the Middle East
has been rather minimal. The vast changes effected in the United States,
Europe, and a few nations elsewhere—in banking and securities, business-
to-business transactions, e-mail communications, entertainment, and
other innovations—have come to the Middle East within extremely
small parameters. Much of this has to do with the way in which Middle
Eastern governmental and other leaders approach the subject and their
consequent attempts to exercise various degrees of control over the impact of the Internet on the cultures, economies, and political systems of
the different countries. This chapter explores some of the specific interrelationships between the Middle East and the rest of the world in
Internet-related matters in an attempt to determine the overall international impact of the Internet on the region thus far and its potential role
into the future.

■ INTERNET RESTRICTIONS AND FILTERING

In most Arab states the principal reason for delay in mounting an effective Internet infrastructure has been concern about the possibility of
wide-open dissemination of information through use of the new technology. Strict censorship, high tax rates on use, and bans on foreign websites are common in the entire Middle East region, with governments

and religious leaders invoking traditional values to call for severe restrictions on Internet use. In Iran, for example, the monthly clerical publication *Sobh* has called for a flat ban on the Internet, and in Israel a *halakhic* ruling issued in January 2000 by a number of prominent rabbis prohibits their followers from using the Internet except where such use is directly work related.[1] Conservative government and religious leaders are concerned with the easy availability on the Web of sexually explicit and pornographic materials, writings viewed as antireligious, the potential for changing the traditional role of women, and the spread of information and other Internet activities that might threaten national security.

The degree of restrictions placed on Internet use in the Middle East varies from country to country, and their effects can be exaggerated because they are often unenforced. Jordan is among the most liberal Arab nations in this regard, with its leadership stressing the benefits rather than the dangers of the World Wide Web.[2] In contrast to most Middle Easterners, Jordanians are not required to register to log on to the Internet or to create a website. Although Jordan's leadership occasionally bans foreign newspapers, it has not taken any action to prohibit access to international websites.[3] The number of people who can access the Internet in Jordan has been limited by the costs involved (minimum monthly expenses for the average user were estimated at U.S.$70 in late 2000, and service must be purchased from Jordan Telecom, a monopoly state telecommunications company).[4] A September 1998 law, although not yet strictly enforced, could have a significant impact in the future (it restricts and fines publications "in any media" that conflict with the "values of the Arab and Islamic nation"[5]). Thus far, however, while Jordanian officials have tried to pressure individuals who use the Internet, they have not prosecuted anyone for improper or illegal use.[6] Jordan's Internet users, therefore, can be considered—along with Egyptians and Moroccans—the least regulated Arabs in Middle East cyberspace.[7]

In sharp contrast, Saudi Arabia and the United Arab Emirates (UAE) stand out as being subject to considerable censorship and control. State regulations in Saudi Arabia prohibit Internet service providers (ISPs) and Internet users from accessing the Net for "pornography and gambling" or "any activities violating the social, cultural, political, media, economic, and religious values of the Kingdom of Saudi Arabia."[8] In 1998, rumors circulated that Saudi Arabia was planning to initiate a policy of white listing Internet sites—that is, blocking *all* sites until each could individually prove it was nonoffensive—in contrast to the more usual approach of blacklisting specific sites. The rumor turned out to be false, with the result that only certain "offensive" sites continue to be blocked in Saudi Arabia by the King Abdul Aziz City for Science and Technology (KACST), the watchdog for these activities.[9] The UAE is experimenting with a system, borrowed from Singapore and currently being tried in Australia as well, that bans restricted sites through proxy servers that constantly update and send out to users lists of undesirable and banned sites, along with information about punishments and potential legal action.[10]

Computer industry sources described the Saudi Arabian Internet filtering system in mid-2000 as follows:

> First, it caches all approved web pages in a 500-gigabyte storage system. Users get these sites from the computer in Riyadh rather than the original source on the web. This means that frequently used pages can be accessed quickly without the system having to check their suitability each time. Requests for pages that are not stored in the cache are passed to the second stage of the system, supplied by a U.S. company, Websense, which lists and can filter out 30 categories of potentially unsuitable sites.[11]

KACST computer experts in charge of the system concede that it is imperfect and difficult to administer and that it frequently "over-censors" (e.g., it cuts out information about breast cancer or AIDS because it is excluding sex sites). Moreover, individuals who want unrestricted access to the Internet can simply obtain a service provider from Lebanon, the United States, or Europe. This can result in conflicts with Saudi authorities, however (in April 2000, for example, a women's Internet café in Mecca, wired to non-Saudi providers, was closed down after a complaint that it was being used for "immoral purpose"). Because of the many different ways in which Internet activity is attacked and limited by government action, leaders of Saudi opposition groups view the overall system as being effective from the government's perspective.[12]

The most restrictive governments in the Middle East are Iraq and Libya, each of which established its own Internet connections to the world only in 1999 for government use, but neither of which offered direct Internet service to its citizens as late as mid-2000.[13] Iraq contends that it does not provide Internet services because of the damage caused by the 1991 war and the subsequent embargo on the import of anything except humanitarian supplies.[14] In 2000, Libya's government monopoly telecommunications provider, General Posts and Telecommunications Company (GPTC), began operating a dial-up and leased line Internet hub in Tripoli, with an international link to Teleglobe in Canada. Somewhat surprisingly, Israel (for what it sees as security reasons) has joined the Saudi government and Tunisia as the only major Middle Eastern nations to restrict the domestic use of encryption software that would enable everyday users to ensure greater privacy on the Internet.[15]

Among the most restrictive countries in the past was Syria—the only connected country in the region that refused to allow local access to the Internet until the death of President Hafez-al-Assad in June 2000. Syria's situation was complicated during the last few years of President Assad's life by the enthusiasm of Assad's son, Col. Bashar Hafez-al-Assad, for computer and Internet cultures. Although Syrian military and Baath Party leaders legally banned access to the Internet throughout the 1990s, they had difficulty enforcing the ban in the face of Bashar's public statements and activities in the last few years of the twentieth century.[16] In February 1999, at his first major press interview following his brother's death, Bashar told the Beirut newspaper *Al-Kifah Al-Arabi,* "Before long, the computer culture is going to become an integral part of our traditions. . . . Just as illiteracy until fairly recently meant a human being's inability to read and write, the latter-day version means an inability to use the computer."[17] A member of Bashar's social circle was reported in a 1999 *Newsweek* story to have said that "[by law] the Net is not allowed, but we're all connected." In addition to Internet connections, use of satellite television mushroomed in Damascus in the late 1990s, even though it was technically illegal. That article reported that "tens of thousands of households can tune in to MTV and Sky News (both beamed to Syria from abroad) as well as a host of non-Syrian Arabic-language programs."[18] Despite the official ban on Internet use, Syria's state-owned telecommunications company started taking applications for e-mail accounts in mid-1999 after officials realized that hundreds of Syrians had signed up with foreign-based ISPs.[19]

When Hafez-al-Assad died in June 2000, there were only an estimated 7,000 Internet portals (i.e., computers connected to the Internet) in a country of 17 million people, with all portals connected to a single government-run server that kept track of every password. Arguing that the country's phone system could not handle more connections, Syrian authorities restricted licenses to institutions, with only a few professors or business owners allowed to have Internet service provided to their homes. Internet cafés were not permitted, and connections to ISPs outside of Syria were technically illegal but occasionally countenanced. Like Internet connections at home or television connections to satellite providers outside Iraq, the head of the media committee of the Syrian Computer Society suggested in mid-2000 that connection to a foreign ISP "is not forbidden, but it is not allowed."[20] Bashar Assad has suggested that he will work to bring a new approach to information technology (IT) in Syria, predicting that the number of Syrian Internet portals would expand to 200,000 in a few years and that eventually every home in Syria would be connected to the Internet.[21] Whether he will be able to carry through with this vision will depend a great deal on his ability to gain control of the institutions that were crucial to his father's thirty-year rule (the Baath Party, the military, and the intelligence organizations) and at the same time sustain peaceful relations with neighboring Israel and Lebanon over an extended period.[22]

■ GETTING MIDDLE EASTERN GOVERNMENTS ONLINE

Most Middle Eastern rulers—even those at the very top levels—are encouraging the development of the Internet, at least for governmental and semigovernmental organizations, because they see it opening up vistas for exercising authority and control or for spreading their government's message to the rest of the world. Under Hafez-al-Assad, Syrian leadership, for example, started in 1997 to arrange introductory computer and Internet training for many government officials and instructed most of its departments to prepare online capabilities that could provide more effective communication links between various parts of the bureaucracy.[23] Syria also established high-level committees under Assad and hired consultants to work with the Syrian Computer Society (SCS) on the development of an Internet structure for Syrian businesses. During Hafez Assad's later years, the monopoly Syrian Telecommunication Establishment (STE) focused on the provision of Internet services to most government departments, a few newspapers and journals, and some scientific and academic organizations while merely promising Internet access to other sectors.[24] This pattern has been followed in other Arab nations as well.

By 2001 all Arab states had launched their own websites (most have several such sites), designed to get information about their countries out to the rest of the world and to counter or balance information provided on the Web by Israel, Iran, and other nations. Saudi Arabia has been the heaviest investor in such sites, which are pitched at an international audience and used routinely to refute material provided by small London-based Saudi dissident groups.[25] Saudi Arabia, Bahrain, Egypt, Iran, Israel, Kuwait, Morocco, Oman, Tunisia, and the Palestinian Authority are among Middle Eastern governments and authorities that provide Web casts of state radio and television networks. In early 1999 both the Iraqi News Agency and Iraq's main newspaper *(Al-Zawra)* launched online editions, and both have since emphasized in "netcasts" the damage inflicted on Iraq by UN sanctions.[26]

The most advanced government websites among Middle Eastern nations are those in Dubai and Qatar, where Sultan Qaboos in Qatar and Sheikh Mohammed bin Rashid Al Maktoum, crown prince of Dubai, are trying to become the first to create an entirely electronic government (where it will be possible to have all government services for individuals and businesses, as well as internal government communications and procedures for all departments and agencies, conducted through the Internet).[27] Crown Prince Mohammed's cyberspace projects (which include the goal of getting all Dubai schools online by 2002) are particularly important for the international involvement of the Arab world because they include aspirations for Dubai to become a world-class e-commerce center in the Middle East and a premier Internet communications link between Arab nations and the rest of the world. To promote these goals, Dubai's Etisalat, the only company providing Internet services in the UAE, has reduced its fees so they are the lowest in the Arab Middle East. At some point in 2001, Etisalat hopes to become the first (or among the first) ISPs in the Middle East to introduce high-speed digital subscriber line (DSL) technology, provide voice-over Internet protocol (IP) technology, and test WAP (wireless application protocol) gateways for mobile Internet use. Etisalat is also building a network of Internet Centers, offering free orientation to the Internet and a hands-on service where the general public can learn to surf the Web and send e-mail (special sections are provided for men and women in these centers).[28]

A handful of Middle Eastern governments, including some at the local level, have started to create interactive sites where citizens can question government authorities and establish other forms of direct communication. Jordan leads in this respect, having created websites for most ministries (including the General Intelligence Services) that invite e-mail correspondence from the Jordanian public. One Jordanian ISP (NETS) has an "Ask the Government" folder on the Internet that specifically encourages subscribers to post questions and address comments to participating government agencies.[29] Governments that have informational websites include Morocco (www.mincom.gov.ma), Egypt (www.mfa. gov.eg), and the Palestinian Authority (www.pna.net). None of the Middle East government websites is very advanced by modern communications standards, however. In the words of Eric Goldstein, "Few Arab governments have embarked on a systematic effort to put online information that would enhance informed political participation by their publics—[e.g.,] materials such as legal and regulatory codes, draft legislation, official reports and statistics, transcripts of press conferences and parliamentary debates, court rulings, and economic data used to define budget allocations."[30]

■ ONLINE BUSINESS AND COMMERCE IN THE MIDDLE EAST

Middle Eastern experience with e-business and e-commerce is even less extensive than government involvement online. In mid-1999 it was estimated that consumers in all Arab countries combined had spent only $95 million on online purchases in the previous fourteen months, with just 18 percent of those purchases made from vendors in the Middle East.[31] The bulk of these purchases (84 percent) were for Internet-related items, including 48 percent on computer programs, 26 percent on computers and peripherals, and 10 percent on domain name registrations. A later survey conducted by Internet Access Worldwide (IAW) (in August 1999) concluded that only forty websites in the Arab Middle East were able to support some form of online financial transaction with any degree of continuity, of which only eleven were fully functional for the fourteen-month period of the survey.[32] In April 2000, Internet banking was described by the *Financial Times* (London) as being "in its infancy . . . in a region where cash is still king," although a *Financial Times* survey had found "anecdotal evidence" that online trading of securities with U.S. security traders was brisk, particularly in the Gulf states.[33]

The state in the Middle East that seems most determined to take the lead in e-commerce is Jordan, under King Abdullah II, who succeeded his father, King Hussein, in 1999. To stimulate the development of an information economy, Abdullah has already appointed the first regulatory authority with financial and administrative independence in the region and is encouraging the development of a new legal and administrative structure for e-commerce.[34] Laws governing e-signatures, consumer privacy, and a host of other e-commerce-related matters began passage through the Jordanian parliament in 2000 and early 2001. In

February 2002, the first e-ministry in the region will be created in Jordan, combining e-commerce concerns with other aspects of telecommunications, post, and information technology. By 2005, Abdullah hopes to bring all government transactions online.

Industry analysts in the Middle East have argued that regional governments and legislators have not done enough to build telecommunications infrastructures and legal safeguards to warrant substantial investments in e-business and e-commerce. Phil Dwyer of Jupiter Communications (a U.S.-headquartered global Internet marketing research and consulting company), for example, suggested at a conference in Dubai in January 2000 that "three drivers" or conditions must be present before significant e-commerce can take place: (1) penetration of the Internet infrastructure to a substantial portion of the population, (2) widespread daily use of the World Wide Web, and (3) online content that makes the Internet appealing and useful for potential subscribers. As Dwyer stated: "The underlying principle is the same [everywhere]. . . . Without content . . . you will not grab the attention of consumers. . . . In the U.S. and Europe we see that as consumers spend more time on the Internet, they spend less time watching TV or reading magazines and papers. . . . You have to engage people in online content [first]. . . . [Only later can] you then engage them in online commerce."[35]

A similar analysis of e-business and e-commerce in the Arab Middle East was provided by Mary Gorman of the Dublin, Ireland–based high-tech firm Nua, who suggests as a consequence of such analysis that companies in the region should concentrate initially on establishing a favorable e-business (rather than e-commerce) presence on the Web. Gorman argues that "the infrastructures for online transactions in the Middle East have not yet reached a stage to support e-commerce hubs in the region."[36] Her suggestion to Arab business firms, therefore, is to "give reason for people to keep visiting their [company] Web sites":

> The question business people have to ask themselves is how they could leverage [information about their company] for added value online, and build their companies to be renowned in certain areas. . . . Issues that need to be addressed are how to add the information value for customers, how to build brand awareness in their target audience, and [how to] portray positive energy about the brand and what the company stands for.[37]

The most successful companies engaging in e-commerce in the Arab Middle East are foreign firms selling computers, software, and

Internet-related equipment and peripherals. Dell—the world's leading direct sale computer company—for example, has been successful in selling its products directly on its international websites and has recently launched a new site located in the UAE, in conjunction with Emirates Computers, designed to attract major Middle Eastern corporate accounts. This model—to establish a strong market presence with local partners and local sites—is also being pursued by Dell in Saudi Arabia (beginning in April 2000), and was previously developed in Israel.[38]

Dubai, the capital of the UAE, is strongly competing to be the leading city in the region for advanced Internet development.[39] In November 1999, Dubai hosted a major international conference on "Completing the Electronic Handshake," which included world-class IT experts from all over the globe.[40] During the first three months of 2000 the Dubai Shopping Festival (DSF)—a global event that was started in 1994, featuring best bargains in commercial items that appeal to people from the Middle East—was available online as well as in person at www.myDSF.com, allowing global customers to take part in the DSF without having to travel to Dubai. The e-commerce site was organized by Lotus, and to ensure high-quality performance, twenty personnel from Lotus, IBM, and the DSF group—including e-business architects, database administrators, security specialists, network managers, technical and content staff—were assigned to oversee the continuing operation of the site once it was up and running.[41] By January 2001, Dubai's "Internet City" announced that it had attracted 194 companies to its corporate complex, supported by the world's largest artificial harbor, the Jebel Ali commercial "free zone," an efficient container terminal, and an airport that serves eighty airlines.[42]

Even without the infrastructure for rapid growth of e-business and e-commerce, Jon Alterman has identified a growing role for the Internet in intra-Arab trade, particularly as it relates to computer and Internet expertise and service.[43] One of the largest Arab infotech companies that has arisen is the Jordanian-based Arabia Online, which designs Web pages commercially, maintains several of its own websites, and is involved in a number of other related ventures. On its gateway sites Arabia Online sells advertising and runs promotions, much like Yahoo! or Netscape or any other such site. Arabia Online also operates a dedicated news site (Akhbar.com) as well as sites for the UAE, Jordan, Qatar, Oman, Lebanon, Saudi Arabia, and the Palestinians. Another Jordanian start-up company that has grown rapidly is Business Optimization Consultants (BOC), which operates, among other enterprises, an Arabic e-mail service on the Internet called Maktoob, which in 1999 crossed the 100,000 mark for subscribers.[44] Among international firms that have made substantial commitments to build e-commerce business in the Middle East is Barnes and Noble, which in April 2000 entered into an alliance with Naseej.com, the largest Arabic portal site, to develop a website that could promote Barnes and Noble products and services among Arabic Internet users.[45]

Surprisingly, some of the most successful entrepreneurs developing online business ventures in the Middle East are women in Saudi Arabia, who have traditionally been hampered in business competition by laws and administrative rulings that severely restrict their ability to move around outside their homes. Use of the Internet, for example, has helped Saudi women overcome some of the obstacles created by rules prohibiting them from driving automobiles or other vehicles on Saudi streets.[46] Through skillful use of the Internet, women have been able to develop self-sufficient business ventures in certain areas—including travel agencies, bakeries, and catering—that lend themselves to Internet learning and transactions. The Internet has also made it possible for women to more easily secure employment with firms, as well as jobs where they can work online from home-based computers.

■ ISLAMIC AND ARAB NATIONALIST WEBSITES

If the Internet is becoming a factor in breaking down cultural barriers in the Middle East, it is also being used by traditional groups in support of religious, cultural, and nationalist causes. Indeed, a major survey of Internet use by Human Rights Watch concluded that "of all the region's political opposition forces, Islamists are among the most active online."[47] The organizations that have invested substantial resources to promote Islam on the World Wide Web include: (1) the Islamic Society of North America (ISNA), which held a worldwide conference in May 1999 devoted to using the Internet "as a tool for effective presentation of knowledge on Islam";[48] (2) a computer institute in the city of Qom that is preparing more than 2,000 Islamic instructional documents for presentation on the Web;[49] (3) numerous groups, companies, and governments that have launched websites designed to assist the world's 1.2 billion Muslims in their efforts to plan a sacred pilgrimage to Mecca, including descriptions of the rituals of hajj in minute detail and sites that offer maps, audio, and even video of many of the places and events associated with hajj; and (4) a large number of other organizations (both governmental and nongovermental) that first met at an international meeting in Cairo in July 1998 to coordinate efforts to promote Islam through the use of new information technologies.[50]

The Iranian government has invested considerable resources to translate the works of the late Ayatollah Ruhollah Khomeini into a number of languages and make them available online.[51] But this effort was being countered in late 2000 and early 2001 by the Ayatollah Huseyn Ali Montazeri, a dissident cleric who was in line to succeed Khomeini as Iran's supreme leader and was forced to resign a few weeks before Khomeini's death in 1989. At age seventy-nine in late 2000, Ayatollah Montazeri published a 600-page memoir in Persian on his website (www.montazeri.com), refuting Khomeini's accounts of events in the 1980s in a series of dramatic revelations. An article in the London-based Arabic newspaper *Al-Sharq al-Awsat,* dated December 14, 2000, reported that Iranian authorities were jamming Montazeri's website and had launched a virus that would be activated in the computers of those who accessed the site in an effort to deny the world public access to the memoirs.[52]

Much of Muslim clerics' interest in the Internet has to do with intra-Islamic theological conflicts, with Sunni websites (based in the Arabic world) attacking Shi'a websites in Iran, and vice versa. A number of cybercafés in Iran are run by Qom's main Islamic seminary, which has its own ISP, Noornet, and makes computers available to scholars and clerics by appointment only.[53] Although the legal status of the Internet in Iran is unclear, some Iranian elites have been allowed to gain access to it, creating a situation one ISP described as "a totally risky business since, for the time being, nobody is responsible for supervision."[54] Muslim clergy in Iran debate how restrictive the government should be in its approach to the Internet. Ayatollah Mahdi Hadavi Tehrani, a professor of Islamic law who is fluent in English and has three e-mail addresses, argues that pornographic sites should be blocked but political opinions should be allowed to circulate fairly widely among the general population. Conservative ideologically minded clerics like Ayatollah Mohammad Taqi Mesbah-Yazdi disagree, suggesting that only clerics and learned people need "instruments such as the Internet" and that its use by ordinary people and youths is "a dangerous path."

All of the Arab governments have participated in and encouraged efforts to develop the Internet and other new information technologies for the promotion of Islam. One of the most ambitious projects of this kind, Islamvision, is specifically designed to resist "electronic colonialism" by developing a long-range coordinated plan among Muslim nations for effective use of IT in support of the Islamic religion.[55] Originally mooted at a meeting of information ministers from Muslim nations in 1988, the Islamvision project is attempting to develop an Islamic Information Strategy that would reduce communications tariffs among Muslim nations, establish an Islamic Union of Journalists and Muslim think tanks, create a new worldwide television channel or network to promote Islam, and foster more balanced exchanges of information about Islam at the regional and global levels. Professor Daniel Pipes has observed that "Islamists," as opposed to traditional Islamic scholars, have been particularly active on the Internet, with several hundred websites.[56]

Arab governments have also been assiduously pursuing ways to get more Arabic-language content on regional television, to develop software that would make the Internet user-friendly for Arabs who do not read and write English, and to promote Arabic nationalism through use of the World Wide Web. The UAE has become a leader in this regard, producing more than 80 percent of its own television and radio programming while playing a major role in advancing Arab-language use on the Internet. Saudi Arabia has invested the largest amount of resources in television and radio programming, particularly to promote Islam. Broadcasting in twelve languages—in an effort to reach almost all Muslims throughout Asia and Africa, Saudi radio and television offers services that conform strictly to Islamic law in three broad areas: (1) cultural programs (on religion, folklore, drama, information, education, and health) that provide interpretations and guidance by Islamic scholars and teachers; (2) a Holy Koran broadcasting service that provides readings, interviews, lectures, and music dealing with the Koran; and (3) popular programs that fit within the boundaries of Muslim law and promote Islamic ideals.[57] In late 1999 and early 2000, the Saudi government launched a series of initiatives on new websites to disseminate over the Internet materials previously presented on radio and television.

IT companies doing business in the Arab Middle East have quickly developed programming and software useful to Arab rulers and citizens seeking to promote Internet capability. Particularly impressive has been the development of a number of advances for use of Arab-language materials, including a new Windows 2000 operating system platform supportive of Arabic (launched in February 2000), an automatic indexer for Arabic texts (made available by Sakhr in January 2000), a palm computer system (the Arabic Palm Operating System [APOS]) that makes palm computing possible for bilingual and localized use in the Middle East, and a number of Arabic portals that offer business-to-business services, consumer services, educational activities, and even "approved" games for children.[58] At the 1999 annual Awards of Excellence banquet held by Dabbagh Information Technology (DIT) Group, a special Lifetime Achievement for an Arabic Technologist award was presented to Nabil Ali, the chief of Sakhr's Department of Research and Development, who developed the first Arabic-language morphology analyzer and a number of other important Arabic-language technologies.[59] The development of software capabilities in the Arabic world has stimulated the Iranian government and Iranian business leaders to explore the possibility of developing a substantial software industry in Iran, but by mid-2001 this effort had not attracted the kind of investment needed to be significant within the region.[60]

Companies have also been pressing Middle Eastern leaders to take a greater interest in industry efforts to develop Arabic Internet capabilities and to use their positions of influence and their resources to build more effective standards and more uniform codes for Arab-language applications. In December 1999, for example, Hussam Eid, the senior Arab software architect from Bi-Directional Products at Lotus in Dublin, Ireland, called for greater attention to the development of a unicode for Arabic developers—similar to the single-code page for English-language applications—that could be used on various platforms.[61] Silki La Silki and ZakSat have been in discussions since the late 1990s with the Saudi Ministry of Communications about a project that would provide high bit-rate digital subscriber lines (HDSLs) for bandwidth-intensive use at Saudi schools and universities, including a new Open University (to be developed using Sakhr software) based on widespread use of the Internet and the World Wide Web.[62] Almost all IT companies in the Middle East have been lobbying governments to take more effective action against piracy and other forms of violation of intellectual property, which are widely viewed as the major reason for the inability of manufacturers to build effective Arabic-language materials and other software.[63]

Some of the most important developments in the use of the Internet for promoting Arabic nationalism, the use of Arabic language, and Islam have taken place in Arab diaspora communities, particularly in England and the United States. As Jon Alterman points out,

> Technology has played a significant role . . . in facilitating the exchange of information between Arabs living abroad and those in the

> Arab world. . . . Arabs abroad can monitor events in the Middle East with unprecedented ease. International Arabic newspapers are available in major European and North American cities, and more than 30 of them can be read daily over the Internet. Arabs can also watch satellite television broadcasts in Europe and, increasingly, in the United States. . . . The Internet is a huge resource for Arabs to plug into news and culture from the Middle East, either by passively reading news and information or by actively participating in any of the numerous discussion groups on topics of interest to Arabs.[64]

Arabs in the diaspora have also contributed directly to Internet and IT development in the Arab Middle East. Indeed, Jon Anderson singles out in his writings a group of Arab emigrants, whom he labels *diaspora pioneers,* as "the first to bring their cultural, political and Islamic interests and content to cyberspace and help define it."[65] Anderson describes these pioneers as "among the creators of Internet technology and among its first users," with interests ranging from "Arabic music to searching for cheap tickets to the Middle East, and from looking for wives to halal grocers and to the closest mosque or church."[66]

■ ARAB-ISRAELI RELATIONS ON THE INTERNET

In contrast to Arab and Israeli efforts to use the Web for religious and nationalist promotion, some of the most active attempts to expand Internet use in the Middle East have been joint efforts between Arabs and Israelis, who see in the new medium opportunities for citizens of the two "enemies" to begin to establish dialogues with one another.[67] Much of this activity has been spontaneous, with Arabs and Israelis logging on to a variety of websites where they can debate and converse with one another in online chat rooms and other interactive Internet forums in ways impossible otherwise because of travel restrictions and the absence of postal and telephone links. Human rights organizations—particularly in Egypt and the Palestinian territories—have been active in organizing e-mail and other Web programs that encourage dialogue between the two sides and disseminate information back and forth in a more effective manner than was possible previously, often with very limited resources.[68] The Arab press has also made good use of Internet news to enhance its coverage of the Arab-Israeli conflict (as with the rest of the world) and has generally been allowed to circulate on the Web stories deemed unpublishable in print form because of political or other pressures. Arabic, English, and French newspapers have routinely posted online stories that had been censored or banned by authorities in one or another of the Arab nations.[69]

A number of attempts to build Arab-Israeli relations by using the Internet are associated with universities, including a major project called the Middle East Virtual Community (MEViC) (at www.mevic. org), initiated by Michael Dahan of the Harry S. Truman Research Institute for the Advancement of Peace at Hebrew University and several Arab partners. The Truman Institute has also tried to promote Internet dialogues between various political science departments on both sides, most prominently between students at Hebrew University in Jerusalem and the American University in Cairo (AUC) (Professor Larry Goodson is the leader of this project at AUC). The largest Jewish studies program in the world, at Bar-Ilan University, has created an online program called the Virtual Jewish University, which is designed to increase understanding of Judaism—including its archaeology, history, and culture—for anyone of any faith.[70]

An Internet service called ICQ (the letters substitute for "I seek you"), developed by a highly successful Israeli start-up company (Mirabilis), has been particularly helpful in linking Internet users from Israel with those from other parts of the Middle East.[71] Four Middle Eastern nations—Egypt, Jordan, Kuwait, and Lebanon—have been especially tolerant of their citizens accessing sites that link them to Israel, and Arabs from all parts of the Middle East have been allowed to purchase and import Internet equipment manufactured in Israel.[72] Language is sometimes a barrier to communication between the two sides, but translation services are provided at Internet cafés and by professional translators. The appeal of Arab-Israeli Internet communication has been described by Aaron Bart:

> The nature of Internet communication allows participants to express their positions freely and without feeling threatened. . . . The Internet forces a kind of engagement that face-to-face talks often fail to produce. Such interactions can occur whether the peace process is moving forward or not. . . . Israelis who communicate via the Internet with Palestinians—and with Arabs in countries with no formal ties to the Jewish state—gain valuable insights into what these people are actually thinking, as opposed to what their leaders relate rhetorically. Israelis who participate in such exchanges encounter a range of views among Arabs on issues such as historical rights to land, security, terrorism, and Jerusalem.[73]

Despite efforts to use the Web to promote online interaction between Arabs and Israelis, the bulk of the expenditure of Web resources on Arab-Israeli relations has been to promote some partisan position in ongoing Middle East conflicts. Arab and Israeli organizations—with government organizations leading the effort—have vied with one another to get their messages across regarding the various points of contention. Both Israel and the Arab governments have spent considerable resources trying to find ways to better monitor and develop partisan websites in an effort to extend their information reach beyond the usual television, print, and radio channels to cyberspace. In 1998, Imad Mustafa presented the results of a Syrian government survey that purportedly identified 1,439,664 documents on the World Wide Web "which deal with the Syrian aspect of the Arab-Israeli conflict." According to Mustafa's nationalist perspective, none of these sites presented material in a manner benign to Syria's interests.[74] A number of Arab leaders have advocated developing a united Arab strategy for Internet use to counteract the increasing presence on Web networks of programs and perspectives that explain and champion Israeli perspectives on contentious issues.[75]

One of the most energetic Internet projects in the Middle East—the Across Borders project—is being organized by Bethlehem's Birzeit University, funded by the Canada Fund, and designed to eventually provide online training to refugees in all Palestinian-populated areas. The project was initiated in mid-1999 at Dheisheh Refugee Camp, on the West Bank near Bethlehem, with the establishment of the first of what has become several "Internet centers" in Palestinian refugee camps. The Across Borders project has purchased computers, provided training, and created websites in English and Arabic to enable displaced Palestinian refugee families to reconnect and correspond with one another through searching services, e-mail, and message boards.[76] In addition, the project seeks to recover and record some of the history that binds all Palestinians, including Palestinian perspectives over the years on major issues in Arab-Israeli relations and significant elements of oral history that can be provided by leaders and elders. Likening their work to the well-established capability of the Zionist movement to use the Internet to forge links between the Jewish diaspora and their biblical homeland in Israel, Across Borders leaders have developed substantial plans to build networked connections between widely dispersed refugees and their homeland in Palestine.[77]

■ THE MIDDLE EAST AND THE NASCENT
INTERNATIONAL REGIME FOR THE INTERNET

The Middle East's involvement with information technology and cyber-space provides rich material for studying of the Internet's impact on international relations and for theorizing about comparative politics. People in Middle Eastern nations have many fewer opportunities to access and use the Internet than citizens of the United States or European nations, but in this respect they are like the vast majority of people elsewhere in the world. Generalizations about the accelerated speed of communications, the drastic lowering of costs, or the thickness of globalization at the turn of the millennium have thus far been directly relevant only for a few scattered elites in the Middle East, although the potential for effecting future societal change has been widely recognized. The great economic benefits so much in evidence in the West—from e-commerce, online banking, Internet security trading, business-to-business transactions, and so forth—have not yet had a significant impact on Middle Eastern nations except to a very limited extent in Israel and the United Arab Emirates. The Internet has also contributed only marginally to the gap between rich and poor in the Middle East, producing some new wealth for entrepreneurs in Israel and investors in the Arab world but having little effect on the wealth of others in Israel or the Arab nations.

Perhaps the most significant impact of the Internet on international relations in the Middle East thus far has been the way in which its capabilities have alerted governments to its intrusive possibilities, causing leaders in all nations to concentrate policymaking efforts and resources on finding ways to control the spread and influence of foreign ideas and data in relatively closed societies through this new communications medium. Both Arab and Israeli leaders initially reacted to the Internet's invention by slowing the pace of its full-scale introduction, although Israeli IT "pioneers" were far quicker than the Arabs to seize on the possibility for Israel to play a world leadership role in developing new Internet-related technology. As in other parts of the world, the Internet has produced a class of "new communicators" in the Middle East, but in relatively small numbers—again with the exception of Israel and the UAE, closer to the numbers in Africa than to those in the United States or Europe.

The new communicators in the Arab Middle East differ from those in Europe, Africa, and Asia in one significant respect: the extent to which they access computers from private homes. A major study conducted by *Internet Arab World* magazine in April 2000 indicated that 72 percent of the people in Arab nations who used the Internet did so in their homes, with only 22 percent logging on in the office, 4 percent at universities, and 2 percent in Web cafés.[78] This pattern differs sharply from patterns of Internet use for parts of the world other than the United States. But the Arab Middle East figures stem largely from cultural and societal mores in which individuals are relatively isolated in their homes, unable to freely express their opinions outside unless those opinions happen to coincide with those of political, religious, and cultural authorities. In these respects the reasons for the Middle Eastern pattern are quite different from those for the U.S. pattern. One finds little evidence of the involvement of Middle Eastern Internet users in the global *publicum* Torbjorn L. Knutsen sees emerging as a result of the Internet, as discussed in Chapter 1. Nor is there evidence that the Internet has given nongovernmental organizations (NGOs) and private voluntary organizations (PVOs) any enhanced power or influence in public policy matters in the Middle East.

Although the Internet has enabled Middle Easterners to communicate more frequently with NGOs, PVOs, and international organizations generally, there is no sign that this has threatened the sovereignty of the Arab nations or Israel. Most Arab states have established clear rules for NGOs and have assigned specific government organizations as both contact points for the NGOs to relate to the government and as focal points for the government to monitor the NGOs. The Palestine Authority has even created a Ministry for NGO Affairs, to ensure that the work of NGOs is "based on probity, transparency, accountability and understanding."[79] The Egyptian People's Assembly passed a controversial new law in 1999 significantly restricting the activities of NGOs, but the law was struck down by Egypt's Constitutional Court as "unconstitutional" in June 2000, causing the Egyptian government to look for ways to amend it to make it more acceptable to the judiciary.[80] In all Middle Eastern nations except Israel, NGOs and PVOs based outside a country in which they choose to work are under strict surveillance and guidance, with limits imposed on where they can work within the country, who they can contact, and what they can do. The intensity of Arabs' distrust of foreign-based NGOs was summarized in February 2000 by Usamah al-Baz of Egypt, a top aide to President Hasni Mubarak in charge of government relationships with NGOs:

The state encourages many NGOs because they have [a] positive influence on the society . . . but these organizations should be national rather than a Trojan horse or a facade for activities of foreign organizations. . . . Some NGOs sometimes reflect visions of Western societies which do not heed the characteristic discrepancies between communities. . . . This [kind of] organization takes certain events as a pretext to interfere in other countries' internal affairs.[81]

Some NGOs have objected to strict government rules and organizations designed specifically to monitor NGO activity, but most have interpreted such actions as indicating receptivity by governments trying to help NGO involvement in development work.[82] A favorable predisposition by NGOs toward governments is particularly evident in the Middle East because substantial government funding often accompanies these arrangements.[83] In many cases, NGOs and PVOs are fully supportive of Middle Eastern governments in their conflicts with others, including the West—as is the case, for example, with most NGOs' support of Iraq in its efforts to lift UN sanctions imposed on Baghdad after Iraq's unsuccessful invasion of Kuwait.[84]

■ CONCLUSIONS

If any region of the world demonstrates the severe challenges involved in trying to establish cyberspace as a sovereign territory in its own right, the Middle East would have to be at or near the top of the list. Arab rulers have fought especially hard to establish and maintain the sovereignty of their nations in relationship to the Internet and thus far seem to have done so successfully. At the same time, there is no question that both Arab and Israeli leaders feel somewhat threatened and challenged by the Internet and its potential consequences for their societies and polities.

It is perhaps for this reason that the leaders in most Middle Eastern nations are just beginning to consider the extent to which they will countenance their nations' involvement in the international regime for the Internet. None has thus far played a major role at the global level in developing the "principles, norms, rules, and decisionmaking procedures" around which actor expectations are converging for Internet use and development, although some Israelis have begun to be involved in establishing world standards in some Internet-related areas, particularly in encryption technology. As Jeffrey Kahn points out, "Israeli engineers and companies have been integral to the development of the Internet since its earliest commercial beginnings. Various backbone technologies—from modems, routers, switches and cables to ISDN, ATM and compression and encryption techniques—have been created or nurtured in Israeli high-tech incubators. Companies such as RAD, NDS, Versaware and Foxcom have each established themselves as industry standards in their respective markets."[85] Because of its substantial interest in becoming a leader in high-tech development related to the Internet, Israel has been willing to negotiate agreements and develop policies related to Internet development that are closer to international regime norms and decisionmaking procedures than those being discussed by the Arab states. One example of this divergence is the agreement concluded by Israel with the World Trade Organization (WTO), which goes much further on trade matters than similar agreements negotiated by the Arab states.[86]

The gap between the Arab states and the West on Internet regime approaches is exemplified by their varying positions on the legal responsibilities of ISPs as opposed to authors and other content providers. The European Commission, the European Parliament, and the Council of the European Union have all endorsed the view that ISPs "should not be targeted by the individual governments and law enforcement bodies where the ISPs have no control of the Internet content."[87] This perspective is also firmly established in section 230(c)(1) of the 1996 U.S. Communications Decency Act, which remains valid even though other clauses of that act have been struck down by the Supreme Court. But in most Arab nations the law is somewhat ambiguous in this respect, so that ISPs or even cybercafé owners might be held responsible for allowing illegal messages to be sent by their clients or customers. Tunisia has even passed laws holding ISPs liable for content, including statutes requiring ISP directors to "maintain constant oversight of the content of the ISP's servers to insure that no information remains on the system that is contrary to public order and good morals."[88]

A second area where Israel and the Arab states diverge is with regard to Internet-related conflict resolution and human rights activities. Although Israel is not entirely without fault in the perception of human rights organizations (as mentioned previously, for example, it is one of the few Middle Eastern nations that severely restricts use of privacy-protecting encryption software by its citizens), Israel's Internet-related human rights record generally receives much higher marks from Amnesty International and other nongovernmental organizations than does the

Arab Middle East.[89] In recent years several international organizations have documented a number of ways in which Arab governments have abridged principles and norms that have long been part of international telecommunication and other communication regimes—norms acknowledged in the West as being fundamental to the nascent Internet regime.[90] The rights abridged by Arab governments have included the right to freedom of expression on the Internet through a variety of administrative rules and police orders, significant restriction of the free flow of information online through legislation and administrative fiat, and a general disregard for many other human rights concerns. In the most severe cases, Internet users in several Arab nations have charged that there has been government surveillance of e-mail, and Amnesty International has publicized the case of a Bahraini engineer, Sayyid'Alawi Sayyid Sharaf, who was "suspected" by Bahraini authorities of e-mailing political information to dissidents abroad, was arrested in March 1997, and was jailed for nearly two years before being released without charges ever having been brought against him.[91]

A third major Internet-related area, one in which some Arab Middle Eastern states have taken an ambiguous position toward international regime norms, relates to new forms of terrorism being waged on the World Wide Web, generally referred to as "Netwar." A 1999 study by Michele Zanini of the RAND Corporation, for example, concluded that:

> Terrorism seems to be evolving in the direction of violent netwar. Islamic fundamentalist organizations like Hamas and the bin Laden network consist of groups organized in loosely interconnected, semi-independent cells that have no single commanding hierarchy. . . . The rise of networked arrangements in terrorist organizations is part of a wider move away from formally organized, state-sponsored groups to privately financed, loose networks of individuals and subgroups that may have strategic guidance but enjoy tactical independence. Related to these shifts is the fact that terrorist groups are taking advantage of *information technology* to coordinate the activities of dispersed members. Such *technology* may be employed by terrorists not only to wage *information warfare* but also to support their own networked organizations.[92]

Although some Middle East terrorist groups are stridently opposed by Arab national leaders (e.g., the Egyptian Islamic Group by the Egyptian government), several modern terrorist organizations continue to receive substantial support, particularly from Syria, Libya, and Iran. Based on financial backing from governments and private sources, several of

these organizations are reportedly creating "a kind of international terrorists' Internet," established over a network known as *Al-Qaeda* (the
Base) as the core structure, funded by Osama bin Laden.[93] The goal of
the bin Laden alliance is to wage global opposition against perceived
threats to Islam, initiated by bin Laden's 1996 declaration of holy war
against the United States and the West.[94] According to reporters who
have visited bin Laden's Arab headquarters in the remote mountains of
Afghanistan, his organization has computers, fairly sophisticated communications equipment, and a large number of disks for storage. Bin
Laden and other Arab terrorist organizations are reportedly attempting
to develop "CIA-proof" networks that rely on the World Wide Web, e-
mail, and electronic bulletin boards to communicate among a number of
bases and outposts scattered throughout the world.

Conflicts on the Web between Arab and Israeli hackers and netizens
became so intense in late 2000 and early 2001 that newspapers and television stations in the Middle East were discussing what they called
"CyberWar-I." By January 2001, more than 100 Israeli sites and an estimated four dozen sites in Arab states had been attacked by hackers and
self-proclaimed partisan groups, bent on destroying or defacing websites considered unacceptable by one side or the other.[95] When Knesset,
Israeli Foreign Ministry, and some Israeli army and other government
sites were either silenced or rendered relatively ineffective over a two-
week period in October 2000, the chair of the Knesset Internet subcom-
mittee, Michael Eitan, called for a truce and suggested that "we should
persuade the international community of the need to create a body
which will insist on strict regulations and enforce them to stop such attacks."[96] When AT&T successfully came to the rescue of the Israeli
ISPs under the most severe attack, some militant Arab-Islamic groups
listed the company as one to boycott, but leading Arab Internet security
experts cautioned that "the Arab world will be seriously damaged if a
true cyber-war begins" because of Israel's superior command of knowledge and resources in computer networking.[97]

Although a nascent international regime exists for building collaboration among Western allies opposed to international terrorism and
Netwar, among Middle Eastern nations only Israel has been centrally involved in the discussions and negotiations leading to the development
of that regime.[98] Arab nations have worked closely with U.S. authorities
to better understand specific terrorist incidents (e.g., attacks on U.S.
tourists in Egypt, the bombing of the Khobar Towers in Saudi Arabia, or
the destruction of the American Embassies in Kenya and Tanzania), but

this has not led to agreement on a set of principles, norms, rules, and procedures characteristic of regime creation. Indeed, disagreement between Egyptian and U.S. authorities concerning possible causes of the crash of Egyptair flight #990 in October 1999 reflected rather different American and Arab approaches to the control of terrorist acts.

In the final analysis, all Arab nations have had difficulties working with international regimes led by the United States and, to a lesser extent, European nations. Strains in the relationship result from Arabs' rejection of some cultural manifestations of the West's secularism, the perceived past wrongs of colonial rule, and the West's role in creating and sustaining Israel. The creation and leadership of international regimes by the West are often viewed by Arabs, in Michael Field's words, as

> the West . . . still trying to dominate the Arab world, manipulate it, and take away its independence. This view may seem absurd to Westerners, who take the independence of the Arab countries for granted and are happy to deal with them on equal terms as long as they are not blatantly hostile to their interests. But in the minds of Arabs the idea of the West's malevolence and of its conspiring against them is deeply rooted and will remain for many years.[99]

For the Arab Middle Eastern nations, therefore, decisions about whether and to what degree to join the international regime for the Internet are related to many other aspects of policy and international politics. Although many of these nations would prefer to have the benefits of the Internet without joining Western nations in a common regime, that option seems unlikely because of the nature of the technology and of international political power relationships.

▪ NOTES

1. See McCullagh, "Mideast Misses the Net," pp. 1–3, and Siegel and Hausman, "Haredim Abuzz," p. 5. See also Machlis, "Israel's Orthodox," p. 6.

2. For an analysis of the early years of the Internet in Jordan, see Abdel-Rahim, "The Impact of the Information Revolution," pp. 160–175. See also Ghneim, "Covering Internet Trends in Jordan," p. 2. Ghneim is associate editor of *Byte Magazine* (Middle East edition) and a correspondent for the *Star* news weekly in Amman.

3. See *The Internet in the Mideast and North Africa*, p. 33.

4. In addition to cutting costs for connectivity, the Jordanian government launched a number of other incentives at the beginning of 2001 to encourage

Internet use, including a major project to computerize all schools and provide them with Internet access and an agreement with local banks to enable Jordan's 57,000 schoolteachers and school administrators to purchase their own personal computers. See "Jordan Telecom Slashes Fees," p. 16. Jordan is hoping to initiate a process of privatizing Jordan Telecom in 2001 as a means of raising revenue for Internet-related development. See Gray, "Jordan," p. 3.

5. Quoted in *The Internet in the Mideast and North Africa,* p. 34.

6. The kind of pressure being applied to Internet users in Jordan was described by Marwan Joma, general manger of NETS (one of the largest private ISPs in Amman), in a May 26, 1998, telephone conversation with Human Rights Watch: "There are very few rules, but NETS, being in Jordan, has to comply with local laws. This means users must not use foul language nor attack public figures. You can attack the policy of a certain minister, but you can't attack [them or other] subscribers personally. NETS doesn't screen [i.e., censor] messages, but we read the messages, like any other user, and if there's a [transgression] we send the user a reminder, and we can suspend them from a [forum]." Quoted in ibid.

7. An excellent analysis of Internet development in the Arab nations of North Africa is Jensen, "Algeria/Egypt/Libya/Morocco/Tunisia," pp. 94–97. See also Allen, "Maghreb Online," pp. 155–164.

8. McCullagh, "Mideast Misses the Net," p. 2.

9. For analysis of the rumor, see "Saudi Arabia's ISPs Filtering/Slash White List," available at www.2bits.com/isp/0013-filtering.

10. The proxy servers in the UAE are maintained by the government monopoly telecommunications company Etisalat. When someone requests a website, the filtering software on the proxy server detects objectionable material and sends a message back to the user, through the proxy server, denying access. Authorities can also use proxy servers to track computer terminals that are accessing websites. See Jehl, "The Internet's 'Open Sesame.'"

11. Saad Fagih, a leader of the exiled opposition Movement for Islamic Reform in Arabia, for example, suggests that despite many websites being available, "millions of others have been blocked, including all the hot political sites, such as Amnesty International." Quoted in Whitaker, "Online," p. 17.

12. Ibid.

13. See Azzam, "Globalization.com," p. 1, quoted in "E-Commerce in the Arab World," p. 15. Iraq's Kurdish political parties, as well as other Iraqi opposition movements and parties in exile, maintain websites through providers outside Iraq. In addition, an Iraqi cultural website, www.iraq.net, is maintained by members of the Iraqi diaspora. For more information, see Napoli, "Iraqi Exiles," p. D5. See also Jensen, "Algeria/Egypt/Libya/Morocco/Tunisia," p. 97.

14. An analysis of early computer and Internet use in Iraq appears in Fox, "Unwired Iraq," pp. 11–18.

15. See McCullagh, "Mideast Misses the Net."

16. Bashar was thrust into the role of championing the Internet in Syria when his older brother, Basil al-Assad, died in a 1994 car accident. Basil was

a civil engineer who founded the SCS as an independent, nongovernmental organization in 1989. Bashar, who had been studying ophthalmology in England, returned to Syria and was elected chairman of the SCS following his brother's death. For more information, see the article by the chairman of the SCS, Amr Salem, "Syria's Cautious Embrace," pp. 49–50.

17. Quoted in Contreras, "Cyber-Savvy in Syria," p. 54.

18. Ibid. Another Middle East figure who has championed the Internet is Sultan Qaboos bin Said, the fifty-nine-year-old supreme ruler of the Sultanate of Oman. Qaboos overthrew his father, Said bin Taimur, in a bloodless coup in 1970 with help from the British army, relatives, and friends. He has since instituted significant modernization programs, including building Christian churches and Hindu temples for Omani minorities, and many women's rights programs (Qaboos appointed the first female ambassador from an Arab Gulf country, has admitted women to his Consultative Council as deputy ministers—also a first for the Gulf—and has built the kingdom's first university in which the majority of students are women). Oman is the only Gulf country to have a Basic Law, or constitution, that guarantees inalienable rights to its citizens. See Daniszewski, "A Former Hermit Kingdom," pp. 1, 5.

19. Begleiter, "Syria and the World Wide Web," pp. 33–34.

20. Kaplow, "Syria Embraces the Internet Gingerly," p. G6.

21. Sennott, "Syria's Leader," p. A4. For an analysis of how far Bashar Assad's regime had progressed toward this goal after Assad junior had been in power for almost a year, see "Syria Online," pp. 42–43.

22. For an analysis of the interrelationships of these factors with Internet-related variables, see Friedman, "Unfinished Business in Syria," p. 29. See also "With the Death of Hafez Assad," p. 24.

23. Williams, "Syria Plods Into Net Revolution," pp. 14–16. Among the Syrian websites that can be accessed by the public are the Syrian Arab News Agency (www.sana.org), the government mouthpiece *Tishrin Daily* (www.teshreen.com), and the Syrian Computer Society (www.scs-syria.org).

24. For a statement of Syria's policy toward the Internet, see Naffakh, "Will Syria Embrace?" pp. 35–36. Naffakh is a member of the Syrian Computer Society and a marketing engineer in Ericsson, Damascus, who studied in the United States under a Fulbright Fellowship in 1999. Naffakh concluded that "the [Syrian] government will help develop the [Internet] in the best possible way. Obviously, this cannot happen overnight; time is needed to study all the proposals and execute them carefully to avoid any unexpected impediments and to assure the smooth and safe implementation of modern telecommunication services."

25. For a list of sites, see www.gksoft.com/govt. For more information, see Lincoln, "Middle East Governments." Saudi dissident groups include the Committee for the Defense of Legitimate Rights (www.ummah.org.uk/cdlr) and the Movement for Islamic Reform in Arabia (www.miraserv.com). See *The Internet in the Mideast and North Africa*.

26. More information on the Iraqi sites is available in "Iraqi Newspaper," available at www.indialine.com/net.news/May99.html.

27. Others in this race for the first electronic government are the state of California, which hopes to reach the goal in 2002, Canada in 2004, and the U.K. in 2005. When Qatar established the goal of autumn 2002, Dubai's government countered with the "end of 2001." See Kamli, "Will Dubai?" and Bokhari, "Internet City," p. 11.

28. In April 2000, Crown Prince Mohammed, then also minister of defense, warned senior civil servants that they had eighteen months to implement the project for an electronic government in Dubai and that they would "face sacking or be rewarded," depending on their performance on the project. The crown prince has committed a large budget for the project and is working with a number of global IT companies, including Oracle, Cisco, IBM, Microsoft, Nortel, Lucent, Hewlett Packard, Ericsson, and Nokia. For more detail, see "E-Government in Dubai" and "Dubai Internet City."

29. See Weiner, "Jordan and the Internet," pp. 49–50.

30. *The Internet in the Mideast and North Africa,* p. 51.

31. The survey on which these figures are based was conducted by the research unit of IAW and is detailed in Jarrah, "Internet Shoppers in Arab World," pp. 1–3, available at www.ditnet.co.ae/itnews/me.

32. Jarrah, "Private Ventures Lead Arab Migration," pp. 1–3. All eleven of the fully functional sites were English-language sites. The twenty-nine non- or less-functional sites suffered from one or more of the following problems: sluggish download of heavily loaded and difficult-to-understand pages, faulty systems of payment, and insecure servers.

33. Drummond, "Middle East," p. 3.

34. Shetty, "Crown Jewel," pp. 13–14.

35. Quoted in Jarrah, "Widespread Internet Use," p. 2.

36. Quoted in Jarrah, "Organizations Urged to Think eBusiness," p. 2.

37. Ibid.

38. See Jarrah, "Dell Launches Online Business in UAE," pp. 1–2.

39. A useful volume providing considerable background on the development of the Internet in the UAE is Al-Suwaidi, *The Information Revolution and the Arab World.*

40. For an outline of the conference contents, see Jarrah, "Practical E-Commerce Conference," pp. 1–3.

41. Plaza, "Lotus Nears Completion," pp. 1–3.

42. Pope, "Why Is the Tech Set Putting Down Roots in the Desert?" p. A15.

43. Alterman, *New Media, New Politics?* pp. 42–43.

44. "Arabic Email Celebrates 100,000 Users," press release of BOC, available at www.pressreleasenetwork.com/mainpr53.html.

45. "Barnes and Noble to Target Internet Users," pp. 1–2.

46. "Online in Saudi Arabia," p. 48.

47. *The Internet in the Mideast and North Africa,* p. 62.

48. Quoted in ibid. For more information see the ISNA website at www.islamicinternet.org.

49. See "Islam, Iran and the Internet," *CNN Interactive,* at www.cnn.com/WORLD/9705/22/iran.tech/index.html.

50. Weiss, "Road to Ancient Muslim Hajj," p. B2. The 1998 meeting is described in Salah, "Al-Azhar wa al-Jam'at al-Islamiyya yatanafasan 'ala al-Internet," quoted in "Egypt's Moslem Authorities."

51. A description of the project appears in "Iran to Put," pp. 1–3. The website for reading the works in English is www.irna.com. See also "World: Middle East Khomeini Immortalised Online," pp. 1–5.

52. For excerpts from the site and English translation quotations from the article in *Al-Sharq al-Awsat,* see "Iranian Authorities," pp. 1–4. See also "Iranian Cleric," sec. 1, p. A1.

53. Dinmore, "Iran's Ayatollahs," p. 12. All quotations in this paragraph are from this source, unless noted otherwise.

54. Quoted from an interview, June 21, 2000, on condition of anonymity. For an attempt to understand the technical operation of Iran's Internet, see the 144-page report "Iran's Telecom."

55. For more detail on the Islamvision project and related government efforts, see Wheeler, "In Praise of the Virtual Life."

56. Plans for the Islamvision project are analyzed in "Experts Group" and "Islamvision." Pipes, "Islam and Islamism," p. 87, explains the difference between traditional Islam and Islamism as follows: "While Islamism is often seen as a form of traditional Islam, it is . . . profoundly different. Traditional Islam seeks to teach humans how to live in accord with God's will, whereas Islamism aspires to create a new order. The first is self-confident, the second deeply defensive. The one emphasizes individuals, the latter communities. The former is a personal credo, the latter a political ideology."

57. A summary of the various approaches of Middle Eastern governments to modern media and communications appears in Hilliard and Keith, *Global Broadcasting Systems,* pp. 136–140. The authors describe prohibitions on the media (including the Internet) by Saudi authorities as follows: "Any materials that could be considered sexually stimulating in any way, or materials that depict women in ways not consistent with Islamic practices, such as playing a sport, dancing, dressed in nonacceptable styles (especially Islamic women appearing unveiled), or materials showing gambling or alcohol use." In addition to the prohibitions, Hilliard and Keith point out that "the clergy and the royal family must be properly praised. Other religions are not mentioned" (p. 139).

58. For more detail, see "Windows," pp. 1–3; "Sakhr," pp. 1–2; Jarrah, "New OS Opens Palm Computing," pp. 1–2; and "New Dabbagh," pp. 1–3.

59. "DIT's Award," pp. 1–3.

60. For analysis of Iran's effort in this regard, see Kiarostami, "Could Iran Rival India?" pp. 1–5. See also Kamli, "ASP Service," pp. 1–3.

61. Jarrah, "Internet Communication," pp. 1–4.

62. "KSA Online?" p. 3.

63. Lacuna, "The Future," p. 6.

64. Alterman, "Shrinking the World," p. 31. Alterman has expanded on this theme in "The Middle East's Information Revolution," pp. 21–26.

65. Quoted from a review of Anderson's book by Ghareeb in *Middle East Insight,* p. 65. See Anderson, *Arabizing the Internet.*

66. Ibid., p. 66.

67. For cooperation between Israeli and Palestinian officials on telecommunications and Internet development, see Luxner, "Digital Bridge," pp. 20–21.

68. Gallagher, "Middle East and North Africa," pp. 1–11.

69. See "La Presse Libre Sur le Web."

70. Flusfeder, "Global Audience," pp. 12–14; Watzman, "A Virtual Jewish-Studies Program," pp. A51–52.

71. While continuing to be active in the Middle East, ICQ was acquired by AOL in 1998 for $287 million and has grown to be the second largest instant messenger service in the world (the other, Instant Messenger, is also owned by AOL Time Warner). In May 2001, AOL announced plans to use ICQ as "a launch pad for our broader web portal strategy," with ICQ, AOL.com, and CompuServe conceptualized as "the company's multibranded Web portal triad." See Hu, "Is the ICQ Experiment Working?" p. 17.

72. Bart, "Israel Online," pp. 47–48.

73. Ibid. See also Ein-dor and Goodman, "From Via Maris," p. 19.

74. With regard to the Golan issue, for example, the Syrian Internet survey, according to Mustafa, found that 71 percent of the Internet documents were "very hostile" to Syria, 12 percent were "typical informative ones that appear to be innocent but conceal malicious points of view," and 17 percent were "put on the network by Israeli organizations which outwardly call for peace with Syria and the rest of the Arabs but in reality seek something else." These and additional details from the survey are available in Alterman, *New Media, New Politics?* pp. 40–41.

75. In February 1998, for example, the Syrian journal *Tishrin* published an article calling for a comprehensive plan to lower rates for Internet connections and "spread Internet culture to all Arabs" for several reasons, primary among them being to compete with Israeli efforts in cyberspace. See al-Ibrahim, "The Internet and Informatics."

76. For a description of the Across Borders project, see "Palestinian Refugees Join the Net," pp. 1–5. More than 4 million Palestinian refugees are scattered in 59 refugee camps in the West Bank, Gaza Strip, Jordan, Syria, Lebanon, and elsewhere in the world—many having been separated from their families for four or five decades.

77. These plans are outlined in "Palestinian Refugees Online," p. 48.

78. For more details on the survey, see Jarrah, "Internet Reaches Layman in Middle East," pp. 1–5.

79. Abu-Sharif, "NGOs Ministry," p. 3.

80. "Egyptian Court Says Law on NGOs 'Unconstitutional,'" pp. 1–3.

81. Quoted in "Egypt: President's Aide Says," p. 2.

82. The most prominent case of an NGO resisting a "pact" with a Middle Eastern government was the refusal of humanitarian organizations working in Sudan to sign an "agreement of understanding" with the Sudan People's Liberation Movement in spring 2000. The European Commission even announced that it was prepared to give assistance amounting to 11 million Euros to southern Sudan if the

rebel forces retracted their "extortionist" demands. See the *BBC Summary of World Broadcasts,* March 28, 2000, based on a report in the Sudanese newspaper *'Al-Ra'y al-Amm,* March 25, 2000.

83. An example of such direct support is a group of women's NGOs, supported by various Arab governments, that in mid-1999 issued a joint report condemning "the widespread plot of the enemies of Islam and the Islamic Revolution" while voicing their "strong support for *Velayat-e Faqih* [religious jurisprudence]." See "Women NGO Group," p. 2.

84. See Joha, "Iraqi Tragedy."

85. Kahn, "Pushing the Cyber-Envelope," p. 45.

86. The weak aspects of Jordan's WTO membership, which was approved by the WTO in January 2000 and must now be ratified by the Jordanian parliament, are discussed in "Jordan WTO," pp. 1–2, a summary of articles from the *Jordan Times* and the *Petra News Agency.* Saudi Arabia is negotiating WTO membership and hopes to be admitted in 2002. See Almotawa, "Kingdom Will Hold." Many Middle East nations, including Syria, Lebanon, and Iraq, are not members of the WTO.

87. Quoted in *The Internet in the Mideast and North Africa,* p. 24. See also *Liberating Cyberspace,* pp. 140–158.

88. Quoted in *The Internet in the Mideast and North Africa,* pp. 43ff.

89. For example, in the Freedom House evaluations of communications and media systems, Israel scored 2 in 1999, on a scale in which 1 indicated the most free and 7 the least free. All Arab nations received scores of 4 or lower, with Israel ranked overall "free"; Jordan, Lebanon, and Egypt ranked "partially free"; and all other Arab nations ranked "not free." Freedom House operates under the auspices of UNESCO. For more detail, see Caspi and Limor, *The In/Outsiders,* pp. 185–187.

90. Nancy Gallagher lists thirty-nine organizations (including a short description of each with addresses and websites) engaged in human rights activism in the Middle East, each with a particular emphasis or focus related to the Internet. See Gallagher, "Middle East and North Africa," pp. 1–11.

91. These and many other Middle Eastern human rights violations are detailed in *The Internet in the Mideast and North Africa.* Amnesty International reported in 1997 that Sharaf had been tortured by intelligence officials while being denied contact with anyone, including his family. See *Amnesty International Urgent Action Appeal 42/97,* March 25, 1997.

92. Zanini, "Middle Eastern Terrorism and Netwar," pp. 247–248; emphasis added.

93. In addition to ibid., see Ottaway, "U.S. Considers Slugging It Out," p. 25, and Weiner, "U.S. Sees Bin-Laden," p. A1.

94. "Saudi Arabia: bin-Laden Calls for 'Guerrilla Warfare' Against U.S. Forces," *Beirut Al-Diyar,* available in FBIS-NEW-96-180, September 12, 1996, quoted in Zanini, "Middle Eastern Terrorism and Netwar," p. 256.

95. The estimates are made by iDefense, an electronic security firm, and are updated on the iDefense website. For a description of CyberWar-I activities,

see Whitaker, "Online," p. 17.

96. Quoted in "'Web-War' Puts Knesset's Internet Site out of Service," p. 2.

97. The quote is from security expert Mirza Asrar Baig, in Ba-Isa, "Cyber War."

98. A preliminary study of regime issues for what the U.S. military commonly labels "the revolution in military affairs" among the United States and its European and Asian allies appears in Laird and Mey, *The Revolution in Military Affairs*. See also Hundley and Anderson, "Emerging Challenge," pp. 231–252.

99. Field, *Inside the Arab World,* pp. 423–424.

4

Information Technology
and Political Cultures in Eurasia

E urasia, like Central and Eastern Europe, emerged in the late 1980s
and early 1990s from more than a half century of Soviet dominance at approximately the same time that the Internet was becoming an unprecedented force for change in world communications
networks. As Lawrence Lessig has pointed out, both of these epic
events gave rise to widespread feelings and hopes that new regimes
could be established with minimal sets of new rules and with little or no
government control. Lessig has characterized this preference for what
should happen in Central/Eastern Europe in the flush of post-Soviet independence as follows: "Just let the market reign and keep the government out of the way, and freedom and prosperity will inevitably grow.
Things will take care of themselves. There is no need, and can be no
place, for extensive regulation by the state."[1] With regard to cyberspace,
Lessig pointed out, libertarian aspirations were even more pronounced
and extensive, giving rise to worldwide claims that "government could
not regulate cyberspace, that cyberspace was essentially, and unavoid-
ably, free. . . . Cyberspace would be a society of a very different sort.
. . . There would be definition and direction, but built from the bottom
up, and never through the direction of a state."[2]

In both cases—for Central/Eastern Europe, and especially the societies of the former Soviet Union (FSU) in the 1990s and early twenty-
first century, and for the Internet—governments and private organizations have been exerting and continue to exert new forms of regulation
and control. Political power has slowly shifted in the various Central/
Eastern European and FSU nations as many former Communist Party,

intelligence, and military leaders have managed to retain or acquire power while recently established national, provincial, and local governments have found themselves subject to the influence of emergent mafiosi and a variety of freshly minted nongovernmental and business interests. In all cases the new governments have experienced the pressures being exerted by international and regional organizations and by U.S. hegemony in the twenty-first century's interdependent global political economy. As part of the general pattern outlined in early chapters, the impressive capabilities—and even more impressive potential—of the Internet have moved it to the center of attention of authorities throughout Central and Eastern Europe and Eurasia, with the result that it is being transformed from a relatively free and open technological wonder to an increasingly controlled international communications facility.

This chapter begins with an analysis of the failure of Soviet communism to successfully compete with the West in the development of information technology (IT) and communications, resulting in telecommunications infrastructures throughout the former Soviet bloc that were either totally unprepared or ill prepared to adopt an Internet culture in the 1990s. The response of the FSU nations, as well as the former Soviet-dominated states of Eastern Europe—once they were freed from Russian dominance—has varied enormously. A few of the new governments have made rapid or at least steady advances toward a meaningful involvement with cyberculture and the economic restructuring necessary for a flourishing Internet environment. All of the evidence confirms that Eastern European nations have progressed much more quickly than the FSU states in this regard, although a few Eastern European countries (e.g., Albania, Macedonia) have barely managed to get started, and the Baltic states have far outstripped the rest of the FSU in IT and Internet initiatives. One major goal of this chapter and Chapters 5 and 6 is to trace the ways in which these varying national experiences with IT have affected the place of Central/Eastern Europe and the FSU states in the nascent international Internet regime. A second goal is to determine the impact of international relations and domestic politics on the evolution of IT and Internet policies in the various nation-states.

■ IT DEVELOPMENT AND THE
FAILURE OF SOVIET COMMUNISM

The failure of the Soviet Union or any of its satellites to maintain even a semblance of parity with the West in the development of information technology is perhaps the most conspicuous failure of the Soviet system, among its many other failures, during seventy-four years of existence. As Frank Ellis has pointed out, the Soviet system was undermined by the information technology revolution on two counts. First, the development of IT simply took off in the West in the second half of the twentieth century, leaving the Soviets and their allies unable to compete or often even to comprehend the breadth and significance of the innovative technological and entrepreneurial changes taking place. To quote Ellis:

> Without buy-outs, start-ups and venture capital, without, in other words, the economic infrastructure which capitalism and private ownership of the means of production make possible . . . [the Soviets and their satellites were unable] to develop computer hardware and software industries capable of rivaling those in America. . . . We can see the development and staggering growth of the personal-computer industry as one of a number of allegories of capitalist success, and equally, an illustrative, single example of what went wrong in the Soviet Union.[3]

A second aspect of the IT revolution that worked cruelly to dissemble the Soviet order was the way in which computer-related development moved inexorably in the West's favor as regards the dissemination of news and information, even in the USSR itself. To quote Ellis again:

> IT enhanced the already superior empirical and flexible practices of the Western media. Add to this the increased volume of data and information that could now be processed and transmitted and the advantages start to look overwhelming. . . . Unable to cope, Soviet delivery systems, domestic and international (TASS and APN), lost the initiative and found themselves on the defensive. The ability of the new electronic media to seep through just about any barrier, and as important, their ability to impose a new *modus operandi* on the dissemination of news, meant that the Soviet Union had, whether the [communist] party liked it or not, been drawn into a global media structure, in which the West—to use the current phrase—was setting the agenda.[4]

In mid-June 1989, President Ronald Reagan was referring to the Soviet bloc when he predicted that "technology will make it increasingly difficult for the state to control the information its people receive. . . . The Goliath of totalitarianism will be brought down by the David of the microchip."[5] As more and more Soviet bloc citizens and dissenters were able to effectively use the fax machine, the Internet, and other rapidly spreading means of modern communication, Reagan's rhetorical prediction became first believable and then fact. Conservative communist rule collapsed in East Germany in October 1989, and the Berlin Wall came down on November 9. Two weeks later more than 300,000 people demonstrated in Prague, leading to the selection of the anticommunist hero Vaclav Havel as the interim president of the Czech Republic in December. A newly elected Polish parliament also met in December 1989 to amend the national constitution of Poland and formally eliminate reference to the leading role of the Communist Party. In March–April 1990, parliamentary elections in Hungary brought an end to forty-five years of totalitarian rule. In August 1991 an attempted coup by Communist Party and military leaders in Russia failed, leaving Mikhail Gorbachev in charge of a fragile Communist Party (CPSU) and Soviet Union (USSR). Both the CPSU and the USSR were dissolved and replaced in Russia by the democratically elected government led by Boris Yeltsin after Gorbachev resigned as president of the USSR on Christmas Day in 1991. In between and following these tumultuous events, communist regimes collapsed throughout Central/Eastern Europe and Eurasia. Within the space of a few months fifteen new nations (some of which joined a new Commonwealth of Independent States [CIS]) replaced the Soviet Union.

A history of the role of information technology in the events of 1989–1991 has yet to be written, but two examples—from Poland and Russia—provide some idea of its significance. In Poland the leader of the anticommunist Solidarity movement, Lech Walesa, has argued that the spread of information technology—both in Poland and among Poles worldwide—even though it was less rapid in Poland than in the West, was crucial to Solidarity's success.

> The truth is, communism exhausted its possibilities. It was based on censorship, but at that time satellite television was introduced, [as well as] the Internet [and] cell phones. And they [the communists] would have to multiply their political police force by five at least [to censor these new communications media]. They had no money to do it. . . . In the past [communist functionaries] could stand with a gun behind a man who had a pick and spade, and tell him to dig a hole 200 meters long. But you can't put a man behind someone working creatively with a computer and tell him "please devise something original." There's no way to do it, and I took advantage of that.[6]

In the case of the Russian coup attempt in August 1991, Heather Hudson has written about the role of nascent Russian electronic networks in breaking the blackout of conventional media imposed by coup leaders:

The coup leaders . . . neglected to take effective steps to isolate Yeltsin electronically. They could have cut off international traffic at the Moscow international gateway switch, the Ostankino relay tower, or the Dubna Intelsat earth station. The Ministry of Defense ordered international communications to be shut down, but the staff did not obey the orders. . . . [Thus], from the Russian White House, Yeltsin could communicate with the West via phone, fax, telex, and electronic mail. Foreign business people brought him cellular phones. New private networks kept channels of communications open within the country and to the rest of the world.[7]

The effectiveness of IT media during the August 1991 coup attempt has been described similarly by Sergei Erofeev:

As a result of a decree issued by the hard-core Communist rebels [in August 1991], the activity of the Russian State Television and Radio Company was banned and it was switched off the air. The Chairman of the company, Oleg Poptsov, who was also a deputy of the Russian Parliament, was put on a priority execution list and labeled a most dangerous person. . . . [But] the company . . . evacuated all available equipment to homes in order to start underground broadcasting. . . . With the help of amateurs, a shortwave radio station [was organized]. Television reporters from Russian Television made live reports for CNN via its Moscow bureau. On the second day of the coup, Russian Television technicians made it possible to broadcast "illegally" via satellite a 20-minute report on the situation in Moscow directed to the Ural Mountains and west Siberia. It was reported later by the press that, within an hour of that broadcast, a crowd of one million had gathered in the central square of Yeltsin's home city of Sverdlovsk in the Urals as a show of support in opposition to the Communist rebels.[8]

■ LEGACIES OF SOVIET RULE AND TELECOMMUNICATIONS INFRASTRUCTURES IN THE FSU

Despite the successful use of new information technology in the overthrow of communism, one of the major legacies of Soviet rule was an assortment of telecommunications infrastructures throughout Central/ Eastern Europe and Eurasia that were woefully inadequate for rapid development of the Internet. At the outset of the twenty-first century, it is still the case in the Russian Federation that almost all telephone lines are analog rather than digital, with demand for telephones far exceeding supply even without Internet usage figured into the equation.[9] Since the cost of telephone lines to consumers was (and is) extremely expensive and the cost to the government of installing modern new telephone lines in the world's most extensive country (which also has some of the earth's most severe climates) is prohibitive for a badly ailing economy, the IT infrastructure in Russia is likely to improve only marginally even with major outside investment. In the words of one observer, "Despite the country's best efforts, the telecommunications infrastructure in Russia is simply unsuitable for modern computer communication needs and is not expected to reach Western standards for many years to come."[10] To greater or lesser degrees, the same situation prevails in all of the fifteen former republics (now nation-states) of the FSU with the exception—for reasons discussed later—of the Baltic countries (Estonia, Latvia, and Lithuania).

Almost all of the FSU states have established Ministries of Informatics, Information, or Communications designed to help establish IT infrastructures, training centers, networks that can facilitate the spread of IT, and administrative and legislative rules and policies for domestic and international connectivity. But funding for such activities has been scarce within FSU states, with the result that they were heavily dependent on largesse from international nongovernmental organizations (NGOs) and other donors to get their Internet infrastructures started. Some of the organizations particularly active in the earliest years of Internet development were:

1. The Open Society Institute (OSI), established by the philanthropic Hungarian billionaire George Soros, which has been responsible for establishing some of the first high-speed local Internet connections in the FSU and Central/Eastern Europe, most of them through satellite[11]
2. The International Research and Exchanges Board (IREX), a U.S.-based nonprofit that has established public Internet sites at universities and libraries throughout the region as part of its Internet Access and Training Program (IATP)
3. The ISAR (formerly Institute on Soviet-American Relations), another U.S.-based nonprofit organization working to improve e-mail capability, provide computer equipment, and train users exclusively for NGOs with environmental concerns in Moldova and to train leaders in the use of e-mail and other computer activities in Kazakhstan, Kyrgyzstan, and Turkmenistan[12]
4. The U.S.-Russia Foundation, which in the 1990s became involved in fifty Internet-related investment projects in Russia and

plans to invest $75 million to $100 million in the early 2000s in the form of credits to Russian start-up companies[13]

5. The Eurasia Foundation, a U.S.-based, privately managed grant-making organization that has made a number of small grants ($10,000–$150,000) for Web-related development, primarily in the Caucasus and Central Asia; by 2000 more than $2 million had been provided for Internet development in the FSU

6. The U.S. Agency for International Development (USAID), which through its Rule of Law program helped link the Georgian Parliament and some government agencies in Tbilisi to the Internet via satellite (both the North Atlantic Treaty Organization and the International Association [INTAS]—a program sponsored by the European Union—have helped the Georgian Academy of Sciences establish a permanent Internet link as well)[14]

7. The Central Asia Development Agency (CADA), a private U.S. organization that established "computer halls" in Tajikistan where anyone who knows the e-mail address of the person he or she wants to contact can go and send a message free (with the limitation that messages over two kilobytes per month have to be paid for by the sender)[15]

8. In January 2001, the World Health Organization (WHO) announced that it would join with a number of private and governmental organizations to develop Internet-based programs in Africa and Central Asia designed to deliver high-quality scientific and medical information to research centers[16]

Despite the efforts of international philanthropists and funding agencies, Internet development has been slow throughout the FSU. In addition to problems associated with outdated telecommunications infrastructures, an insufficient number of telephone lines to meet demand, and the high cost of telephone service, other factors holding back Internet growth include the high cost and lack of availability of computer equipment and software, the paucity of websites in Russian and other languages of the area, the inability of the vast majority of people in the area to speak English (the language of most World Wide websites), and the difficulties involved in Internet development, planning, and maintenance in an environment where funding is at best erratic and management skills are in short supply.

In an effort to overcome some of these problems, a group of seven FSU nations banded together in 1993 to establish a common Central and Eastern European Networking Association (CEENet) to promote academic research on cyberspace. Working through CEENet, Moldova was able to establish permanent Internet access for the first time in 1995 by leasing a line to Bucharest, Romania.[17] The seven nations in CEENet have also benefited through exchange of operational, directory, and technical information and have created joint technical working groups and jointly funded projects that have attracted small amounts of outside financial support. Many other efforts to assist Internet development—by private, governmental, and international agencies—could be mentioned, but none has been close to the magnitude necessary to create world-class networks in any of the FSU states except in the Baltics.

Some idea of the enormity of the financial challenges involved in building modern telecommunications infrastructures in the FSU and Central/Eastern Europe (FSU/CEE) can be gained from mid-1990s figures developed by Robert Campbell.[18] The largest single investment in telecommunications infrastructure in any part of the FSU/CEE in 1995 (and to date in 2001) has been $30 billion provided by Germany to modernize the old East German networks, but investment on that scale was possible only because East Germany was being reintegrated with the wealthiest country in Europe. In comparison to this massive investment, the World Bank and European Bank for Reconstruction and Development (EBRD) had invested only $1 billion or so in telecommunications projects in the entire region stretching from Central/Eastern Europe throughout Eurasia by 1995. Campbell concluded that "assistance on either of these scales is a drop in the bucket in relation to the [needs of] the ex-USSR, and the few loans made so far to the CIS countries are tiny." An example of a "tiny" loan, in Campbell's perspective, was $38 million the EBRD provided to the Belarus Ministry of Posts, Telecommunications, and Informatics for an overlay network in Belarus that would serve only 10,000 subscribers and give them an external link.[19]

Minimal investment requirements for providing modern telecommunications infrastructures in the FSU alone were estimated by Hudson in 1997 to cost $254 billion, which would have provided 120 million lines capable of digitalization at 1997 prices.[20] This figure would be much larger today, but the amount of government investment in telecommunications has actually been declining in many FSU states with the weakening of the economies throughout the area. With the exception of the Baltic states, which have managed to attract investment from the Scandinavian countries to build telecommunications infrastructures (discussed below), the telecom sectors in most FSU nations have faced what Campbell calls "a disastrous income and cash-flow position and [have] no funds of [their] own to finance investment."[21] As a state-owned industry throughout the FSU, the telecom sector is expected to earn money for the state, so there are no plans for substantial privatization.[22] And yet, telecommunications is not generally considered a core sector for state investment because of the limited amount of investment monies available and the enormous demands on available funds from other sectors.

The Russian government has projected what it calls a "telecommunication boom" during the first decade of the twenty-first century and is planning to spend $33 billion on telecommunications projects by 2010.[23] Most of this investment, which is relatively inconsequential when compared with the figures that would be required to build a satisfactory national network, will be in developing high-speed, secure lines for military and security purposes or for the oil and gas industry rather than for nonstrategic domestic use. Relatively small amounts of foreign investment by world standards—primarily from Scandinavia and Germany— have been attracted to the development of mobile phone technology in Russia, but in ways that have limited applications for computer networks.[24] Attempts to develop satellite telecommunications networks suffered a number of setbacks just as they were getting under way in 2000.[25] Projected cable links to Western Europe have been difficult to complete because of the legal and political difficulties encountered when trying to lay cable through Eastern Europe.[26]

Self-financing of the telecom sector, which has been possible in other parts of the world, has failed miserably in the FSU because of what Campbell calls "the crazy quilt of inflation, free/restrained prices, subsidies, and interenterprise arrears."[27] For example, prices for local and intercity telecommunications services in Russia increased by 14 and 20 times, respectively, in 1992 alone, but that was well below the inflation rates of most of its inputs (energy prices, for instance, rose by 80 times during the first two years of post-Soviet rule). Because the FSU economies are in such poor shape, telecommunications services in many places dwindled rather than grew in the 1990s as potential customers were unable to pay increasingly higher costs. Telecom companies have also been unable to collect revenue from organizations using their services, including in many cases government organizations; and emergency decrees (such as that passed by the Russian government in 1993) requiring that all accounts with government enterprises for services provided be settled "on demand" have been only partially implemented. In the absence of flourishing economic prospects, banks in the FSU will not generally lend long-term to the telecommunications sector. Capital markets for the sector have not yet developed to any significant degree in any FSU nation.[28]

Foreign investment in FSU telecommunications has thus far been minimal, with most foreign companies undertaking cautious joint ventures that enable them to gain knowledge of the area and establish a presence that might eventually be expanded should economic prospects in the FSU improve. One of the earliest such investments was an $18 million project of U S West, initiated in 1988, that helped establish cellular telephone services in St. Petersburg, three international gateway switches (in Moscow, St. Petersburg, and Kiev), and other minor facilities. U S West owns between 22 percent and 45 percent of the facilities resulting from these various projects, with the remainder owned by the Russian Ministry of Posts and Communications and the St. Petersburg City Telephone Company (50–55 percent) and other partners (e.g., Millicom International Cellular of Luxembourg).[29] In the 1990s, investment lagged increasingly as the Yeltsin government became less and less successful, but the elevation of Vladimir Putin to the Russian presidency in 2000 produced a boomlet in international investment in Internet-related sectors. By August 2000 a series of relatively small foreign investments had already added up to more than $100 million for the year, a rather routine amount for many Internet companies in the West—which think of large-scale investments in terms of billions rather than millions—but the most significant amount ever invested in Russia in a single year.[30]

▪ INTERNET DEVELOPMENT IN RUSSIA

The extent to which Russia and the FSU states (excepting the Baltics) have fallen behind in Internet development is dramatically illustrated in Table 4.1, where Russia ranks above only Romania among the major countries of Eastern Europe regarding Internet use in January 2001. All other FSU states (again with the exception of those in the Baltics) rank well below Bulgaria, Romania, and the rest of Eastern Europe except for the two desperately poor East European states of Macedonia and Albania. This has to do primarily with the very poor telecommunications infrastructures inherited by the FSU states, as outlined earlier, and is unlikely to change significantly until massive investments can be brought in to build telecommunications infrastructures and get computers, software, and modems into offices and homes. With the Russian economy devastated by corruption and lack of direction and the economies of the

Table 4.1 Teledensity and Internet Hosts in the FSU and Central/Eastern Europe, January 2001

Country	Population[a] est. year 2000 (in millions)	Telephone Lines per 1,000[b]	Internet Hosts[c]	Internet Hosts per 1,000 people
Estonia	1.4	337	40,909	29.20
Czech Republic	10.3	326	159,319	15.50
Slovenia	1.9	333	21,868	11.50
Hungary	10.0	312	104,415	10.40
Poland	38.7	212	339,816	8.80
Latvia	2.4	302	19,925	8.30
Slovakia	5.4	232	37,921	7.00
Lithuania	3.7	301	17,804	4.80
Croatia	4.6	309	16,602	3.60
Bulgaria	8.2	338	18,429	2.20
Russian Federation	145.2	175	304,613	2.10
Romania	22.4	140	41,523	1.90
Kyrgyzstan	4.9	75[d]	4,115	0.84
Macedonia	2.0	170[d]	1,588	0.80
Ukraine	49.5	251	35,787	0.72
Armenia	3.8	154[d]	2,663	0.70
Kazakhstan	14.8	116[d]	7,383	0.50
Georgia	5.5	105[d]	1,734	0.30
Turkmenistan	5.2	74[d]	1,231	0.23
Belarus	10.0	208[d]	2,033	0.21
Azerbaijan	7.7	85[d]	1,542	0.20
Albania	3.4	17[d]	209	0.06
Tajikistan	6.4	42[d]	273	0.04
Moldova	4.3	140[d]	n/a	n/a
Uzbekistan	24.8	67[d]	n/a	n/a
Yugoslavia	10.7	n/a	n/a	n/a
(incl. Bosnia)	3.8	n/a	n/a	n/a

Sources: a. Population figures are estimates for 2000 from the Population Reference Bureau, Washington, D.C., available at www.popnet.org.

b. Telephone lines per 1,000 population are based on government figures provided by the Washington, D.C., embassies of the countries listed, unless otherwise noted. These are standardized figures provided to the United Nations by national governments.

c. An Internet host is a computer connected to the Internet with a Domain Name System (DNS) entry that identifies it. Individual machines can service more than one host. For detailed information on how Web hosts are counted, see the "Hostcount FAQ" at www.ripe.net. Figures for Internet hosts in this table are from this source as of January 10, 2001.

d. Figures for telephone lines per 1,000 population for these entries are from *Human Development Report 1999* (New York: Oxford University Press, 1999), pp. 53–56. These are standardized figures provided to the United Nations by national governments.

Note: n/a = reliable figures not available.

other FSU nations (excluding the Baltics) lagging far behind even the Russian economy, potential foreign investors in Internet-related projects are rare. The extent of the problem for Russia was summarized by Lee S. Wolosky in early 2000:

According to Anatoly Chubais, the principal architect of Russia's privatization program, Russia needs hundreds of billions of dollars for industrial restructuring and modernization. Yet private investors have abandoned the country because, among other things, their legal and economic rights are abused there with consistency and impunity. Investor fear has a ripple effect. . . . Widely publicized misconduct involving Russia's largest companies and most prominent business leaders scares away international investors from all Russian companies—including those with no intention of defrauding anyone. The problem is compounded by staggering capital flight, which removes further funds from the cash pool available for investment in Russian industry. In recent years, Russia has received less direct investment than has Peru. At the beginning of 1999, daily trading volumes on the Russian stock market were less than $1 million and have since risen to only $15–$20 million. The total market capitalization of all companies listed on the Russian stock exchange is approximately $36 billion. By contrast, the market capitalization of Yahoo alone exceeds $90 billion.[31]

In the entire Russian Federation, which has a population of approximately 145 million people, only an estimated 1.2 million were Internet users in mid-1999 and 1.4 million in mid-2000, with "user" defined liberally to mean anyone who logs on once a week or more.[32] The vast majority of Russian Internet users are scientists, scholars, and those entering cyberspace to contact friends or organizations abroad, but both e-commerce and e-business are still virtually nonexistent.[33] In 1999, income generated from Internet services other than access payments to Internet service providers (ISPs) amounted to less than $14 million for the entire year for all of Russia. Advertising income from the Internet in Russia totaled only $500,000 in 1998, was less than $1 million in 1999, and was projected to increase to as much as $3.5 million in 2000—but 80 percent of that amount is accounted for by only five websites.[34] Reflecting on such figures, Bernard Sucher, the managing director of trading and sales at the Moscow brokerage firm Troika Dialog, predicted in mid-2000 that the vast majority of online shops in Russia were destined to fail, telling the *Wall Street Journal,* "I don't know how more than a handful of these folks are going to earn the revenues to survive."[35]

Russia's limited Internet development is to a significant degree a function of a political culture that has traditionally viewed advanced communication as a form of privilege and a means of control. Following the collapse of the Soviet regime, for example, only 55 percent of the telephones in Russia were connected to a public network, with the remaining 45 percent dispersed among a larger number of private or branch systems belonging to government ministries, political parties, military and security organizations, large industrial conglomerates, and "unofficial" networks created in the "informal" sector. Rafal Rohozinski has traced the development of some of the early "unofficial" networks that introduced the Internet into Russia—including Relcom/ Demos, which established the first international connectivity (through Finland) in September 1990, and Fidonet, a computer bulletin board system that declined in use everywhere in the world except Russia shortly after it was introduced to the Internet in 1991.[36] Rohozinski described the process of creating the Internet in Russia:

> As state enterprises dissolved and former government and party offices were sold or rented to generate revenue for their new owners, their independent Soviet-era telephone networks became available as alternative sources of connectivity for ISPs that wanted to distance themselves from the existing local, regional, and national telephone operators. By 1998, Russia had more than 200 ISPs, many of whom acted as "upstream" providers to a multitude of local outfits. . . . While this changed somewhat in the wake of the collapse of the Russian economy in 1998—which forced consolidation in the commercial ISP industry—by global standards the Russian ISP market remains remarkably fragmented, and much more tolerant of cottage ISPs than is the case elsewhere.[37]

Rohozinski and others have pointed out that the fragmented origins of the Russian Internet, particularly when coupled with government attempts to ban use of encryption technology and to devise means for monitoring Internet traffic (discussed later), have been conducive to the growth of both private networks and "hacker" Internet cultures—both of which have a vitality in Russia unparalleled almost anywhere else in the world.[38] Emma Kiselyova and Manual Castells have described how fragmentation continued and even intensified in the 1990s as banks, financial institutions, trading groups, corporate services, and business conglomerates have created their own satellite-based Internet links: "As the various systems were privatized in a disorderly fashion, the results have been lack of coordination, uneven quality of service, and absence of an integrated telecommunications grid providing a basis for universal access."[39] To quote Rohozinski again:

> Despite its limited penetration of Russian society, the Russian Net provides a technological level for individuals to "route around" the old and new obstacles of Russia's geographic enormity, its relative

underdevelopment, and its post-Soviet economic and political dispar-
ities. True, the Net's growth cannot be divorced from the global importance of information and communications technologies . . . [but]
the continued relevance of unofficial networks in Russia suggests they
remain an important cultural back channel for all important personal
networking.[40]

▪ E-COMMERCE AND INVESTMENT

Both the Russian national government and international business and
government leaders have been concerned about the fragmentation and
lack of development of the Russian Internet, in part for security reasons
(see Chapter 6) but also because of the difficulties posed for Russia's
integration into the global Internet regime. At the end of the 1990s, for
example, the European Union publicly recognized the lack of development of e-commerce and e-business in Russia as a problem when it concluded an agreement to cooperate with Russia to boost public-sector cooperation and collaboration for Internet-related investment.[41] After
Putin's election, German Chancellor Gerhard Schroeder proposed at the
summit of the group of 8 (G-8) nations in July 2000 that a comprehensive program be initiated to cancel the debts of the world's poorest
countries, including Russia, with the understanding that this would enable those countries to undertake large-scale investment programs in
Internet-related technology. At the summit, Japan pledged $15 billion
for investment in Internet projects in poorer countries, including Russia,
to be expended during the five-year period 2001–2006.[42]

The largest single Internet-related investment in Russia prior to the
mid-2000 boomlet amounted to only $20 million, with funds coming
from Russkiye Fondy and Orion Capital Investors for expansion into a
portal for communications and e-commerce of the Russian online service Rambler Search Engine, run by the Russian company Stack.[43] Other
large investments, which have also come from Russian investors, include the establishment of the MeMoNet Company (Media-Most Networks) by Vladimir Gusinsky's Media-Most group and Internet Media
House Russia (IMHO), the largest Russian Internet advertising agency,
which controls around 50 percent of the advertising market in the infant
Russian Internet (or Runet, as it is known in the Russia Federation). The
greatest Internet resources in Russia at the turn of the twenty-first century were the technical skills of Russian engineers and scientists, particularly those who graduated from IT programs. In the words of Esther

Dyson, who headed the Internet Corporation for Assigned Names and Numbers (ICANN) organization and is one of a few dozen venture capitalists with projects in Russia, "[Russian] programmers [are] much better than Western ones because they [do] things [on a shoestring], with limited amounts of memory."[44] Dyson is also quick to point out that the business and management skills of Russian workers "woefully lag [behind] those of their Western counterparts." Companies establishing operations in Russia, she concludes, "won't need to offer much technical training for programmers and system administrators [but] will need to make a significant investment in training people to use business applications."[45]

Dyson and other investors in Internet-related ventures in Russia are primarily interested in developing business-to-business projects, linking the Internet within and between companies, rather than projects designed to extend Net or Web access to the general population.[46] A prominent example of this approach is the investment by Interfax Information Services Group, Russia's Gazprom, Britain's Middlesex Holdings, and the Swiss company Crown Resources A.G. to create an "Oil-On-Line" electronic platform that can service the rapidly developing oil and natural gas extraction industry in Russia, which is one of two sectors of the economy that have attracted large-scale international investment.[47] The Oil-On-Line project has been helped along with support from major foreign oil companies, which see in it a worldwide communications component without which the extraction of Russia's vast oil reserves would proceed at a significantly slower pace.[48] The oil companies and other Russian and foreign businesses were also instrumental in pressuring the government to support a project to extend high-speed Internet technology to five major Russian cities in mid-2000 and to bring the first optical Internet technology, based on dense wavelength-division multiplexing, to Russia through long-haul networks from other parts of the world by way of Sweden.[49]

Internet investor enthusiasm for Putin stems in part from his avid interest in the Internet and his determination to pursue more aggressive information technology policies. When he first became acting president in December 1999, Putin immediately established a new government website (www.pravitelstvo.gov.ru) that has since been used to communicate with businesses and government officials. An introductory statement on the site's home page declared: "The significance of this development [i.e., creating the website] is well beyond another official public information channel taking off in the Internet. In fact, that means a fundamental turnabout in government information policies."[50] Putin's initial year running the Russian economy—first as prime minister under Yeltsin and then as acting president and president—produced a number of imaginative proposed programs for Internet development for the general population, accompanied by less than effective implementation.[51] Where government has invested in Internet-related technology, funds have gone into programs designed to enhance the abilities of officials and military leaders to communicate with one another, an approach consistent with the predisposition of Putin's administration in other areas.[52]

■ RUSSIA'S "INFORMATION SECURITY DOCTRINE"

Central to Putin's policies vis-à-vis the Internet is an "information security doctrine" adopted by Russia's secretive Security Council in June 2000, designed (in Putin's words) to "strengthen the government's role in monitoring information flow."[53] Putin's government has argued that the doctrine (which has not been made public in written form) will "safeguard journalists' rights, help crack down on computer crime, and support the telecommunications industry." Putin has attempted to justify the doctrine by saying that "the state has lost the capability of informing society" and that the information security doctrine will "create the appropriate state mechanism."[54] He has also said that the doctrine will replace a "phony freedom" with "a civilized information business."[55] But journalists and supporters of a free flow of information on the Internet have been alarmed by the actions that have accompanied the promulgation of the "doctrine," which have included:

1. Measures that require Russian ISPs to link their systems to the Federal Security Service (FSB) at their expense ($40,000 or more), which is expected to both reduce the number of ISPs and give government considerable power to monitor Internet content
2. January 2000 amendments to legislation that allow security services to legally intercept a variety of communications, including postal deliveries, cellular telephone conversations, and Internet traffic
3. A May 2000 law that allows Moscow's security organizations to tap into e-mail messages and other Internet content using procedures that include mention of a search warrant but are otherwise not clearly defined
4. Administrative regulations that allow data collected from the previous two sources to be shared by several Russian agencies,

including the Foreign Intelligence Service, the Federal Tax Police, the Kremlin Security Service, and the Presidential Security Service[56]

Several groups of journalists from around the world—primarily from the World Press Freedom Committee and the Committee to Protect Journalists—visited Moscow in the first half of 2000 to try to persuade the Putin government to back away from a policy toward press and Internet freedom that runs directly against international norms calling for a free flow of information. But these overtures were met with Russian government raids in May 2000 on the offices of Media-Most, a private Russian communications giant that had opposed Putin's scorched-earth policies in the Chechnya war, and the arrest in June 2000 of the head of Russia's only major independent television station (NTV), Vladimir Gusinsky, on vague charges of embezzlement.[57] The editors of thirty-two of Russia's leading newspapers issued several statements throughout 2000 protesting raids and arrests of journalists. Ted Turner, vice president of America Online Time Warner, offered to invest $300 million in Media-Most to pay off Gusinsky's debts if Putin were willing to drop fraud charges against Gusinsky and proffer a "personal guarantee" to Turner that he (Putin) would allow Gusinsky's company to remain free of state interference.[58] Oleg Panfilov, a media expert who formerly worked for the Glasnost Defense Fund, summarized the fears of large numbers of people in Russia's journalism, media, and communications communities when he told the *Washington Post* in February 2000: "Such an aggressive attack on journalists like there has been under Putin never could have happened under Yeltsin. . . . This is the beginning of a tragic epoch."[59]

But most analysts of Russian politics agreed that Gusinsky's fall from grace was popular within Russia, reinforcing the likelihood that government controls on communications media, including the Internet, will remain prominent in the Russian landscape for many years to come. A January 2001 opinion poll by the respected Russian Center for Public Policy and Market Research (VCIOM, a joint project with the Centre for the Study of Public Policy, University of Strathclyde) found that 57 percent of Russia's citizens thought Putin's actions were entirely the result of Gusinsky's financial wrongdoing and only 15 percent saw them as an attempt by Putin to stifle criticism. The same polling organization found in its 2000 polls that more Russians would consider the media less independent if controlled by an "oligarch"—such as Gusinsky—than if controlled by the state. By May 2001, Gusinsky was living in exile and Media-Most had been taken over by Gazprom, the most powerful economic entity in Russia, formerly a Soviet government ministry controlling Russia's vast reserves of natural gas, which accounts for 5 percent of Russia's GDP, 15 percent of export earnings, and 20 percent of federal tax revenues.[60] Putin justified his role in establishing increasing government control over Media-Most and other Russian media by pointing to an unexpected inflation rate of 10 percent in the second year of his presidency, with official projections of 12 percent by the end of 2001 (unofficial projections went as high as 20 percent). "Unless we begin to act intensively," Putin warned in May 2001, "tomorrow we might fall into a long-term economic stagnation."[61]

■ INTERNET DEVELOPMENT IN OTHER FSU NATIONS

Ukraine, Belarus, and Moldova lag far behind even Russia in Internet development, with each having far less than one Internet host per 1,000 people (see Table 4.1). In all three cases, severe economic problems have made it impossible for governments to invest significantly in telecommunications and Internet-related infrastructure, and privatization programs that might attract foreign investment either have been unsuccessful or have failed to take place. The result is that investors have lacked enthusiasm for, or in some cases have been repelled by, the investment climate for Internet and IT ventures in these areas, as in Russia and elsewhere in the FSU.

■ *Ukraine*

As indicated in Table 4.1, Ukraine is slightly better off than Belarus in terms of telecommunications development, and both Ukraine and Belarus are a step ahead of Moldova, but in all three countries far less than 1 percent of the population has access to a computer, and only an elite few are able to log on to the Internet. Ukraine—the second-largest state (after Russia), with 49.5 million people—has been unable to privatize its economy to any significant degree or to enact substantial free market reforms. This results largely from the continued political strength of the Communist Party in the country, which receives substantial support from the large Russian minority (around 40 percent of the total population). Russia is protective of this minority and is determined to use Ukraine's dependence on Russian oil to pressure the leadership in Kiev to abandon its hopes for closer relations with the European Union (EU) and the North Atlantic Treaty Organization. The EU, the World Trade Organization, and other world economic organizations have made it clear that they would welcome Ukraine's membership but only if its leadership is able to enact and implement effective privatization and market reforms. But a major portion of the Ukrainian economy as it enters the twenty-first century has come to be dominated by oligarchs, like those found in Russia, who are essentially extremely corrupt new business tycoons who control the political process and rarely reinvest their ill-gotten wealth at home. The result is what the *Economist* (London) calls "a stricken economy": "Ukrainians are paid late and earn little; average wages are half even those of Russia. Industry is largely unreformed, foreign debts all but unpayable. . . . Relations with the IMF [International Monetary Fund] are chilly. Corruption is pervasive."[62]

Computer and software companies are particularly reluctant to invest in or even do business with Ukraine because of the reputation it has acquired as "the prime source of illegal product in Europe."[63] But Ukrainian leaders are often unwilling to implement intellectual property antipiracy laws or even to recognize the existence of piracy and corruption because of their dependence on them for political office. In December 1999, for example, Ukrainian president Leonid Kuchma visited Washington, D.C., for meetings with President Bill Clinton after Kuchma had won a second four-year term in elections in which he reportedly depended for funds on a number of Ukraine's leading oligarchs.[64] When asked by a *Newsweek* reporter whether he would be willing to carry out reforms sought by the Clinton administration, Kuchma only dodged the question and appealed for more U.S. aid, saying, "Ukraine could be compared to a sick person, lying on a table, cut up by a surgeon who lacks proper tools to finish the necessary treatment. If the world—and the U.S. in particular—waits to see what happens, the patient dies. Ukraine needs massive Western assistance."[65]

■ *Belarus*

Belarus built its first permanent Internet connection through a dedicated line from Minsk to Warsaw in 1994, with the assistance of the Polish Academic and Research Network, but by 2000 its leadership had still not developed an effective telecommunications infrastructure outside its capital city (Minsk). Belarus telecommunications are dominated by the monopoly government company Beltelekom, which owns and operates the country's communications infrastructure and licenses all related organizations.[66] All Internet ISPs are licensed by the government, with the understanding that their networks must flow through BelPAK, the Internet division of Beltelekom. As part of their licensing agreements, ISPs and other IT organizations must submit to periodic unannounced "technical inspections" by the Ministry of Communications.[67] Tight government controls on telecommunications by the monopoly provider are creating a situation where high prices and poor service, in the words of one Internet leader in Belarus, are "strangling Internet growth."[68] A second consequence of state controls, particularly when coupled with the sorry state of the Belarus economy, is that although some U.S. and European companies are involved in small joint ventures in Belarus, there has been no major foreign investment in Belarus for IT or Internet development.[69]

The economy of Belarus is in even greater difficulty than those of Ukraine or Russia, in part because of the nuclear plant meltdown that occurred on April 25, 1986, in the Ukrainian city of Chernobyl, which has since irradiated one-fourth of Belarus. A recent demographic study found that the Belarus population *declined* by 4.6 percent between 1991 and 1997 because mortality rates rose from 8.8 per 1,000 population to 13.4 per 1,000 over that same period.[70] The occurrence of illnesses of all types has risen alarmingly in Belarus since 1991, including, for example, a more than fiftyfold increase in the incidence of thyroid-gland cancer among children, thirtyfold increases in the incidences of lung cancer in some parts of the country, and a doubling of the number of child invalids for the country as a whole. The Belarus health minister, I. B. Zelenkevich, estimated in 2000 that only half of the hospitals and polyclinics in the country were able to meet minimal sanitary or technical norms, and a large number of medical facilities lacked a safe and regular supply of water—indications of the degree to which the medical infrastructure has been overstretched. About half of the Belarus population in 2000 was forced to consume low-quality water—especially in the rural areas—and pollution by harmful substances in the larger cities exceeded "permissible maximums" by several times.

The president of Belarus (since 1994), Aleksandr Lukashenko, is convinced that the way to improve the Belarus economy is to closely link Belarus to Russia, thereby gaining easier access to Russian oil and gas and replacing with the Russian ruble the collapsed Belarussian currency (known popularly as "bunny money" after the little rabbit that used to appear on it and because it has multiplied so fast under triple-digit inflation). In January 2000, Lukashenko and then acting president Putin of Russia signed a treaty creating a "union state" that would reunite the countries in some respects, although the treaty was not widely supported in Russia and was not specific enough to determine the extent to which the new "union" might be effective.[71] The measure was popular in Belarus, however, among a population that has never developed a strong sense of nationalism and has consistently indicated in polls substantial support for the opinion that Belarus was much better off under the old Soviet Union.[72] As a result of such attitudes, as well as other positions of the Lukashenko government and a moribund economy, international investors—in IT and other industries—have not been coming to Belarus.[73]

■ *Moldova*

Moldova established its first permanent Internet access in 1995 through a leased line to Bucharest, Romania, and a year later created the Republican Center of Informatics (RCI) as the main node of a national network. Much of the early development of the network was funded by the Open Society Institute of the Soros Foundation, which originally provided technical support to connect five Moldovan campuses—including the State University, the Technical University, and the Academy of Economical Studies—to the State Academy of Sciences, the Soros Information Center, and RCI.[74] At later stages OSI–Russian Internet Project (RIP) helped connect Moldovan secondary schools and NGOs to the Internet using satellite technology. ISAR and IREX have provided training and technical assistance for a variety of Internet projects, including purchase and maintenance of computers and modems. A private U.S. organization, Apriori, has concentrated on the development of capabilities by Moldovan banks to use the Internet for international transactions and information, with the hope of eventually instituting Internet banking.

One of the most creative Internet projects in Moldova is the brainchild of John Harris, an expatriate Canadian living in Florida who noticed that the domain name for Moldova is .md—the same initials medical doctors use to signify that they hold a degree in medicine. Harris created his own firm (Domain Name Trust) and entered into a twenty-five-year contract with the Moldovan government to run the country's Web address registration. In 1999 alone Harris registered more than 10,000 sites, including www.urologist.md, www.platicsurgery.md, and www.pfizer.md. He plans to continue registering many more each year, selling them to doctors and medical or pharmaceutical organizations throughout the world. Harris charges the doctor or association that buys the domain name from his company $299 and gives Moldova a share of the profit after he pays the small fees for each name he registers on the Internet. In a six-month period in 1999, Moldova earned $200,000 from the venture. Domain Name Trust earned a profit in its first year of operation.[75]

Building on the minuscule Internet network that has been created in Moldova will be difficult because of a lack of investment and government capital. A country the size of Maryland with 4.4 million people, Moldova's total economy is valued at only $1.6 billion a year—about the same as a small U.S. city—with only Albania being poorer among European nations. Moldova's external debt in 1999 reached $1.1 billion, which caused Russia to cut off oil and gas supplies fearing an inability of Moldovans to pay their bills (current services charges on the debt constitute two-thirds of Moldova's budget revenue).[76] The World Bank and the IMF have offered to help restructure the Moldovan economy if large-scale reform and privatization programs are undertaken, but Communist Party members (who make up a sizable minority in the Moldovan parliament) refuse to allow such programs. With a political system that saw eight governments come and go in the eight-year period 1992–2000, it is little wonder that international capital is not attracted to Moldova.

■ **INTERNET CULTURES IN
CENTRAL ASIA AND THE CAUCASUS**

Problems similar to those of the FSU nations already discussed are also being confronted by the three countries of the Caucasus (Armenia, Georgia, and Azerbaijan) and the five nations of Central Asia (Kazakhstan, Turkmenistan, Kyrgyzstan, Uzbekistan, and Tajikistan). Without going into great detail for each country, clearly none has been able to attract investment capital for telecommunications or IT development, all retain government monopoly telecommunications providers, and none has developed a significant Internet capability. Six of these eight countries (all but Armenia and Georgia) are on the list of Enemies of the Internet developed by the Paris-based organization Reporters Sans Frontieres (RSF), a list human rights activists prepared to single out countries whose governments have not only failed to develop the full potential of the Internet but have intentionally limited access to it by censoring websites and taking prosecutorial action against users who violate government censorship rules. In the report Turkmenistan was described as "the very worst" of the seven FSU nations on the list of twenty (Belarus was the other nation on the list), with Turkmenistan being singled out as "a virtual Internet black hole."[77]

Low penetration rates for the Internet are directly related to government policies—in both Central Asia and the Caucasus—which in turn correlate closely to degrees of democratization.[78] In a major article on the topic in 1999, for example, Erik Herron found that Kazakhstan and Tajikistan were pursuing a policy of "benign neglect" regarding information technology, whereas Uzbekistan and Turkmenistan (the two least democratic states in Central Asia) were actively opposed to increased Internet access for citizens. By mid-2001, the European Bank for Reconstruction and Development (EBRD) had stopped all public-sector lending to Turkmenistan and the IMF had suspended operations in Belarus and Uzbekistan as well as in Turkmenistan. Both institutions considered a further scaling back of financial support for countries in the Caspian Sea region, in part because of the failure in these nations to undertake economic reforms but also, in the case of the EBRD, because of a renewed mandate to emphasize the importance of political reform and communications technology policies in lending programs.[79]

In 1999 Herron and other observers held out hope that Kyrgyzstan (the most democratic of the five nations of Central Asia) would be able to make rapid progress in developing the Internet for public use and open discourse, and until 2000 the country impressed a number of observers as it developed its telecommunications and Internet capabilities at a faster pace than any other nation in Central Asia or the Caucasus while maintaining a nascent democratic political system.[80] But these hopes were dashed in February 2000 when most opposition parties were excluded from Kyrgyzstan's parliamentary elections, which were won largely by pro-government parties and the only sanctioned opposition— the communists. The subsequent arrests of opposition leaders and the introduction of highly restrictive measures alarmed a number of Kyrgyz political and societal leaders to the point where they sought asylum in the West in fear of further crackdowns on dissent in preparation for the presidential election in Kyrgyzstan in December 2000.[81]

In a part of the world that has never known democratic government, all of the nations of Central Asia and the Caucasus are dominated by single leaders determined to remain in office, most of whom have created personalistic and autocratic regimes that have failed to deliver on messianic promises.[82] These leaders' attention is focused on the competition for extracting oil, diamonds, and other minerals and controlling the pipelines and distribution channels from this resource-rich part of the world to the rest of the globe. For Central Asian and Caspian leaders this not only involves a need to exercise close control over internal religious, ethnic, and factional clan rivalries but also requires constant manipulation of intraregional alliances; of relationships with Russia, Europe, and the various nations of the Middle East; and, increasingly, of diplomatic dealings with the United States, Japan, and South Asia.[83] In this atmosphere it is perhaps not surprising that Internet development is not a priority for national leaders and is often viewed as potentially too intrusive for both domestic and international relations to be helpful in the perpetuation of domestic political coalitions.

The number of people surfing the World Wide Web in Central Asia in mid-1997 was estimated at 500 each for Kazakhstan and Kyrgyzstan, 250 to 1,000 for Uzbekistan, and none for Tajikistan and Turkmenistan. The numbers of e-mail users at that time were estimated at 25,000 for Kazakhstan, 5,000 each for Kyrgyzstan and Uzbekistan, 800–1,000 for Tajikistan, and 200–500 in Turkmenistan.[84] Although reliable later figures are not available, none of the Central Asian nations has added significant Internet capabilities since these estimates were made in 1997. Figures for the number of Internet hosts in Table 4.1 indicate that Internet use may have increased marginally for some Central Asian countries, however—most notably Kyrgyzstan (figures for Internet use are usually two to three times those for Internet hosts because more than one person usually uses a domain name address connection). Nonetheless, whether counting Internet hosts or Internet users, the figures for all Central Asian nations combined indicate about as many users of the Internet in all of Central Asia as there are on one or two large U.S. university campuses.[85]

In the Caucasus nations (Armenia, Azerbaijan, and Georgia), figures for Internet use are comparable to those for Central Asia but are below those for Russia and far below those for Eastern Europe (see Table 4.1). The Armenian Internet Users Association (AIUA) estimated Internet use in Armenia in March 2000 at 10,000–12,000 people, using a definition of "user" that included anyone who had logged on for any length of time.[86] Georgia and Armenia dispute which has more Internet users, whereas Azerbaijan, which is on the RSF "Internet enemies" list discussed earlier, definitely ranks third in the competition over which nation has more users.[87] Georgia has received the most international assistance in building an Internet infrastructure, but all of it has come in small amounts.[88]

None of the Caucasus nations has been able to attract significant foreign or private investment for IT or Internet-related infrastructure.

One of the most remarkable aspects of Internet development in the Caucasus is the recent outbreak of what many news agencies have called "the first cyberwar" between Armenia and Azerbaijan. The electronic war broke out in January 2000 when a group of Armenian hackers broke into more than twenty Azerbaijani sites—including those of the American Embassy in Baku, Azerbaijan National Television, and several international organizations—to post incorrect information about Azerbaijan president Heydar Aliyev and other misinformation and propaganda concerning the many conflicts between the two countries. Armenian news groups argue that the attack was made in retaliation for a previous attack by Azerbaijani computer experts on the website of Armenia National Television, but that is disputed by Azerbaijani authorities who have subsequently established an Internet Security Council to deal with future hacking incidents as well as cybercrime. A group representing a number of Armenian journalist organizations held a news conference in February 2000 to dramatize the joint public request that Azerbaijani hackers stop engaging in cyberattacks, arguing that "the Internet cannot be a vehicle for blackmailing and settling of accounts. . . . No one has the right to restrict people's access to information. The Internet does not belong to a certain separate country, and no one can claim a dominating role in it."[89]

■ CONCLUSIONS

The picture that emerges from an analysis of Internet development in Russia and the FSU nations (excluding the Baltics) is one of an entire world region struggling to find ways to make the transition from a relatively isolated past and to adapt to an increasingly interconnected, globalizing world. If globalization can be measured by degrees of thickness, then Russia and all of the FSU states (excluding the Baltics) are thinly globalized. This becomes especially clear when one compares the extent to which their citizens have access to the Internet (particularly in contrast to the developed areas of the world) and the paucity of telecommunications infrastructures to support future Internet growth. Although Russia is developing high-speed Internet capability to service its scientific endeavors, space technology, and the emerging oil and natural gas extraction industries, almost 98 percent of the population lacks access to the Internet, and neither the government nor international investors have targeted dramatic change for the Internet's general users as a priority matter. In other FSU states (excluding the Baltics) the Internet is used even less than in Russia, and leadership groups have little interest in building Internet capability in nonstrategic sectors.

As a consequence of a common pattern of information technology introduction and use, the Internet has had relatively little impact on Russia and the former Soviet Union. In some dramatic instances the Internet has played a role in political events, most notably at the very end of Soviet rule and in the work of NGOs in the post-Soviet period.[90] But the Internet *publicum* in the FSU, if one could identify such a phenomenon, would be far smaller than in Europe, the United States, and much of Asia because the number of "new communicators" on the Internet in this region is lower than in most other parts of the world. This is reflected in the relative lack of development within the FSU of distance learning, the stuttered way in which NGOs function in Russia and the FSU states, and the questionable utility of the concept of civil society—particularly as it might be applied to an online community in any part of the region.[91] National governments in this part of the world have been highly conscious of both IT developments taking place elsewhere and the emerging importance of the Internet, but they have been so busy coping with internal disruptions, the rebuilding of elemental parts of their economies, and intraregional conflicts and civil wars that they have not been able to turn their attention to or spare scarce resources for a new technology whose promise lies further into the future than they have the luxury to consider. International relations, therefore, is still being played out in this part of the world with relatively little consideration of the Internet as a significant factor in its conduct.

▪ NOTES

1. Lessig, *Code and Other Laws of Cyberspace*, pp. 3–4.
2. Ibid., p. 4.
3. Ellis, *From Glasnost to the Internet*, p. 60. Even as late as May 2000 there were only 33 computers per 1,000 people in Russia, compared with more than 500 computers per 1,000 people in the United States. See Sokolov, "Million-Dollar Investments."
4. Quoted in Ellis, *From Glasnost to the Internet*, p. 61, and Ellis, "The Media as Social Engineer," p. 221.
5. Ronald Reagan, "Speech at London's Guildhall," *Los Angeles Times*, June 14, 1989, p. 10. Quoted in Ellis, *From Glasnost to the Internet*, pp. 61,

223. In that same speech Reagan said, "electronic beams blow through the Iron Curtain as if it were lace."

6. Quoted in Burns, "Walesa," p. 1.

7. Hudson, *Global Connections*, p. 234. For additional analysis of the role of the electronic media in the 1991 coup attempt, see Travica and Hogan, quoted in Ellis, *From Glasnost to the Internet*, pp. 62, 223.

8. Erofeev, "Russia," p. 181. See also Moffett, "Gorbachev."

9. In 1997 an estimated 16.2 of every 100 people in Russia had telephones in their homes, and waiting lists for telephone installation were backed up from two to seven years in different parts of Russia; see *World Telecommunication Development Report*, 1998. See also Fossato, "Russia." Other information in this paragraph is from Moffett, "Russia: Evolving."

10. Moffett, "Russia: Demand." An idea of the extent of the computer technology gap between Russia and other nations in the early years, provided by Moffett, is as follows: with a population of 145 million people, Russia had an estimated 20,000 computers connected to the Internet in 1997, compared with 200,000 computers connected to the Internet in Finland, with a population of only 5 million in 1997.

11. The OSI Regional Internet Program and other Soros programs have concentrated primarily on Internet connectivity to universities, secondary schools, and nongovernmental organizations, providing modems, e-mail, and other Internet services—including in some cases computers—to make possible access to satellite facilities. For more information, see the Soros website at www.soros.org. See also Ivanov, "Kasyanov Discusses."

12. See Moffett, "Moldova," and Moffett, "The Internet in Central Asia."

13. "U.S.-Russia Foundation to Invest in Russia."

14. For other AID-sponsored projects, see Platt, "Fund Backed by AID," pp. 9–10.

15. Aioubov, "Tajikistan."

16. For details of the WHO plans see Voelker, "Bridging the Digital Divide."

17. Moffett, "Moldova."

18. See Campbell, *Soviet and Post-Soviet Telecommunications*, pp. 179 ff.

19. Ibid., p. 179.

20. Hudson, *Global Connections*, p. 238.

21. Campbell, *Soviet and Post-Soviet Telecommunications*, p. 197.

22. In the early years some attempts were made to create joint ventures between monopoly government telecommunications companies and foreign companies, most notably in Russia (Hudson, *Global Connections*, pp. 252–253) and in Armenia, where a new telecom company called Armentel is a joint venture of the Armenian Ministry of Communications and Transworld Corporation of the United States. See Moffett, "Armenia." In Georgia, in 1996, the Ministry of Communications began working with several foreign companies—from South Korea, Japan, Turkey, and Greece, among others—to modernize the telecommunications infrastructure. See Moffett, "Georgia."

23. *Nezavisimaya Gazeta* (Moscow), January 19, 2001, translated and published in *The Russian Business Monitor*, January 22, 2001.

24. Varoli, "A Wide Open Mobile Phone Market," p. W1.

25. See "Russians Lose," p. A9.

26. Stephen, "Polish Peasant Holds Key," p. 13.

27. Campbell, *Soviet and Post-Soviet Telecommunications,* p. 198.

28. An excellent analysis of the Russian economy at the beginning of the twenty-first century is Hedlund, *Russia's "Market" Economy.* See also Popov, *The Currency Crisis in Russia.*

29. Hudson, *Global Connections,* pp. 241–243.

30. Analysis of this investment boomlet, generally attributed to the relative stability brought to Russian politics with the elevation of Vladimir Putin to the presidency, appeared in a series of *Wall Street Journal* articles. See Borzo, "Investors Look," p. 1; Whalen, "Russians Seek Investment," p. A23; Borzo, "Net Start-Ups," p. 1. See also Tavernise, "Dot.Com Deals," pp. 188–189.

31. Wolosky, "Putin's Plutocrat Problem," p. 24. See also Cullison, "Shareholders Get Short Shrift," p. A22, and Borrell, "Investing in Hope," pp. 170–178.

32. The figures are from an International Data Corporation survey. See Borzo, "Russian Internet Usage." Although Internet use in Russia tripled between 1996 and 1998 as a result of major projects by international organizations (most prominently the Soros Foundation), investors in these projects began to pull out in 1998, and Internet use subsequently leveled off at around the 1 million user level.

33. A mid-2001 survey by The Economist Intelligence Unit and Pyramid Research ranked Russia forty-second on an "e-readiness" scale, out of sixty countries surveyed (the sixty largest countries by economy were included in the survey). Russia's worst score was in connectivity and Internet infrastructure, which accounted for 30 percent of the points in the scale. It was also low in business environment and presence of e-commerce mechanisms (20 percent each) and only somewhat higher in the remaining factors (e.g., legal and regulatory environment, support for e-services like portals and Web hosting, and social/cultural infrastructure, which includes education and literacy). An analysis of the survey appears in Wolfe, "Russia Ranks 42nd," p. 8.

34. Based on reports from the Russian newspaper *Segodnya* (January 6, 2000), as reported in the *BBC Monitoring International Reports Series,* January 10, 2000, available at the *Financial Times* website, www.globalarchive.ft.com. See also Sokolov, "Million-Dollar Investments."

35. Quoted in Borzo, "Russia's Fledgling E-Commerce," Eastern edition, p. 1.

36. Rohozinski, "How the Internet," pp. 334–338. See also Rohozinski, *Mapping Russian Cyberspace.* "Fidonet," invented by Tom Jennings in 1983, is described in Moschovitis et al., *History of the Internet,* pp. 112ff.

37. Rohozinski, "How the Internet," p. 338.

38. See, for example, Varoli, "In Bleak Russia," p. G10. See also Chazan, "A High-Tech Folk Hero," p. A28.

39. Kiselyova and Castells, "Russia in the Information Age," p. 133.

40. Rohozinski, "How the Internet," p. 338.

41. See Borzo, "Russian E-Commerce," and Anthes, "IT Walls Come Tumbling Down," p. 4. The agreement was immediately overshadowed by Russia's economic ills and has therefore had little effect.

42. "Germany to Push." See also Landers, "G-8 Creates 'Dot Force,'" p. A21.

43. See "Russian Firm," p. A26.

44. Quoted in Anthes, "IT Walls Come Tumbling Down," p. 4.

45. Ibid.

46. Henderson, "Russia's Online Enigma," p. C12.

47. The other sector is space technology. See Leary, "U.S. Company Sets Space-Station Venture," p. A33.

48. "Russian Internet." See also Hoffman, "Itera," pp. H1, 5.

49. See "MMDS Systems," and "Sonera, Nortel."

50. Quoted in Matloff, "Bargain Beets, Babushkas," pp. 1, 9. Putin also impressed the leaders of the G-8 countries, meeting in Japan in July 2000, with his suggestion that they begin to correspond with one another by e-mail. See Chandler, "Putin Makes Strong Bid," p. 8.

51. A project to create fifty regional centers to train secondary school teachers to use the Internet was launched in mid-1999, for example, but the first of the fifty centers (in St. Petersburg) was not established until July 2000. See "Russia Opens." The great tradition of Russian jokes about the ineffectiveness of the government has been established on the Internet by a number of websites, including most prominently www.anekdot.ru.

52. See, for example, Caryl, "Catch a Rising Czar," pp. 32–34, and Hoffman, "Putin Pits Politics," pp. 1, 20.

53. Kramer, "Russian Government Approves," p. 1.

54. Ibid., p. 2.

55. Randolph, "Russia's New President," sec. 4, p. 14.

56. Bronskill, "'Big Brother' Gets Free Rein," p. A8.

57. For thoughtful analyses of the arrests, see two editorials in the *Christian Science Monitor:* "Slipping Backward," p. 8, and "Lessons," p. 10. Gusinsky was later released by Putin and fled to Spain, where he was placed under house arrest by the Spanish government pending a decision whether to extradite him to Russia. For details, see "The Very Long Arms," pp. 57–58.

58. See Glasser, "Ted Turner Wants Assurance," p. A24, and Higgins, "Turner Sets Investment," p. A16.

59. Quoted in LaFraniere, "Russian Media Fear," p. A19. See also Hoffman, "Russian Media," pp. 16, 22.

60. Peel, "From Glasnost to Gazprom: NTV," p. 21, and Lipman, "Putin Won," p. A23.

61. Lipman, "Putin Won," p. A23. Lipman was associate editor of *Itogi,* a weekly news publication that was part of the NTV group.

62. "Ukraine's Grim Choice," p. 55. For scholarly articles that reach similar conclusions about industry, despite privatization, see Estrin and Rosevear, "Enterprise Performance," pp. 442–458, and Lhabitant and Novikova, "Doing Business," pp. 571–595.

63. The phrase comes from publications of the International Federation of the Phonographic Industry (IFPI), which set up an office in Kiev in 2000 to assist the Ukraine government in combating intellectual property piracy. IFPI and other organizations have found that many piracy activities were moved from other parts of Europe, especially Bulgaria (the previous piracy capital of Europe), in the late 1990s. Ukraine's policy toward such activities is analyzed in Solomons, "IFPI," pp. 7–11. See also Goldstein, "Ukraine to Step Up," p. 27.

64. The 1999 elections and their consequences are analyzed in "The Ukrainian Question," pp. 19–20. See also Warner, "Lessons for Foreign Investors," p. A18.

65. Weymouth, "'We Need Massive Assistance,'" p. 26. A Harvard economist, David Snelbecker, in Kiev at the time with the Harvard Institute for International Development, more or less agreed with President Kuchma when he told the *Wall Street Journal* that "foreign debt is the least of Ukraine's problems. You have an economy that essentially is ceasing to function." See Whalen, "Ukraine President," p. A22.

66. Moffett, "Belarus." Belarus does have an enclave of scholars who have computer capabilities, but they are limited primarily to advanced mathematical, scientific, and engineering institutes. See Stolyarov, "Computers in Belarus," pp. 61–65.

67. Moffett, "Belarus."

68. Quoted in ibid.

69. Some of the Belarus ISPs that have U.S. or European involvement include SprintNet (a joint venture of U.S. Sprint and a number of communication enterprises from the FSU), the German Research Deutsches Elektronen Synchroton (DESY) satellite being used by the High Energy Physics Institute in Minsk, and OverDrive, Ltd., a British firm that provides satellite service to the Belarus ISP NetSat/DirecPC. See ibid.

70. Marples, "The Demographic Crisis in Belarus," pp. 16–28. Other statistics in the paragraph are from this source.

71. Shortly after the Belarus-Russia union agreement was signed, Yugoslavia's president Slobodan Milosevic expressed an interest in bringing Yugoslavia into the new union. On February 26, 2000, Belarusian Radio announced that the chairman of the Council of the Republic of the Belarus National Assembly, Pavel Shypuk, would travel to Belarus and Russia for exploratory discussions concerning the possibility of Yugoslavia joining the new union. See "Belarusian Parliament."

72. Prior to 1991 the present-day territory of Belarus had never been a nation-state, so it is perhaps not surprising that in a 1995 referendum engineered by Lukashenko, 82 percent of those voting supported some form of union with Russia. For an analysis, see Tayler, "Back in the USSR?" pp. 62–72.

73. An example of Lukashenko's strident anti-Western bias, particularly toward economic organizations that are central to a globalized economy, was his statement to a reporter in January 2000, chiding the Russians for "getting on your knees before those crooks at the International Monetary Fund." Quoted in "Belarus: An Ambivalent Couple," p. 19.

74. Moffett, "Moldova."

75. The project is described in Yang and McNatt, "The Net Frenzy," pp. 8–9. See also Wharry, "Sorry, thebest.md Is Gone," p. 66.

76. Jordan, "Struggling," p. 7. See also "Nowhereland," pp. 61–62.

77. See Goble, "An Internet Enemies List," p. 2.

78. For an early analysis of such correlations, see Bichel, "Contending Theories of Central Asia."

79. LeVine, "As Turkmenistan Stalls," p. A15; "EBRD in Strategy Talks with Ukraine and Azerbaijan," pp. 1–2; and "An Eastern Promise," p. 19. See also Pope, "Corruption Stunts Growth in Ex-Soviet States," p. A17.

80. The thesis is laid out in Herron, "Democratization," pp. 56–69. A discussion of the modernization and expansion of telecommunications facilities in Kyrgyzstan and Kazakhstan appears in Smith, "The Bridge from East to West," pp. 179–182. For analyses of Kyrgyzstan's attempt to build democratic institutions, see Guttman, "Kyrgyzstan: Breaking Out," pp. 21–26, and Anderson, "Creating a Framework," pp. 77–93.

81. See Whalen, "Kyrgyzstan Poll," p. A26; Otorbayeva, "Entire Kyrgyz Opposition Locked Up," p. 15; Panfilova, "Opposition Activists," pp. 16–17. See also Pope, "Why Is the Tech Set?" p. A15; and LeVine, "In Kyrgyzstan, Flawed Election," p. A26.

82. The extreme case is Saparmurad Niyazov, president of Turkmenistan and former first secretary of the Soviet Communist Party, who insists on being called *Turkmenbashi* (Father of the Turkmen People) and has received "eternal authority attributes" and has been granted "presidential powers for an indeterminate period" by the Turkmenistan parliament. Glorified in minishrines, his picture appears on every street corner, on Turkmenistan's currency, on alphabet charts for children, on calendars, and much else. A 197-foot statue is being constructed in his honor, and yet his policies have resulted in a declining economy and increased isolation from the rest of the world, as outlined in the article "Dream On," p. 40. See also "Saparmurad Niyazov," pp. 43–44.

83. An excellent basic book on the impact of international relations on Central Asia is Rashid, *The Resurgence of Central Asia*. Useful contemporary articles are Lubin, "Pipe Dreams," pp. 66–71, and Carney and Moran, "Imagining Communities in Central Asia," pp. 179–199.

84. For details on the 1997 estimates, see Moffett, "The Internet."

85. The consequence of this situation for Central Asian intellectuals and professionals is explored in Slakey, "In Central Asia," p. B8.

86. Reported in "Internet Business." The same AIUA report described the state of IT development in Armenia as "embryonic," with future prospects "vague." The head of the Armenian governments's Internet Union had said earlier that Armenia had 20,000 Internet users on about 150 Internet sites.

87. "Number of Internet Users."

88. An excellent summary of international donors to Georgia's Internet development appears in Moffett, "Georgia." The major reason usually given for Georgia's edge in securing international assistance is the international experience of Edouard Shevardnadze, the current president, who was foreign minister

under Gorbachev in the last days of the USSR. For an analysis of Shevard-nadze's presidency, which was renewed for five years with his reelection in 2000, see "Charlemagne," p. 52.

89. The Azerbaijani position in this "Netwar" is described in detail in a report by Azerbaijani television station ANS, available in "Azeri-Armenian." The Armenian position appears in a report of the Armenian press agency ITAR-TASS, dated February 18, 2000, available in "Armenia Calls." See also "Azerbaijan: Internet."

90. A substantial list of the NGOs active in seven FSU states (Armenia, Azerbaijan, Belarus, Georgia, Moldova, Russia, and Ukraine), including their Internet activities, is available in Ruffin et al., *The Post-Soviet Handbook*.

91. For informative studies, see Kirillova, "Prospects of Distance Learning," pp. 14–17; Abramson, "A Critical Look at NGOs," pp. 240–250; Bogolubov et al., "The Challenge of Civic Education," pp. 523–541.

5

The Political Economy
of the Internet in Eastern Europe

The position of Eastern Europe with regard to telecommunications infrastructures is rather different from that of the FSU, although both regions were left with woefully inadequate facilities when the 1989 and 1990 "revolutions" took place.[1] Major differences result from (1) the more rigid hierarchical overall framework within which Soviet telecommunications systems were modeled, in contrast to the heterogeneity of telecommunications systems in Eastern Europe that were not directly part of the Soviet government and bureaucracy; (2) the much greater extent to which many Eastern European nations have moved since 1990 to adopt Western-style economic systems dominated by private enterprise, with free capital markets replacing state budgets in the allocation of resources; and (3) perhaps most important, the pressures for modernization and reform of telecommunications placed on Eastern European nations as a result of negotiations in anticipation of their joining the European Union (EU).

This chapter seeks to analyze the diffusion of the Internet in the parts of Eastern Europe where such development has been most rapid and, consequently, where there is a thicker degree of globalization. The focus is on nine of the ten countries in Table 4.1 that had more than two Internet hosts per 1,000 people in 2000 (the Czech Republic, Hungary, Poland, Slovenia, Slovakia, Estonia, Latvia, Lithuania, and Bulgaria), all ranking above Russia in this respect. Most of these countries also had high teledensity rates (seven of the nine had 300 or more phone lines per 1,000 people in 2000). With the exception of Croatia, these are the only countries in all of Central/Eastern Europe (CEE) and the FSU states with such teledensities.[2] Chapter 6 will discuss the countries of Eastern Europe that have been less successful at Internet development, all (with the exception of Croatia) ranking below Russia with fewer than 0.2 percent Internet hosts and (again excepting Croatia) teledensity figures under 200.

▪ TELECOMMUNICATIONS INFRASTRUCTURES IN EASTERN EUROPE

In 1998, Eastern European telecommunications infrastructures were estimated to be twenty-five years behind those of Western Europe.[3] Chronic underinvestment in telecommunications by pre-1989 regimes was the consequence of Stalinist economics, in which services were not considered a form of production and were therefore assigned as costs to the economy.[4] In addition, the growth of communications systems was purposely limited and constrained by the government so the state could more easily control information, and revenues from telecommunications were routinely used to subsidize other sectors of the economy. Further limitations on telecommunications development resulted from patterns of economic self-sufficiency in the Eastern bloc (Comecon) countries, where prior to 1989 only 4 percent of goods consumed in Eastern Europe were imported from the outside world and only 2 percent of indigenously produced goods were exported. This penchant for self-sufficiency uncoupled the Eastern bloc from the global economic mainstream in the second half of the twentieth century—a development especially damaging to East European economies in sectors such as information technology and telecommunications, where exploding growth rates were beginning to take place in the United States, Western Europe, and East Asia. Like the FSU, the Comecon nations—by resisting becoming interdependent with the rest of the world—were simply cut off from the benefits of burgeoning international trade flows and a number of the other interlinked forces usually described as "globalization."

The amount of investment required to build modern telecommunications infrastructures in Eastern Europe was estimated at $76 billion (to build "high-end quality") in 1997.[5] At that time Heather Hudson found that Poland, Hungary, and the Czech Republic were already proceeding with telecommunications plans and policies at a fairly rapid pace, whereas other Eastern European nations were moving more slowly. Most East European nations are convinced—to a much greater degree than is the case in the FSU—that they will need to privatize the telecommunications sector, but most have been unable to develop the secure legal and regulatory frameworks that would allow foreign countries to invest with complete confidence. With few exceptions, Eastern Europe's insecure lending and contractual regimes, its widespread lack of clarity with regard to ownership and transfer of assets, and the incidence of outdated or inadequate regulatory frameworks have combined to scare away foreign investors or have forced them to move slowly in building relationships with potential Eastern European partners.

Nonetheless, some telecommunications companies and venture capitalists from the United States and Western Europe have made large long-term investment commitments to particular countries in Eastern Europe, and most large foreign companies active in Western Europe have also established a presence in the East—primarily to gain experience and be involved if IT development takes off at some point in the future. Siemens, for example, has joint ventures to manufacture equipment in all countries of Eastern Europe, with the local partner generally providing land and buildings while Siemens provides production equipment and know-how. Other companies with meaningful involvement, among many others, are Telecom Finland, Telia (Sweden), Tele-Danmark, Norwegian Telecom, France Telecom, Telefonica de España, Deutsche Telekom (Germany), PTT Telecom (Netherlands), and several U.S. companies (e.g., Bell Atlantic, Ameritech, AT&T, and US West).[6] Many of these companies have received encouragement from the EU, international organizations, Japan, and the U.S. and European governments because of the presumed strategic and future economic importance of this part of the world.[7]

Eastern European nations' aspiration to join the European Union has placed particular pressure on these countries to liberalize and privatize their IT and telecommunications sectors. A major factor in this regard is the European Economic Community (EEC) "Green Paper," finalized in 1987, requiring that EU member nations adopt steps to liberalize telecommunications monopolies—a requirement that also applies to EU aspirant nations. The steps include separation of regulatory authority from the operation of telecommunications systems; open interconnection of user equipment to lines to encourage free flow of information; liberalized use of leased lines; liberal licensing and other controls on private value-added networks to enable them to compete; privatization of highly competitive specialized services, such as cellular and mobile; tolerance of facilities-based private networks; government allowance of competition in long-distance service; and encouragement of competition in basic local or regional service.[8]

Further pressures on CEE nations for privatization and competition in telecommunications emanate from the policies of the World Bank and other development banks, which routinely insist on reductions in the size of government operations, debt, and expenditures in sectors of the economy (like telecommunications) where private operators and investors can be found. Finally, users and customers of telecommunications services in Eastern Europe—individuals, organizations, and businesses—are pressuring governments to lower prices while providing more efficient services and to offer a range of services (cellular telephony, digital overlay networks, computer-enhanced or value-added services, and VSAT or other satellite services) government cannot afford to initiate on its own. Such pressures sometimes push government and political leaders toward advocacy of privatization and liberalization as a way to quickly attract at least a significant portion of the capital, technology, and expertise needed to provide such services.

■ APPROACHES TO PRIVATIZATION: HUNGARY, THE CZECH REPUBLIC, AND POLAND

At the turn of the millennium, most Eastern European nations had made some attempt to liberalize telecommunications and information technology—if only to attract foreign investment, meet the lending requirements of international banks and donors, and prepare themselves for entry into the EU. But only two countries (Hungary and the Czech Republic) had at that point relinquished state control of the basic network. Hungary began its privatization program in 1993 by selling 30 percent of the monopoly telecommunications operator (MATAV) to a consortium called MagyarCom, led by Deutsche Telekom and Ameritech, for $875 million. Although by law the Hungarian government was still required to retain a 50 percent plus one vote stake in MATAV, MagyarCom secured veto rights over major decisions taken by MATAV's board of directors and a leading role on the operating committee responsible for day-to-day functioning. In 1995, MagyarCom acquired an additional 35 percent stake in MATAV (at a cost of $852 million), reducing the Hungarian government's share to 25 percent plus one vote. Another dramatic leap toward liberalization and competition is expected in Hungary in 2002, when MATAV's international long-distance monopoly ends.[9]

The acceptance by Hungarian leaders of significant control over day-to-day telecommunications operations in Hungary by a German-U.S. consortium was influenced in part by the experience Deutsche Telekom had accumulated in the modernization and expansion of networks in East Germany.[10] But it also reflected a basic Hungarian foreign policy decision to build long-term economic and political ties with Germany, its largest trading partner by far, accounting for more than 25 percent of both imports and exports.[11] Other factors that influenced the arrangement were enthusiastic support from the German government, which helped to secure a number of loans from international banks; the central location of Hungary as a potential "transit" hub for telecommunications activities throughout Central and Eastern Europe, which further encouraged the banks; and significant tax benefits granted by newly enacted Hungarian tax laws, including a 100 percent tax holiday for the first five years of the twenty-five-year deal and 60 percent for the next five years.[12]

In the Czech Republic privatization of some commercial subsidiaries and construction and production functions of the monopoly telecommunications provider, SPT Telecom (Sprava Post a Telekomunikace Praha), took place around the period of the "velvet divorce" between the Czech and Slovak Republics, bringing to an end the old Czechoslovakia federation on January 1, 1993. A major privatization step in the Czech Republic was taken in 1994 when 30 percent of SPT stock was sold to individuals and an assortment of investment funds. The next stage of the privatization process, managed by J. P. Morgan Investment Bank, resulted in a 27 percent equity stake in SPT Telecom being sold to a Dutch-Swiss consortium named TelSource (with AT&T as a nonequity partner) for $1.45 billion. As in the case of the selection of MagyarCom in Hungary, TelSource was chosen as the government's "strategic investor" in the Czech Republic not only because of the amount of money it was willing to invest but primarily because it had established good working relationships in Eastern Europe and had network development plans for meeting annual quality service targets and other obligations designed to improve telecommunications efficiency. Larger international political considerations also played a role, since Prague's foreign policy establishment at the time was reluctant to become too economically dependent on Germany or France and therefore argued against accepting bids from consortia from those nations (the successful Dutch-Swiss consortium was not only composed of smaller equity partners, it was also from smaller European powers).[13] As part of the bidding process for the 27 percent stake, the TelSource consortium, as a "strategic investor," was required to spend $3.5 billion to modernize the network and double the number of lines by 2000.[14]

The privatization process in Poland proceeded at a much slower pace in the 1990s than in Hungary or the Czech Republic, for several reasons. First, Poland is the largest and potentially most powerful country in Eastern Europe, but it ended up with one of the weakest telecommunications infrastructures of the Central and Eastern European countries at the end of communist rule. Only Albania had a lower penetration rate (number of telephones per person) under the communists, and Poland's 1990 successful call rate (the rate of calls successful on first dialing) was among the most embarrassing in the world (only 20 percent for local calls and 28 percent for long distance). Even as late at 1997 the number of lines per 100 inhabitants averaged only fifteen across Poland, with the vast majority of those lines still lacking digital networks and optical fiber cable. With a minuscule portion of GDP committed to telecommunications and without substantial potential revenue from a network severely lacking in infrastructure, Poland faces one of the most challenging tasks in Central and Eastern Europe as it attempts to develop modern information technologies.

Poland's telecommunications challenge is compounded by the powerful political and bureaucratic presence of a state-run monopoly telecommunications company (Telekomunikacja Polska S.A. [TPSA]) that in the 1990s was able to resist privatization while at the same time being unable to improve performance to anything resembling modern standards.[15] The Polish government made a basic decision to privatize TPSA in 1992, but seven Polish governments in the eight-year period 1992–2000 were unable to conclude an arrangement with foreign investors acceptable to the Polish parliament. Finally, in May 2000 the government entered into "exclusive negotiations" with a partnership of France Telecom and a Polish conglomerate (Kulczyk Holding) for the sale of a 35 percent stake in TPSA for $4 billion, with the understanding that the stake could be increased to 51 percent in subsequent share offers in 2001 and 2002 depending on performance and future negotiations.[16] Thirty percent of TPSA stock is held by managers and employees of the company, who were allowed to purchase shares through a public offering in 1998.[17]

The sale of 35 percent of TPSA for $4 billion, once finalized, will be the largest privatization ever for Eastern Europe. In mid-2000 investors hailed the sale as fundamentally sound because it includes guidelines on tariffs, fees, and market liberalization that should make it possible for the France Telecom–led partnership to run the company with much less government intrusion than had been the case previously. Karol Dzialo-szynski, head of the parliamentary committee that drafted the new tele-com law providing legal and regulatory support for privatization in Poland, summarized the sense of urgency felt by many Polish govern-ment officials and legislators: "If we had privatized back in the early '90s when the Czechs and Hungarians did, we'd be years ahead of the game now. . . . This is our last chance to make up for lost time and to give serious support to the information economy."[18]

Privatization of government-monopoly telecommunications compa-nies in Hungary, the Czech Republic, and Poland has created new op-portunities for these countries to attract foreign investment.[19] One ana-lyst in April 2000, for example, projected that the IT needs of customers in these three countries could be expected to grow annually at 15 to 20 percent in hard currency during the first decade of the twenty-first cen-tury, primarily because privatization would drastically pull down the cost of Internet access and vastly increase the desire among Poles to purchase PCs, software, and other IT products.[20] Poland and Hungary seemed particularly well placed in 2000 to take advantage of privatiza-tion to attract foreign investment, whereas enthusiasm among investors toward the Czech Republic cooled in late 2000 and early 2001 in re-sponse to political events considered troubling for the economy.[21] These included an act of the Czech parliament that delayed long-planned ad-ditional privatization measures for the SPT (renamed Cesky Telecom in late 1999) for two years (from 2000 to 2002) and a commitment by the ruling Czech party to pass electoral reform legislation that would boost parliamentary representation of the larger parties beyond their share of the electoral vote, thereby opening possibilities for large gains by a re-vitalized Czech Communist Party in the 2002 elections.[22]

Between 1996 and 2000, Hungary's economy grew by 5 percent or more each year, making it the fastest-growing Eastern European economy during that period. Fueled by $20 billion in direct foreign investment in the 1990s, with 70 percent of exports going to the European Union, the Hungarian economy was judged by most analysts to be in a better posi-tion than any of its neighbors in 2000 to support privatized telecommu-nications and Internet-related growth.[23] A major goal of Hungary's lead-ership in the early years of the twenty-first century is to use IT and Internet-related development to repair the "fault line" that developed in the 1990s between Hungary's capital, Budapest, and the rest of the country, with Budapest accounting for only 20 percent of Hungary's population in 2000 while garnering 70 percent of all foreign investment.[24]

Having moved near the top of the list of East European countries with domestic Internet capabilities, Hungary has set its sights on becoming a world-class manufacturing center for computer software and other Internet-related products. Motorola and Siemens located major research and development facilities in Hungary in the 1990s, General Electric had manufacturing facilities employing more than 10,000 people in Hungary in 2000, and Flextronics International was operating three industrial parks where contractors were manufacturing, among many other products, printers for Hewlett-Packard and routers for Cisco Systems.[25] Nokia completed the location of its largest research and development operation outside of Finland in Hungary in 2000.[26] Even more impressive have been the growth and international linkages of Hungarian companies such as Cygron, a firm focused on artificial intelligence software that struggled with only three full-time employees and about $40,000 in annual revenue until it was purchased by California-based MindMaker for $2 million in 1998. Under MindMaker (whose CEO is Jozsef Kiraly, a Hungarian), Cygron began marketing its Data-Scope software worldwide, expanded its employee base to thirty-three, and had an estimated worth between $20 million and $40 million in April 2000.

Kiraly and other Hungarian entrepreneurs, as well as government officials, are convinced that they can be extremely strong international competitors because of Hungary's large numbers of well-educated scientific and engineering personnel willing to work at relatively low salaries and an economic and government regulatory framework conducive to innovation by the private sector. By 2000 more than 80 percent of the formerly state-owned companies in Hungary had been privatized, and 85 percent of Hungary's GDP was produced by private-sector firms.[27] A favorable regulatory environment is particularly important for investment analysts and CEOs of potential investors and international partners such as MindMaker. Kiraly, for example, has suggested that a crucial difference exists between those companies investing or partnering with India—one of Hungary's major global competitors for software manufacturing—and those doing so with Hungary. Because of India's less favorable regulatory environment and poor data protection laws, he argued, "most of the firms that start offices in India are not really doing critical development there. They will just use that office as a headhunting pod."[28]

Like the Czech Republic, Poland lost some of its luster for international investors at the turn of the millennium because of political uncertainties and its rather stutter-step approach to privatization compared with Hungary.[29] Potential investors were buoyed by Polish government measures in 2000 that promised to conclude privatization processes initiated years earlier in both the telecommunications and banking sectors. Moreover, Poland had gained favor in international circles by enacting bold tax and pension reform programs in the late 1990s while slashing state spending, bringing inflation rates down, and proceeding expeditiously with its negotiations to join the European Union.[30] In early 2001, however, a decision by Poland's Treasury to seize control of a large insurance group (Powszachny Zaklad Ubezpieczen [PZU]) by ousting representatives from foreign and private investors, including the Dutch insurance group Eureko, was said by the *Wall Street Journal* to have "sullied the government's reputation among foreign investors."[31]

■ EU MEMBERSHIP AND INFORMATION TECHNOLOGY INVESTMENTS

Approaches to both privatization and EU membership vary among the other Eastern European countries, depending on a number of factors. Although ten East European nations are being considered for EU membership, the European Commission has warned that enlargement of the EU cannot be considered a foregone conclusion, particularly in light of several contentious and potentially explosive issues relating to the impact of enlargement on employment, trade competition, and migration. Despite these warnings, a survey by the *Financial Times* (London) in 2000 concluded that "many hundreds of companies have already been acting for years on the basis that it [EU enlargement] is almost certain to happen."[32] This has led a number of observers to liken the way economic integration has been taking place between Eastern and Western Europe in the 1990s and early 2000s to the process followed when the EU was created several decades ago, at which time the interests of the French and German coal, iron, and steel communities were gradually brought together in a seemingly willy-nilly way until the formation of a "community" eventually seemed to become inevitable. By pursuing their own economic interests, companies and governments in Eastern Europe brought about increasing economic integration in the 1990s, particularly in areas related to telecommunications and IT. As Stefan

Wagstyl has pointed out, this process is furthest along for the five countries already involved in accession talks (the Czech Republic, Estonia, Hungary, Poland, and Slovenia) and is generally less advanced for those that have just started to engage in serious negotiations (Bulgaria, Latvia, Lithuania, Romania, and Slovakia).[33]

A major pathway for both privatization and integration with Western Europe has been the growth of mergers and acquisitions, primarily in the telecommunications and IT sectors, which reached a record $16.86 billion for deals in Eastern Europe in 1998 and has continued to grow larger each year. This has given rise to substantial fears that foreigners, among whom Germans and Americans are usually singled out, will end up with excessive influence in Eastern Europe—in IT industries, banking, and elsewhere. A poll conducted by the University of Ljubljana's Research on the Internet in Slovenia (RIS) organization found that more than 50 percent of respondents tended to agree with the proposition that the Internet was creating a form of "cyberimperialism," but a majority of the same respondents also saw this as something that would "improve the situation" both in developing countries and in Slovenia.[34] Wagstyl has pointed out that attempts by Eastern European governments to resist mergers, acquisitions, and other forms of integration and collaboration with Western European firms by trying to "go it on their own" have been uniformly unsuccessful.[35]

In some cases, telecommunications infrastructures are supported by international banks and East European governments in conjunction with private enterprise, more for the purpose of building international and regional networks than for developing internal infrastructures. Perhaps the most striking example is Bulgaria, which has a surprisingly high telephone density for Eastern European nations of 34 percent (34 phones per 100 inhabitants) but with fairly unsatisfactory local performance and a lack of capacity for handling modern information technology domestically. Bulgaria's lead in teledensity is largely a function of its history as the nation originally designated to be the "Silicon Valley" of the Soviet empire in Eastern Europe.[36] A major reason for the inadequacies of the Bulgarian telecommunications infrastructure is the lack of digital networks (in 1999, for example, only 5.8 percent of Bulgaria's local networks were digitalized, whereas 66.3 percent of its international networks had digital switching and 55 percent of its international networks could carry digital transmissions).[37] The Bulgarian government has no extensive plans to digitalize local networks in the next few years but instead is concentrating on the digitalization of the networks and transmission lines passing through Bulgaria. This is in keeping with its aspirations to become a major regional telecommunications hub, connecting northern portions of Eastern Europe to Greece and Turkey in the south and Western Europe and western parts of Eastern Europe to Russia and other points east.[38]

The process of digitalization in Bulgaria received a significant boost in the 1990s with the completion of the Digital Overlay Network (DON) project, providing seventeen modern digital exchanges with a total capacity of 70,000 trunk lines and 106,000 subscriber lines plus 1,700 kilometers of optical lines and 1,300 kilometers of digital radio relay links. With the completion of the DON project, approximately 10 percent of Bulgaria was provided with digital capabilities. Digital networks for the entire country are expected to be built by 2010.

The DON project has made it possible for Bulgaria to become part of other international telecommunications projects, most of which have been funded by international financial institutions (e.g., the World Bank, the European Bank for Reconstruction and Development, and the European Investment Bank). They include (1) the Trans-Balkan Line, which starts from Istanbul and crosses Bulgaria, Macedonia, Albania, and (through undersea cable) into Italy; (2) the Undersea Cable System Under the Black Sea, connecting Romania, Turkey, Ukraine, and Bulgaria with parts of Russia and Italy; (3) the Black Sea Fibre-Optic Cable System, projecting a fiber-optic network that would run from Russia through Ukraine, the Caucasus, and Bulgaria on to Greece and Cyprus; (4) the Trans-European Network, initiated in 1988 under the auspices of the International Telecommunications Union (ITU), designed to create an up-to-date network starting in the Czech Republic at Brno and running through Slovakia, Hungary, Romania, Bulgaria, Greece, and on through Cyprus into the Middle East; and (5) the Trans-European Line, starting in Frankfurt, Germany, and running through fifteen Central and Eastern European countries until it ends in Kishinev, Moldova.[39]

Like Poland, Bulgaria has enacted legislation that would move the country in the direction of the guidelines for telecommunications operations required for membership in the European Union.[40] The Bulgarian National Assembly also committed the country to the liberalization of telecommunications in ways required by the World Trade Organization (WTO) when it ratified Bulgaria's WTO membership. But a 1996 decision by the government to "privatize" the monopoly Bulgarian Telecommunications Company (BTC) has not yet been implemented, and there are a number of indications that the Bulgarian government is trying to brake the pace of Bulgarian Internet growth in ways that might create difficulties in the EU membership negotiating process.[41] In early 2001 supporters of privatization were buoyed by a series of decisions in Bulgaria's petroleum industry to award contracts for new exploration and production to private and foreign companies.[42]

Bulgaria first became connected to the Internet in a manner somewhat different from other Eastern European countries, with the lead role assumed by a small private company of Bulgarian entrepreneurs (Digital Systems) beginning in 1989. Digital Systems established a permanent link in December 1992, but it was not until 1995 that the Bulgarian Academy of Sciences and several leading universities received enough money from the government to establish their own permanent links. Because the government has concentrated its telecommunications modernization efforts on becoming an international hub but without modernizing its internal networks, Internet access domestically is still difficult and expensive, with the BTC retaining its legal monopoly over all areas of telecommunications.[43]

Reports of the International Press Institute (IPI) have speculated that key figures in the Bulgarian government and parliament may be trying to stall privatization processes until legislation and administrative measures might be put into place to establish permanent control over domestic Internet content.[44] IPI's speculation resulted from a December 1998 proposal of the Bulgarian Committee on Posts and Telegraphs (CPT) to require all private ISPs to use BTC lines and to pay a substantial fee to the CPT for Internet access. In addition, the CPT chief executive, Antoni Slavinski, announced in December 1998 that Internet content "may be scrutinized by the CPT."[45] In response to the CPT proposal and announcement, the Bulgarian Internet Society (ISOC) was formed as a nongovernmental organization and immediately filed a complaint against the CPT, stating that the proposal would make the Internet prohibitively expensive for many Bulgarians and would leave the door open for government control of Internet use. After several confrontations between ISOC and representatives of the Bulgarian media, the prime minister announced in mid-1999 that he would no longer give press conferences because of the media's "lack of respect" in its questions about the country's economy.[46]

Concerns over Internet freedom in Bulgaria reflect a public debate about press and media freedom that raged throughout the 1990s. The Bulgarian parliament continues to debate a number of media laws introduced in early 1996, but they have been strenuously opposed by a coalition of academics, journalists, and business and professional organizations. In 1998 parliament passed a media law that would have given state broadcasting organizations exclusive domain over news and public affairs, leaving private radio and television companies with rights only to broadcast music and entertainment. That bill was vetoed by President Petar Stoyanov. In the absence of specific media legislation, Bulgarian reporters continue to be prosecuted under old libel laws, and more than fifty private radio and television stations are broadcasting clandestinely (without proper licensing) despite their being subject to periodic closure by the government.[47]

■ INTERNET DEVELOPMENT IN THE BALTICS

As indicated in Table 4.1, the extent to which the Internet is being used by people in Central/Eastern Europe and Eurasia (represented in the table by the number of Internet hosts relative to population) is fairly consistent with individual countries' development of telecommunications networks (as exemplified in the table by the number of telephone lines relative to population). Even more important has been the amount of money each country has invested specifically in Internet development, which is not reflected in the table. From the table it is clear that the Baltic countries (Estonia, Latvia, Lithuania) are among the most advanced with regard to Internet use, with the three largest Eastern European nations (Hungary, the Czech Republic, and Poland) ranking with and among them. The only other Eastern European countries that had more than two Internet hosts per 1,000 people in 2000 were Slovenia, Slovakia, Bulgaria, and Croatia—reflecting a degree of Internet development analyzed for each country in this chapter and Chapter 6. All but one of the larger Eastern European nations (Romania is the exception) ranked above Russia in terms of Internet use, and literally all Eastern European nations except Albania and Macedonia ranked above the other FSU states.

The reason the Baltic nations are so advanced with regard to Internet use has much to do with substantial investments in telecommunications and Internet development made by the Nordic countries (especially Finland, Sweden, and Norway) and the Soros Foundation in the early 1990s, beginning shortly after the Berlin Wall was torn down.[48] In 1993 the Nordic Council initiated a program called BALTnet, which provided assured funding for computer networks, as well as research, training, equipment, and software for Internet development in the Baltic region. The most dramatic and immediate effect of these initiatives was the establishment of invaluable high-quality computer and Internet links between the Baltic countries and their Scandinavian neighbors at a very early stage of Internet development.

Within the Baltics, Estonia has led the way in Internet growth, in part because it has managed to construct digital telecommunications lines for a greater portion of the country than has been the case in Latvia or Lithuania but also because Estonia has a more substantial base of technological, entrepreneurial, and managerial resources.[49] Much of the Internet capability in Estonia results from the creation of the Estonian Education and Research Network (EENET), which has linked almost all of the nation's universities, schools, cultural institutions, government offices, nongovernmental organizations, medical facilities, and libraries to a common cyberspace network. Several electronic media centers have been established in the country—primarily at universities—where people can gain experience using computers, log on to the World Wide Web, and enroll in more advanced training programs in Internet use.[50] According to Soros Foundation figures, all of Estonia's secondary schools were connected to the Internet by the end of 2000 as a result of a Soros project called "Tiger-leap."[51] In contrast to Estonia, Internet connectivity in Latvia and Lithuania is confined primarily to the area around the capital cities (Riga and Vilnius), and neither country has made as much progress as Estonia in developing media centers or programs for universities and school systems.

Estonia also leads the other Baltic nations in the development of a legal and administrative framework that would facilitate the growth of the Internet into the future. A new telecommunications act is expected to liberalize the entire telecommunications sector by 2002, including privatization of the government monopoly company, Estonian Telecom, and allowance for foreign and private investment in competitive companies. These measures are designed to lower prices for Internet use and improve the efficiency of Internet-based services. To support these goals, additional legislation has created a Communications Board that is independent of the Ministry of Transport and Communications and should therefore be able to act as an effective regulatory agency. These and other measures have moved Estonia to the list of the "top five" candidates from Central and Eastern Europe likely to satisfy the regulation requirements that will enable them to be admitted to the European Union.[52] Indeed, Estonia's rapid rise to the position of perhaps first on the list of those likely to be invited into the EU has resulted in a movement within the country to slow the pace of integration with Europe.[53]

Key figures in Estonia's rapid Internet development have been President Lennart Meri, the country's senior statesman at age seventy-two in 2001, and Prime Minister Mart Laar, both avid followers of Internet technology. In mid-2000 these two leaders were responsible for constructing a meeting room in Tallinn that makes possible what they call a "paperless cabinet," where twenty government ministers can sit around a table with keyboards, "mice," and other paraphernalia and have instant access to videoconferencing with government officials, links to legal and statistical databases, and use of other modern communications facilities.[54] Sessions of the Riigikogu (parliament) are broadcast in real time over the Internet, new laws are immediately available in cyberspace once passed, and plans are under way to provide digital links to all 250 of Estonia's municipal governments. Similar progress has been made in the private sector in Estonia and to a somewhat lesser extent in Latvia and Lithuania.[55] Telebanking and Internet banking, for example, are so well developed in all three nations that a 1999 survey by Euromoney Publications concluded that "the Baltic consumer now has almost the same [online banking and credit card] options as the American or British consumer."[56]

■ INTERNET GROWTH IN HUNGARY, THE CZECH REPUBLIC, AND POLAND

Among the larger Eastern European countries, it is not surprising that Hungary and the Czech Republic are the most advanced in terms of Internet use, since they were the first two nations to undertake significant reform and privatization of telecommunications systems. Once Ameritech and Deutsche Telekom acquired 60 percent of MATAV—the previously state-owned telecommunications company in Hungary—MATAV quickly eliminated 4,000 jobs, raised local telephone rates and other fees by 25 percent, and used the additional revenues to improve service and lower rates in the long-distance and international sectors. Since these are the two sectors that relate most directly to effective worldwide Internet service, the quality of Hungary's Internet connectivity tends to be superior to that found elsewhere in Eastern Europe and the FSU. In addition, waiting lists for phones have been eliminated in some parts of Hungary and reduced significantly elsewhere, and other aspects of Internet access—from both homes and businesses—are being streamlined and made more efficient. As a result of its improved reputation and management capabilities, MATAV is growing faster than any other Hungarian company, its stock having appreciated by 85 percent between 1997 and 2000. In 1999, MATAV started paying dividends to investors, something unprecedented for any Eastern European telecom company.[57]

Investment analysts and other observers are expecting even more significant improvement of Internet services and other aspects of IT in Hungary, as well as a lowering of rates, as a result of the highly competitive environment developing among Hungarian and international private and government firms.[58] Hungary's newly created Competition Council has been designed as a regulatory body to try to ensure fairness and competition among the large number of aspiring entrants to this newly liberalized market. Among the firms strategically considering entry into Internet-related areas are the Hungarian oil and gas company (MOL) and the national railway company (MAV), both of which have extensive telecom networks that might be expanded to provide public telecommunications services. MAV is already partnered with KPN Telecom of the Netherlands and KFKI, the Hungarian Academy of Sciences, to handle data services for corporations but is seeking to become a major provider of a number of different local, long-distance, and international IT services in the future. Many smaller IT companies (e.g., Antenna Hungaria, Novacom, Hungarian Telephone and Cable Corporation, CG Sat, and GTS Hungary) are also trying to carve out niches in particular IT markets—especially in the rural areas—often on the supposition that they can offer more personalized, flexible, and quicker service than is possible for large companies like MATAV, MOL, or MAV.[59]

Internet use in the Czech Republic is roughly comparable to that in Hungary, although the partially privatized Czech telecommunications company, SPT Telecom (renamed Cesky Telecom in 2001), has not had nearly the success (financially, technically, in terms of public relations) as MATAV. In November 1998 more than 2,000 protesters turned out in blowing snow in Prague to protest proposed rate hikes by SPT Telecom (with similar numbers protesting in the cities of Brno and Zlin). Arguing that the rate hikes would place the Internet "out of reach of schools, local and regional governments, and small and medium-sized enterprises," the demonstrators forced SPT Telecom to provide special lower rates for Internet users and reconsider plans for IT development previously proposed to the government.[60] The demonstrations were widely considered to reflect the disenchantment of Czech citizens with the quality of Internet service, although the impact of the protests is often cited as an indication that the Internet has already become a force to reckon with in Czech society.

At the turn of the millennium there were an estimated 300,000 Internet users in the Czech Republic (a country of 10.3 million people), with nearly half of them college and university students. Most Czech companies are on the Internet—even if they use it only to receive and send e-mail—and large businesses have their own websites for corporate presentations. The Czech Republic was the first country in Central/Eastern Europe and Eurasia to spawn both an Internet broker and an Internet bank. The bank (Expandia Banka) is trying to promote e-commerce as a means of enlarging its 1999 base of 13,000 customers to a hoped-for 100,000 by 2003. In early 1999, Expandia sponsored a "virtual city on the Web" Internet event, visited by 17,000 people during its first three days and more than 100 companies and 90,000 users during the succeeding months.[61] Although total turnover of Czech e-commerce, e-banking, and e-business has been less impressive than in Estonia, that is expected to change rapidly in the first decade of the twenty-first century. The major new factor in the development of the Internet in the Czech Republic at the turn of the millennium was the acquisition of Czech On Line, the Czech Republic's largest ISP, by Austria Telekom in April 2000 for an undisclosed amount but one that ranked "as easily the largest Internet transaction to date in Central and Eastern Europe."[62]

As indicated in Table 4.1, Poland lags significantly behind Hungary and the Czech Republic in Internet development, with only a third as many Internet hosts per 1,000 population. Table 4.1 also points out the extent to which Poland is trailing Hungary and the Czech Republic (as well as most other major countries in Eastern Europe) in telecommunications infrastructure. Because of the continued delays in its privatization program for telecommunications, Poland's Internet-related infrastructure is still inappropriate for efficient modern IT use, and the TPSA management continues to be hamstrung by a factional Polish politics with many carryovers from its bureaucratic and socialist past. Inadequate basic service and high user rates have spawned a number of Polish nongovernmental organizations that lobby the government to step up its Internet development efforts.[63] The situation has also led to fierce competition among Poland's ISPs to deliver value-added services (such as making long-distance phone calls or sending faxes through the Internet at lower costs) as companies try to find ways to distinguish themselves in an atmosphere where they can do little to provide more efficient basic service.[64]

A major survey of Polish Internet users by the newspaper *Gazeta Wyborcza* (Warsaw) in February 2000 found that more than 90 percent of those logging on to the Internet did so through the TPSA infrastructure, but the vast majority complained that the quality of the connections were poor, downloading of data and routine response times were extremely slow, and service was often subject to interruption or disruption.[65] Because of the poor quality of Internet connectivity, the survey found Poles were reluctant to purchase computers or pay for an Internet facility in their homes, with the vast majority of users logging on at their office or educational institution. Poles who regularly used the Internet were overwhelmingly in the eighteen-to-twenty-five age group, a majority of whom were students. Only one in ten of those surveyed used the Internet for more than thirty minutes a day (most used it far less than thirty minutes per day), and only 8.8 percent lived in rural areas. The principal uses of cyberspace for Poles, as detailed in the survey, were not for business or commerce or everyday use but rather for computer science news, information about new software, current domestic and foreign news, and academic material. The *Gazeta Wyborcza* editors concluded that the survey documented the extent to which Poland is lagging behind the rest of the world in Internet development because of its poor telecom infrastructure.[66] As indicated earlier, there is a widespread expectation in Poland that Internet service will improve considerably when the TPSA is finally privatized.

▪ INTERNET USE IN SLOVENIA AND SLOVAKIA

Two of the most surprising figures in Table 4.1 are the relatively high percentages of Internet hosts and telephone lines in Slovenia and Slovakia. The figures put both countries ahead of all nations of the former Soviet Union (except Estonia and Latvia) with regard to Internet development, with Slovenia trailing only Estonia and the Czech Republic among Eastern European nations.[67] Slovenia's lead in Internet use results largely from its successful transition to democratic rule and a well-managed economy following its secession from the former Yugoslavia in 1991–1992.[68] With a population of 1.9 million people in 2000, built around the capital city of Ljubljana, Slovenia is the most industrialized and urbanized of the former Yugoslav republics and is also the most homogeneous (Slovenes constitute almost the entire population, which is also overwhelmingly Catholic and of Western heritage). The transition to a market economy has been helped along by support from the EU, which has been involved in accession negotiations with Slovene leadership since the European Commission and the Slovenian government signed an EU accession agreement in 1996. The transition has been so successful that Slovenia has come to be recognized, in the words of one observer, as "easily the wealthiest of all the former communist states."[69]

Slovenia's privatization legislation was enacted in 1996 and is distinguished from others because Slovenian privatization schemes were based primarily on employee buyouts, possible in part because of the higher standard of living already present in the country. A 1999 *Business Week* article praised Slovenia for the way in which it had privatized "large swaths of its economy" but also for the way it had "knocked state finances into shape, freed prices, deregulated markets, and curbed inflation."[70] As early as January 1998, more than 1,200 of the 1,598 enterprises included in the government's privatization program (including the government monopoly telecommunications provider, SiOL) had been privatized, and the number of private enterprises increased from 7,935 in 1990 to 35,786 in 1996. The rapid decrease in the number of employees in former government enterprises (from 652,669 in 1990 to 467,238 in 1996) is perhaps the most dramatic indication of the economic efficiencies gained very early in the privatization process.[71]

Blessed with a fairly high standard of living, a favorable geographic location next to Western Europe, a functioning democratic political system, and a stable growing economy, Slovenia has had little difficulty building substantial telecommunications and Internet links into Europe while attracting foreign investment in a variety of Internet-related ventures on a regular basis. Favorable geography and a high standard of living have also made it easier for Slovenes to purchase computers and software, pay user fees for Internet access, and otherwise explore cyberculture.[72] Particularly valuable have been opportunities for Slovenes to undertake training programs in Internet use and development in Western Europe combined with the growth of a number of educational and training centers for Internet use in Slovenia.[73] Newly emerging private companies in Slovenia have played a major role in Internet development, particularly since many are in the IT sector.[74] In mid-1999 it was estimated that 80 percent of Slovenia's large companies, 67 percent of its medium-sized companies, and 50 percent of small companies were online; and the government had launched a large-scale program to get the Slovenian government and parliament online.[75] By early 2000 a larger percentage of people in Slovenia were estimated to log on to the Internet on a daily basis than was the case in Austria or Italy.[76]

Some indication of the relative political stability of Slovenia compared with most other governments in Eastern Europe came with the collapse of the government of Prime Minister Janez Drnovsek in April 2000, forcing new elections.[77] This was the first governmental crisis since Slovenia's independence from Yugoslavia in 1991, bringing down a prime minister who had led the country since 1992. Nonetheless, as a major article in the *Financial Times* of London stated, "much of Slovenia's ordinary political life [continued] almost unaffected by the crisis," largely because of the widespread consensus in the country behind an economic restructuring program designed to make Slovenia one of the first European nations admitted to the European Union.[78] By April 2000 the Slovenian parliament had passed eleven of the seventy-six pieces of legislation required to meet the criteria for EU membership, and the remaining legislation was expected to be passed regardless of who formed the next government. To quote the *Financial Times* again, "Such issues played no part in the fall of the government. . . . With EU and NATO [North Atlantic Treaty Organization] accession agreed on by all the main parties, the biggest questions for [Slovenia] are already decided."[79]

Slovakia is not nearly as far along in Internet development as Slovenia, but it is often ranked above Poland, other parts of Central/Eastern Europe, Russia, and all FSU states except the Baltics. Slovakia was half of one of the three socialist federations in the communist empire (the other two were Yugoslavia and the USSR), all of which failed almost immediately after the Berlin Wall was torn down. Slovakian nationalism reasserted itself after the collapse of communism, resulting in the so-called velvet divorce from the federal arrangement with the Czech Republic and the creation of an independent Slovakia on January 1, 1993.[80] Until 1998 Slovakia was led by a prime minister, Vladimir Meciar, whose government was heavily dependent on Russia for cheap energy and diplomatic support. Meciar ruled in a manner the *Economist* described as "thuggery, incompetence and contempt for the law."[81] When Meciar was defeated in the 1998 Slovakia elections, the EU opened negotiations for possible EU entry with the new government under Mikulas Dzurinda, who proposed to restructure the banks, sell off state-owned firms, drastically reduce public debt, and otherwise reform the Slovak economy to conform to EU guidelines. J. P. Morgan and

Company was brought in to advise Slovakia on the privatization of its two largest banks, and a number of restructuring programs were launched.[82]

The relatively robust computer and Internet cultures already present in Slovakia before the change of government in 1998 were primarily a result of three factors: (1) a telecommunications infrastructure inherited from the old Czechoslovakia that, despite its many shortcomings, was among the best in Central/Eastern Europe; (2) consistent support from the government of independent Slovakia (even under Meciar) for the purchase of computers and the spread of computer-Internet capabilities in Slovak scientific and educational institutions; and (3) the creation within Slovakia of a citizens network, built around the World Wide Web, that has sought to promote a civic culture and open channels for discussion between citizens in Slovakia and the Slovak diaspora. The 1998 election of a more reform-minded government that is more acceptable to the EU has created an even stronger climate for Internet development and has started to attract significant foreign investment.[83]

Some of the most important work in early Internet development in Slovakia was carried out by the Computing Center of the Slovak Academy of Sciences, which has conceived of its work as "an attempt to make the world of [the] Internet accessible to citizens of Slovakia and provide a bridge to Slovakia for citizens of the world."[84] Using government funding, the Slovak Academy of Sciences (through the Slovak Academic Network [SANET]) provided initial support for training, facilitating contacts among people, and making some hardware and software purchases—making it possible for Slovak newspapers, television and radio stations, government offices, embassies, schools and colleges, book publishers, religious organizations, theaters, art galleries, and many other institutions to log on to the Internet for the first time. In addition, the academy promoted the concept of the Internet as an important vehicle for advancing Slovak national interests by establishing and maintaining links among Slovaks in the European, Canadian, Australian, and U.S. diasporas. This campaign has attracted financial support from Slovak leaders worldwide and from international organizations.[85]

With the installation of a reform-minded government in 1998 and the initiation of negotiations for entry into the EU in 1999, Slovakia piqued the renewed interest of foreign investors in Internet-related ventures, including France Telecom (which recently increased its stake in Globtel Global System for Mobile Communications [GSM] of Bratislava from 34 percent to 64 percent) and Telenor Nextel (TN), the Internet branch of the leading Norwegian data and telecommunications company Telenor.[86] In early 2000 TN acquired the Internet division of Slovak Netlab Plus, one of Slovakia's five top ISPs, in a move TN viewed as "an important step towards becoming a major Internet provider in the central European region."[87] Internet Securities (IS) of Boston reaffirmed Telenor's endorsement of Slovakia as an important Internet link in Central/Eastern Europe in September 1999, when it launched a new service called "Slovak" that provides financial news and company and industry information from Slovak sources to the IS world network.[88] In May 2000 the Slovak government agreed to the privatization of Slovak Telekom, the government monopoly telecommunications provider, and on August 4, 2000, a 51 percent stake in the company was sold to Deutsche Telekom for 1 billion Euros (U.S.$900 million).[89]

▪ CONCLUSIONS

Analysis of Internet growth in those countries of Eastern Europe that have been most successful in gaining access to cyberspace necessarily begins with the significant changes taking place in the telecommunications sector in the region. The contrast with the FSU states is striking, with some East European nations clearly beginning to attract the foreign capital necessary to break out of the old Soviet-enforced telecommunications mold, whereas none of the FSU nations except the three Baltic states has been able to move Internet-related matters to priority policy status or to develop the requisite domestic economic and political environments that might attract large-scale foreign direct investment (FDI). The result is that FDI in Internet ventures in Central/Eastern Europe and the FSU states has focused lopsidedly on only six or seven East European nations.

Even in these few nations, however, the fact that they are beginning to attract capital does not mean the impediments to Internet access have disappeared or that the Internet will suddenly function in a miraculously new way. Where substantial privatization has been agreed to, the transition to an entirely privatized telecom environment often will not be complete for several years. This is the case, for example, in Hungary, where privatization of MATAV was initiated in 1993 but is not scheduled to be fully implemented until 2003. In all other East European countries privatization of telecommunications monopolies was initiated later than in Hungary, and in the vast majority of the nations it has not yet begun. The result is that despite considerable change, with more to come as wireless and other advanced Internet technologies are introduced, many of the old problems remain: the cost of computers and software is coming down but is still high enough that barely 10 percent of the population owned computers in 2000, even in the most progressive Internet states; inadequate competition keeps telephone charges for access and online operating time high and quality of service low; and e-commerce is minuscule because consumers are not used to buying goods and services they cannot inspect, few have credit cards, face-to-face transactions dominate life, and legal protections against fraud are weak. Dina Iordanova has pointed out that in 2000, "only a relatively small number of academics, social activists, media professionals, and businessmen regularly use[d] the Internet for online research and for dissemination of information. The Internet has not yet become an integral part of everyday life."[90]

To suggest in this atmosphere that the Internet is already creating a *publicum* that embodies meaningful civic discourse on a day-to-day basis seems premature. John Horvath, a writer based in Hungary, is perhaps more accurate when he suggests that civic discourse in the Eastern European countries with the most advanced information technology (which he calls "the New Europe") is "limited to an elite minority, who hold values and discuss issues that are usually closed." Horvath believes that "despite appearances and the euphoric promises of a greater expression of democracy and extensive civic discourse through new media technologies, the medium has so far exercised a reverse potential to drown the message."[91]

Many East European scholars would go even further, arguing that the Internet in "the New Europe" has been more effective in promoting extremes that are anathema to the idea of a *publicum,* strengthening enormous factional divisions within Eastern European societies. Elliot Glassman of Eotvos Lorand University in Budapest, for example, traced the growth of websites, chat rooms, listserves, and other evidence of "hate groups" on the Internet in Eastern Europe and found that in 1999 and 2000 their numbers were doubling every few months and were increasingly in native languages. Glassman's conclusions suggest that the possibility that Internet development will be a nonintegrative factor in the future development of Eastern European societies must be taken seriously:

> In an area with a history of ethnic strife, a resurgence of nationalism after the fall of Communism, and a return of political popularity for parties of the right, the New Europe remains ripe for intolerance to sweep the region. . . . Many of the cyber hate mongers are émigrés living in the West in a wealthier society where Internet access is relatively

cheap. They tend to target their compatriots in the region, especially the young, who most readily use the Internet. These young are also very impressionable, and such propaganda can influence them, especially as the political system moves to the right.[92]

Regardless of whether the Internet eventually becomes a force for democracy and the integration of societies, it is clear that international relationships will play a major role in its future in Central and Eastern Europe. The major driving force for Internet development in the region thus far has come not from internal societal pressures for development but rather, as this chapter makes clear, from the desire of national leaderships to join the European Union, which has developed admission guidelines that include a central role for IT and the Internet. Accession to the European Union is seen as desirable primarily because it promises more assured access to the large amounts of foreign capital essential to modernization across the entire spectrum of Eastern European economies and societies. Aside from the desire to join the European Union, as Iordanova points out, "most governments in Eastern Europe . . . do not have a clearly defined position on the issues of the information society, and issues of Internet access and regulation have not yet become an integral part of their media and telecommunications policy."[93]

▪ NOTES

1. For purposes of this discussion, Eastern Europe is defined as those states that were not part of the FSU but were part of the Soviet bloc—Poland, the Czech and Slovak Republics, Hungary, Romania, Bulgaria, Macedonia, Albania, the new Yugoslavia (including Bosnia-Herzegovina), Croatia, and Slovenia—plus the Baltic countries. The Baltics are included here even though they were part of the FSU because their pattern of Internet-related development since 1989 has been closer to that of most Eastern European countries than to the FSU states. But Eastern Europe was still far behind Western Europe when it freed itself from Soviet rule (e.g., it was estimated in 1990 that Eastern Europe had about one-quarter as many telephones per 100 inhabitants as Western Europe, one-fifth to one-sixth as many fax machines and data terminals, and virtually no mobile communications; some rural regions had no communications facilities whatsoever). See Kaske, "Eastern Europe," p. 89.

2. Croatia also ranked just above Russia in Table 4.1, but I have chosen to discuss it in Chapter 6 rather than in the present chapter because its international relationships are closer to the other countries discussed in Chapter 6 than to the nations discussed here.

3. Kontkiewicz-Chachulska and Phan, "From Path-Dependent Processes," pp. 317 ff.

4. Nolan, "Development of Satellite Services," pp. 98–104. Figures in this paragraph are from this and ibid.

5. Hudson, *Global Connections,* p. 238. This would include new digital international switches, digital overlay networks, the skeleton for long-term infrastructural modernization, licensing of cellular operators, and packet-switched data networks for large data users.

6. Ibid., pp. 243–244.

7. For example, the European Council Summit in Essen (December 1994) concluded that cooperation with Eastern Europe could best be promoted if "countries in transition" were able to participate fully in the emerging "information society," along lines suggested in the report by Bangemann, *Europe and the Global Information Society.*

8. These steps are spelled out in detail in discussions of the EEC "Green Paper" in Ungerer and Costello, *Telecommunications in Europe,* pp. 185–226. The summary of steps listed in the text is taken directly from a summary in Straubhaar, "From PTT to Private," p. 15.

9. Kontkiewicz-Chachulska and Phan, "From Path-Dependent Processes," pp. 319–320. See also *Communication for a Better World.*

10. Canning, "Privatization and Competition," p. 114.

11. Okolicsanyi, "Hungarian Telephone's," pp. 41–43.

12. As Canning, "Privatization and Competition," p. 116, has pointed out, "Partial privatization and the implementation of a new tariff regime conforming to international practice rapidly boosted [MagyarCom's] creditworthiness, and attracting the requisite development finance has not posed a problem. In 1994 a DM 85 million loan [U.S.$38 million] was proffered by the Export-Import Bank of Japan, an international consortium of 27 banks granted a five-year syndicated loan of U.S.$150 million, while the European Investment Bank (EIB) provided the equivalent amount in *ecu* [Euro-dollars]. During 1995 the company's investment arm, Investel, secured a further loan of U.S.$300 million—the biggest loan granted to a CEE enterprise without the backing of a government guarantee from a consortium comprising the EBRD, the IFC [International Finance Corporation], and Deutsche Bank, along with thirty-five commercial banks."

13. "Record Dollars." A later Czech government accepted a bid from Germany's Deutsche Telekom to buy a majority stake in the second-largest Czech mobile operator, Radiomobil, for $565 million in March 2000. See Anderson, "Deutsche Telekom in Czech Deal," p. 25.

14. Details of the telecommunications privatization process in the Czech Republic are available in Michalis and Takla, "Telecommunications in the Czech Republic," pp. 88–102.

15. For an account of TPSA's resistance to privatization, see Jasinski, "Competition Rules," p. 137. See also Wagstyl and Bobinski, "Poland Pays," p. 3.

16. Williamson, "Poland to Name Bidder," p. C11E.

17. See "Four to Bid."

18. Quoted in Reed, "Better Late Than Never for TPSA," p. 4.

19. A comparison of Internet-related investments in the three countries appears in Reid, "IT Craze," pp. 46–47. See also Hoelscher, "The Next Step," pp. 76–78, 82.

20. Quoted from interviews with Sean Murphy, Nomura's technology analyst, in Reid, "Web's Tentacles," pp. 39–41. Murphy's projections were based largely on the gap between IT development in these three nations and that in Western European nations (e.g., approximately 10 percent of the population in Hungary, Poland, and the Czech Republic owned PCs in 2000, compared with 30 percent in Germany and 23 percent in Austria).

21. See, for example, Holdsworth, "Czechs 'Losing Internet Race,'" pp. 13–15; Hilsum, "No Revolution," pp. 13–15; Green, "A Czech Internet Venture."

22. For details, see Anderson, "Prague Delays," p. 8, and Finn, "Czech Communism," p. A30.

23. See, for example, the Associated Press 2001 report on Hungary in "Hungary Improving," and the reports on Hungary on the website of PricewaterhouseCoopers at www.pricewaterhousecoopers.com. See also "Venture Capital."

24. The term *fault line* was used by Prime Minister Victor Orban in January 2000 when he pointed out that unemployment in Budapest was only 5 percent at the time while it was as high as 19 percent in eastern Hungary, an area where before 1990 the communist government had located much of its heavy industry. See Finn, "Hungarian East," p. A22.

25. In October 2000 a *Business Week* article described Flextronics as "the Continent's largest electronics manufacturing operation." For details, see Echikson, "Taking Hungary," pp. 148B–148F.

26. Langencamp, "High-Tech Hungarians," p. 6.

27. Niccolai, "Hungary." For details on telecommunication manufacturing in Hungary, as well as in Poland and the Czech Republic, see Sadowski, "The Myth of Market Dominance," pp. 323–345.

28. Quoted in Langencamp, "High-Tech Hungarians," p. 6. On the relationship between Internet development and national regulatory environments, see Melody, "Internet Development," pp. 85–87.

29. For analyses of Poland's somewhat unstable political situation, in which a resurgent Communist Party is also (as in the Czech Republic) a factor, see Finn, "Party Pullout," p. A17, and "Europe: The Changing Poles."

30. Thurston, "Poland," pp. 71–72.

31. Williamson, "Poland Seizes Insurer," p. A19. See also Erlanger, "Despite Soaring Prosperity."

32. Wagstyl, "Survey—Eurozone Economy," p. 5.

33. Ibid. See also Winestock and Kaminski, "Preparing for the Enlargement," p. A23.

34. See *RIS News 99 Survey Results,* available at www.ris.org/news30.html.

35. The most salient example of resistance was by the government of Vaclav Klaus in the Czech Republic in the early 1990s, which "put control of

important groups such as banks and big manufacturing companies into the hands of local business people, often collaborating with existing managers. These investors usually proved unable to develop and finance effective plans. The current Czech government is now struggling to refinance [these] companies with the help of foreign capital." See Wagstyl, "Survey—Eurozone Economy," p. 5.

36. In the 1960s and 1970s the Kremlin tried to position Bulgaria to be the center of computer development in Eastern Europe. Although this policy was abandoned in the 1980s, it resulted in levels of telecommunications infrastructure and human resources capabilities above those of most East European countries and led to policies, even before the collapse of communism, to promote Bulgaria as a telecom center for international and regional networks. See Bennahum, "Heart of Darkness," pp. 227–277.

37. Triffonova and Kashoukeeva-Nousheva, *Regional Infrastructure Projects,* p. 345.

38. In pursuit of this goal, Bulgaria was a lead organizer of a two-day ministerial conference in Cyprus in January 2000 designed to promote cooperation among seven countries (Albania, Bulgaria, Macedonia, Romania, Turkey, Yugoslavia [Serbia-Montenegro], and Cyprus) in the fields of telecommunications, postal service, and information technology. See "Telecommunications: Cooperation," p. 159.

39. Details on these networks are available in Triffonova and Kashoukeeva-Nousheva, *Regional Infrastructure Projects,* pp. 348–354.

40. The central piece of legislation is the Telecommunications Act, passed on July 27, 1998. See Leonard, "Bulgaria Aims," pp. 4–5. See also "Bulgaria Continues," p. 67.

41. For details, see Kanev, "Bulgaria Tangles with Web," pp. 14–15. See also Stones, "Bulgaria," pp. 95–96, and "Europe: A Bulgarian Way."

42. An analysis of these decisions appears in "Bulgaria: Muddling Through," pp. 36–37.

43. For an analysis of the early years of Internet development in Bulgaria, see Moffett, "Bulgaria."

44. See Kanev "Bulgaria Tangles with Web."

45. Quoted in ibid., p. 4.

46. Ibid., p. 5.

47. For an analysis of the twists and turns of Bulgaria's media and press freedom debate, see Rubin, "Transitions," pp. 62 ff.

48. Under the guidance of the Nordic Council, each of three Nordic countries "adopted" a Baltic country for Internet development. Thus Latvia received support for equipment and connectivity from Sweden, Estonia from Finland, and Lithuania from Norway. For an analysis of post–Cold War relationships between Finland and Estonia, which have been a major factor in Estonia's economic development, see Sander, "A Tale of Two Countries," pp. 61–73.

49. For a comparative analysis of resources for Internet and IT development in the Baltics, see Mayhew-Smith, "Entrepreneurs," pp. 18–19. See also Maheshwari, "Lithuanian City," p. 14.

50. By the end of 1999, businesses and nongovernmental organizations had financed more than seventy Public Internet Access Points across rural Estonia, most of which were located in old farm buildings, where farm families and schoolchildren could come to send e-mail, surf the Web, and play computer games. Much of this activity has been supported by the Archimedes Foundation and the European Survey of Information Society (ESIS). Additional details of Estonia's IT legislation and policy are available in Arak, "Estonia."

51. Most of the support from the Soros Foundation has come through the work of the Soros-managed Open Society Institute–Internet Program (OSI-IP), which was the first major Soros program for Internet development in Eastern Europe and was coordinated in the Baltics with some of the early work of the Electronic Frontier Foundation. For details, see the OSI-IP article "Internet Policy in the Baltics," available at www.soros.org/internet/policy/parliament-human-rights.html. For additional information on the earlier years of Internet development in the Baltics, see Moffett, "Baltic States."

52. In late 1999 a survey of Central/Eastern European nations by *Business Week* concluded that five countries—Hungary, the Czech Republic, Poland, Slovenia, and Estonia—would be the first admitted to the European Union (as early as 2003). In the words of the survey summary: "They have already been preparing. The lion's share of their exports now goes to Western Europe. The rules and regulations governing their economic life increasingly come from Brussels. Their economies are rapidly being integrated into the vast and prosperous EU market" (p. 3). See Fairlamb, Smith, and Condon, "How Far, How Fast?" p. 64.

53. Smith, "In Drive for EU," p. A18.

54. The project is described in "Estonian Cabinet."

55. See, for example, "Estonian E-Sales," p. 5, and Maheshwari, "Small Could Be Profitable," p. 14.

56. "First with the Newest," p. E6; see also "Estonian E-Sales," p. 5.

57. "Setting a Fast Pace," p. 31.

58. See "Analysts Predict."

59. Some of the problems confronted by investors in smaller media enterprises in Hungary are outlined and analyzed in Hiebert, "The Difficult Birth," pp. 34–36.

60. The demonstrations were organized by Ondrej Neff, publisher of the Internet daily *Neviditelny Pes* (Invisible Dog), and leaders of two Czech Internet search services. Banners read "Stop Telecommunism" and "With Telecom forever and ever, but not an impulse longer" (a play on the slogan of the Velvet Revolution's slogan "with the Soviet Union forever and ever but not a day longer"). See Naegele, "Czech Republic."

61. Figures in this paragraph are from Anderson, "Trail-Blazers." See also Bahensky, "Czech Mobile Carrier."

62. Bushrod, "DBAG Exits," p. 1.

63. Many of these NGOs have been brought together in a program called Fight for the Internet, led by the Internet Association of Poland (Polska

Spolecznose Internetu), which is described on the website: www.cto.us.edu.pl. Some of the legal constraints on the development of the Internet in Poland, particularly on e-commerce, are outlined in Zalewski, "Poland," pp. 37–39.

64. See Simpson, "Internet Providers."

65. *Gazeta Wyborcza* (Warsaw), February 8, 2000, as reported in "Poland: Internet Market." The survey was conducted by two leading marketing research companies—ARS Market and Opinion and Global eMarketing SA—and was the first systematic large-scale survey on Internet use conducted in Poland. That the poor quality of Internet connectivity in Poland is attributable to the TPSA infrastructure is clear from the survey, which found that Internet users complained of poor service regardless of the portal they used for access. In the survey 44.5 percent of respondents used the Onet.pl portal, 26.4 percent used Virtual Poland, and 13.7 percent used Yahoo!

66. Patterns identified in the *Gazeta Wyborcza* survey were confirmed by a number of other surveys on Internet use conducted throughout 2000, which are analyzed in detail in "Internet Users in Poland."

67. Figures for Internet use were even more sharply divergent in a highly detailed survey conducted by the Analysys Company in 1999, which found that Internet "penetration levels" (a more sophisticated index measuring the amount and quality of time spent on the Internet) for Poland were only 5.7 percent, whereas those for Slovakia were 9.5 percent and for Slovenia 15.1 percent. The Analysys survey is not publicly available but can be purchased through the website www.analysys.com. Figures quoted here are from the PR Newswire, as reported in the *Financial Times* (London), December 20, 1999.

68. Slovenia declared independence from the old Yugoslavia on June 25, 1991, but it was not recognized by the European Community and the United Nations until January 15, 1992.

69. Bukowski, "Slovenia's Transition," p. 69. See *Slovenia Weekly* (February 22, 1997, p. 16) for a statistical comparison of Slovenia's economy with other economies in the FSU and Central/Eastern Europe.

70. Fairlamb, Smith, and Condon, "How Far? How Fast?" p. 64.

71. Figures are from Bojnec, "Privatisation," pp. 77–78. An excellent overview of the Slovenian economy at the turn of the twenty-first century is Ash, "Slovenia Update," pp. 1–4.

72. A major factor cited by Slovene leaders for the rapid increase in Internet use in Slovenia is the widely accepted principle in government and academic circles that "the schooling generations" should have "free public access." Quoted from correspondence with Vasja Vehovar of the RIS organization. I am grateful to Professor Vehovar for pointing me toward substantial information on Internet use in Slovenia.

73. One of the most important is RIS in the Faculty of Social Sciences, University of Ljubljana. For more information about the development of the Internet in Slovenia, see the RIS website at www.ris.org. See also DeChant, "U.S. Firm," and Trofimov, "Mobile-Phone War," p. B13A.

74. Keynes, "Slovenia's Very Own," p. 22.

75. See *NUA Internet Surveys,* 4:22 (January 6, 2000), available at www. tagish.com/ethos/news/lit1/1570e.html. See also Vintar and Decman, "Telematics," pp. 451–464.

76. This is an estimate of ESIS, available on its website at www.ispo.cec. be/esis/.

77. For details of the collapse, see "Slovenia's Government Collapses."

78. Wright, "Slovenia Looks to Liberalisation," p. 2.

79. Ibid.

80. One of the most succinct analyses of the event is Hilde, "Slovak Nationalism," pp. 647–666.

81. "Mikulas Dzurinda," p. 48.

82. See Kraus, "J. P. Morgan Will Advise," pp. 17–20, and Appel and Gould, "Identity Politics," pp. 111–132.

83. Stones, "Slovakia," pp. 98–100.

84. Vystavil, *Internet,* p. 3.

85. A description of one of the Slovak Academy of Science projects with the Slovak diaspora appears in Vystavil, *Virtual Community.*

86. For a description of France Telecom's interests in Slovakia, see "France Telecom." A report on Slovakia's negotiations on EU entry appears in "Revision of Slovak Programme."

87. "Telenor Nextel Invests in the Slovak Internet Market," a press release of Telenor Nextel (March 7, 2000), available at www.nextel.no/english/news/archive/916309278.20805.html.

88. "Internet Securities Unveils New Services," pp. 29–30.

89. "White and Case Advises," p. 13. See also Anderson, "Slovakia," p. 2.

90. Iordanova, "Mediated Concerns," pp. 110–111.

91. Horvath, "Alone in the Crowd," p. 97. Both quotes in this paragraph are from this source.

92. Glassman, "CyberHate," p. 161.

93. Iordanova, "Mediated Concerns," p. 110.

6

Internet Politics in the Former Soviet Union and Other Central/Eastern European States

This chapter concludes the case studies of Central/Eastern Europe and the FSU states by focusing first on the East European nations that have been somewhat less successful at Internet diffusion than those discussed in Chapter 5. These include several of the successor states to the former Yugoslav Federation, which have been embroiled in war and other forms of intense conflict since the breakup of the federation in the early 1990s. The second half of this chapter draws some overall conclusions from the three case study chapters. An important component of this analysis is an attempt to place this extensive region in the context of international relations generally, including a discussion of the region's potential for involvement in the emergent international regime for the Internet constructed by advanced IT societies.

■ ALTERNATIVE PROSPECTS FOR THE INTERNET IN ALBANIA AND ROMANIA

The parts of Eastern Europe that have experienced the greatest difficulty in building an Internet infrastructure are Albania, Romania, and most of the former Yugoslavia. Albania has by far the worst telecommunications infrastructure in the FSU/CEE, with a penetration rate of only seventeen telephone lines per 1,000 people at the beginning of the twenty-first century (this also ranks among the worst rates in the world). There are no digital lines in Albania, and telephone service is erratic, subject to the vagaries of a violence-prone, unstable political system and a collapsed economy. Foreign direct investment in Albania was estimated at only $12 per capita in 1993 and has been declining since that time in the wake of a total collapse of the Albanian economy. In 2000, Albania had only twelve ISPs, with just 250–300 Internet hosts operational at any given point, for a country of 3.4 million people.[1]

Throughout the 1990s and into the early twenty-first century the Albanian economy has lacked an effective banking system, financed largely, in the words of a *Keesing's Contemporary Archives* report, "through remittances from Albanians working abroad and from smuggling."[2] Any hope of building confidence in Albania's privatization process among potential investors was quashed in 1997 when a number of financial pyramid schemes—promoted by both government and private enterprise—collapsed. Subsequent investigations by the International Monetary Fund (IMF) and other international organizations concluded that the Albanian government had used the schemes throughout the 1990s "as a money-recycling operation and, with the high interest payments, as 'a way of buying political support from the people.'"[3] Most of the Albanian population participated in the schemes with substantial knowledge of how they worked but with the belief that the illegal contrivances could continue because their collapse would mean the destruction of the entire ruling order. Many of Albania's fastest-growing private-sector companies, such as Vega Holdings, had used the pyramid schemes to finance spectacular growth but were protected by the government through corrupt practices and because they were the largest employers outside of the government.[4]

In this atmosphere, the major substantial attempt to promote Internet development in Albania has been a program of the Open Society Institute of the Soros Foundation, which has worked in collaboration with the United Nations Development Programme to obtain Albanian government approval for satellite connectivity to establish a small e-mail network for NGOs, universities, the media, and a few other organizations.[5] The founder and director of this project, Jonathan Peizer, described its minimalist expectations:

> Albania, Europe's poorest country, just going through a process of further decay and (self)destruction, was in an urgent need of communication to the outside world. The isolation, even at this moment, is stunning. The Soros Internet center, now running well, is using a satellite link and package radio connections inside Tirana, to link up university buildings. Still, one gets the impression there of a heroic project with little or no use for common people. For security reasons such

buildings look like fortresses. In such harsh poverty and [politically] unstable situation, how do you imagine the Internet to grow? And what will happen if, within a few years, there won't be any more Soros funding?[6]

Aside from the Soros initiatives, a handful of companies in Tirana, Albania's capital city, have established Internet connections. The first cybercafés and "cyberhalls" were established in Tirana in 1999, usually near high schools and universities, catering almost exclusively to young people and to journalists or aspiring journalists who cannot afford computers at home and do not have a computer or an Internet connection at their offices. One of these cyberhalls was described as having twenty "very up-to-date-looking computers . . . lined up on tables," where patrons could access the Internet for 120 lek (about 90 cents) an hour.[7] An operator of another cyberhall described his patrons as follows: "They come either before or after school and work, and the first question they ask once they set foot here is: 'Is there electricity?'"

Romania inherited a telecommunications infrastructure a step above Albania's, but it is still in poorer condition than those of all other nations in Eastern Europe (see Table 4.1). Because of its inadequate telecommunications capabilities, particularly when coupled with factional politics in the 1990s that failed to produce bold leadership of the economy, Romania also lags behind all but two of the other Eastern European nations (Albania and Macedonia) in Internet development. During the period 1996–2000 there were a number of indications that this situation might change significantly, largely because of three factors. First, elections in November 1996 brought to power a government, led by Emil Constantinescu, that pursued a more assiduous privatization policy and built closer relationships with the West than its predecessor governments, with an emphasis on investment in sectors related to information technology. Second, U.S. and European companies started to move into Romania with significant investments, primarily to take advantage of the highly skilled, well-educated, and technologically capable Romanian labor pool that is available at low wages. Third, government programs designed to modernize IT networks—including digitalization, expanded use of satellite technologies and fiber-optic cable, and improved Internet access capabilities—made it much more appealing, possible, and useful for companies and a small band of netizens (centered in the universities) to use the Internet productively.[8]

The optimism of the 1996–2000 period was diminished following the December 2000 elections, which returned to power a government led by Ion Iliescu, who during his previous seven years in power (1989–1996) had exhibited a lack of enthusiasm for both domestic economic reform and foreign investment.[9] Although the World Bank and the IMF have pressured the second Iliescu government to privatize government enterprises and implement reform, Iliescu has argued that his first priority will be to relieve the enormous economic strain on the population that resulted from previous reform efforts. Iliescu has tried to articulate a "vision" for economic growth and has indicated that he would like to lead Romania into the EU, but a European Commission report card published in December 2000 placed Romania dead last among Eastern European countries when assessing their economic progress.[10]

The December 2000 report indicated that more than 40 percent of Romania's 22.4 million people were living in poverty, with inflation galloping along at a rate of 40 percent per year. The one major attempt at privatization—selling the dominant telecommunications carrier, RomTelecom, to the Hellenic Telecommunications Organization (OTE) of Greece for $675 million in 1999—became the subject of a parliamentary investigation in 2000 following revelations of widespread corruption in the finalization of the privatization agreement. Because of the poor economy and previously botched privatization efforts, Romania's State Ownership Fund—the body in charge of auctioning off state assets—still had a portfolio of sixty-four large enterprises to sell in early 2001 but had been unable to sell them for lack of buyers. Shortly before Iliescu was returned to power, the Senate passed a resolution halting all privatization until the new government could establish a more coherent economic reform policy.

With more than 22 million people, Romania is the second-largest country in Eastern Europe, but it has a collection of bad legacies that held it back in the twentieth century. Both a Nazi ally and a member of the Soviet bloc, Romania lived with a "cult of personality" under Nicolae Ceauşescu—from 1965, when he became first secretary of the Romanian Workers Party, until his death in 1989—unlike any other during that period. Ceauşescu prided himself on being relatively independent from Moscow, but he was a great admirer of Joseph Stalin. He governed Romania through the secret police (Securitate), in a manner that led to what Vladimir Tismaneanu has called "isolation and desperation."[11] Romania was the only Eastern bloc nation where a communist government was overthrown with violence when Ceauşescu's own party cadres joined some sections of the military and large masses of the Romanian people to revolt; captured Ceauşescu, his wife, and some trusted associates; gave them a mock trial; and then executed them on Christmas Day 1989. Ceauşescu was succeeded by Iliescu, who abolished the Communist Party and formed a National Salvation Front (NSF) that was essentially a slightly transformed version of the old communists. Iliescu continued to rule through Securitate, with considerable repression of press freedoms, until the NSF was defeated in the 1996 elections.

The post-1996 government—led by former geology professor Emil Constantinescu—stopped persecution of critics and opponents, inaugurated an ambitious privatization program for state enterprises, and initiated Romania's negotiations to join the EU. The EU responded to this in late 1999 with an $800 million package of loans, grants, and other economic investments in the Romanian economy that made possible some IT initiatives that temporarily improved prospects for Internet growth. A survey by *Romania Business-Economics* in mid-1997 found that the years 1996–1997 marked a major turning point in the development of the Romanian Internet, with a vast expansion taking place particularly in the number of companies appearing on Web pages. Andreea Dutescu described the change as follows:

> Computer and telecommunication firms were among the first to have sites on the Internet . . . but other industries are now emerging. Manufacturing companies, banks, law firms, transport companies, hotels and consulting/marketing firms have sites displaying their products and services. Most of the universities and research centers are also present, and various Romanian embassies, government institutions, and chambers of commerce are starting to surface on the Internet. . . . Close to forty different Romanian newspapers and magazines, six radio and four television stations, are now online.[12]

In the final analysis, however, the Constantinescu government failed to effectively carry out its proposed transition to a reform agenda, producing widespread dissatisfaction with the economic sacrifices it attempted to exact from the population while failing to solve problems of corruption and fiscal indiscipline.[13]

Stemming from plans initiated in its IT reforms in the 1990s, in 2001 the Romanian government inaugurated a world-class "Romania Gateway" Internet portal, providing detailed descriptions of the economic, political, social, and cultural life of Romania as well as news, "transaction centers" for conducting business with Romanian organizations, and much else. The Romania Gateway project is part of Romania's larger privatization program and is financed jointly by the government and the

World Bank with the cooperation of a number of private companies (e.g., Microsoft Romania, Compaq Computer Romania, ICL Romania, and Oracle Romania).[14] In an effort to create more open access to Romania's financial records, in May 2000 the Romanian National Bank (RNB) inaugurated a series of Internet pages, accessible at www.bnro.ro, that include sections on macroeconomic indicators for Romania, data regarding monetary indicators, monetary and state security markets, major legislative measures governing RNB operations, specialized analyses, and much else.[15]

Until Romania's privatization program gathers steam, its government monopoly telecommunications provider, RomTelecom, is widely blamed for the country's inability to maintain a faster pace of Internet development. Nicolae Oaca described the situation:

> RomTelecom [has] faced strong criticism in the Romanian media. This criticism was sometimes sustained by politicians, so at the beginning of this year an increase in tariffs was renounced for 2000. . . . RomTelecom still has problems in dealing with its clients, in solving a long waiting list, in increasing its productivity and service quality, and in implementing a new corporate culture. However, the main problems come from the fact that in 1999 RomTelecom did not concentrate on diversifying its business portfolio. Fixed-line telephony is the majority of its business in an industry that worldwide is losing ground.[16]

In early 2000, Romania had 250 ISPs and 70,000 Internet users (0.3 percent of the population), with users paying average monthly access fees of U.S.$35 ($24 of which went to RomTelecom, in a country where the average monthly income is around $100). In September 1999 a Romanian investment fund backed by the European Bank for Reconstruction and Development (EBRD) paid $1.5 million for a 40 percent stake in Romania's most successful ISP (with 18,000 subscribers), PC-Net—the first foreign investment in a Romanian ISP.[17]

Perhaps the most significant development in the evolution of the Internet and IT in Romania was the willingness of U.S. and European companies to locate portions of their operations there when the Constantinescu government was in power (1996–2000). Some of these companies envisage Romania as a center of connectivity for other remote regions of Central/Eastern Europe, as is the case, for example, with a joint Romania-Moldova project of Global One Communications and Romania Logic Telecom that hopes eventually to introduce wireless

Internet services to areas along the Romania-Moldova border.[18] A less ambitious project was launched in June 2000—with support from the EU and a handful of multinational firms—by the Chambers of Commerce of Bekes County, in southeastern Hungary, and Arad County in western Romania, designed to provide a joint Internet-based information system for the two counties. This is the first time in history that the two counties have been able to initiate a joint economic relations project.[19]

The major attraction for foreign companies with interests in Romania has been the great number of engineers and other technologically trained Romanians willing to work for less than $5,000 per year at highly skilled jobs that would command annual salaries of $60,000 or more in the United States or Europe. The Romanian-American Capital and Trade Development Group, which has promoted the location of U.S. firms in Romania, estimates that Romania has twice the number of computer science graduates per capita as the United States and seven times the rate in India. Companies like Raytheon, Cambric Consulting of Draper, Utah, Harza Engineering of Chicago, and many others have found Romania particularly fertile for employing engineers because so many are competent in foreign languages (including English, Russian, and the major languages of Europe), are well trained, and tend to take more initiative and be more creative than engineers from Asia. The work being done for U.S. and European subsidiaries in Romania has been described by Donald McNeil:

> Engineers here [in Romania] worked simultaneously with teams in Princeton, New Jersey, and Thailand on the design of a new Thai power plant; the model could reside on a computer in any country and the Romanians could work on it while the Americans were eating breakfast and the Thais were fighting the evening rush hour. . . . [The Romanian engineers] helped design a polystyrene plant for Poland, a chemical plant for Equatorial Guinea, detergent and cigarette factories for Romania, and a Pringle's potato chip factory for Belgium. . . . Overhead is low in Romania and companies [save] money on computers and software licensing fees by having its [Romanian] work stations in use 18 hours a day (employees work nine-hour shifts).[20]

Because of their role in attracting foreign investment to Romania, engineers in computer-related fields have become a scare resource—with the result that they have been able to command larger and larger salaries, thereby contributing substantially to the widening gap between rich and poor. At the same time, Romanian computer specialists are increasingly being courted by companies in advanced IT societies—particularly Germany, the U.K., and other parts of Europe—and are leaving the country in larger numbers each year. The chairman of the Bulgarian Association of Information Technologies, Vassil Hristovich, expressed the fear of many Romanian leaders when he told the *Wall Street Journal* in late 2000 that Bulgaria's industry faced the prospect of being "left in a technological backwater," despite the presence in the country of first-rate engineers, because of the inability of the economy to sustain wage levels high enough to retain the most capable specialists.[21]

■ THE FORMER YUGOSLAVIA AND INTERNET DEVELOPMENT

Internet development in the former Yugoslavia has been dependent almost entirely on the extent to which the various parts of the former communist nation were able to avoid warfare in the 1990s. As indicated previously, Slovenia has managed to become one of the most advanced nations in Eastern Europe with regard to IT development, reflecting its healthy economy and close relationships with Western Europe. This has been possible for a relatively homogeneous nation of 1.9 million people (91 percent Slovene) because it escaped almost entirely any direct involvement in the wars that took place in the former Yugoslavia in the 1990s, having gained international recognition as an independent nation as soon as it declared independence in 1992. Other parts of the former Yugoslavia have not been so lucky.

■ *Croatia*

Croatia was able to gain international recognition as an independent nation in 1992, but its post-1992 transition has been complicated by its substantial Serb, Muslim, Hungarian, and Slovene populations (Croatia has 4.6 million people, of whom 3.5 million are Croat, 600,000 Serb, and the remainder primarily Muslim, Hungarian, and Slovene). Because of its large Serb population, Croatia was drawn into the conflicts that resulted from attempts by the Serb-dominated Yugoslav Federation to hold the old Yugoslavia together. Internet and other IT development in Croatia was held back in the 1990s by the stringencies of wartime budgets and lack of investment by European and U.S. companies repelled by the strident nationalism, democratic failures, and economic mismanagement and corruption associated with the regime of Croat strongman

Franjo Tudjman. A former general, Tudjman created a cult of personality around himself in the 1990s after he declared Croatia a separate nation in June 1991, turned on Bosnian Muslims in 1993 in an attempt to carve out a "greater Croatia," and in the period 1991–1995 successfully defended Croatia's borders by "liberating" territories held militarily by rebel Serbs opposed to Croatian independence. Tudjman's HDZ Party (Croatian Democratic Community) exercised strict control over the media, police, army, and courts right up until Tudjman's death in December 1999.[22]

Although Tudjman was not opposed to IT or Internet development, throughout his regime Croatia essentially remained dependent on the premodern telecommunications infrastructure inherited from the old Yugoslavia—largely because as long as Tudjman was in power, Croatia was not appealing to Western investors. Croatia was excluded from nearly all EU development programs in the 1990s, and its attempts to join the World Trade Organization were blocked by the United States. All of this could change rather dramatically in the first decade of the twenty-first century, since Tudjman's HDZ Party was defeated rather soundly in the January 3, 2000, general elections by a more liberal, democratic-minded, and Westward-leaning coalition. A new reform-minded president (Stipe Mesic), elected on February 7, 2000, has moved the country sharply in the direction of democracy and has demonstrated that he is much more amenable to building relationships with Western Europe and the United States—particularly in areas related to IT, global business, and communications.[23] In June 2000 the EU established a Joint Consultative Task Force, designed to provide Croatia with expertise and technical assistance in developing programs and to develop an agreement that might put Croatia on a par with other East European nations for eventual EU membership.[24] In May 2001 a survey by the *Financial Times* (London) journal *The Banker* examined a number of CEE economies and concluded that "Croatia is making steady progress."[25]

Observers have been cautious to point out, however, that neither the promotion of investment nor the development of IT and an Internet culture will be easy in Croatia because of the legacy of confusion and distrust left by Tudjman's privatization program, which has created an uncertain legal environment and widespread perceptions that privatization was designed only to benefit HDZ supporters.[26] The new government is attempting to impose painful but necessary financial measures to restore the economy, but these measures have weakened ties among the six political parties in the coalition led by Mesic. With severe balance-of-payments problems looming, Croatia's current account deficits of

6 percent or more in mid-2000 were considered unsustainable by most economists without large-scale foreign investment. A record unemployment rate of 21.3 percent in early 2000 was perhaps the most troubling aspect of both the economic and political environments in Croatia.[27]

▪ *Yugoslavia*

Information technology and the Internet are more developed in the new Yugoslavia (sometimes called the Yugoslav Federation of Serbia and Montenegro)—which includes Serbia, Montenegro, and Vojvodina—in part because the inherited telecommunications infrastructure around Belgrade (the capital of the new Yugoslavia) was the best the old Yugoslavia had to offer and in part because the new government has spent resources building an Internet capability it can use for propaganda and control of the population.[28] The new Yugoslavia's telecommunications infrastructure has also been less affected than those in other parts of the old Yugoslavia—even though Yugoslav Serbs have been heavily involved in almost all of the conflicts—since on-the-ground fighting has occurred primarily in territories other than the new Yugoslav Republic (primarily in Bosnia and Kosovo). Nevertheless, by 1999 it was estimated that fewer than 50,000 people in the new Yugoslavia had access to the Internet, with government ISPs providing very slow service because of their excessive dependence on terrestrial and nondigital lines.[29] Some private companies, including the largest bank in Serbia, have ISPs that are linked to satellites and thus provide much better service; and many organizations and individuals in present-day Yugoslavia are connected to the Internet through ISPs from outside the country, primarily in Amsterdam.

Control of the Internet and other forms of communication was of central importance to the new Yugoslavia's government in the 1990s because of its aggressive policies toward its non-Serb neighbors and non-Serb minorities. After the death of the avowed Stalinist president Josep Broz Tito (a Croat) in 1980, Yugoslavia became dominated by the Serbs, who quickly alienated the non-Serb populations by their strong assertions of Serbian nationalism. Following the election of Slobodan Milosevic as president of the Serbian Republic in 1988, the Serbs sought to unite most of the former Yugoslavia into a new Serbian-controlled nation by building political unity among Serb minorities while seeking dominance over other ethnic groups. The republics of Serbia, Montenegro, and Vojvodina (all with Serb majorities) have been able to remain banded together as the new Yugoslavia, but aspirations of Serb dominance have led either to secession or to civil wars in the former republics of the old communist Yugoslavia where Serbs are not a majority.

▪ *Bosnia*

Civil war in Bosnia-Herzegovina resulted in its secession as an independent nation (usually referred to as Bosnia) in 1992. In the Yugoslav republic of Kosovo, the Albanian population (constituting the most substantial minority, with 44 percent of the population) elected its own parliament and president and declared Kosovo an independent nation in May 1992 in the face of contested assertions by the Serbs that doing so was illegal. Kosovo has not gained international recognition as an independent nation, its future status unclear because of the protracted civil war that continues there in which the United States and Europe are deeply involved as part of NATO's 1999 decision to intervene. In an analysis of the role of the Internet in the wars in Bosnia and Kosovo, Florian Bieber found it had helped connect people from the various warring organizations across national divides but had also contributed to the spreading of rumors and animosity. He concluded that "both trends are important," but because the Internet is "a small and elite medium [it] should not be overestimated in assessing the impact on developments in Yugoslavia."[30]

The government of Slobodan Milosevic (1988–2000) tried to gain control over what is communicated on the Internet, with limited success. A 1999 law imposed a large tax on owners of satellite dishes and Internet users, but the government has been unable to identify Serbian Internet users with any precision. Because so many ISPs in Yugoslavia are located outside the country, it is impossible for the Yugoslav government to control all ISPs directly. In 1998 the Serbian government installed filters on the websites of the independent-minded media (radio stations and press) and the Serbian Academic Network (SAN), thus preventing Serbian Internet users from accessing those sites. But the media and SAN countered by setting up "mirror pages" (alternative Internet sites that provide the same information as the original sites).[31] By early 1999 the establishment of mirror pages had proceeded at such a prolific pace that the Serb government began to lift its filters on original sites, realizing its inability to block information from being disseminated. In July 2000 legislation took effect requiring that all ISPs contract with the Serbian government to determine the conditions of remaining in business.[32]

The most dramatic instance of an institution in present-day Yugoslavia successfully coping with government attempts to control the Internet has been the continued efforts of radio station "B92" to mobilize resistance to media censorship. B92 was formed in May 1989 when a small group of academics and journalists started broadcasting from a ramshackle room in Belgrade that the Central Committee of the Yugoslav Communist Party had previously used for storage. The station offers a mix of what it calls "objective news, urban music and irreverent critiques of the reigning powers of the moment."[33] The Internet became an important part of Radio B92 in 1994 when the station's leaders decided they would combine radio and Internet communications to "create a world parallel to that established by the regime in order to feel that we were living outside the authoritarian, criminal state." By 1999 the station's leaders estimated they had a "subscriber list" of more than 30,000 people, to whom they will send occasional e-mail messages to rally support against government intrusions on press freedoms and human rights. Much of the financial support for the B92 effort comes from the Soros-backed Open Society Institute.[34]

B92 gained international notoriety in 1996–1997 when government authorities cut the radio station's transmissions and the station reacted by simply redirecting its feeds to send live broadcasts over the Internet. After fifty-one hours the Milosevic government rescinded its ban on Radio B92, a measure that attracted worldwide attention and support for the station. By mid-1997, Radio B92 had established a network of thirty local radio stations in Serbia and Montenegro and, with the help of the British Broadcasting Company (BBC), had set up a "rebroadcasting scheme" that provides four hours of B92 news over the Internet from Belgrade, which the BBC then uplinks to the world through satellite. Local stations in Yugoslavia download the Internet broadcasts and rebroadcast them on the air.[35] In May 2000, however, B92's Internet operation—along with its radio, television, and newspaper offices—were seized by the government using armored personnel carriers and riot police with automatic weapons stationed in a number of buildings in downtown Belgrade.[36]

Although B92 was able to regain control of its property during the waning months of the Milosevic regime, it is still facing challenges to its operations from the new government elected in September 2000, led by Vojislav Kostunica.[37] Following rejection of its proposal to build a new TV studio in the building where it has operated since its inception, B92 issued a statement in January 2001 that it was being "forced to look for premises elsewhere."[38] Until it can find new facilities, B92 has no television studio of its own and has inadequate transmitting capabilities; therefore, it is able to reach only half of the Belgrade area with its programs. Its ability to maintain its Internet operations is also dependent on relocation to an appropriate physical space.[39]

▪ *Kosovo*

Since NATO's intervention in the civil war in Kosovo, beginning March 24, 1999, the war has come to be known in the international media as "the first Internet war" (note the claim of Azerbaijani and Armenian hackers and journalists to the epithet "the first cyberwar," mentioned earlier, and similar claims by India and countries in the Middle East). The extensive use of the Internet in areas of battle under wartime conditions has been possible largely because of new, powerful data scrambling technologies that keep the identity of online informants and reporters secret, thereby protecting them from authorities. One of the major initiatives of the Electronic Frontier Foundation (EFF)—in collaboration with the private company Anonymizer.com and the American Association for the Advancement of Science—has been the Kosovo Privacy Project, designed to get Anonymizer browsers into the hands of journalists, NGO leaders, human rights activists, and others in Kosovo engaged in reporting on the war.[40] Another innovation that has spread the use of the Internet under battlefield conditions has been the location of "Internet trailers" throughout Kosovo—maintained by news organizations, relief organizations, NGOs, and human rights organizations—in which computers and connectivity are provided. With sufficient funding and a secure location, Internet trailers can be set up fairly quickly, particularly where it is possible to establish a satellite link to the rest of the world.[41]

Using encryption technology, Internet trailers, and satellite links, journalists from around the world (including those in Eastern Europe) have been able to cover the Kosovo war in ways not possible in previous wars.[42] Leaders in Kosovo refugee camps have used the Internet to find and relocate refugees who have been separated from their families.[43] People in refugee camps have also been able to stay in touch with relatives through the Internet and the cell phone, both of which have helped many to arrange moves to locations beyond camp life.[44] A number of telecommunications, computer, and other IT companies—from Europe, the United States, and elsewhere—have contributed equipment, software, telecommunications lines, and in some cases funding to help build cyberspace networks to and from the refugee camps.[45] In addition, there have been a handful of attempts to create small private ISPs, such as Internet Project Kosovo (IPKO), led by an Albanian Kosovar, Akan Ismaili (a former employee of the United States Information Agency), and a number of U.S. human rights activists and leaders of U.S. and international NGOs.[46]

The war in Bosnia took place at an earlier stage of Internet development, so the impact of new Internet-related technologies was less great there than in Kosovo.[47] Moreover, the ravages of war and its aftermath have prevented the rebuilding of Bosnia's telecommunications infrastructure, thereby making it virtually impossible for the vast majority of people living in Bosnia-Herzegovina to learn and engage in an Internet culture.[48] Those who have been able to log on to the World Wide Web are usually dependent on direct access to military, government, or foreign organizations that are able to maintain the necessary computers, software, and links to secure telecommunications lines. Examples include an Internet program called Bosnia Link, established by military forces in Bosnia;[49] a project of the Villanova and Chicago-Kent University law schools to help journalists in Bosnia communicate with one another over the Internet;[50] and a second Villanova University project, led by Professor Henry H. Perritt Jr., designed to help the Bosnian legal community gain access to legal resources in cyberspace.[51] At least some of these efforts were inspired by President Bill Clinton's admonitions in his State of the Union Address in 1997 that "we must be shapers of events, not observers" and his subsequent support for voluntary efforts abroad like those that grew out of the Summit of Service Clinton attended in Philadelphia, at Villanova University, in April 1997.[52]

As in Kosovo, international relief agencies and NGOs working in Bosnia have found the Internet useful for organizing and keeping track of their activities, although they have had difficulties controlling the urge of some volunteers (and even local mission directors) to use the Internet to rally support for particular, sometimes partisan causes related to their work. The humanitarian aid group Oxfam, for example, took a stand in defense of Bosnia's Muslims against the Serbs on its Web page in 1995, prompting the president of the International Committee of the Red Cross (ICRC) to propose a code for humanitarian organizations that "aid not be used to further a political or religious viewpoint, or as an instrument of government foreign policy."[53] Western journalists have reported widespread feelings among people living in Bosnia and elsewhere in Yugoslavia that a combination of new journalistic styles of reporting on the Internet and the use of the Internet by private groups has tended to misinform and give a dramatically false impression of events on the ground in Eastern Europe.[54]

▪ *Macedonia*

Full Internet connectivity was established for the first time in Macedonia on June 15, 1995, by MARnet, a national academic and research network organized with the assistance of the Soros-supported Open Society Institute (OSI) Internet Program. Members of the network include the only two universities in Macedonia—Skopje and Bitola—as well as the Macedonian Academy of Sciences and Arts, a handful of independent and corporate research institutions, and some government ministries and agencies. Sporadic financing has been provided by the government and by nascent attempts to develop advertising.[55] In 1997 OSI sponsored a national campaign to provide connectivity to medical centers, secondary schools, NGOs, and libraries—particularly in the area around Skopje—by providing grants for modems, e-mail/Internet servers, and connectivity. Since 1998 OSI has been working with the Macedonian Foundation to try to connect "civil society institutions" throughout the country to the Internet.[56]

Significant future development of IT, telecommunications infrastructure, and the Internet in Macedonia will be dependent on the ability of the government elected in November 1999 to straddle many diplomatic fences at the same time to allay fears of instability that have been prominent among international business and other international organizations, especially the EU. Macedonia became essentially an independent nation in early 1992, although it was not given international recognition until two years later, largely because of Greek insistence that it be recognized under a name other than Macedonia.[57] Macedonia's economy has been faced with desperate conditions because of the highly volatile nature of its relationships with its four neighboring countries. (1) Greece has imposed an economic blockade on Macedonia (estimated to have resulted in losses of $1 million or more) in continued protest against the new nation's use of the word *Macedonia.* (2) Macedonia's large Albanian minority (at least 22 percent of the population, although the Albanians claim 40 percent) has called for autonomy in the westernmost portion of Macedonia where it resides and has made no secret of its dream of a future "Greater Albanian state" that would include Kosovo and the Albanian portions of Macedonia. (3) Milosevic's

Belgrade regime expropriated all of the weaponry and other military equipment in Macedonia, as well as other economic and financial assets, in the years just prior to Macedonian independence; Macedonia's trade with the new Yugoslavia (its principal export market) has since collapsed.[58] (4) To the east, significant political groups in Bulgaria continue to claim large portions of Macedonian territory, consistent with a historic Bulgarian view that "the Macedonians are ethnic Bulgarians separated from their motherland only by an artificial frontier and an ersatz Macedonian language," although the Bulgarian government has officially relinquished these claims.[59]

The president of Macedonia since the November 1999 elections, Boris Trajkovski, is a forty-three-year-old United Methodist pastor who graduated from Skopje University and went on to become Macedonia's deputy foreign minister for nine years in the 1990s.[60] He hopes to prevent the secession of Macedonia's Albanian community by building bridges between the two communities, a feat that for a time appeared to have some credibility since Trajkovski did secure electoral support from both sides by gaining the backing of Arben Xhaferi, leader of the main Albanian political party (the Democratic Party of Albanians). But an insurgency launched by rebel Albanians in late February in the border areas inflamed relations between the Macedonian Slavs, who make up almost 70 percent of Macedonia, and Macedonian Albanians, who account for most of the rest of the population, resulting in massive violence and migrations of people along ethnic lines in a manner reminiscent of the Bosnia and Kosovo conflicts.[61]

Prior to the 2001 insurgency Trajkovski had initiated a lobbying campaign in Western Europe designed to get European leaders to accept Macedonia as a serious candidate for membership in both NATO and the EU, with the hope that this might increase possibilities for securing much-needed investment in the economy.[62] Toward that end, the Trajkovski government launched a privatization program in 2000, including the sale of 51 percent of Macedonia's previously government-owned monopoly fixed-line and mobile telecommunications company, Makedonski Telekommunikacii (Maktel), to a consortium led by Hungary's MATAV for $341.3 million, with the further agreement that MATAV would invest $241 million in additional funds to operate Maktel over the two-year period February 2001 to February 2003.[63] The Trajkovski government is also lobbying international agencies and other potential investors to locate their offices and venture capital in Skopje.

▪ INTERNATIONAL REGIME ISSUES IN THE FSU AND CENTRAL/EASTERN EUROPE

With few exceptions, the countries of Central/Eastern Europe and the FSU have not yet been involved to any significant degree in Internet development, in the invention of Internet technology, or in the formation or maintenance of the international regime for the Internet. Matters that lie at the core of the regime, such as the establishment of the Internet's technical standards and norms, the principles and rules adopted to ensure its daily functioning internationally, and the procedures used to ensure cooperation among providers and users or to resolve conflicts between them, all have thus far been established and promoted by organizations located outside Central/Eastern Europe and Eurasia. For the most part, such organizations have been located in the United States and Europe—originally in the U.S. Department of Defense, the National Science Foundation, and in some of the offspring of these initial creators of the Internet. Especially in the 1990s, private corporations, private associations, and an increasing number of international organizations have attempted to shape the regime in one direction or another in pursuit of their own interests.

The FSU states in particular have had little to say about the ways in which the international regime for the Internet has been created and shaped. Woefully behind in information technology and without reliable networks for e-commerce or even in most cases for simple e-mail, the FSU nations have had limited detailed awareness of the technological and policy advances that have made possible the functioning of the Internet at the global level. Although a minuscule number of scientists and computer experts have managed to maintain skills and contacts at world-class levels, policymakers and economic leaders in the FSU nations have been so concerned with the development of the economy's broader infrastructure and resources that they have had little time or money to train and develop the kinds of human resources necessary to become significant players in international regime formation and maintenance.[64] Literally no indigenous IT companies in any of the FSU states have played a major role in shaping global Internet regime issues. The states have no powerful ISPs or regional associations of ISPs, and few people from the FSU are members of key private international Internet organizations (like ISOC and the IETF)—reflecting both the relatively small number of users and their lack of funds for joining international organizations.

One key area of international regime formation that illustrates the dichotomy that has evolved between the emerging international regime for the Internet and the FSU states is the widely acknowledged principle in advanced IT societies that the Internet regime, like other international communications regimes, should be based on a "free flow of information."[65] A sharp contrast also exists between the FSU states (with the exception of the Baltics) and most of Eastern Europe, which has been much more comfortable in accepting the free flow of information as an Internet regime norm (the major exceptions in Eastern Europe are the parts of the former Yugoslavia and the Balkans most heavily involved in military conflicts). A second key area of international regime formation that reveals sharp contrasts between the FSU states (again with the exception of the Baltics) and most Eastern European nations (again with the exception of war-torn areas) is their degree of willingness to conform to regime principles, standards, rules, and procedures being developed to regulate and build cooperation in the international business and commercial arenas. Primarily because of their desire to join the European Union as full members, the Eastern European states have been much more willing than the FSU states to enact legislation and establish administrative regulations and policies consistent with those found in Western Europe, the United States, and other advanced IT societies.

The remainder of this chapter will outline some of the more salient issues that have emerged in the FSU and Central/Eastern Europe relating to both of these aspects of the international Internet regime.

▪ Free Flow of Information

When the FSU states and former Soviet bloc nations of Eastern Europe emerged from a half century of communism, they were overwhelmed with advice from the West regarding their transitions to democracy and a market economy. Underlying much of this advice was the premise that open access to information is a critical component of the political life of democracies.[66] As Erik Herron has pointed out, each of these nations confronted three major issues that have always been inherent challenges for international communications regimes:

1. Each nation had to choose the types of information that would be made available to the public and the types that would remain secret, which in turn raised major questions about confidentiality

for security or commercial reasons, the degree of protection of confidentiality that should be accorded to policymakers and party members who had run the government in the old communist days, and the adoption of new policies to protect the privacy of individuals into the future.

2. Each state had to determine what information would be collected and how to collect it under the postcommunist governments—including information about the socioeconomic characteristics of the population, population movements, participation in the political process, and other sensitive matters.

3. States had to decide to whom information collected by the government would be disseminated or made available.[67]

Based on an elaborate index he developed, Herron concluded in mid-1999 that Russia and the Baltic states were the only countries in the FSU that had begun to develop Internet capabilities and policies responding to these three challenges.[68] Herron's index combines scales for the number and proportion of government offices that have developed Internet sites, the range and quality of government information provided by those sites, ease of access to the sites, and provision of contact information at the sites. In Herron's study Georgia and Ukraine constitute a second tier of FSU nations with some Internet capability in these regards, but neither is yet approaching the quality, range, and scope of Russian and Baltic websites in responding to the challenges of developing information policies appropriate to a democratic politics. All other FSU nations fall into a third tier, which is still quite unprepared to establish modern IT communications policies and effect Internet development, and a fourth tier (consisting of only two countries, Tajikistan and Turkmenistan), which is totally unprepared.

Although the Baltic nations are in step with Western notions that value a free flow of information in future Internet use, Russia and all other FSU countries have indicated that their perceptions of what constitutes a free flow of information will be at variance with this fundamental principle of the Internet regime. In Russia the successor to the KGB—the Federal Security Service (FSB)—has written a package of "bylaws," issued in the form of departmental orders and regulations, that allow it to conduct surveillance of websites without a prosecutor's warrant or a court ruling whenever the security agency is suspicious of criminal activity, tax evasion, or corruption.[69] Known as SORM-2 (a system for operational and investigative activities at documentary electronic communication centers), the FSB bylaws run directly counter to Russia's basic "law on communications," adopted in the State Duma (parliament) and signed by the president of the Russian Federation in 1993, which was designed to provide and protect a minimal right to privacy.[70]

Beginning in early 1998, the FSB began asking ISPs to sign documents introducing SORM-2 at ISP communications centers at ISP expense. Under these arrangements Russian ISPs are to provide to the FSB a communication line, a portable control panel, a communication scheme with all of the passwords, and a full list of all the ISP's clients and their personal passwords.[71] When one major ISP, Bayard Slavia Communications, refused to sign the FSB documents on grounds that they violated the constitution of the Russian Federation and the 1993 law on communications, Bayard began to encounter a series of problems with various government agencies. According to a *Moscow News* report:

> [Bayard's] license was not taken away—that would have been too blatantly unlawful. Instead . . . there were endless inspections by the fire security service, the State Communications Inspectorate, public utilities, electric companies, and so forth. The automatic telephone exchange where Bayard leased premises announced all of a sudden that it wanted its premises back—at once. . . . Then came more serious problems. First [Bayard was] cut off from the Internet for six weeks . . . ostensibly because they had failed to pay their bills for using communication channels. It was only after numerous letters and appeals to various organizations and threats of legal action that access [was] restored. Meanwhile, Bayard lost half of its clients.[72]

A second major instance where an FSU government has thrown its weight solidly against attempts to develop an Internet regime based on a free flow of information occurred in Belarus in 1997, when the Belarus government levied a $3 million fine against the Soros Foundation. The OSI of the Soros Foundation had been prominent throughout the 1990s in its attempts to develop guidelines for an Internet regime in the FSU that would promote civil societies and democratic institutions. By 1997, OSI had spent more than $44 million in Russia and $13 million in Belarus in support of these objectives. In March 1997, however, the government charged the U.S. executive director of the Soros Foundation in Belarus with "interference in domestic affairs" after attending an opposition party rally, and he was subsequently expelled from the country.

On April 23 Belarus tax inspectors concluded that nineteen grants made by the Soros Foundation were not covered by the foundation's tax-exempt documents, and a $3 million fine was assessed.[73]

A third instance in which an FSU government has set itself against development of a free flow of information as a principle for the Internet regime was the assignment by presidential decree of a monopoly of all Internet services to Ukrtelekom, the Ukrainian monopoly telecommunications provider. As Anton Nosik has pointed out in his analysis of this measure, state monopoly of Internet access—the predominant pattern throughout the former Soviet Union—is considered normal by rulers of almost all of the formerly totalitarian FSU societies, but a continuation of this pattern also makes it extremely difficult to effect change in the direction of more civil societies and more democratic communications structures.[74] In the postcommunist era, Nosik explained, attempts by authorities in the FSU states to control the contents of communications in cyberspace are being buttressed by their ability to consolidate the entire Internet infrastructure into the hands of a certain group of companies (or in the case of Ukraine, a government company) favored by the political establishment.

▪ *International Business and Commercial Aspects of Regime Formation*

As discussed earlier, most of the nations of Eastern Europe have been able to enact laws and develop policies relating to Internet use that are much more consistent with the international regime principle of a free flow of information than has been the case in all of the FSU states except the Baltics. At the same time, the nations of Eastern Europe that have not been directly involved in recent military conflicts in the former Yugoslavia and the Balkans have been able to initiate significant policy change toward conformity to the international business and commercial aspects of regime formation. In this latter arena, most of Eastern Europe also differs sharply from all of the FSU states except the Baltics.

The major impetus for the movement of Eastern European states toward international regime norms has been the prospect of their joining the European Union, with all of the benefits that would accompany membership. Of the thirteen countries currently negotiating with the EU for eventual membership, ten are from Eastern Europe (the other three are Turkey, Cyprus, and Malta). The Czech Republic, Estonia, Hungary, Poland, and Slovenia opened formal negotiations in March 1998. Bulgaria, Latvia,

Lithuania, Romania, and Slovakia began negotiations in January 2000. To qualify for admission to the EU, countries will need to adopt twenty-five Internet regime–related EU directives, including several that require substantial privatization of national telecom providers and others that will require independent telecom regulatory authorities. As indicated in discussions of each of the Eastern European countries in this chapter, the process of restructuring economies and telecommunications systems—particularly as they relate to Internet development—is fraught with political conflict and partisanship.

For most of Eastern Europe, unlike the FSU states, there is still a societal consensus to build toward international regime norms, but that has not lessened the intensity of the political debate surrounding the implementation of specific legislation.[75] Although most of the pressure to adopt international regime norms has come from the EU, the United States has been highly supportive of the effort. Indeed, when EU enlargement commissioner Gunter Verheugen stated in late 1999 that "the most advanced" applicant countries could be admitted to the EU as early as 2003, financial leaders in the United States responded that this pace is too slow, pointing to the speed at which NATO acted to take in three new Eastern European members (Hungary, the Czech Republic, and Poland) as an alternative model of integration.[76] But the EU has stood firm on its requirement that any candidate country admitted must enact and implement *all* EU rules. Enlargement negotiations therefore consist essentially of determining how far along a given applicant is in meeting requirements, with "transition periods" granted to allow members extra time to restructure their economies and telecom systems. Each of the Eastern European countries is confronting problems in developing and implementing new laws, and estimates of the cost of integrating CEE nations have ballooned, with the result that a series of 1999, 2000, and 2001 assessment reports by the EU Enlargement Committee have remained firmly committed to the original EU resolve that all ten countries "have a long way to go before successfully aligning their telecommunications laws with EU regulations."[77]

■ NOTES

1. See the host count in www.ripe.net and information provided by the United States Agency for International Development (USAID) at www.info.usaid.gov.

2. *Keesing's Contemporary Archives,* vol. 43 (January 1997), p. 17.

3. Ibid., p. 18.

4. Vega Holdings—a conglomerate with a wide range of operations—was described in the *Financial Times* (London), February 1, 1997, as a "state within a state." For an analysis of the pyramid schemes, see Abrahams, "The Albanian House of Cards."

5. For a description of the program, see the Open Society Institute–Internet Program website at www.soros.org/internet/foundations/ALBANIA.html.

6. Quoted from an interview with Jonathan Peizer conducted by Geert Lovink in *First Monday: Peer-Reviewed Journal on the Internet,* iss. 4 (April 1999), available at www.firstmonday.dk/issues/issue4_2/interview/index.html.

7. See "Tirana's Link," pp. 9–10. All quotations in this paragraph are from this source.

8. For an analysis of recent improvements in Romania's connectivity, see Serban, "Wired Romania," p. 6, available at www.novell.com/nwc/nov.97. Serban and others point out that major obstacles still need to be overcome if Internet use is to surpass that in other parts of Eastern Europe, including slow and unreliable telecommunications service, the high cost of computers (a modest PC presently costs more than 1,100 percent of the average monthly salary), and rampant piracy of software and intellectual property.

9. Russell, "Romania Places Future," p. 18.

10. Karnitschnig, "As Romania Nears," p. B12A. Iliescu's vision is outlined in Johnston, "Romanian President."

11. The quote is from a Tismaneanu presentation to the Fulbright seminar at the University of Maryland in April 2000. For more detail, see Tismaneanu, *Fantasies of Salvation.*

12. Andreea Dutescu, available at www.isr.co.ro/publications/rapid.fire.htm. A description of earlier stages of Romanian Internet development appears in Woodard, "Transylvania."

13. Karnitschnig, "Romanian Vote," p. A23.

14. The project is detailed in a July 6, 2000, report of the independent Mediafax News Agency, available in English in "Website."

15. "Romanian National Bank."

16. Oaca, "Romania," p. 94.

17. McMillan, "Romania: Wireless Spurs," p. 92. See also ibid., p. 95. Statistics on Romanian Internet use, updated to April 2001 with comparisons to Western Europe, are available in "South Eastern Europe: Digital Divide or Digital Opportunity?" pp. 2–6.

18. McMillan, "Romania: Wireless Spurs," p. 94.

19. MTI News Agency (Budapest) report of June 22, 2000, available in English in *BBC Worldwide Monitoring,* June 22, 2000.

20. McNeil, "Opportunities in a Rusting Romania," p. 9.

21. Quoted in Hamilton, "Balkan Information-Technology Firms," p. 1.

22. An excellent article on the cult of personality surrounding Tudjman is Jordan, "Croatians Ready," p. 8. See also Erlanger, "Croatia Elects," p. A12.

23. The potential impact of the elections in Croatia is analyzed in "New Start?" pp. 50–51. See also Smith, "Croatia," pp. A23, A28, and "Premier 'Moderately Optimistic.'"

24. "Croatia's New Beginning," pp. 248–249. See also Wright, "Croatia."

25. Timewell, "With Many of the World's Economies," p. 4.

26. For privatization efforts in Croatia in the 1990s, see Cohen, "Embattled Democracy," pp. 89 ff. Competition among foreign investors is analyzed in "Croatian ISPs."

27. Langenkamp, "Free of Its Iron-Fisted Rule," p. 8. See also "Hard Choices," pp. 48–49.

28. Commenting on the quality of Yugoslav Internet development, the *Economist* (London) described official websites as "surprisingly slick" and the Yugoslav government's English-language websites as "well organised and the English . . . almost impeccable." See "The War," p. 8.

29. Ironically, one of the major reasons Internet use is so low in present-day Yugoslavia is Western bans on sale of computer equipment and Internet services there. See Engardio et al., "Activists Without Borders," pp. 144–146, and Brown, "After More Sanctions," p. 7.

30. Bieber, "Cyberwar or Sideshow?" p. 128.

31. For a discussion of government efforts to control Internet sites in present-day Yugoslavia, see Moffett, "Big Brother Watches."

32. Speculation about the possible consequences of this measure appears in "Serbia: Government to Take over Control."

33. Matic and Pantic, "War of Words," p. 34. Quotations in this paragraph are from this source.

34. See Pantic, "Internet in Serbia," available at www.firstmonday.dk/issues/issue2_4/pantic/index.html. Drazen Pantic, one of the key founders of B92, is a professor of mathematics at Belgrade University.

35. As soon as the Kosovo war started in March 1999, the Milosevic government took over the Radio B92 Web address and began to publish government propaganda on the website. Radio B92 then set up a new website under another Web address, and cautioned those who logged on, "Don't believe anyone, not even us," pointing out that many people had been duped into thinking the station was supporting the Serb government after hearing broadcasts traced to news items from the captured website. See Matic and Pantic, "War of Words."

36. Smith, "Belgrade Shuts TV Station."

37. For an analysis of the Kostunica government in Yugoslavia and its relationships to new governments in the provinces of Serbia and Montenegro, see Gall, "What's Ahead in Yugoslavia," p. A8.

38. "B92 Denied Permission," p. 1.

39. B92's hardships over the years have been analyzed as a "saga component of Symbolic Convergence Theory" in Csapo-Sweet and Shields, "Explicating the Saga," pp. 316–334.

40. The technology used in the Kosovo Privacy Project has been described in *Interactive Week* as follows: "Visitors can send encrypted messages to the

Anonymizer sites without fear of being identified easily. From there, the Anonymizer strips out records of the path the e-mail took to get to the Web site and sends the message to the appropriate newsgroup or e-mail box. . . . To be sure, a highly sophisticated eavesdropping regime can trace which local users have visited the site. But short of seizing the computers used to write the messages in the first place, there's virtually no way authorities can know what it is people are writing." See Rodger, "Kosovo Project," p. 1.

41. The role of the U.S. military in setting up telecommunications, computer, and Internet capabilities in support of tactical and humanitarian operations in and around Albania, Macedonia, and Yugoslavia (particularly Kosovo) is detailed in Brewin, "DOD Boosts Telecom," pp. 3–5.

42. Detailed descriptions of the role of the Internet in reporting the Kosovo conflict appear in Lasica, "Conveying the War," pp. 76–79; Moses and Strupp, "Press Mobilizes," pp. 9–11; and Woodard, "No Heroes," pp. 8–14.

43. For a description of the process, see Guernsey, "For Kosovo's Scattered Refugees," p. G9.

44. Jordan, "New Refugee Aid Worker," p. 7.

45. Power, "For Refugees, a Cellular Lifeline," pp. 34–37.

46. For a description of the IPKO project, see Shapley, "Rebuilding the Web in Kosovo's Ashes," p. H14.

47. The civil war in Bosnia resulted from Bosnia's secession from the old Yugoslavia in 1992, when Bosnia became an independent nation supported by Bosnian Muslims and Croats, who had voted overwhelmingly for independence, whereas the Serb minority (40 percent of the population) opposed it. For an analysis of the factors that led to Bosnia's secession and its failure to successfully establish a stable new nation, see Burg, "Bosnia Herzegovina," pp. 122–145.

48. Although organized fighting in Bosnia stopped in 1995 as a result of the Dayton accords, hammered out with U.S. intervention in the negotiating process, Bosnia's 3.2 million people were left partitioned among three warring ethnic groups, often called "entities" (Serbs, Croats, and Muslims), leaving Serbia's ethnic cleansing policy a fait accompli. Massive movements of people from the refuge areas of the three entities and into neighboring states, combined with unfair elections and severe economic deterioration, have made it necessary for NATO to maintain forces in Bosnia to keep the peace. Much of the administration of the country is being shepherded by UN organizations, NGOs, and relief agencies. For a recent overall analysis, see Mandelbaum, *The New European Diasporas*.

49. Schmitt, "Military Puts Bosnia on the Web," p. 14.

50. Machlis, "Intranet Project," pp. 57–58.

51. Guernsey, "Villanova Effort," p. A33.

52. For a discussion of Clinton's influence, see Ingis, "Law Students with Laptops," p. 19.

53. Prince, "World's Aid Groups," p. 6; see also Kiernan, "Net Search Could Reunite Refugees," pp. 7–10.

54. Steven Erlanger of the *New York Times,* for example, quoted a Yugoslav student, Vuk Micovic, who had found reports on the Internet that "8,000 to 12,000 Albanian refugees were crossing the border (from Kosovo into Macedonia) every hour." Micovic pointed out that "first, it's impossible to know. But in 10 hours that's 100,000 people, and in four days that's a million people. And in seven days, all of Kosovo is empty." See Erlanger, "Even Milosevic," p. A10. See also "The War on the Web," p. 8.

55. For a description of the development of the Internet in Macedonia, see Thurber and Djonova-Popova, "The Spirit of the Internet."

56. For more detailed descriptions of these and other Soros activities, see the Soros website at www.soros.org/internet/foundations/FORMER-YUGOS-REPUB. html.

57. Thus the name under which it has been recognized by the United States is Former Yugoslav Republic of Macedonia, one of Greece's preferred appellations. Greece views the word *Macedonia* as Greek and fears the creation of an independent nation with that name will promote irredentism among people in Greece's northernmost province, which also has the name Macedonia. The U.S. Post Office uses FYR Macedonia as the official address of the new nation. An excellent discussion of the media's role in fueling Macedonian nationalism appears in Demertzis, "Media and Nationalism," pp. 26–51. For an analysis of Macedonia's international position, see Harris, "Macedonia: The Next Domino?" pp. 42–46.

58. The Serb minority in Macedonia (at least 7 percent of the population, although the Serbs claim 10–12 percent) has become more nationalistic since independence and has sought increased influence in Macedonian government circles, causing the Macedonian population (65 percent of the population) to fear intervention from Serbia in defense of Serbian interests. See Harris, "Macedonia: The Next Domino?" p. 45.

59. Ibid., p. 43. See also "Europe: Fresh Hope."

60. A biography of Trajkovski appears in "Briefs: The World," pp. 29–30.

61. Gall, "A Trail of Misery," p. A8. See also Kaminski, "Macedonia Moves to Quell the Albanian Rebels," p. A12.

62. "Europe: Methodical Man," pp. 59–60.

63. See "Matav Purchases," p. 24, and "Macedonia's Communications Minister."

64. This was the conclusion of a major conference on Internet developments in the FSU states sponsored by the Electronic Frontier Foundation in 1998. For a summary, see www.soros.org/internet/policy/parliament_human_rights.html.

65. For a detailed analysis of this principle as it was created and evolved over the past century and more, see Zacher and Sutton, *Governing Global Networks,* especially pp. 127–211.

66. A summary of many of these recommendations, outlining international norms among democracies relating to a free flow of information, was put together by the so-called Blue Ribbon Commission—composed of Hungarian leaders, expatriate Hungarians, and international advisers—as part of a project

to develop a "plan of action" for the newly democratic Hungary in 1989. Although they focused on Hungary, the recommendations (with adaptations) were taken up by groups in other nations as well. See *Hungary: In Transition.*

67. Herron, "Democratization," p. 57.

68. Ibid., pp. 61 ff.

69. For an analysis of the FSB as compared with the KGB and of a Russian website that attempts to cover FSB activities, see McGrane, "A Web Site."

70. An outline of the bylaws appears in Borzo, "Russia Considering." See also Moffett, "Russia: Secret Policy," and Caryl, "Big Brother Covets All the E-Mail," pp. 46–47.

71. Yevreinov, "Encrypt Your Messages." See also Moudrak and Zimmerman, "Newsfront," pp. 11–14.

72. Yevreinov, "Encrypt Your Messages."

73. A detailed analysis of the incident appears in Miller, "Belarus Fines Soros," p. A3. The Soros Foundation has refused to pay the fine and has charged that the Belarus government is simply interested in closing down the foundation and its work in the country.

74. Nosik, "How to Ban the Internet."

75. Some of the issues involved in the debate are discussed in a case study of Eastern Europe in Chamoux, "After Privatization: Neocolonialism?" pp. 343–350.

76. Pond, "Come Together," pp. 11–12.

77. deBony, "EU Applicants." See also Kaminski and Williamson, "EU Balks," p. A22; Wagstyl, "Eastern and Central Europe," p. A13; and Dempsey, "Adding New States," p. 2.

7

China and India
as Potential Internet Superpowers

In contrast to the more than 100 countries located in regions discussed in previous chapters, two of the less developed countries (LDCs)—China and India—merit special attention as particularly important actors in global information technology regimes. Together comprising almost 40 percent of the earth's population, each of these countries has more people than the vast area stretching across Russia through Central/Eastern Europe and Western Europe. Or to use an even more dramatic comparison, China and India together have *more than twice* the population of the entire Western Hemisphere. Many analysts are predicting a major shift in international power toward Beijing and New Delhi in the twenty-first century, but there is an additional significant reason for focusing on the future development of these two Asian giants with regard to the topics covered in this volume.[1] In information technology matters, especially with regard to development of the Internet, both nations are determined to pursue alternative ways of structuring the world than those being established by emerging international regimes.

With regard to computer networking, China is expending considerable resources on efforts to wall off significant portions of the global Internet from domestic use and to create a colossal countrywide intranet that would be more amenable to control by central government and party leaders than the shared global Internet most of the world knows. India is less interested in creating a firewall between itself and the rest of the world, but its leadership has established as a major goal that the nation become an "Internet superpower."[2] India's aspiration stems in part from its overall quest for superpower status, but it is also driven in significant ways by the desire of Indian leaders to adapt Internet functioning to meet India's domestic needs and ensure its security. In a separate manuscript I have explored in detail the policies of China and India toward the Internet and information technology in the context of their rivalry and international power aspirations.[3] The present chapter summarizes some of the conclusions from that study in a more concise manner, with particular attention to their relevance for concerns of this volume.

■ BASIC PRC POLICY: ENCOURAGEMENT AND CONTROL

Encouraging the growth of the Internet has been part of Beijing's conscious policies, dating from the early 1980s, to build a first-rate national information technology infrastructure. Much of this has been done on an almost commercial basis, with subscribers paying government fees that in turn generate revenue to build more infrastructure and provide more fee-generating services. China's telecommunications infrastructure grew at an annual rate of more than 30 percent throughout much of the 1990s, with growth driven by technocrats and economists who perceive IT as the key to economic development as well as political stability and continuity.[4]

An important aspect of the Internet's introduction into China is the way in which it has been linked to what Chinese leadership calls the "informatization" process, which is designed to use information technology to simultaneously decentralize decisionmaking and enable the central government to exercise more effective control over policymaking in the vast and increasingly decentralized provinces of China. This concept is somewhat akin to the idea prevalent in the USSR in the 1980s that IT could be used to make central planning more effective and to better manage the Soviet economy. A major study by the University of Arizona's Mosaic Group has attributed the failure of the Soviet strategy to the inefficiency of Moscow's version of centralized control and the limitations of Soviet technology.[5]

China's communist leaders are convinced that their situation is different from that of the former USSR and that they can develop an informatization strategy that will succeed where the Soviets failed. A major reason for this conviction is that China's party and government leaders have been able to exercise almost unprecedented control over the country's intranet activities while facilitating those aspects of international networking Chinese leaders consider positive. In contrast to all other large nations, the PRC has been able to channel almost all Internet participation at the international level through one small physical and bureaucratic bottleneck controlled by a single government monopoly telecommunications provider, China Telecom, which has dominated China's Internet development since its inception. Although other interconnecting networks in China are directly linked to the global Internet through international leased circuits, China Telecom's "China-Net" is far larger than all others combined and in effect has dominant control over Internet technology throughout the country with relatively little competition.[6]

Prior to 2001 only six networks had been granted licenses by the State Council to lease international circuits (lines on the "foreign leg" are leased from a number of international carriers, including AT&T, Global One, and Teleglobe).[7] But all six are required to lease their Chinese network segment—connecting them to their international lines—from China Telecom, and none of the other networks is allowed to construct its own physical international lines. This has given China Telecom considerable control over all international Internet activities from the earliest days of the Internet's introduction into the PRC. Possibilities for central government control were further solidified in early 2000 with the completion of a Network Access Point (NAP) project, under the direction of China Telecom, that makes it possible for computers within China to communicate readily with one another without having to transmit messages outside the country and back. This project is extremely popular with Internet users because it means the time required to upload or download materials is considerably reduced much of the time, with a reduction as well in the costs of remaining online for extensive periods, but it also contracts the bottleneck connecting the PRC with the global Internet and enhances the government's capability to monitor Internet communications.

China Telecom's control over Internet technology was further strengthened during the 1990s because it had a virtual monopoly to sell Internet access on the local loop on commercial terms to other Internet service providers (ISPs). Both ChinaNet and GBNet were legally empowered to sell such access in 1999, but since only China Telecom had an extensive infrastructure in place it was effectly given a monopoly position, which it used to extract large fees for services. Most ISPs in China (520 were licensed to operate in mid-2000) pay rental fees directly to ChinaNet for use of its facilities, with fees accounting for nearly 80 percent of the ISP's operating expenses in mid-2000 (for comparison, U.S. rental fees averaged only 5 percent of ISP expenses at the time). Foreign corporations and joint ventures have been prohibited by Chinese law from being ISPs and have been banned from participation in all telecommunications services, a policy scheduled to change in 2002 after China officially becomes a member of the WTO and as a condition of membership will be required to allow more liberal foreign investment in telecommunications.

Prior to 2001, substantial revenue from fees allowed China Telecom to add to its infrastructure at an almost geometrically increasingly rate, thus enhancing its monopoly position. That position was further reinforced by a payment system that linked rental costs to the amount of revenue received per line. As Peter Lovelock explained:

> Instead of rental declining with volume, it rises, making an ISP less profitable the more it increases its user base or usage. Given a playing field tilted so steeply against them, most independent ISPs have not only found it impossible to compete with ChinaNet, they have found it impossible to stay in business without receiving some degree of assistance or lenience from China Telecom. . . . So, much as many people might like to think the Internet is part of a bottom-up explosion of individualism in China, it is not. It is instead a highly centralised network, largely running through a single carrier, China Telecom, and a monolithic infrastructure.[8]

Within the PRC's political and administrative structures, the Ministry of Information Industries (MII) has full authority over China's international interconnections for information networks, including the Internet. The MII was created in March 1998 out of the State Council's former Steering Committee on National Information Infrastructure, which had been charged with responsibility for operating the Internet under Order 195 in 1996. Order 195 was intended to end any speculation that the Chinese government would maintain anything resembling a decentralized or "hands-off" attitude toward control of the Internet, as these excerpts make clear:

> The State is in charge of overall planning, national standardization, graded control, and the development of all areas related to the Internet. . . .
>
> Any direct connection with the Internet must be channeled via international ports established and maintained by the Ministry of Post and Telecommunication. No group or individual may establish or utilize any

other means to gain Internet access. . . . All organizations and individuals must obey the respective state laws and administrative regulations and carry out rigorously the system of protecting state secrets. Under no circumstances should the Internet be used to endanger national security or betray state secrets.[9]

▪ PRC ACCOMMODATION TO THE INTERNATIONAL REGIME

Companies and foreign governments involved in substantial IT investments in China are hoping China's entry into the WTO will result in a breakup of the monopoly of China Telecom, establish a telecommunications environment with fewer restrictions, and eventually result in more cooperative participation by the PRC in the global Internet regime. But Chinese leaders have been reluctant to proceed hastily with WTO membership, preferring instead to put in place a series of policy measures and institutional changes designed to strengthen Chinese institutions in the face of the new waves of foreign competition expected to result from WTO membership rules and procedures.[10] With control of over 95 percent of fixed-line telecommunications activity and more than 66 percent of mobile telephony, China Telecom is still the major IT force to be reckoned with in the PRC in 2001, but it is also clear that China's leadership is highly conscious of the need for significant adaptation to the powerful forces of globalization if it is to maintain anything resembling the degree of government and party control of telecommunications and the Internet that has been possible in the pre–WTO membership period.

In January 2001 a series of policy changes designed to prepare PRC telecommunications for entry into the WTO promised to enhance competition with China Telecom in a number of ways. A new potential nationwide competitor was launched when China Railway Telecom (Railcom) was licensed and began operating in January 2001.[11] Both Railcom and China Netcom (also owned by the Railway Ministry) were reported to be setting up high-speed fiber-optic networks that could compete with China Telecom's advanced technology, particularly if the newcomers are able to attract foreign investment after China's entry into the WTO. On other fronts, several smaller companies (including especially China Unicom, Jitong Communications, and China Mobile) were beginning to compete with China Telecom in the mobile communications area, being increasingly advantaged by government-imposed measures to slash service fees in the telecommunications sector by as much as 50 percent in some areas.[12] China Telecom responded to the new initiatives in 2001, in preparation for WTO entry, with plans to streamline its operations (including a planned downsizing of its workforce by 250,000 over the course of 2001–2002) and by preparing a listing in overseas stock markets that could raise as much as $15 million (the largest initial public offering ever by a Chinese company).[13]

▪ Free Flow of Information

During the early years of Internet development, the major obstacle to Chinese acceptance of an international regime for the Internet was related to the principle, common in all international communications regimes, calling for "free flow of information." Leaders of the government of the PRC and Chinese Communist Party leaders do not accept "free flow of information" as the norm for international communications regimes. In fact, they believe that information technology can "give them *both* modernization *and* enhanced powers of central control and stability." Mueller and Tan have summarized PRC leadership perspectives on this issue as follows:

> From the point of view of the Communist Party, China's situation *requires* it to retain a significant degree of control over the flow of ideas and information. . . . Open political competition and freedom of speech are incompatible with Communist Party control of the reform process. China's desire to control electronic communication, maintain state ownership of mass media and telecoms systems, and keep out foreigners is neither arbitrary or inconsistent, but a prerequisite of the development path it has chosen.[14]

Based on this perception, the Chinese Communist Party often publicizes its position that the free flow of communications would be "destabilizing for China." At the same time, when speaking at diplomatic functions or when trying to move closer to a Western position on this issue in negotiations, Chinese officials have frequently tried to depict their policies regarding the Internet (or on international trade and commerce) as moving toward an ideal of openness. Zhao Xiaofan, deputy director of MII's division for promoting computerization, for example, has said that China's national policy toward the Internet is "one of opening up" but that "this has to be done in stages."[15]

In recent years many world information technology leaders have been willing to accept blockage of the free flow of information by the

PRC so they could continue to do business in China. A prominent example of a communications firm submitting to China's penchant for control of information was the case of Rupert Murdoch, the owner of StarTV—an Asian satellite broadcasting network—who reached an agreement with China's leadership in 1996 to collaborate on a satellite TV venture, including transmission of state-backed Chinese television programs over the StarTV network. Whereas Murdoch had previously taken the position that satellite broadcasting would help liberate China's citizenry from state control of broadcasting, in 1996 he agreed to drop BBC programming from StarTV's broadcasting menu into China in response to Chinese Communist Party concerns that the programming was not a healthy influence on Chinese society.[16] Beginning in September 1996 the Chinese government blocked access to almost a hundred sites on the World Wide Web—including *Playboy,* the *Economist* (London), the Web pages of most U.S. newspapers, sites run by Tibetan exiles and the Taiwan government, and many more—but in 1997 restrictions on accessing some media sites (including CNN and the *Wall Street Journal*) were relaxed by Chinese authorities. These Western media have also become far more conscious of Chinese sensitivities to what is presented on their websites.

A further indication that multinational companies are not inclined to resist Chinese government interference with the free flow of information over the Internet is the fact that many of the most prominent among them routinely develop and sell to China the hardware and software needed to filter or block Internet sites. Microsoft's Chinese-version Windows NT 4.0 software, launched in January 1997, for example, was specifically designed to make possible controlled access to particular sites within China, but Microsoft's regional marketing director defended this by arguing "you could call it censorship . . . [but] there's nothing different in our Chinese product than in our English versions."[17] Among the many other companies that provide software that makes possible filtering systems (called "preventative interference" by one Communist Party leader) are Sun Microsystems, Cisco Systems, and Bay Networks.[18] In July 2000, NetScreen—one of the world's leading manufacturers of comprehensive Internet firewall hardware—established a major branch operation in Beijing.[19]

In the final analysis, it is impossible for any government to completely block access to Internet sites. Even the best software can often be circumvented by experienced computer users, and if only one unauthorized user gets materials onto an uncontrolled site, that user can spread messages throughout the rest of the system. In the Chinese case, an uncontrolled PRC user will often gain access to a foreign computer network—including those in Hong Kong or Taiwan—download information from that network onto a home computer, and transmit that material to many others in the PRC. With more than 200,000 different routes around the major nodes of the Internet, attempts by Chinese authorities to program blockages in large numbers of routers would render Internet service almost unusable.[20] China has banned the import of encryption software capable of blocking the government's supercomputer monitors, but such software is frequently smuggled into the country or downloaded from foreign computers. For many years organizations such as Human Rights Watch have even provided training to nongovernmental organizations in China on the use of encryption programs like Pretty Good Privacy (PGP) despite a U.S. State Department export ban on such programs throughout most of the 1990s.[21]

Because of the impossibility of physically blocking or filtering information passing through the Internet, Chinese authorities have also sought control by maintaining information on Internet users through a variety of bureaucratic devices. These include an application form for registering with an ISP, which requires an identification card and a Police File Report Form filled out in triplicate (one for the ISP, one for the Public Security Branch, and the third for the provincial-level Computer Security and Supervision Office). Accompanying the application is a Net Access Responsibility Agreement in which the applicant pledges "not to use the Internet to threaten state security or reveal state secrets" and swears "not to read, reproduce, or transmit material that endangers the state, obstructs public safety, or is obscene or pornographic."[22] The application includes considerable personal data about the applicant, including key information about residence and work, as well as details about computer equipment, modem type, and permit numbers. Users at Internet cafés are technically required to run the same bureaucratic path—filling out a Police File Report Form, Net Access Responsibility Agreement, and ISP contract—but this set of hurdles is sometimes avoided by café operators who argue that they are simply "training potential purchasers of computers" or "providing demonstrations to potential buyers" on the use of the Internet and are not providing customers with Internet service. A crackdown on Internet cafés in the capital city of Beijing in March 2000, however, led to enactment and more disciplined enforcement of Internet café regulations in several of

China's largest cities, which has been intensified and extended throughout China in 2001.[23]

▪ *Free Flow of Electronic Commerce*

The PRC's rejection of the free flow of information as an Internet regime norm is paralleled by its rejection of a totally free flow of electronic commerce. China's leadership is quick to point out that rejection of these international norms, which are widely accepted in advanced IT societies, should not be confused with discouragement of the growth and development of global networking—particularly in business and economic matters. Although the Internet is expected to grow and spread rapidly throughout China, Beijing wants to be assured that the central government and Communist Party leadership can carefully manage the way it spreads and continue to exercise control over its basic functioning. What distinguishes the PRC's global computer networking involvement—even with regard to e-commerce—is that it continues to be a top-down initiative, controlled and dominated by the government. To be sure, some small retailers and IT entrepreneurs are gaining relatively minor parts of the action in specific areas of opportunity, but the central players in the Internet's evolving interplay with the PRC economy are almost exclusively government ministries, agencies, and organizations.[24] Rather than allow e-commerce to grow from a series of bottom-up activities involving local entrepreneurs or from private foreign companies that are granted considerable leeway and private authority, the Chinese government has promulgated a number of initiatives designed to establish an infrastructure that can, in the words of one official, "provide suitable conditions before they can succeed."[25]

In part because it has not been integrated into the global Internet's embryonic commercial infrastructure, e-commerce in China at the outset of the millennium is still woefully underdeveloped, falling far short of its seemingly vast potential for the future. In mid-2000 a Goldman Sachs report described the volume of China's e-commerce activity as "insignificant" from a world perspective and suggested that this was not likely to change until at least 2003 or 2004.[26] Major obstacles to the growth of e-commerce in China—in addition to the absence of computers in more than 99 percent of Chinese homes—include foreign exchange currency regulations, a lack of consumer protection, concerns about privacy online, the lack of managerial and transportation capabilities to deliver products over the entire expanse of such a vast country, a confused legal and taxation policy for e-commerce, absence of a tradition of advertising, and untrustworthy guarantees for return of products by dissatisfied customers. Perhaps the greatest obstacle to a flourishing e-commerce environment, however, is the absence of a satisfactory credit card verification system.[27]

In an effort to enhance possibilities for expanded e-commerce and other Internet-based financial transactions, the People's Bank of China has constructed a national financial communications network, the Centralised National Automated Payments System (CNAPS), which serves as a national bank clearing system, taking over work previously carried out by provincial branches and regional offices. New network architecture has made it possible for the People's Bank of China to completely restructure the administration of the banking system, centralize decisionmaking, and reduce administrative interference from local authorities. As a result, the People's Bank is not only contributing to future possibilities for e-commerce, but as Lovelock has pointed out, "the central bank's headquarters is slowly but surely achieving far greater control over monetary policy than it has had in the past, thereby realising an increase in administrative efficiency and economic control."[28] The ability of the People's Bank of China—to simultaneously develop enhanced commercial capability for the Internet and increased bureaucratic efficiency and control—is often cited by government sources as a model of the kind of Internet development the PRC leadership is trying to achieve.[29]

MII's alternative to a regime that would allow the free flow of commerce over the Internet has been developed in the form of an all-encompassing e-commerce strategy, outlined in a draft document entitled "Draft Guidelines for China's Ecommerce Development," submitted to the Information Technology Leadership Group of the State Council in April 2000.[30] Although the draft guidelines were widely criticized—primarily because they introduced substantial unprecedented taxation of the Internet—their more significant future impact is likely to stem from a set of measures laying out legal and financial frameworks for e-commerce that include commercial laws and regulations governing intellectual property rights, Internet domain name arrangements, privacy and security matters, tariffs, and online payments.[31] The complex set of regulations contained in the draft guidelines, particularly when combined with the corpus of rules and laws that are already part of China's legal and soft law framework, dooms for the present any hope that

China might accept even a relatively unregulated free flow of electronic commerce as a regime principle.[32]

▪ PRC SECURITY CONCERNS

Although Chinese Communist Party and government leaders have balked at regime norms for the free flow of information and commerce, they have negotiated continually to accommodate private and public authorities in advanced IT societies that have shaped the physical infrastructure of the Internet—primarily because Beijing is dependent on the financial investments and technical know-how needed to get the Internet up and running in China and to sustain international connectivity. In the long run, the PRC is clearly bent on changing the underlying structure of power in international affairs to lessen China's dependence on the rest of the world and establish what a *Washington Post* editorial (November 14, 1999) called "a muscular new position across a broad swath of Asia and perhaps beyond." Among the many indications that China plans to use enlarged military capabilities to expand its influence in Asia are the development of (1) in-flight refueling technology to enable fighter jets to patrol to the outer edges of the South China Sea; (2) plans to transform the navy from a coastal force into a world-class organization with blue water capability; (3) missile forces that can strike throughout Asia, tested successfully in the summer of 1999; (4) limited deterrence against U.S. use of missiles (e.g., in a conflict involving Taiwan) through the development of its own missile systems and purchase of Russian missiles; and (5) research on satellite and information warfare.[33]

Specifically with regard to the Internet, reports in the Chinese press in mid-2000 indicated that both the Chinese military and the Ministry of Public Security are concerned that over 90 percent of China's websites lack security and are "highly vulnerable to sabotage."[34] In response to such concerns, there is growing support within Chinese military circles to train a cadre of "cyberwarriors" who could establish defenses for Chinese computers against foreign attacks and be ready to launch attacks against enemies.[35] A U.S. CIA official, John Serabian, appearing before the Joint Economic Committee of the U.S. Congress in February 2000, quoted an unidentified Chinese general as saying: "We can make the enemy's command centers not work by changing their data system. We can cause the enemy's headquarters to make incorrect judgment[s] by sending disinformation. We can dominate the enemy's banking system and even its entire social order.[36]

Although the PRC leadership is clearly at odds with international regimes in many issue areas, particularly those related to defense and intelligence activities, Chinese government and military officials are also pursuing opportunities to discuss international cooperation in areas related to cyberterrorism and infowar. Daniel Kuehl, a military strategy and national security professor at the Information Resources Management College of the Pentagon's National Defense University, told the congressional committee mentioned earlier, for example, that "both the Chinese and Russians have expressed interest in some form of international effort to place curbs on [cyber]attacks. . . . The Russians have gone so far as to formally propose via the Secretary General of the United Nations the development of 'an international legal regime' to combat information crime and terrorism."[37] Perhaps the most that can be said at this point is that China's leadership is determined to project the PRC as more and more of a major player in developing international regimes.

■ PRC ASPIRATIONS FOR AN INDEPENDENT CHINESE INTERNET REGIME

In recent years the PRC's search for a way to wall itself off at least in part from vast parts of cyberspace has focused on the possibility of creating an intranet for the Chinese language, to be governed from Beijing. The PRC began experimenting with networks that could be shielded from the rest of the world in the mid-1990s. By 1998 it was able to launch the China Public Multimedia Network, also known as the "169 network" after its dial-up access number, which is distinguished from other networks because everything on it is in Chinese. Because 169 is difficult to access from outside, it is far more secure (from the perspective of the PRC leadership) than the global Internet, although it does permit users to have access to the Internet outside China under controlled conditions. Thus far, the 169 network is used primarily by ministries and other government organizations for secure intragovernmental communications, but some officials view it as having possibilities for a more general Chinese-only version of the Internet that might help confine large numbers of Chinese users to shielded online participation with confined global access.[38] Among more conservative officials, the goal in developing nationwide intranets is to create a network or networks that could offer predominantly Chinese-language content, e-commerce, banking, and other commercial services but without "undesirable" content like pornography and "spiritual pollution."

A number of private and government projects and undertakings have been designed to facilitate a Chinese-language network, and to vastly increase the use of Chinese on existing networks. Since in the modern world more than twice as many people speak Chinese than speak English, the potential market for language and other facilitating materials for use of Chinese on the Internet is enormous. Most major computer software and hardware manufacturers (including Microsoft and the Chinese computer giant Legend), as well as websites (like Yahoo!) and ISPs (like AOL), have either developed or are developing Chinese-language capabilities, with one of the most comprehensive projects a joint venture of Motorola Semiconductor and San Francisco–based TurboLinux. The Motorola-TurboLinux project will use a Chinese-language version of an embedded Linux operating system, running on the PowerPC 8240 microprocessor, to target a variety of Internet applications—including interactive television, global positioning of satellite receivers and cellular phones, and most of the Internet "appliances" currently being developed. Motorola/TurboLinux promises full Chinese-language support for hardware, including CD-ROMs, floppy disk drives, network interface and display cards, and much more.[39]

The number of people surfing the Web in Chinese is still relatively small, even on a worldwide basis, and is projected by sinanet.com—the largest Chinese-language website—to have grown to only 19 million in 2001. One of the major reasons there is not more Chinese-language activity on the Internet is the difficulty of inputting Chinese materials, as outlined by Matthew Yeomans:

> In order to input Chinese into a computer, writers must rely upon a Western, Romanized keyboard. Unfortunately, Chinese is so complex and contains so many characters that there's no way to include them all on one keyboard. To type online, most Chinese speakers use a number of different Chinese-language input software programs—Richwin and Chinese Star are two of the most popular—that allocate a number of characters to individual Roman letters and enable users to construct Chinese sentences through a laborious series of key strokes. While many Chinese computer users simply memorize which characters match the Roman keys, another way of writing Chinese characters is to

use Hanyu Pinyin. This is the Roman alphabet version of Chinese, a straightforward system that allocates a phonetic definition to each character. . . . Refined by the Chinese Communist Party from an earlier Western method, Pinyin was developed to help the Romanized speaking world reproduce Chinese words. As such, it is mainly understood by westerners and educated Chinese who interact with westerners.[40]

One of the most promising developments for enhancing the use of Chinese online has been the keypad or palm devices that make it possible to physically handwrite Chinese characters or that vastly reduce the number of keystrokes necessary to enter a Chinese character because the software's memory will often complete the character once a few keystrokes are made. Based on such technologies, Chinese-language e-commerce activities have been increasing gradually, as has the popularity of Chinese-language websites. But this has not solved problems encountered by those who would like to acquire and use Chinese-language domain names, who have been thwarted by the absence of a consensual accepted authority for allocating domain names and addresses.[41]

Competition to become the international authority for registering and supervising Internet domain names in Chinese has developed among a number of organizations, most notably I-Dns in Singapore and the China National Network Information Center (CNNIC) in Beijing. Both I-Dns and CNNIC, plus a number of other Chinese and non-Chinese private firms, have been registering literally hundreds of thousands of domain names in Chinese over the past few years despite people's relative inability to use such domain names with any regularity until a framework can be developed to facilitate their routing on local and international networks.[42] One might assume the CNNIC would have the advantage over others in the competition to become the authority for establishing a Chinese-language domain name framework, if only because CNNIC is the management organization designated by ICANN to oversee the "cn" country domain in English and is the government organization within the PRC that will likely play the most prominent role in setting a standard for Chinese-language domain names for all of the mainland. But many Chinese speakers outside the PRC are reluctant or simply refuse to register domain names with the CNNIC because of its official connections to the communist government in Beijing (which requires and stores substantial information from those applying for domain names and addresses) or for other reasons as well.

Complicating the worldwide use of Chinese on the Internet was the November 2000 decision of Network Solutions, Inc. (NSI) VeriSign—in its capacity as the leading registrar of domain names authorized by ICANN—to begin accepting domain names in Chinese, Korean, and Japanese characters for the first time. Chinese authorities immediately struck back, with CNNIC announcing a rival—and incompatible—system for registering Chinese-language names, prompting widespread concern among Chinese-language Internet users.[43] Pindar Wong—the first Chinese person elected to the ICANN board, a former vice chairman of ICANN, and a leading figure in Hong Kong Internet circles—warned that the conflict between Beijing's leadership and ICANN on this issue risked "balkanization of the Internet." Trying to pull them back from a protracted conflict, Wong asked both sides to remember that "global connectivity is the most precious aspect of the Internet. Anything that might jeopardize that needs to be considered very carefully."[44]

Within the PRC Internet community, however, registration of domain names in Chinese by NSI/VeriSign is often viewed as an effort to "recolonize" China in cyberspace, a sentiment often accompanied by assertions that the Chinese language "belongs to the Chinese" and "should not be run by a foreign company in cyberspace." Leading Chinese IT authorities have been quoted in the state-run press, arguing that foreign registration of domain names violates the PRC's sovereignty, will result in "a rush of foreign exchange outflow," creates "potential threats to state security," and is "humiliating."[45]

Those who oppose capitulation by the world that would allow Beijing authorities to establish the standards for and run the global domain name system for the Chinese language point to the threats to free speech and privacy already evident in the domain name system CNNIC has devised. Free of cost, the system requires that users download special software that routes all requests to a central "dictionary" located on computers in Beijing. With complete authority over this dictionary, those controlling the system in Beijing could in effect decide who is and is not able to use the Internet in Chinese. As a *Wall Street Journal* article stated, "China's system is a home-grown method of handling Chinese-language domain names completely separate from those currently in use—a change as fundamental as if China decided to use a globally incompatible system of telephone numbers."[46] Matthew McGarvey, senior Internet research analyst for the IDC in Beijing, has described the system as "a classic case of China trying to develop the Internet the way it suits them rather than what suits the rest of the world."[47]

▪ BUILDING A UNIQUELY CHINESE INTERNET

An even more ambitious attempt by China's leadership to create a uniquely Chinese Internet was announced in a Xinhua News Agency article in January 2001. Conceived initially in 1999 as a "completely new, second-generation proprietary communications and data network that is intended to replace the global Internet," the new network is being organized by a consortium of PRC hardware and software companies, in conjunction with government ministries and research institutes, in a project called the C-Net Strategic Alliance.[48] The president of one of the alliance partner companies, Xia Chuanyou, suggested in the Xinhua article that the backbone system for the C-Net network could be completed by early 2002, connecting China's major cities to branch nodes in both provincial capitals and to major prefectural cities.[49] The article repeated at several points that the new C-Net venture had support from "authorities," as follows: "Authorities have determined that the global Internet has various inherent bandwidth and security shortcomings and is unable to satisfy the needs of the Chinese government and domestic commercial enterprises. . . . Authorities believe that the proposed China C-Net will be a better fit for the country's 'reality' with specific advantages such as tighter security, better efficiency, and larger capacity."[50]

Should the PRC leadership achieve significant technological breakthroughs in walling off or shielding the Chinese population from the global Internet, it would undoubtedly produce a dynamic that would have consequences for China's relations with the international Internet regime. Perhaps the major difficulty this would create for the rest of the world would be the inevitable contradictions encountered in day-to-day business transactions, both by world business leaders with interests in the China market and by Chinese business leaders with interests in the world market. Thus far many world business leaders have invested in the development of the Internet in China with the understanding that they will somehow have access to the markets that the Internet will create in the future. As an article in London's *Financial Times* commented in the context of the evolution of the international trade regime:

> [Given] China's long history of diplomatic isolation . . . it may come as something of a shock to Beijing that countries' influence in the WTO depends more on the scale of their imports and the size of their home market than on their export performance. On that measure, China still looks like a political lightweight. Despite its vast population, it boasts

merchandise imports roughly equivalent to those of Belgium or the Netherlands, and well below those of Hong Kong.[51]

From the opposite perspective, Chinese business and government leaders have a huge potential stake in selling Chinese products to the rest of the world over the Internet, but the degree of success they can aspire to in this regard will be highly dependent on the ability of Chinese producers and sellers to communicate in cyberspace in a relatively free and open manner with potential customers, suppliers, and business partners in the rest of the world. It may be possible for a clever PRC leadership to find ways to resolve these contradictions at the fringes while maintaining an international Internet firewall, but the likelihood is that a Chinese intranet that is walled off and shielded from the rest of the world's Internet regime would create serious impediments to a flourishing e-commerce. Experience from other international regimes indicates that relations between the PRC and the global Internet regime would become increasingly strained over time in the absence of agreements with the rest of the world about essentials in the early stages of Internet development. Alternatively, regime theory tells us that cooperation, resulting in a firm and early understanding about the norms and rules to be followed in developing the Internet's relationship with China, could result in a feedback mechanism that would reinforce and strengthen both the regime itself and China's position in the regime.[52]

■ INTERNET DEVELOPMENT IN INDIA

In contrast to China's fast start in the 1980s and 1990s, India has been a much more enigmatic actor in developing information technology. Although the city of Bangalore, in southern India, has developed into a leading world-class manufacturing and invention center for computer software innovation since the early 1980s, and, a good portion of the Internet entrepreneurs in the Silicon Valley of California (in some years as many as 20–25 percent of newcomers) are of Indian origin, most of the rest of India has lagged far behind the United States, Europe, Japan, and China in the development of Internet infrastructure and use. At the turn of the millennium, the figures for India's Internet involvement were as dismal as for any major country. At the beginning of 2000, India had only a dozen fully functioning ISPs and was just beginning to allow private firms to become ISPs. A major e-Asia survey estimated in May

2000 that the number of Internet connections in India was 1.9 million (less than 0.2 percent of the population), compared with 8.9 million in China. The same survey projected that connections would grow to 9 million in India and 21 million in China by the beginning of 2003.[53] International Data Corporation ranked India fifty-fourth in the world among the fifty-five countries listed in its 2001 Global Information Society Index, placing India just ahead of its subcontinental rival, Pakistan, which finished last on the list.[54]

A comprehensive University of Arizona study comparing Internet development in China and India concluded in 1999 that "the Chinese Internet has equaled or surpassed its Indian counterpart in every dimension."[55] In 1999, China provided commercial Internet access in more than 200 cities in all Chinese provinces, whereas Internet Points of Presence (POPs) were available in a little more than 50 cities in only 17 of the 32 Indian states and union territories. There were approximately four times as many Internet accounts in China as in India. Over 300 Chinese universities and more than 200 Chinese research institutes had direct connectivity in 1999, whereas very few Indian universities and research institutes were online. If anything, the Internet infrastructure gap between China and India has widened since 1999. China has been using both satellite and terrestrial links to build an extensive and robust domestic backbone for the Internet, whereas India had very little backbone capacity even in 2001.[56] Much of this is a result of the head start and more effective planning in China compared with India. The University of Arizona study concluded, for example, "ChinaNET connects its centers with 155 Mbps [megabytes per second] circuits and connects to its 200 POPs at speeds between 2 and 34 Mbps. Nothing close to this exists in India . . . [where] there has been no effective backbone planning."[57]

There are many reasons China has been more successful than India in mounting a robust Internet environment. China has invested far more in telecommunications infrastructure and has attracted more than ten times as much direct foreign investment as India during the 1990s.[58] The Chinese telecommunications system also scores better on efficiency of operation, generating more than four times the revenue per employee—a phenomenon the Arizona study attributes to a decentralized decisionmaking process in China that pushes investment and service decisions to provincial or city levels.[59] Comparing India to China in this respect, the Arizona study argues that "India's legendary bureaucracy hurts efficiency. For example, radio spectrum allocation in India is not handled centrally, but [is] parceled out to government agencies, each of which manages its own slice, leading to sub-optimization."[60] Computer sales in China have far outstripped those in India, with an estimated 18.1 million PCs having been sold in China at the start of 1999 in comparison with only 2.32 million in India (in January 2001, India finally reached a milestone when 5 million PCs *total* had been installed, at a point when more than 5 million PCs were being sold in the PRC *each year*).[61]

Although both China and India have imported almost all of the equipment necessary to build and operate their Internet infrastructures, China is far ahead in developing a domestic network equipment industry. This has been aided by China's massive export advantage over India, with Chinese telecommunication equipment exports alone being twenty-five times greater than India's in 1997.[62] In 1999 the vice president of India's Manufacturers Association for Information Technology, Vinay Deshpande, contrasted the buoyant position of India's software industry with the computer hardware and electronics manufacturing sector in India in general, which he called "a demoralized one."[63] Differences between China and India with regard to foreign direct investment are equally striking. A study by the Institute of International Finance reported in January 2001 that China had gained 26 percent ($40 billion of $154 billion) of the total worldwide private financial flows to emerging markets in 2000, including 77 percent of all such investments in East Asia, whereas India had received less than 1 percent of such funds over the same period.[64]

■ LIBERALIZATION POLICIES AND FOREIGN INVESTMENT

A key factor in reducing Internet costs to users in India has been the government's liberalization policies, which have made it possible for private companies to become ISPs and have opened other areas for competition in the provision of Internet services. In November 1998 the Department of Telecommunications (DoT) awarded 75 ISP licenses to Indian organizations, many of them private companies, and has since announced plans to grant at least 100 additional ISP licenses by the end of 2001.[65] By January 2000 only three companies had been able to use their new licenses to offer Internet access, however, primarily because the terms the government granted for their operations produced insurmountable regulatory hurdles and costs. More than two dozen of the licensees (informally called the "bandwidth club") have since joined together to form the Internet Service Providers Association of India

(ISPAI) to lobby for better terms and for greater reduction of government control and regulation regarding the Internet.[66]

The two Internet-related areas where foreign investors have been most recently attracted to India are in satellite-based ISPs and cable and wireless networks, in both instances because government liberalization policies in these areas have enhanced prospects for businesslike development and profits. In the case of Internet satellite connections, the government announced in February 2000 that it would issue licenses to eight private companies, beginning with Dishnet of Chennai, that would grant them rights to use private satellite uplinks for their Internet servers. Previously, all international Internet traffic passed through a single Bombay gateway, run by the government. Particularly when the announcement was accompanied by the appointment of a business-friendly technocrat to head DoT, the legitimation of the eight privately run gateways was greeted with enthusiasm by the Indian and foreign business communities. The head of India's National Association of Software and Computer Companies, Dewang Mehta, for example, was quoted as saying, "We are moving from an information superfootpath to a superhighway."[67]

Running broadband computer networks over cable lines is particularly attractive to potential investors in India because of the way cable television developed in a totally unregulated (albeit illegal) manner prior to 1994. The Cable Operators Federation of India claims it represents 60,000 to 70,000 small firms, most in urban areas where they still run cable from housetop to housetop and resell programs the small-scale entrepreneur has gathered from satellite broadcasts to a few hundred homes each. Since most if not all of these small firms underreport the number of their customers and the scale of their operation by at least 50 percent to avoid taxes and use a number of other guises to circumvent government rules, it is difficult to know the extent of India's existing cable connections. Including reported and unreported cable operations, the miles covered by cable in India may exceed the miles covered by telephone lines.[68] This striking fact, particularly when coupled with the potential advantages of broadband cable networks, has produced plans by a number of foreign and Indian companies to attach their fiber-optic networks to the snarl of rooftop cable lines that already exist to create a series of broadband Internet networks of the future.

Credit Lyonnais Securities Asia has projected that Internet use in India will multiply by a factor of 15 to 20 by 2004 (a figure larger than all Asian countries except China), with the "key driver" for such growth being cable networks. Making such systems work will be dependent on the economic viability of what are known in India as multi-system operators (MSOs), essentially middlemen (and women) who can take signals from broadcasters and international Internet networks and pass them on to local operators, who in turn charge users for their services. The MSOs fear being caught between international providers charging high fees for their services and local operators, unwilling to pay much to the MSO or regularly defaulting on payments. To provide better profit margins, which would make the position of the MSOs more comfortable and would help the system function more effectively, in 1999 India's National Association of Software and Service Companies (NASSCOM) launched a campaign (called "operation bandwidth") to boost India's Internet bandwidth eightyfold by 2003 and get the government to remove regulatory obstacles such as the 49 percent cap on foreign ownership of telecommunications companies and the ban on Internet telephony.[69]

Largely on the basis of relatively liberalized environments for satellite- and cable-based Internet development, significant numbers of international and Indian investors either renewed or initiated new interests in India in 2000. Enron, a U.S. energy firm, began negotiating an arrangement in which it might install at least 10 gigabits of bandwidth among seven Indian cities by 2002, which would equal one-tenth of the NASSCOM target mentioned earlier. Some of the larger local Indian cable operators (e.g., IN CableNet, owned by the Indo-European Hinduja family, and SitiCable, which is part of Zee Telefilms) have plans to invest more than $500 million in new money in efforts to build competitive networks of cable MSOs over the next few years (Intel was impressed enough with this idea that it has committed $49 million to the effort).[70] Korea's LG Group has allocated $185 million for Internet-related investment in India between 2000 and 2005, with $100 million marked for electronics, $50 million for telecommunications, and $35 million for software.[71] Among the companies seeking regulatory approval for operating satellite gateways are Cyberstar and PanAmSat, with Cyberstar's proposal including an offer to provide 100 new megabits of international Internet traffic. The Asia Cellular Satellite System (AceS)—51 percent of which is owned by Shyam Telecom and 49 percent by AceS International, including investors from Hong Kong, Indonesia, and the Philippines—is expected to be operational in the Delhi region by late 2001.[72]

In response to an unprecedented influx of new private investment in Internet-related ventures in the first half of 2000 and under the influence of a new chairman, in May 2000 the DoT recommended to India's Telecommunications Commission that "the foreign equity cap of 49 percent be removed and foreign equity up to 100 percent be permitted."[73] The DoT estimated that as much as $60 billion in investment would be needed over the five-year period 2001–2006 to bring India's Internet-related sectors up to world standards, and argued that funds on such a scale could be attracted only with assured high incentives for those willing to risk capital (even the enhanced investment of 2000 falls far short of the $60 billion pace). Although some leaders in the current Indian government favor the DoT proposal, the main opposition party (the Congress, which has ruled India for most of its independent history) is publicly opposed, as are substantial portions of the Indian bureaucracy.

In addition to its efforts to attract investments from foreign companies, the Indian government has launched a major effort to attract foreign direct investment (FDI) by working with Indian leadership and with Indians who have taken citizenship in other nations in an attempt to interest investors from abroad. In January 2000, Finance Minister Yashwant Singh has established a goal of $10 billion in FDI per year for the first decade of the twenty-first century, more than three times the annual average in the 1990s.[74] One strategy for reaching this goal is to enlist the support of the leadership of the six states (Delhi, Maharashtra, Karnataka, Tamil Nadu, Gujarat, and Andhra) that attracted most of the $18 billion in FDI in the 1990s to encourage the states to follow up on their contacts and possibilities for attracting additional investment. Included in an earlier Bharatiya Janata Party (BJP) budget was a proposal to create special bond and mutual fund programs to attract investment from the 15–20 million Indians living abroad (the numbers vary depending on whether one counts people of Indian origin with different types of citizenship). A new innovation, introduced by Singh, is the idea of creating an Indian "green card" that would entitle nonresident Indians (NRIs) who qualify to hold dual citizenship where it is permitted by the foreign country involved. The card would also enable NRIs to travel to and from India without a visa and might provide other rights of citizenship as well. These proposals were prompted by statistical trends that indicate an almost continuous decline in investment in India by NRIs since 1996, reaching an all-time low of 7.5 percent of total FDI in 1999.[75]

▪ INDIA'S LEAD IN SOFTWARE TECHNOLOGY

The one bright spot for India in its economic competition with China has been the ability of Indian software manufacturers to far outproduce Chinese manufacturers and to produce and market software on a much larger scale than in most other countries of the world as well. The most telling demonstration of India's software superiority is in its trade statistics, with India exporting almost 100 times as much software as the PRC ($4.6 billion worth of software products compared with $50 million for China in 1999, the last year for which complete statistics are available).[76] Beijing's leaders have been so impressed with India's increasing capability to outperform the rest of the world in software technology that they have initiated programs to send Chinese delegations to India to explore ways the two countries might build cooperation in this area and to determine whether PRC software industries might learn ways to improve their production and export capabilities.[77]

India's lead in software technology is generally traced to 1984, when Rajiv Gandhi succeeded his mother as prime minister of India, recognized the importance of information technology for future economic growth, and began to adopt the first liberal economic policies designed to develop this sector. Encouragement provided by liberalization policies was particularly important to Indian government and business leaders who had been battling uphill for several years to lay the foundations for growth in this sector. Many of the earliest software companies located in Bangalore, created by Jawaharlal Nehru in the 1950s as India's "city of the future," where efforts had been made to create a very special legal structure and business climate that would be as conducive as possible within the Indian context to scientific enterprise. Already in the 1980s Bangalore boasted three universities, fourteen engineering colleges, forty-seven polytechnic schools, and a wide variety of research institutes (including the prestigious Indian Institute of Management) and was the main operations center for public-sector high-tech companies like Hindustan Aeronautics, Bharat Electronics, Indian Telephone Industries, Hindustan Machine Tools, and the Indian Space Research Organization.[78]

As part of the reforms of the early 1990s, a Software Technology Park was established near Bangalore as an economic free trade zone, operating under bylaws that have enabled companies to function with far fewer regulatory constraints than firms operating under the normal

Indian legal and business structure. Once it became clear that software exports were going to be a major foreign exchange earner for India, the Indian government began to provide income tax exemptions on profits from such exports, as well as other special concessions, to software companies. Both the state and central government have also tried to provide world-class infrastructural facilities—e.g., roads, fiber-optic telecommunications lines, health and recreational facilities—to attract and retain the best engineers and managers and their families. Companies have offered additional perks, including zero-interest home loans and Western-style apartment communities for visiting professionals, and local businesspeople have been attracted to Bangalore as a place to invest and set up shop (it is estimated, for example, that Bangalore had more than 700 cybercafés in fall of 1999).[79]

The enormous success of the Indian software industry, in Bangalore and a few other such centers, demonstrates the vast potential for economic growth when the maze of government rules associated with India's older socialist pattern of society is removed. As one of the most successful IT centers in Asia, Bangalore has not only enticed the world's largest and most successful companies—e.g., Texas Instruments, Motorola, Microsoft, to name just a few—to locate major world-class facilities within its industrial parks; it has also spawned hundreds of Indian companies that have either remained within Bangalore or spread out to the rest of the country and the world. The largest of these, Infosys, has more than 8,000 employees worldwide, of whom more than 400 are millionaires (in U.S. dollars). In 2000, Infosys finished building a new 44-acre campus on the outskirts of Bangalore that employs more than 4,300 engineers.[80]

Bangalore is not free from problems, however. The city has expanded from a relatively sleepy town of less than half a million in 1981 to more than 1.5 million in the 1991 census and to more than 5 million people at the turn of the twenty-first century. As property prices have skyrocketed and wages have steadily risen, a quality life in Bangalore has become more expensive and the attainment of such a life more difficult. Whereas it took only five to ten minutes to travel from downtown Bangalore to the first software park fifteen years ago, it now takes more than an hour, and disruptions caused by power outages and breakdown of telephone connections are increasing. The wealth of the city has attracted large numbers of rural migrants who have not found adequate housing and jobs, introducing neighborhoods with substantial poverty and slum conditions that did not exist in the 1960s and 1970s. As Bangalore loses the cost advantage relative to other cities that was one of the principal reasons for its early success, both multinationals and Indian software companies are turning to other Indian cities—such as Hyderabad, Chennai (formerly Madras), Noida (a suburb of New Delhi), and Pune—to locate their production facilities.

One of the most widely heralded attempts by an Indian state to attract software production facilities away from Bangalore is being led by the chief minister of Andhra Pradesh, N. Chandrababu Naidu, who came to world attention in 1997 when he cornered Bill Gates, who was visiting India, talked him into hearing a PowerPoint presentation on Andhra's IT interests, and ended up convincing Gates to locate a Microsoft software development center in Hyderabad (which Naidu calls "Cyberabad"), the capital of Andhra Pradesh. Naidu has since attended the annual summit of world business and economic leaders in Davos, Switzerland; arranged for President Bill Clinton to visit Hyderabad; and otherwise promoted Hyderabad's software exports to the point where they have tripled since 1995 to more than $280 million per year.[81] Naidu came to power in 1995 by outmaneuvering his father-in-law, a former film star, and eventually taking over his father-in-law's regional political party. He daringly campaigned in 1999 on an unusual platform for an Indian politician—arguing openly that subsidies to farmers and others should be reduced or eliminated, that computers should be introduced into every Indian village and all government records should be accessible online to reduce bureaucrats' ability to cajole and induce bribery for government services, that foreign companies should be allowed into India on the most liberal terms, and that taxes and regulations imposed on Indian businesses should be drastically reduced.

Naidu won the 1999 election against an opponent, the head of the local Congress Party, who during the campaign openly urged farmers to stop paying their electric bills, promising them that his party would not only waive those charges once he was elected but that he would rescind charges for electricity and water instituted by the Naidu state government.[82] In the 1999 state election in Andhra, Naidu's party (the Telegu Desam Party) also became the second largest in the governing coalition at the national level. But a year later, in September 2000, Naidu was faced with massive protest movements against his programs designed to eliminate subsidies, particularly those that resulted in an average 27 percent increase per person in the cost of electricity. To make matters worse, Andhra suffered the heaviest rains in forty-six years in August and September 2000, resulting in 150 deaths from floods. Protests against the government turned bloody when police killed four demonstrators in late August 2000, prompting enhanced mobilization against the government.[83]

Although many politicians in other parts of India are watching Naidu's dogged efforts to promote economic liberalization and information technology to see if such measures can be implemented in a manner that is politically palatable, the World Bank has tried to assist the Naidu government in this effort by making Andhra its first "focus state." In 2000 the Bank approved loans of $2.8 million to Andhra for nutrition, education, power reform, and other programs. Critics argue that Naidu's policies are contributing to an already serious state debt problem and that the state government is investing in high-tech infrastructure and training while neglecting basic needs for food, water, and health facilities in poor rural and urban areas. But Naidu argues that his vision is for the long-term development of the state, which can only come about through technological advances. He and his supporters argue that India missed the industrial revolution when it was occurring and cannot afford to miss out on the IT revolution already well under way.[84]

■ SOFTWARE DEVELOPMENT IN CHINA

Software development in China is at the opposite end of the spectrum from that of India. Beijing's effort to build a sophisticated software production capability did not begin until the mid-1990s, and the Chinese government provided little state support for this effort until the very end of the decade. A June 2000 survey of the PRC's government-run China Information News Agency (CINA) reported that China finished last among all Asian countries in both its indigenous development and use of IT resources and its level of state support for IT professionals.[85] The creativity and technical capabilities of China's IT professionals are generally assessed as among the lowest in Asia, largely because of their lack of English-language skills in a medium where the most sophisticated inventions are taking place in English. Restrictions on Internet use, as outlined later in this book, have also hindered Chinese computer programmers and inventors when compared with their Indian counterparts, not only in their attempts to gain and exchange information to develop new software programs but also in their attempts to sell new ideas to government officials in the PRC and to potential investors from abroad.

One result of the differing patterns of software development in China and India is that China has become far more successful as a staging area for international companies to produce high-tech products for export, whereas India has been able—at least in software production—to become a significant global manufacturer and exporter in its own right. Whereas production in China's more globally integrated information industry grew by 20 percent in 2000 and is projected to grow by as much as 25 percent a year over the next five years, India's homegrown software industry is growing at a rate of 50 percent or more each year—far outstripping the growth of its Chinese counterpart as well as other high-tech sectors in India as well. According to some estimates, IT exports in India—led predominantly by the software industry—accounted for 35 percent of the country's total exports in 2000 and 7.5 percent of its GDP.[86]

Among the reasons PRC leaders have become concerned about the gap between China and India in homegrown software capabilities are the potential uses of such technology for military purposes. Damon Bristow, the head of Asia programs at the Royal United Services Institute for Defence Studies in London, has suggested, based on Western intelligence sources, that China and India are two of the very few LDCs that have embarked on extensive programs to explore such potential, particularly for information warfare.[87] Bristow suggested that some Western intelligence assessments "emphasize the fact that in the key areas of high-performance computing and software development," including "the ability to attack and disable the military and civilian communications networks of potential adversaries," China "lags behind India."[88] Bristow quotes Washington-based intelligence as concluding that "neither country comes close to catching up with the U.S.," but cites these same sources to the effect that "India's information-warfare capabilities—were it to decide to use them—are broadly superior to those of its neighbor."[89]

Chinese attempts to catch up to India in indigenous software development have focused in large part on language and training, areas in which India has had a decided edge. Indian universities in 2000 graduated more than 124,000 engineers with competence in the English language, almost twice as many as in the United States and significantly more than China. According to Yin Zhihe, executive chairman of the Beijing Software Industry Association, most Chinese software engineers "can operate effectively in an English-based computer environment, and are proficient users of Western software programs," but are unable "to present ideas, negotiate the deal and write manuals" in a manner competitive with their Indian counterparts."[90] Attempts to interest the brightest young people in China to become software engineers has run up against Chinese cultural values that tend to associate writers of software with traditional scribes. In the words of Bethany Chan, the head of technology and Internet research at the UBS Warburg investment bank in Hong Kong, "China is very far away from challenging India in software development" because "China's emphasis was never on software." Chan cites China's history of industrial development, which has tilted heavily toward machinery and infrastructure as the focal areas for development, as contributing to a de-emphasis on software.

In an effort to jump-start the PRC's indigenous computer software industry, Beijing is trying to lure Chinese and Chinese American software developers living in the United States back to China and is trying to establish venture capital firms and two new stock markets for tech start-ups and to create privately owned companies with access to capital markets, along the lines of institutional arrangements that have been so successful in launching start-up software companies in the United States and India.[91] One of the most successful of these early experiments is Shanghai Venture Capital Corporation (SVC), which was given $72.5 million by the city of Shanghai in August 1999 to identify the most promising homegrown technical innovations and develop them into commercial enterprises. Sixteen months later SVC had parlayed its original funding into a quarter-billion-dollar war chest by investing in fifty-three companies—with a heavy emphasis on IT firms in Shanghai—having screened them from among more than 2,000 proposals.[92] SVC's success has been attributed at least in part to its willingness to ally with foreign fund management companies such as Venture TDF Company, a Singapore-based fund with close ties to the Singapore government's National Science and Technology Board. The Shanghai government has allowed SVC to let the much more experienced Singapore company control the fund in an arrangement that marks an important transition from direct Chinese government control. In return for this concession, SVC has gained a global network of venture capital contacts.

▪ INDIAN PERCEPTIONS OF SECURITY/ NATIONAL INTERESTS AND THE INTERNET

The Indian government has committed itself to policies promoting domestic high-technology manufacturing in one area, and that has to do with national interests, security, and defense. In such matters as parallel computing, nuclear, and satellite technology, for example, a commitment has been made to develop local industries capable of producing world-class products. With regard to the Internet, the Indian defense establishment has set up its own secure intranet for communicating internally on military matters and has begun to explore the dynamics that might be involved in future infowars. Of particular concern to Indian strategic thinkers are reports that China is among a handful of states that have undertaken "extraordinary" steps to develop an Internet warfare capability.[93]

▪ State Security and the Internet

Indian military and security personnel concerns first assumed public prominence in June 1998 when a group of international hackers calling themselves "MilwOrm" broke into the website of the Bhabha Atomic Research Center in Gujarat through a series of Telnet connections that enabled them to travel in cyberspace to India through servers in the United States belonging to the National Aeronautics and Space Agency (NASA) Jet Propulsion Laboratory, the U.S. Navy, and the U.S. Army.[94] In October 1998, Indian Defense Ministry officials reported that suspected Pakistani intelligence operatives had hijacked the Indian army's only Internet site, designed to present the Indian point of view on Kashmir, as part of a cyberwar launched in advance of Indo-Pakistani border talks. Indian defense officials blamed the break-in on problems resulting from the absence of a satisfactory Internet policy at the ministry level and called for greater coordination between civilian and defense agencies on Internet matters. When a group of rebels in northeastern India belonging to the banned United Liberation Front of Assam opened an effective website in September 1999 attacking Indian military activities, the Indian army decided to open its own website in Assam to counter what it called "a cyberwar launched by militants."[95] A year earlier, a major report of the Indian navy had suggested that coordination between Indian military and intelligence agencies was "regrettably ineffective" and called for a series of measures to improve IT capabilities and link them to other intelligence activities.[96]

▪ The Internet and Domestic Security Issues

In addition to the security of military websites and computer infrastructure, Indian government leaders have been concerned with three other aspects of state security, outlined by Ronald Deibert: (1) the challenge to the preservation and maintenance of the symbols of nationalism, including culture, language, and other symbols of identity; (2) challenges to the security of the individual, embodied especially in the right to privacy; and (3) challenges to the maintenance of network security.[97]

India is one of a number of countries that are particularly concerned about threats to their cultural identity in the Internet environment. Because India is a flourishing liberal democracy, its leadership has not resorted to the kinds of measures one finds, for example, in China, Vietnam, Iran, or Syria, where the state has employed a wide variety of authoritarian measures to control Internet content and access. But Indian political leaders are jockeying with one another to respond to a widespread feeling among the Indian populace to "Indianize" the Internet, and state and local leaders have become especially active in trying to find ways to make the Internet available to India's numerous language groups. Indianization of the Internet thus far has meant encouragement by the federal government to put Indian-content materials on websites or to translate or rewrite foreign materials so they can be understood by local Indian audiences. Indianization also refers to attempts to diffuse Internet use to the rural areas and to develop Indian networks in specialized areas like telemedicine.[98]

The most ambitious development of an Indian language on the Internet is in Tamil, which is being promoted by the International Forum for Information Technology in Tamil (INFITT). Although INFITT's secretariat is based in Singapore—which has a substantial Tamil-speaking minority—it has members from India, Sri Lanka, Malaysia, Australia, Switzerland, and the United States. It views itself as "a thought-leader, providing expertise in charting the future for Tamil-based Internet technology" for the 65 million Tamil speakers in Asia.[99] Working closely with the Singapore government (through the Tamil Internet Steering Committee of the Infocomm Development Authority of Singapore), INFITT's secretariat is headed by the deputy director of Singapore's Institute of Policy Studies. It has worked closely in India with the Tamilnadu government and a number of organizations in Chennai (formerly Madras) to launch the first Indian-language ISP in Tamil by 2002.[100]

■ Internet Use and Private Security

India's democratic form of government has forced its leaders to join other liberal democracies in the search to find ways to couple Internet use with privacy safeguards, although the current Indian government—a coalition of parties reelected in 1999 and led by the Hindu nationalist BJP—has gone further than any previous government in attempts to control the Internet. In July 1999, for example, cabinet leaders directed the government Internet provider Videsh Sanchar Nigam Ltd. (VSNL) to block access on international Internet gateways to the online news sites of the Pakistani newspaper *Dawn* (www.dawn.com). Although VSNL did block the Pakistani site, Indians were able to gain access to it fairly easily through the use of redirecting services like www.anonymizer.com.[101] On a much grander scale, the Information Technology Bill that was introduced in January 1999 and passed into law by the BJP-led parliament in May 2000 included provisions to monitor all traffic passing through servers and to make such traffic available to "properly constituted authorities" for "valid reasons of security."[102]

Although encryption software is allowed under the May 2000 legislation, the bill retained clauses empowering any government agency to "intercept information transmitted through any computer resource if it is necessary in the interests of the sovereignty or integrity of India, the security of the state, friendly relations with foreign states or public order, or for preventing incitement to the commission of a cognisable offence." Under Clause 79 of the IT act, the police are given the power to "enter any public place and search and arrest without warrant any person found therein who is reasonably suspected of having committed or of committing or of being about to commit any offence under this Act." Defending the bill in parliament, the BJP's minister of information technology, Pramod Mahajan, suggested that only police officers above a certain rank would be authorized to allow searches of "public premises," which would not include newspaper offices and private establishments, but these clauses have met with wide protests among human rights organizations in India concerned with their potential for government intrusion into private correspondence and record keeping on the Internet.[103]

■ Network Security

A third challenge to Internet security, aside from the obvious military-defense challenge, results from the increasing dependence of modern economies on networked information infrastructures, resulting in the need to protect the networks themselves from system crashes, loss, theft, corruption of data, and other disruptions of information flows. As Deibert has pointed out, network security needs have two related dimensions, focusing on (1) protecting the flow of information internal to specific businesses and corporations and (2) securing flows of information between producers and consumers.[104] Perhaps the most extensive intra-corporation security network in the world is General Electric, which expects at some point in 2001 to have all of its worldwide business units purchasing its internal nonproduction and maintenance, repair, and operations security materials through the Internet for a total of $5 billion.[105] No India-based corporation has approached such an extensive internal network security effort, but the larger corporations and industrial houses, as well as the larger Indian banks, have started to invest substantially in this area.

The secure flow of information between producers and consumers goes to the heart of the commercialization of the World Wide Web but is also bound up with many other aspects of marketplace informatization. Entering the world of networked commerce (e.g., electronic access banking, use of smart cards, stored value devices, digital credit systems) requires increasing investments in security protocols that include both software and hardware (modem pools, compact discs, leased lines, secure servers, access control mechanisms, to name only a small number of devices needed), as well as the expense of computer security and network consultants. Neither the Indian government nor Indian companies have amassed internally, or attracted from outside India, the kind of investment needed to compete with other nations in the race for developing secure networks for e-commerce and other forms of worldwide online business and trading.[106] In a world where security is considered the key to the success of network business transactions, this is likely to be a severe disadvantage for India (for both the government and private corporations) for many years into the future.

■ INDIA AND THE INTERNATIONAL REGIME FOR THE INTERNET

As in many other areas of international activity, India is involved with the international regime for the Internet but is not playing the kind of central leadership role advocated by supporters of globalization.[107] Although Indian Internet activists and officials have participated in the work of organizations centrally involved in developing worldwide Internet rules of the game—for example, the ISOC, the IETF—they have not been key Internet players on the world stage, largely because the volume of Internet activity in India is minuscule, even for Asia.[108] Only one major international organization concerned with the Internet has a significant office in India, the International Council for Computer Communication (with forty countries as members), whose website is hosted by India's National Centre for Software Technology (NCST).[109] A number of contributions have been made by Indian and Indian-born engineers and computer scientists to regime standards and protocols adopted by the global Internet, particularly in the software sector.[110] But in contrast to China, India is not represented on the ICANN board or on ICANN committees.

Although recent policies of liberalization and privatization promise to quicken the pace of IT and Internet development in India, past experience with telecommunications reform and the structure of political interests suggests caution in expecting a rate of growth much faster than that experienced in the past. The halting pace of modernization efforts in India is associated largely with the solidly entrenched democratic system that has been established in this extremely complex and diverse nation. Despite its problems and shortcomings, India is a remarkably full-fledged practicing democracy and by far the largest (perhaps the only one) of the world's true democracies with a massive rural population that is predominantly illiterate and highly traditional. Although a fairly sizable portion of the population is as well-off, educated, and integrated into modern life (including the Internet) as any comparable segment anywhere in the world, that segment of the population is encapsulated within the rest of India, able to wire itself to cyberspace only to the extent (and in ways) Indian politics and bureaucratic regulations will allow.

With this as background, India's relationship to the international regime for the Internet might be expected to grow gradually over time, as it did in the 1990s. To be sure, the international regime is being constructed for the most part without significant Indian participation, but young Indian Internet entrepreneurs have had some global impact, and their potential in that regard is even greater for the future. For India to begin to realize the goal of the 1999 telecommunications policy—to become an Internet superpower—massive capital investment would be needed to provide the infrastructure, hardware, software, and human resources necessary for such a denouement. Given the domestic political and bureaucratic constraints outlined earlier, India's ability to attract the proportion of the world's IT investment needed for Internet superpower status is likely to fall short for years, if not decades, into the future. Although this will undoubtedly be disappointing to netizens and IT enthusiasts in India, it will give comfort to the substantial traditional sectors of Indian society and to a good portion of the bureaucracy whose children and grandchildren may be more inclined to view the Internet with favor but who, in this generation, are suspicious of it and are hesitant to push it along at a rapid pace.

▪ NOTES

1. The editor of the *Journal of Strategic Studies,* Amos Perlmutter, for example, wrote in an op-ed piece, "The twenty-first century will witness a dramatic change in the world's balance of power from Europe to Asia. There are two major aspiring powers—India and Japan—and one hegemonial power: China." See Perlmutter, "Shifting Balance of World Power," p. A15.

2. The idea was first conceived by national policymakers who argued in *New Telecom Policy 1999* (p. 2) that rapid development of the Internet would "propel India into becoming an IT superpower." Whether India can or should become an Internet superpower has become an issue in political campaigns. See, for example, "IT—Superpower Hype."

3. See Franda, "China and India Online."

4. President Jiang Zemin, for example, was quoted as early as 1991 to the effect that China "must develop electronics as eagerly as we developed atomic bombs." *South China Morning Post,* April 10, 1991, quoted in Mueller and Tan, *China in the Information Age,* p. 56.

5. Analysis of the Mosaic findings is available in Goodman et al., *The Global Diffusion of the Internet Project.*

6. In January 2000, ChinaNet had a total bandwidth of 487 million bits per second, whereas GBNet (Golden Bridge Network, servicing some corporate accounts) had 67 million, CSTNet (the science and technology network, operated by the Chinese Academy of Sciences) had 22 million, UniNET and China Netcom (commercial networks created in 1999) had 20 million total between them, and CERNET (the education and research network, run by the State Education Commission) had a mere 8 million bits of bandwidth. For a comprehensive and detailed discussion of China's network infrastructure, see Foster, "China and the Internet, pp. 45 ff.

7. See Lovelock, *E-China,* pp. 14 and 16. A second authorized carrier—China Unicom—has a total bandwidth of 12 million bits per second and is concentrating on building mobile telephone services within urban areas, but China Unicom has only a nascent long-distance network, and its infrastructure is not able to provide Internet services. See Tan, Foster, and Goodman, "China's State-Coordinated Internet Infrastructure," pp. 45–47.

8. Lovelock, *E-China,* pp. 16–17. China Telecom now has a national infrastructure with fiber-optic lines as its backbone, supplemented by a national satellite network with thirty-eight major earth stations and a microwave network to cover remote areas. See Tan, Foster, and Goodman, "China's State-Coordinated Internet Infrastructure," p. 47.

9. Quoted directly from Order 195 in Barmé and Ye, "The Great Firewall of China," p. 154.

10. For a detailed analysis of these measures and changes as they relate to the Internet, see Franda, "China and India Online," especially chaps. 2 and 3.

11. This paragraph is based on reports from the *People's Daily* (Beijing), as interpreted in the English-language press. For a summary article, see, for example, "China Unveils."

12. For a summary, see "China Telecom Feeling Increasingly Embattled."

13. "China Telecom, China Unicom."

14. Mueller and Tan, *China in the Information Age,* p. 12. The previous quote in this paragraph is from the same source.

15. Quoted in O'Neill, "Beijing Commits," p. 1.

16. Brauchli, Kahn, and Witcher, "Murdoch's Plans," p. 4.

17. Dickie, "Microsoft Launches," quoted in Taubman, "A Not-So World Wide Web," p. 265.

18. Barmé and Ye, "The Great Firewall of China," p. 151.

19. "Feeding the Flame."

20. Dickie, "Microsoft Launches," quoted in Taubman, "A Not-So World Wide Web," p. 266.

21. Engardio et al., "Activists Without Borders," pp. 144–150. See also Laris, "China Presses," p. A20.

22. Barmé and Ye, "The Great Firewall of China," pp. 155–156. Information and quotations in this paragraph are based on this source unless otherwise noted.

23. In March 2000, Beijing's municipal Departments of Public Security, Telecommunications, and Culture, jointly with the government's Administration for Industry and Commerce, enacted new registration and compliance regulations—including the penalty of confiscation of "illegal" earnings. According to a March 21 report in *Zhongguo Xinxi Bao* (China Information News), there were Internet cafés throughout Beijing, but only eight had obtained the necessary licenses and certification. Officials had charged that these cafés were inspiring illegal acts (Internet theft, credit card forgery, sale of pornography, infiltration of secure computers by hackers, and the like). The municipality has now established a special bureau to send inspectors to Internet cafés on a regular basis and assess penalties on the spot. Following this lead, other cities in China enacted similar regulations in the following months. See "China's Beijing Cracks Down." For analysis of the intensified drives against cybercafés in 2001, see Wade, "China's War Against Internet Cafs," pp. 1–3, and Pan, "China Opens a Broad Drive Against Dissenters," p. 1.

24. A number of surveys have indicated that although government websites dominate e-commerce and significant economic and financial discussion within China, more than 80 percent of the information held by government departments is not accessible by the public. See, for example, the summary in "It's a Long Road to E-Commerce."

25. The quote is from Chen Wenling, assistant director of the Industry, Transport, Trade, and Economic Development Department of the State Council, in "Conditions Not Yet Ripe."

26. "Goldman Sachs."

27. These are the conclusions of a survey conducted by Shanghai's Field Force Group and reported in "Survey of Obstacles to E-Commerce."

28. Lovelock, *E-China*, p. 11.

29. See, for example, "Getting Organized" and "China to Introduce Credit."

30. Reported in "China Government."

31. In May 2000, China's *Caijing Shibao* (Financial Daily) reported that "China's fledgling Internet industry is in an uproar over the possibility that the Chinese government intends to tax this still-vulnerable sector" because of a statement made by Finance Minister Xiang Huaicheng growing out of the draft guidelines document. The director of the Ministry of Finance's Department of Taxation Rules and Regulations bureau, Shi Yaobin, later told reporters that "traditional taxes"—such as the value-added tax, consumption tax, and commercial contract stamp tax—would be collected on e-commerce transactions as in other commercial spheres. Shi explained the minister's comments by saying that "e-commerce could very well replace traditional models of commerce and become the leading or even the only model," and "because of this, the need to establish tax collection and regulatory methods especially for e-commerce is growing increasingly urgent." An English version of the article is available in "Will China Tax?"

32. The extensive regulations contained in the draft guidelines were published in the *People's Daily,* August 28, 2000, and took effect on September 1, 2000. They are reprinted in "China Posts New Business." See also Gesteland, "China's Business Environment."

33. A discussion of recent Chinese plans for a strengthened air force appears in Pomfret, "China Plans." For analysis of China's naval development, see Lewis and Litai, *China's Strategic Seapower.* Discussion of PRC goals with regard to information warfare appears in Pufeng, "The Challenge of Information Warfare," pp. 317–327.

34. Reported in "Hack Attack."

35. This idea has been championed by the leadership of the People's Liberation Army and is probably being implemented. See, for example, the editorial in *Liberation Daily* (the newspaper of the People's Liberation Army), quoted in "Chinese People Can Say."

36. Quoted in McCarthy, "China, Russia," p. 2.

37. Ibid.

38. For a more complete discussion of the several attempts by the PRC leadership to develop a Chinese-only intranet in the 1990s, see Lovelock, *E-China,* pp. 21–22.

39. The project is described in detail in Liu, "Motorola Partners."

40. Yeomans, "Planet Web," p. 30.

41. "Lack of Net Standards."

42. See, for example, "China Introduces Chinese Character Web Site." See also "Business China Offers Deal"; Greenberg, "Domain Registrars"; and "China Channel, CNNIC."

43. "42,000 Chinese Domain Names." A seven-page outline of CNNIC's domain name system appears in "Complete CNNIC Rules."

44. Quoted in Manuel and Chang, "Will Language Wars Balkanize the Web?" p. C22.

45. See, for example, "Give Me Back My Name!" pp. 1–2, and "And They're Off!" pp. 1–2.

46. Manuel and Chang, "Will Language Wars Balkanize the Web?" p. C22.

47. Quoted in ibid.

48. The original Xinhua News Agency Report describing the C-Net project appeared in *Xinhuashe* (Xinhua News Agency), January 6, 2001, translated and published in "'Uniquely Chinese Internet,'" pp. 1–2. See also Oyama, "China Aims at Its Own Internet Network," p. A3.

49. Xia Chuanyou, president of Sichuan Zhongcheng Network Development Company Limited, is often called the initiator of C-Net. He and other supporters of the C-Net network idea argue that China must establish its own national network, independent from the global Internet, "to break the monopoly of foreign countries on information resources." Quoted in "Management Split on Future," p. 2.

50. "'Uniquely Chinese Internet,'" p. 1.

51. de Jonquieres and Kynge, "Beijing's Big Gamble," p. 26.

52. On the functioning of feedback mechanisms in regime theory, see Young, "Regime Dynamics," pp. 110ff.

53. See "New eAsia Report."

54. The IDC index is based on twenty-three variables and attempts to benchmark the standing of various nations with regard to their ability to access, absorb, and effectively take advantage of IT. India was ranked in the last of four categories, as a "stroller" on the information highway (along with eleven other countries, including Pakistan, Jordan, China, Indonesia, Egypt, and Peru), far back of countries ranked as "skaters" (e.g., Sweden and the United States), "striders" (e.g., Belgium, Ireland, and New Zealand), and "sprinters" (e.g., Poland, South Africa, the United Arab Emirates, and Venezuela). For more information about the index, contact wwelch@worldtimes.com or see the *World Paper,* January–February 2001, pp. 8–9.

55. See chap. 5 in Press, Foster, and Goodman, "The Internet," pp. 1–16. Figures in this and the following paragraph are from this source.

56. See "Internet Infrastructure Needed."

57. Press, Foster, and Goodman. "The Internet." Government plans to build a national Internet backbone for India are outlined in Aggarwal, "Building India's National Internet," pp. 53–58. For a report on the lack of implementation of these plans, see "Internet Infrastructure Needed."

58. The Arizona study, for example, quotes the ITU's *Asia Pacific Telecommunication Indicators* figures for 1996, when India's capital expenditures for telecommunications were $1.8 billion and China's were $13 billion. The foreign investment ratio is from the World Bank's *World Development Indicators* (1997), also quoted in the Arizona study. In February 2000 the *Wall Street Journal* reported that foreign direct investment in India had actually declined for two straight years and was down 17 percent in the first eight months of that fiscal year; see Karp, "India's Finance Minister," p. A19. A second *Wall Street Journal* article pointed out that Indian government spending on infrastructure had also declined over the two-year period, and "red tape, policy changes and legal hassles continue to deter foreign capital." See Karp, "Reform Raj," p. A10. For an analysis of India's budgetary approach to IT in 2000, see "Waiting for the New India," pp. 18–19.

59. See also Chibber and Eldersveld, "Local Elites and Popular Support," pp. 350–374.

60. Press, Foster, and Goodman, "The Internet."

61. Pai, "India's PC Industry," p. 26.

62. *World Telecommunication Development Report,* 1997, quoted in ibid.

63. Quoted in Chendakera, "Software-Rich India," pp. 1–2. See also Chendakera, "New Delhi's Budget Plan," pp. 30–35. Chendakera quotes an IDC study to the effect that of more than 800,000 computers sold in India in 1999, *none* was manufactured in India. More than half were assembled in India, all with imported components. India's import duties on computers and computer parts in 1999 added $900 to the cost of an average-priced PC that would otherwise have sold for $1,125.

64. Downs, "A Quarter of Private Investment."

65. See Rao, "ISP Boom in India," p. 2.

66. Rao, "Indian ISPs Form Alliances," p. 2.

67. Quoted in Marquand, "From Farms to Firms," p. 7.

68. See "The Wiring of India," pp. 63–64.

69. For more detail, see ibid., p. 64.

70. Ibid. See also "India's IT Growth," and Chendakera, "AT&T Enters," pp. 43–47.

71. Chendakera, "Korea's LG Group," pp. 38–41.

72. For additional satellite-related investments, see Mecham, "India Opens Door," pp. 54ff.

73. Quoted in Krishnada, "India Eyes Foreign Telecom," p. 46.

74. Dhume, "India's Awakening," pp. 32–33.

75. Figures are from Karp, "BJP Makes Patriotic Pitch," p. A10.

76. *Fortune* magazine estimated that Indian software computer exports for 2000 (compiled on the basis of unofficial figures in December 2000) were

$6.5 billion, projecting out to $30 billion by 2004. See Whelan, "Emerging Markets," pp. 184–187.

77. Sender, "Nations Strengthen Ties in Software," p. A7.

78. Stremlau, "Bangalore," pp. 50–51.

79. Patni, "Silicon Valley of the East," pp. 8–9.

80. David, "Infosys City," p. 40.

81. Levander, "By Its Bootstraps," p. R16.

82. "Booting Up in Andhra Pradesh," pp. 46–47.

83. "The State That Would Reform India," p. 38.

84. For a biography of Naidu, see Marquand, "Fast-Rising Leader," pp. 1 ff.

85. Quoted in Cooper, "Look at India," pp. 1–5.

86. Cooper, "China and India's IT Connection," pp. 1–5.

87. Bristow, "India May Eclipse China in IT," pp. 29–30.

88. Ibid., p. 30.

89. Ibid.

90. Quoted in Li, "Great Software Divide," p. 12. Quotes from Bethany Chan, later in this paragraph, are also from this source.

91. Smith, "China at Gate." See also Leggett, "China Plans Two Stock Markets," p. A13, and Pecht, Liu, and Hodges, "Semiconductor Companies in China," pp. 148–154.

92. Sender, "China Flirts with Venture Capitalism," p. A3.

93. *Extraordinary* was the word used by George Tenet, director of the CIA, in a report to the U.S. Senate. See "A Prelude to Info War." See also Gompert, "Right Makes Might," pp. 69 ff.

94. Denning, *Information Warfare and Security,* pp. 229 ff.

95. The news was announced by the Press Trust of India and reported by the BBC and the Indian press.

96. *Strategic Defence Review: The Maritime Dimensions,* a Naval Vision report prepared under the guidance of Chief Admiral Vishnu Bhagwat, quoted at www.infowar.com, November 17, 1998.

97. Deibert, "Circuits of Power," p. 235.

98. For descriptions of some of these Indianization activities, see Rao, "First South Asian Internet," and Rao, "Internet Is Emerging." See also "India: New Telecom Technology."

99. Goh, "Global Body for Tamil," p. 53.

100. Based on interviews and on Rao, "Indian Portals." See also "English Losing Monopoly."

101. The incident is described in "Indian ISP VSNL Ordered."

102. Quoted in "Cyberbill-II." Quotations in this and the following paragraph are from this source.

103. Mahajan also defended the bill by arguing that the final legislation had rejected suggestions by the parliamentary standing committee that all cybercafés must register with the government and another suggestion by members of parliament for compulsory registration of all websites or portals hosted in India. Mahajan promised parliament that "we will not act against someone who

is innocent or is visiting certain websites without an ulterior motive"; "Parliament Okays IT Bill," p. 2. See also "Regulating the Internet."

104. See the discussion of network security in Deibert, "Circuits of Power," pp. 258–265.

105. See *The Emerging Digital Economy,* cited in ibid., p. 259.

106. "Cyberlaw: E-Commerce for Babus."

107. The director-general of the WTO, Mike Moore, for example, has argued that "the world needs a strong, successful and competent India," both to help lead the developing world and as "one of the great marketplaces of the future." See the interview with Moore in Parthasarthy, "'The World Needs a Strong India,'" p. 110.

108. For greater detail on India's involvement with the international regime, see Franda, "China and India Online," chap. 5.

109. Ramani, "Humble Beginnings." Ramani is director of the NCST and president of the Computer Society of India.

110. In 2001, for example, the Internet Protocol Version 6 (IPv6) Forum, based in Luxembourg, promoted India as a solutions provider for applications based on the IPv6 next-generation version of Internet protocol (IP) in recognition of the considerable contribution of Indian scientists and engineers to its development. For more information about IPv6, see Franda, *Governing the Internet,* chap. 1.

8

The Internet in Comparative International Perspective

The case studies in this volume cover five large and diverse regions of the world where the Internet has penetrated much less deeply than in the United States and Europe. The manner in which the Internet has been received and developed varies enormously from one country to another within each region or, in the cases of China and India, from one part of these vast countries to another. For a large number of rulers in the five regions, the Internet has been viewed as politically intrusive, culturally threatening, or both. For less than a handful its invention was rather quickly adopted as something that might help a nation modernize, become part of an accelerating process of globalization, or simply communicate better within its borders and with the rest of the world. Perhaps in most cases, leadership has shared something of both kinds of responses, being hesitant to invest heavily in Internet-related sectors of the economy before fully understanding the consequences of such investment while at the same time recognizing that the Internet is an invention unlike almost any in the past, with enormous potential for changing the world into the future.

Regardless of the responses of rulers, the Internet is regularly used in 2001 by more than 6 percent of the population in only four of the ninety-six countries in the five regions included in the case studies in this volume (South Africa, Estonia, Israel, and the United Arab Emirates are the four exceptional countries). In more than eighty of the ninety-six countries, less than 2 percent of the population had any access to the Internet at the onset of the third millennium. In more than two-thirds of the ninety-six countries, far less than 1 percent had access.

227

International forces can be seen as the main factors influencing adoption of Internet use in all of the case studies. The way the technology was invented, the standards adopted for its dissemination, and its promulgation through computers that had just started to gain fairly substantial worldwide distribution in the 1990s were elements put in place by forces extraneous to the countries in all five case study regions. And in most cases the pressures to adopt Internet technology in the five regions have been very powerful, driven by the appeal of websites and portals in the United States and Europe, by opportunities for exchanging e-mail or engaging in e-commerce and e-business transactions instantaneously almost anywhere in the world, by the potential opportunities to gain capital investment for domestic modernization projects from large transnational and multinational corporations seeking a more globalized presence, and by the security threats (real, imagined, and potential) that the global Internet poses.

■ THE INTERNET, SOVEREIGNTY, AND DEMOCRACY

Responses to the invention and spread of the Internet by the leaders of nation-states in the case studies have been consistent with sovereign states' international relations behavior over the past three centuries. Robert Keohane and Joseph Nye concluded a quarter century ago that "modernists point correctly to . . . fundamental changes now taking place, but they often assume without sufficient analysis that advances in technology and increases in social and economic transactions will lead to a new world in which states, and their control of force, will no longer be important."[1] Writing twenty years later, Keohane and Nye found their conclusions from two decades earlier particularly relevant to the Internet, where, in their words, "prophets of a new cyberworld, like modernists before them, often overlook how much the new world overlaps and rests on the traditional world in which power depends on geographically based institutions. . . . Rules will be necessary to govern cyberspace . . . [and] rules require authority, whether in the form of public government or private or community governance. [But] classic issues of politics—who governs and on what terms—are as relevant to cyberspace as to the real world."[2]

Faced with the global spread of the Internet—in a rapid, disorderly, and unpredictable manner in the 1990s—national leadership groups in most countries were immediately cautious about accepting it fully and were determined to make sure its introduction was consistent with national interests. In well over half of the states under review, leaders responded to the invention of the Internet by pursuing an isolationist position, trying to confine Internet use primarily to a small elite portion of the population (usually military, scientific, and administrative-intelligence circles) while severely controlling the circumstances under which the bulk of the population was able to gain and use Internet access. As is pointed out in Chapters 2 and 4, a third of the countries in the Middle East, Eurasia, and Central/East European case studies (fourteen of the forty-two nations) have been included among twenty nations worldwide as "enemies of the Internet" by Reporters Sans Frontieres (RSF)—including six of the eight countries in Central Asia and the Caucasus (Azerbaijan, Kazakhstan, Kyrgyzstan, Tajikistan, Turkmenistan, and Uzbekistan) plus Belarus and, in the Middle East, Iran, Iraq, Libya, Saudi Arabia, Sudan, Syria, and Tunisia. These fourteen nations have been classified as Internet enemies because they "control access totally or partially, have censored websites, or [have] taken action against users."[3] In most nations in the case studies, leaders have pursued isolationist strategies by simply neglecting to invest in Internet-related technologies or refusing to change the legal and administrative investment climates in ways that would attract the kind of capital needed to generate significant Internet growth.

Economics has been, and will continue to be, a major inhibiting factor for the vast majority of international states when considering programs to provide the telecommunications infrastructures that would make Internet access possible for larger portions of national populations. In the case studies in this volume—especially in the FSU states and Africa—the sheer poverty and isolation of most countries, particularly when combined with the many conflictual and demoralizing carryovers from past international relationships, have often thwarted attempts by leaders who have tried to move their nations more aggressively into the world of twenty-first-century information technology. In some instances—primarily in the Middle East and India—potential resources could be either developed domestically or imported from abroad to facilitate more rapid Internet-related development, but leaders convinced of the value of IT and the Internet have been hampered in their ability to exploit such resources in the face of what they see as more pressing and immediate needs that are closer to their perceived national interests. In the Middle East these needs are often underpinned by political exigencies related to the preservation of religious and cultural communities. In India powerful constituencies that view the introduction of the Internet as a threat to their interests (e.g., rural interests, labor unions, small business, and the world's largest bureaucracy) have effectively slowed and circumscribed the introduction of Internet-related technology and investment.

Instead of undermining the sovereignty of the state, in the case studies in this volume the Internet has come up against the nation-state as the gatekeeper of technological innovation, particularly in matters related to information technology.[4] To be sure, national leadership has not been able to totally control who gains access to the Internet and under what circumstances, nor is that the goal in most countries. Where it is the goal—in much of Central Asia, in Azerbaijan, and in some parts of the Middle East (e.g., Iraq and Libya)—Internet access has been effectively denied to all but a tiny select portion of the population. In most nations such severe isolation is not seen as being in the national interest, with the result that most national leaderships have sought to allow Internet penetration into their nations on a controlled basis.

Because of international states' determination to assert control over the Internet as a medium of communication, the expectations of those who had hoped to establish cyberspace as a sovereign territory in its own right have not approached realization. Methods of control pursued by nation-states in the case studies include:

1. Passing of laws restricting or censoring Internet use in matters related to security and defense, pornography, the bounds of political debate, criticism of rulers and their families, writings and religious discussion that might cause dissension, social and sexual mores, and more (laws in at least one of these areas have been enacted in forty of the forty-two countries in the Middle East, Eurasia, and the CEE studied in this volume)
2. Requiring users to register with the government to gain Internet access (this is the case in most Middle Eastern nations and more than half of those in the FSU)
3. Imposing fines for publications on the Web that violate national laws (several nations in the Middle East and FSU)
4. Banning restricted sites through proxy servers and elaborate filtering systems (e.g., UAE, Saudi Arabia)
5. Closing down cybercafés and other public places where Internet behavior and content violate national laws (e.g., Albania, China)

6. Restricting use of encryption technology (Israel, Saudi Arabia, Tunisia)

7. Restricting licenses for Internet use to institutions (e.g., universities, publication houses) and then holding the institutions responsible for the behavior of individuals using the Internet within those institutions (Albania, several countries in the Middle East)

8. Requiring ISPs to link their systems to government intelligence and security networks while allowing security networks to tap into e-mail messages and other Internet content and to share such content with other government agencies (e.g., Russia, China)

9. Holding ISPs responsible for Internet content and use that contradicts national laws (e.g., Russia, Tunisia)

10. Permitting surveillance of e-mail, chat rooms, and other Internet content by intelligence agencies (perhaps more than half of the ninety-six countries in the five regions)

11. Sending reminders, escalating to threats, to disconnect service in the event of violations of laws governing Internet content and use (e.g., Jordan, the Yugoslav Federation, Russia, China)

12. Arresting those violating laws (e.g., Bahrain, Yugoslav Federation)

13. Establishing a complete government monopoly over everything having to do with the Internet—from telecommunications through Internet service—to facilitate government control (e.g., Ukraine, Turkmenistan, Yugoslav Federation, Iraq, Libya)

In addition to these methods, a forty-five-page study of e-commerce in developing nations, prepared for the U.S. National Intelligence Council by the Washington, D.C., law firm of Booz-Allen and Hamilton, identified a number of other practices of the more oppressive LDCs that intruded on widespread Internet development. Among these are (1) *traffic analysis,* keeping track of senders, recipients, message volume, and related data, often using floating servers or false identities; (2) *hacking techniques* that cause malfunctions in targeted websites, inject viruses, or otherwise disrupt the computers of anti-government Internet activists; and (3) *dissemination of disinformation and attractive misleading information* "planted" in a variety of ways (sometimes ostensibly from trusted associates) to sow confusion and dissemble relationships among leaders and followers of dissident groups and parties. The Booz-Allen study concluded that increasing Internet access at the local level in the developing world would generally be "a positive factor politically," but warned that "it will not by itself bring about individual liberty or democratic government."[5]

Individuals and organizations have occasionally been able to fight governments to assert their right to privacy—most often by using encryption technologies, mirror pages, anonymizers, and other technological devices able to diminish the effectiveness of government surveillance equipment—with varying degrees of success. Many of the laws designed to control Internet behavior and content are simply disregarded on a widespread basis, sometimes giving users and foreign ISPs the impression that the laws are meaningless; but the feeling of assurance has lasted in those countries only until a seemingly lax law is suddenly enforced. Most human rights and commercial organizations in the three regions argue that attempts to control Internet behavior and content are fairly effective in meeting government goals, resulting in a serious diminution of Internet use by almost everyone concerned (including for e-commerce, e-business, and other functions where trust and assurance of privacy are essential).

A number of nongovernmental organizations (NGOs) in the three case study regions are working—either with governments or against them—to try to facilitate and build support for the diffusion of the Internet and in some cases to allow greater freedom of access. As pointed out in the case studies, perhaps the most impressive and courageous work in this regard has been done by journalists, media leaders, and human rights organizations—such as the B92 enterprise in Yugoslavia and Amnesty International in all of the regions—but including many others as detailed in previous chapters. Journalists throughout the region have clearly benefited from the existence of the Internet by suddenly finding themselves in a position to gather information from throughout the world to a degree not previously imaginable. In several countries in the Middle East and the FSU where governments have placed strict bans on what the print and broadcast media publish for domestic consumption, such restrictions have been relaxed slightly for journalists writing primarily for external audiences over the Internet—with the result that the outside world is often better informed about these countries' political and economic affairs than are those inside without access to global Internet technology.

But in those cases where NGOs, journalists, and human rights organizations have tried to take on government organizations in attempts to get them to change their behavior, they have almost always been able to do so only with the support of foreign organizations, which has led to many charges by governments in the case study regions that such private organizations are used by enemy governments to destabilize or disrupt international relations. To a much lesser extent, governments have occasionally objected to the role of private entrepreneurs, grant-making foundations, and international organizations in their attempts to spread Internet use—as, for example, when Belarus broke off relations with the Soros Foundation in 1997 or when the People's Assembly in Egypt passed laws in 1999 severely restricting the ways in which NGOs could relate to indigenous organizations over the Internet. On a day-to-day basis, the vast majority of NGOs, journalists, and human rights organizations with interests in extending the reach of the Internet have chosen to work with rather than against authorities in the three regions, and most governments have designated specific agencies to both coordinate and monitor NGO, journalistic, and human rights activities. As pointed out in the case studies, such government agencies are increasingly appointed at higher and higher policymaking levels, with the Palestine Authority the first to establish a ministry devoted solely to NGO affairs.

Although many visionaries have seen the kernels of future civil societies and democracies in the creation of "new international communicators," particularly where such new communicators are beginning to be linked by the Internet across national borders through NGO organizations or as journalists or human rights activists, the number of such new communicators in the three regions under review is still minuscule. The costs of accessing the Internet in the case study regions, particularly when combined with the paucity of information available about indigenous matters, make it extremely difficult for citizens within these societies to use the Internet to become better informed about what is going on locally. In this atmosphere it would be difficult to identify in the case study regions (with the possible exception of Estonia) anything resembling the *publicum* Torbjorn Knutsen associates with Internet communities that seem to be emerging in some parts of Europe and perhaps in economically developed countries elsewhere, as discussed in Chapter 1.

In theory, one can imagine the Internet eventually bringing together like-minded people from many countries to help build more open communications networks, thicker patterns of globalization, and eventually more open civil societies or even democracies. Such is the hope of one analyst, for example, who has called on U.S. president George W. Bush to appoint a chief information officer to his cabinet to create a worldwide

"digital Marshall Plan" that would eventually produce a "global information commons."[6] Similar ideas have been proposed in other contexts,
with the hope that such efforts might be led by international organizations or intergovernmental organizations such as the group of seven
(G-7) or perhaps by private-sector alliances.[7] But the present reality in
most nations is rather different than an idealized information commons
or a global digital democracy. Faced with hard choices, large numbers
of world leaders conclude that they have much higher priorities than the
building of domestic Internet capabilities, to such an extent that many
poorer nations have even refused to pay the minor fees assessed by
ICANN to manage country domain names.[8]

The frustrations of younger leaders who do appreciate the possibilities inherent in a digital future are perhaps illustrated most dramatically
in the case studies by the ascendancy to the presidency of Syria in 2000
by Bashar Assad, who aspires to allow greater public access to the Internet—in sharp contrast to the views and policies during his deceased
father's regime. Younger-generation rulers like Assad have run up
against the interests of the military and intelligence communities in
their nations, as well as against an older generation of diplomats and
domestic political and administrative elites who are less enthusiastic
about the expansion of cyberspace and less willing to agree to rapid introduction of the Internet within domestic society.

Evidence from the case studies indicates that the possibilities of
using the Internet to promote more open societies and democracy are
greater in those parts of Eastern Europe and in India where fairly
healthy democratic systems already exist and governments are more
willing to countenance a relatively free flow of information than is the
case in the less democratic parts of Eastern Europe, the Middle East,
and the FSU states. Even in the most democratic nations in the case
studies, however, there is often a deep-seated reluctance to allow unrestricted dissemination over the Internet of the kind of information citizens would need to convert the Internet into a driver or an engine of
civil society. In India, for example, local officials have seldom allowed
land records to become available over the Internet, fearing publication
of such records might lead to a rash of court cases and fuel local political conflicts. With the exception of Estonia, governments in Central and
Eastern Europe have been unable to overcome political obstacles that
would make it possible for them to create websites and portals that
might provide lawyers and citizens with convenient access to legal

codes, parliamentary reports and discussions, up-to-date economic data, summaries of the administrative rules of domestic regulatory regimes, and other information essential to making informed judgments in democratic polities.

In this atmosphere the idea that the Internet could somehow be the venue for a democratic town meeting in cyberspace seems still in the realm of science fiction, at least for the vast bulk of the countries in the five regions studied in this volume. If one conceives of each of the forty-two countries in the case study regions and the fifty-four countries in Africa as a "neighborhood" represented at a "town meeting" to be organized in cyberspace, eighty of these neighborhoods (countries) would be represented by less than 0.2 percent of their populations, and four of the neighborhoods would be represented by more than 6 percent of their populations. Lacking Internet access, the vast majority of the people in all neighborhoods (countries) would be barred from the cyberspace town meeting. To complicate matters further, there would be a good chance that Internet users from outside the territorial jurisdiction of the countries in the case studies (e.g., from the more advanced IT societies in North America and Europe, from international NGOs, and from international business) would want to weigh in on town meeting discussions, and they would be considerably advantaged because of their superior numbers and capabilities in cyberspace.

Rather than witnessing the emergence of cyberspace democracy or the incipient triumph of the Internet in promoting civil society and democracy, the countries under review are experiencing the use of the Internet by elite minorities representing a fairly narrow spectrum of political discourse relative to local context. The Internet is expanding in the sense that the dialogue over e-mail and websites is increasingly in languages other than English, but this often enables governments to become more proficient in their attempts to control what is said and how far it reaches. Indeed, possibilities for gaining greater control over Internet content and use are a major reason China's leadership has so assiduously pursued the idea of creating an entirely separate Internet for the Chinese language, as described in Chapter 7.

Perhaps the most accurate prediction of how the Internet would be integrated into the lives of most of the world's population in the early twenty-first century was made by one of the founders of the field of political communications, Ithiel de Sola Pool, in the last book he published before his death:

Electronic media, as they are coming to be, are dispersed in use and abundant in supply. They allow for more knowledge, easier access, and freer speech than were ever enjoyed before. They fit the free practices of print. The characteristics of media shape what is done with them, so one might anticipate that these technologies of freedom will overwhelm all attempts to control them. Technology, however, shapes the structure of the battle, but not every outcome. While the printing press was without doubt the foundation of modern democracy, the response to the flood of publishing that it brought forth has been censorship as often as press freedom. In some times and places the even more capacious new media will open wider the floodgates for discourse, but in other times and places, in fear of that flood, attempts will be made to shut the gates.[9]

▪ INTERNATIONAL POLITICAL ECONOMY, THE INTERNET, AND GLOBALIZATION

In addition to the impact the Internet has had on the nature of the political dialogue within nations in the case studies, it has also affected the nature and extent of the dialogue between elites within the nations under review and various diasporas around the world. Jon Anderson, as quoted in Chapter 3, has identified "diaspora pioneers" originally from the Arab Middle East who were the first to create Internet sites and software of high value to Middle Eastern issues and culture, were the first to use the Internet, and were instrumental in its introduction into Middle Eastern settings. For Slovakia, a "citizens network" built around the World Wide Web was a key factor in mobilizing the numerous Slovak communities in countries around the world to raise funds and provide expertise for the development of computer and Internet technology within Slovakia's borders. Indians living abroad were instrumental in developing most of the initial websites with Indianized content during the early years when the Internet was not encouraged by authorities in New Delhi, and the Indian entrepreneurs who first began to build the country's world-class capabilities in software design and manufacturing got their start in the Silicon Valley (California) and other foreign sites rather than in India. Israel's pattern of Internet use has been more rapid than India's, and its software manufacturing capabilities grew from a more solid domestic base from the outset of the Internet's invention, but Internet growth for Israel (as is clear from Chapter 2) has nonetheless been heavily dependent on Israel's multifaceted relationships with the Jewish diaspora and with Israelis living abroad.

Based on the successful use of diaspora communities in helping to build the Internet elsewhere, a number of countries in the case study regions—most notably Hungary—are beginning to explore ways to emulate the success of other nations. The leaders of several of the nation-states in the case studies have also tried to work with diaspora leaders and communities to develop Internet materials in languages other than English and to build Internet websites and portals aimed specifically at the language groups and cultures of specific nations. One of the most successful such attempts, as discussed in Chapter 7, is being carried out by leaders of the Tamil-speaking community in India, working in conjunction with substantial members of Tamil community leaders in Singapore, Malaysia, Sri Lanka, Australia, Switzerland, and the United States.

Apart from the relationships between diaspora communities have been the various migrations taking place between nations as they try to meet the human resource needs for introducing Internet-related production and manufacturing facilities in highly competitive markets. Literally tens of thousands of Indians with engineering and computer skills have flocked to the United States and Europe, where they have played major roles in effecting the computer and Internet "revolutions" during the past few decades. An indicator of the extent to which such migration is taking place was the recent decision by the Japanese government to issue a blanket administrative order, providing 10,000 visas for Indian software engineers beginning in mid-2000, to encourage Japanese firms to hire Indians to fill domestic needs.[10] Chapter 2 detailed some of the ways almost 200,000 computer-literate Russian émigrés, including many engineers, played key roles in developing Israel's IT and Internet industries.

At the turn of the twenty-first century, however, it is becoming more common for Internet-related companies to locate new plants and businesses in places where engineering and computer skills exist rather than trying to lure people with skills to migrate from one geographic location to another. This is more usual today than it was in the 1980s and 1990s because investment climates are more often conducive to such business decisions. As discussed in Chapter 6, for example, a number of Internet companies decided in 1999 that it had become economical (and politically possible) to locate plants in Romania rather than continue to hire Romanians to migrate elsewhere, largely as a result of a change of governments in Romania that produced new investment laws and procedures making it easier for foreign firms to locate there.

As the case studies make clear, attracting international investment is perhaps the major factor in the development of Internet-related infrastructures, which in turn are the beginning point for lowering the cost of Internet access while providing high-speed and reliable Internet service, thereby increasing Internet use. Where substantial and timely international investments relative to a country's size are assured, as in Estonia (Chapter 5) or Israel (Chapter 2), use of the Internet has mushroomed quickly and future IT growth seems certain. But the cost of building Internet infrastructures (including basic telecommunications) is so high and the technology sufficiently complex that no single government or combination of governments is wealthy enough to find the resources to build world-class Internet backbones on its own. In fact, the only way any country has found it possible to become significantly wired to cyberspace is to attract the large multinational and transnational corporations that have already gained major footholds in the telecommunications and Internet-related industries, which can either provide or help attract the capital needed.

Attracting the IT multinationals and the capital that comes with them requires a stable political situation, legal and administrative frameworks conducive to the functioning of a healthy private sector, and policies directly related to telecommunications and the Internet that provide for the privatization of major portions of previous government monopoly companies and encourage competition among service providers. The case studies describe a number of instances (e.g., Croatia, Syria, India) where a change of government has led to a more stable and conducive atmosphere that has attracted foreign investment in IT and Internet-related areas. They also discuss instances (e.g., the Czech Republic and Poland) where hints of instability or government change have at least temporarily slowed foreign investment in these same areas.

Telecom and Internet sectors are particularly vulnerable to rapid shifts of investment flows because the enormous demand for capital in these sectors makes it possible for investors to find alternative places to quickly move investment capital. In addition, companies and international investors have learned to be highly flexible in shifting investments in rapidly changing global IT environments.

As indicated in Chapter 5, most of the policies required for attracting international capital in the IT and Internet-related sectors are spelled out in the steps required to gain membership in the EU, as detailed in the European Community's 1987 Green Paper. These include (1) separation of regulatory authority from the operation of telecommunications systems; (2) open interconnection of user equipment to lines to encourage a free flow of information; (3) liberalized use of leased lines; (4) liberal licensing and other controls on private value-added networks, such as the Internet, to enable them to compete; (5) privatization of highly competitive specialized services, such as cellular and mobile; (6) tolerance of facilities-based private networks; (7) government allowance of competition in long-distance service; and (8) encouragement of competition in basic local or regional service. Although these requirements act as direct incentives only for those countries in Eastern Europe striving to become EU members, similar provisions can be found in the agreements already drawn up between the WTO and its members and in agreements being negotiated with countries aspiring to join the WTO in the future. Many of these policies are also part of World Bank conditions for providing loans in the telecommunications sector and are supported by the actions and guidelines developed over the years by international organizations like the OECD and the G-8 meetings that have played key roles in developing the international regime for the Internet.

In the case studies in this volume, the WTO agreement with Israel on basic telecom has been especially important in moving Israel in the direction of privatization and liberalization, although that movement has been slowed by international political factors and, more recently, by instabilities resulting from the failure of the peace process initiated by the Clinton administration. Domestic political constraints have also dogged India's attempts at privatization, which began to take on serious dimensions in 1994 when the World Bank insisted that India launch programs of telecommunications reform, privatization, and liberalization as part of a major lending effort by the Bank.[11] In both cases—in Israel and India—an initial lack of government willingness to introduce policies that would permit relatively unrestricted open competition in Internet-related sectors by private companies has meant that indigenous entrepreneurs with wonderful ideas for start-ups have either flocked to the Nasdaq exchange in the United States (more than eighty Israeli companies, for example, are listed on the Nasdaq) or—particularly in the case of Indian entrepreneurs—have simply founded their companies as American companies, incorporated and located in the United States.

One of the most interesting attempts to gain foreign investment from sources other than the large multinational and transnational companies and the banks and financial centers that follow them has been the program India launched in 1999 to attract investments from the 15–20 million Indians living outside India. In this case the Indian Finance Ministry has promised either dual citizenship or special green card citizenship privileges for people of Indian origin who have become citizens of other nations in return for investments in India.[12] Every indication thus far is that the program has produced relatively small gains in comparison to the amount of international capital needed to modernize India's Internet delivery sector, with investment by nonresident Indians (NRIs) actually declining rather than accelerating in recent years.[13] This project is an excellent example of a government miscalculating the massive amounts of investment funds required to significantly impact the development of information technology and the growth of the Internet, especially in a country the size of India.

■ PERSPECTIVES ON FUTURE DEVELOPMENT

The one aspect of the Internet in which almost all national governments in the case studies have taken a serious interest and initiated action to become significantly involved is in security-related matters. The countries that have aspirations to be either world or regional powers—Russia, India, Israel, Saudi Arabia, Yugoslavia—have already experienced attacks on their computer networks and have asked specific military and intelligence agencies to explore and initiate preparations for Internet warfare. In four regions in the case studies, conflict between countries over the Internet has been described by journalists and participants as "the first Internet war" (Armenia versus Azerbaijan in the Caucasus, India versus Pakistan and rebels in Assam versus India in the subcontinent, Arabs versus Israelis in the Middle East, and the war in Kosovo in the Balkans), although none of these skirmishes approaches the potential of infowar as defined by military analysts in the United States and Europe.[14] Data about readiness for various levels of Internet warfare are not available for specific countries, but most nations in the case study regions are clearly taking steps to build much more sophisticated Internet capabilities for their military and intelligence communities than are accessible by the general public and educational systems.

Many of the smaller and less powerful nations in the case study regions may not be preparing for a full-blown infowar but have nevertheless started to establish capabilities designed to cope with potential attacks on national electronic infrastructures or the spread of computer viruses in their countries, the delivery of malicious coding to key Internet installations, and theft or destruction of data over the Internet by hackers or terrorists. As is the case in other security matters, for example, Arabs worry about Israeli Internet dominance, Israelis want to provide security for their citizens against many possible forms of hostile action by Arabs, and both are concerned that terrorist groups or lone terrorists in the region (or perhaps even from outside the region) might inflict severe damage on strategic Internet facilities inside the borders of Middle Eastern nations. Similarly, India has established military and intelligence units for the express purpose of understanding and being able to counter hostile computer network activities by traditional international rivals Pakistan and China, as well as potential terrorist attacks from elsewhere on major infrastructural installations (such as stock exchanges, nuclear and telecommunications facilities, and air traffic control networks).

Security concerns have been paramount in all of the case study regions where the leaders of several nations have proposed or introduced policies to either ban or restrain the use of encryption software. As discussed previously, security and control considerations have prevailed to such an extent that no more than a half dozen countries in the three regions have been able to put in place systematic policies for protecting privacy for purposes of e-commerce. In some cases Internet security concerns have resulted in policies directly counter to what might be best for the growth of e-commerce and e-business transactions. What is viewed as excessive concern with security precautions by the governments of several countries in the five regions has often led to charges from international human rights organizations that such precautions constitute invasions of privacy and other violations of human rights. In Eastern European decisions involving international investment, security considerations (e.g., whether to allow Germans or Russians to invest on a large scale) were significant factors at several points in the case studies.

Perhaps more important than narrow security concerns in building an atmosphere of distrust around the expansion of the global Internet is the widespread belief throughout the regions under review that the Internet could and might be used to extend the political, economic, and cultural dominance of the United States and Europe over the rest of the world. This belief is held perhaps most intensely in the Middle East, where Arab nations have had difficulties in the past working with other international regimes led by the United States and Europe. Strains in relationships result from Arabs' rejection of some of the cultural manifestations of the West's secularism, the perceived past wrongs of colonial rule, and the West's role in creating and sustaining Israel. But fear of foreign dominance through use of Internet technology was also seen in several Eastern European countries in the case studies, particularly those involved in the wars in Bosnia and Kosovo, and is a major factor in China's aspiration to somehow create a wall in cyberspace between itself and the global Internet. The desire to gain strength vis-à-vis the advanced IT societies is also a driving force behind India's attempt to become an Internet superpower.

India's cautionary concerns about the international regime for the Internet reflect the perspectives of many developing countries, including perhaps most of those in the five case study regions in this volume. As discussed elsewhere, Indian leadership perceives in the global spread of the Internet a highly unfavorable competitive position for the developing world, whether in technology, finance, or other resources needed to be successful.[15] Indian leaders also resent their lack of representation and positions in key organizations involved in international regime formation where global norms, rules, and procedures are being decided and discussed. Among more radical Indian critics, the nascent international regime for the Internet is viewed as the latest in a series of powerful privatized knowledge-based regimes, backed by globally enforced standardized intellectual property law, that could lead to a new era of imperialism.[16]

Survey data referred to in Chapter 5 confirm that most Eastern Europeans simply assume that the spread of the Internet will contribute to U.S. global dominance, although unlike most Indian leaders they do not necessarily see this as having a totally negative effect on their future well-being. As is the case with other countries in the case studies, Eastern Europeans have not been significantly involved in such matters as the establishment of the Internet's technical standards and norms, the principles and rules adopted to ensure its daily functioning internationally, and the procedures used to ensure cooperation among providers and users or to resolve conflicts between them. This has perhaps been less of a concern to Eastern European leaders than it has been elsewhere because most East European nations have been extended the hope that they might eventually become full members of the EU, which in turn could give them ample opportunity to become involved in the international regime as part of an integrated Europe. Among the FSU states, the only nations that have been involved to any significant degree in building the international regime for the Internet are the Baltic countries, which are also the only FSU nations being considered for admission to the EU. No other FSU nation is significantly involved with the international regime, and several view it with some degree of hostility.

At this early stage of regime formation, it is not essential to the future of the global Internet that all of the countries in the five regions discussed in this volume be fully supportive of the regime. The regime allows for diversity of perspectives and does not require conformity by all nations— particularly smaller nations with little Internet capability—all of the time.[17] As was pointed out in Chapter 1, the international regime for the Internet is based on norms of interoperability, diversity, and heterogeneity of networks and on the principles that authority for operationalization be decentralized and that the process for developing standards be inclusive rather than proprietary or directed by any single government or world organization. It is precisely because of the regime's flexibility and tolerance of decentralized diversity that the Internet became operational on a worldwide basis, almost spontaneously, in the 1990s.

Although the governments studied in this volume have not been involved in any essential way in creating the nascent global Internet regime, most have found those principles and norms that have evolved within it to be compatible with sovereignty and perhaps in most cases potentially supportive of nationalist goals. For the regime to become more robust into the future, it will be necessary to build on this initial success by finding ways to attract to more prominent positions in global Internet affairs—and in more central ways—the leadership of the nations in the five world regions studied in this volume.

■ **NOTES**

1. Keohane and Nye, *Power and Interdependence,* p. 263.
2. Keohane and Nye, "Power and Interdependence in the Information Age," p. 82.
3. "Tight Controls," p. 1.
4. A particularly useful volume for understanding the many ways nation-states necessarily mediate between international economic forces and the local introduction of technological innovation is Braczyk, Cooke, and Heidenreich, *Regional Innovation Systems,* especially pp. 196–197. See also Brunn and Cottle, "Small States and Cyberboosterism," pp. 240–258.
5. "E-Commerce at the Grass Roots," p. 34, 42–43.
6. Steele, *On Intelligence,* pp. 44 ff.
7. See, for example, Arnold, "Hook Up Rural Asia," and "The Global Public," especially pp. 47–49.

8. Bridis, "Internet Body," p. B12.

9. Quoted from de Sola Pool, as excerpted in Etheredge, ed., *Politics in Wired Nations,* p. 363.

10. "Indo-Japan Joint Meeting."

11. Chadha, "Decontrolling India's Telecommunications Sector," especially chap. 1.

12. Karp, "BJP Makes Patriotic Pitch," p. A10.

13. For more detailed analysis of India's investment policies as they relate to NRIs and information technology, see Franda, "China and India Online," chap. 5.

14. A useful general analytical article on Netwar is Arquilla and Ronfeldt, "The Advent of Netwar."

15. Franda, "China and India Online," chap. 5.

16. Thomas, "Trading the Nation," pp. 275–293.

17. For detailed analysis, see Franda, *Governing the Internet.*

Acronyms

AAAS	American Association for the Advancement of Science
AceS	Asia Cellular Satellite System
ADC	a large multinational corporation connecting broadband networks, founded in 1935 as Audio Development Corporation
ADSL	asymmetric digital subscriber line
AIDS	acquired immunodeficiency syndrome
AIUA	Armenian Internet Users Association
AOL	America Online
APN	Novosti Press Agency (in the former Soviet Union)
APOS	Arabic Palm Operating System
ARS	a multinational marketing research company
AT&T	American Telephone and Telegraph
ATM	asynchronous transfer mode
ATU	African Telecommunications Union
AUC	American University in Cairo
AUFS	American Universities Field Staff
AZT	a commonly used medication for HIV and AIDS patients
BALTnet	Baltic Network Project (of the Nordic Council)
BBC	British Broadcasting Company
BIRD	Binational [Israel and the United States] Industrial Research and Development Foundation
BJP	Bharatiya Janata Party [Indian People's Party]
BMC	one of the world's largest software vendors, headquartered in Houston, Texas

BMI-T	BMI-TechKnowledge Company
BOC	Business Optimization Consultants (Jordan)
BTC	Bulgarian Telecommunications Company
CADA	Central Asia Development Agency
CD-ROM	compact disk–read-only memory
CEE	Central/Eastern Europe
CEENet	Central and Eastern European Networking Association
CEO	chief executive officer
CG Sat	Hungarian company that operates two local telecommunications providers
CIA	Central Intelligence Agency
CIDCM	Center for International Development and Conflict Management
CINA	China Information News Agency
CIS	Commonwealth of Independent States
CNAPS	Centralised National Automated Payments System (China)
CNN	Cable News Network
CNNIC	China National Network Information Center
CPSU	Communist Party of the Soviet Union
CPT	Committee on Posts and Telegraphs (Bulgaria)
DA	Democratic Alliance
DBAG	Deutsche Beteilgungs AG
DESY	Deutsches Elektronen Synchroton (Germany)
DIT	Dabbagh Information Technology
DNS	Domain Name System
DOD	Department of Defense
DON	Digital Overlay Network (Bulgaria)
DoT	Department of Telecommunications (India)
DSF	Dubai Shopping Festival
DSL	digital subscriber line
EBRD	European Bank for Reconstruction and Development
EC	European Community
ECA	Economic Commission for Africa
EEC	European Economic Community
EENET	Estonian Education and Research Network
EFF	Electronic Frontier Foundation
EIB	European Investment Bank
EIM	Emirates Internet and Multimedia (UAE)
ESIS	European Survey of Information Society
EU	European Union

FAQ	frequently asked question
FDI	foreign direct investment
FSB	Federal Security Service (Russia)
FSU	former Soviet Union
FYR	former Yugoslav Republic
G-7	group of seven countries (United States, Japan, Germany, France, UK, Italy, Canada)
G-8	the G-7 and Russia, on those occasions when Russia is allowed to participate in meetings as an observer
GDP	gross domestic product
GE	General Electric
GFCF	gross fixed capital formation
GNP	gross national product
GPTC	General Posts and Telecommunications Company (Libya)
GSM	Global System for Mobile Communications
GTS	an IT company in Hungary
HDSL	high [bit-rate] digital subscriber line
HDZ	Croatian Democratic Community
IATP	Internet Access and Training Program (of IREX)
IAW	Internet Access Worldwide
IBM	International Business Machines Corporation
ICANN	Internet Corporation for Assigned Names and Numbers
ICQ	an Israeli company (letters substitute for "I seek you")
ICRC	International Committee of the Red Cross
ICT	information and communications technologies
IDC	International Data Corporation
IEA	International Association for the Evaluation of Educational Attainment
IETF	Internet Engineering Task Force
IFC	International Finance Corporation
IFPI	International Federation of the Phonographic Industry
IMF	International Monetary Fund
IMHO	Internet Media House (Russia)
INFITT	International Forum for Information Technology in Tamil
INTAS	International Association (of the EU)
IP	Internet protocol
IPI	International Press Institute
IPKO	Internet Project Kosovo
IR	international relations
IREX	International Research and Exchanges Board

IRIS	Institutional Reform and the Informal Sector (University of Maryland)
IS	Internet Securities (of Boston)
ISAR	Institute on Soviet-American Relations
ISI	Information Society Index
ISNA	Islamic Society of North America
ISOC	the Internet Society
ISP	Internet service provider
ISPAI	Internet Service Providers Association of India
IT	information technology
ITAR-TASS	Information Telegraph Agency of Russia, succeeded TASS in 1992
ITO	International Trademark Organization
ITU	International Telecommunications Union
KACST	King Abdul Aziz City for Science and Technology
KFKI	Hungarian Academy of Sciences
KGB	Soviet intelligence agency
KIPCO	Kuwait Investment Projects Company
KPN	the major telecommunications company of the Netherlands
KSA	Kingdom of Saudi Arabia
LDC	less developed country
LG	Lucky Goldstar (Korea)
MAI	Multilateral Agreement on Investment (of the OECD)
Maktel	Makedonski Telekommunikacii (Hungarian consortium of telecom companies)
MATAV	Hungarian national telecommunications operator
MAV	Hungarian national railway company
MCI	a large multimedia multinational
MeMoNet	Media-Most Networks (Russia)
MEViC	Middle East Virtual Community
MII	Ministry of Information Industries (China)
MIT	Massachusetts Institute of Technology
MMDS	Multichannel Multipoint Distribution System
MOC	Ministry of Communications (Israel)
MOL	Hungarian oil and gas company
MSO	multi-system operator
MTI News	Hungarian news agency based in Budapest
NAP	Network Access Point (China)
NASA	National Aeronautics and Space Agency
Nasdaq	National Association of Security Dealers Exchange

NASSCOM	National Association of Software and Service Companies (India)
NATO	North Atlantic Treaty Organization
NCST	National Centre for Software Technology (India)
NDS	Network Directory Services
NETS	a leading ISP in Jordan
NGO	nongovernmental organization
NOC	Network Operating Center (Saudi Arabia)
NRI	nonresident Indian
NSF	National Salvation Front (Romania)
NSI	Network Solutions, Inc.
NTV	Russia's only independent television station
NUA	An Ireland-based company specializing in Internet surveys, development of Web pages, and other Internet applications
OECD	Organization for Economic Cooperation and Development
OSI	Open Society Institute
OSI-IP	Open Society Institute–Internet Programs
OTE	Hellenic Telecommunications Organization (Greece)
PC	personal computer
PGP	Pretty Good Privacy
POP	Point of Presence
PRC	People's Republic of China
PTT	Post, Telephone, and Telegraph (Netherlands)
PVO	private voluntary organization
PZU	Powszachny Zaklad Ubezpieczen (Poland)
R&D	research and development
RAD	RAD Data Communications
RCI	Republican Center of Informatics (Moldova)
RIP	Russian Internet Project (of the OSI and the Soros Foundation)
RIS	Research on the Internet in Slovenia
RNB	Romanian National Bank
RSF	Reporters Sans Frontieres
Runet	Russian Internet
SAA	South African Airlines
SAN	Serbian Academic Network
SANET	Slovak Academic Network
SAPA	South African Press Association
SCS	Syrian Computer Society
SORM	system for operational and investigative activities (Russia)

SPT	Sprava Post a Telekomunikace Praha Czechoslovakia)
STC	Saudi Telecommunications Company
STE	Syrian Telecommunication Establishment
SVC	Shanghai Venture Capital
TASS	Russian news agency
TDF	a Singapore-based venture capital company
TN	Telenor Nextel
TPI	technology permeation index (of EMFocus Company)
TPSA	Telekomunikacja Polska S.A. (Poland)
UAE	United Arab Emirates
UN	United Nations
UNDP	United Nations Development Programme
UNESCO	United Nations Educational, Scientific, and Cultural Organization
USAID	U.S. Agency for International Development
USSR	Union of Soviet Socialist Republics
USTR	U.S. Trade Representative
VSNL	Videsh Sanchar Nigam Ltd. (India)
WAP	wireless application protocol
WHO	World Health Organization
WIPO	World Intellectual Property Organization
WTO	World Trade Organization

Bibliography

Abdel-Rahim, Saqer. "The Impact of the Information Revolution on Society and State in Jordan," in *The Information Revolution and the Arab World: Its Impact on State and Society,* ed. James S. Al-Suwaidi. Abu Dhabi: Emirates Center for Strategic Studies and Research, 1998, pp. 160–175.

Abrahams, Fred. "The Albanian House of Cards." *Dollars and Sense,* iss. 212 (July-August 1997), pp. 11–13.

Abramson, David M. "A Critical Look at NGOs and Civil Society as Means to an End in Uzbekistan." *Human Organization,* 58:3 (fall 1999), pp. 240–250.

Abu-Sharif, Karma. "NGOs Ministry Establishes New Concept." *Middle East Newsfile,* August 1, 1999, pp. 1–4.

Accone, Tanya. "Digital Dividends for Journalism in Africa." *Nieman Reports,* 54:4 (winter 2000), pp. 67–70.

Ackerman, Gwen. "Ben-Eliezer: Bezeq Is Becoming a Monopoly That Will Be Hard to Shake." *Jerusalem Post,* November 7, 2000, p. 11.

———. "Bezeq's Tender Schedule Is 'Irrelevant.'" *Jerusalem Post,* January 12, 2001, p. 12A.

———. "Latest Debate Over Bezeq Privatization Referred to Ministerial Committee." *Jerusalem Post,* May 7, 2001, p. 17.

"African Debt, European Doubt." *The Economist* (London), April 8, 2000, pp. 46–51.

"After Seattle: The Non-Governmental Order." *The Economist* (London), December 11, 1999, pp. 20–21.

Agassi, Gal. "Bezeq Deliberately Holds Up Progress." *Jerusalem Post,* December 29, 2000, p. 12A.

———. "Bezeq's Internet Monopoly Hurts Consumers—and, Ultimately, Bezeq." *Jerusalem Post,* December 22, 2000, p. 12A.

Aggarwal, P. K. "Building India's National Internet Backbone." *Communications of the ACM,* 60:6 (June 1999), pp. 53–58.

Aioubov, Salimjon. "Tajikistan: Email and Internet Make Headway." *Radio Free Europe/Radio Liberty,* November 19, 1997.

"ALA to Play a Role in the New Markle Foundation Project for Cyberdemocracy." *Computers in Libraries,* 20:1 (January 2000), pp. 12–13.

al-Ibrahim, Husayn. "The Internet and Informatics in the Arab-Israeli Conflict." *Tishrin* (Damascus), February 23, 1998.

Allen, Chris. "Maghreb Online: A Guide to Internet Resources on North Africa." *Review of African Political Economy,* 27:83 (March 2000), pp. 155–164.

Almotawa, Abdul Rahman. "Kingdom Will Hold New Round of WTO Talks." *Middle East Newsfile,* April 1, 2000, pp. 1–2.

Al-Suwaidi, Jamal S. (ed.). *The Information Revolution and the Arab World: Its Impact on State and Society.* Abu Dhabi: Emirates Center for Strategic Studies and Research, 1998.

Alterman, Jon B. "The Middle East's Information Revolution." *Current History,* 99:633 (January 2000), pp. 21–26.

———. *New Media, New Politics? From Satellite Television to the Internet in the Arab World.* Policy Paper no. 48. Washington, DC: Washington Institute for Near East Policy, 1998.

———. "Shrinking the World and Changing the Rules." *Middle East Insight,* March-April 1999, p. 31.

Amin, Hussein Y., and Leo A. Gher. "Digital Communications in the Arab World Entering the 21st Century," in *Civic Discourse and Digital Age Communications in the Middle East,* eds. Leo A. Gher and Hussein Y. Amin. Stamford, CT: Ablex, 2000, pp. 109–140.

"Analysts Predict Internet Use, Electronic Trade Boom in Hungary." *MTI News Agency* (Budapest), trans. and published in *BBC Monitoring International Reports,* January 30, 2000.

"And They're Off! Domain Names in Chinese Characters Trigger Stampede." Trans. and summarized from an article in *Zhongguo Qingnian Bao* [China Youth Daily], November 8, 2000, in *China Online,* November 9, 2000.

Anderson, John. "Creating a Framework for Civil Society in Kyrgyzstan." *Europe-Asia Studies,* 52:1 (January 2000), pp. 77–93.

Anderson, Jon. *Arabizing the Internet.* Dubai: Emirates Center for Strategic Studies and Research, 1999.

Anderson, Robert. "Deutsche Telekom in Czech Deal." *Financial Times* (London), March 31, 2000, p. 25.

———. "Prague Delays Telecoms Liberalisation by Two Years." *Financial Times* (London), March 6, 2000, p. 8.

———. "Slovakia: Privatisation Mode Engaged." *Financial Times* (London), May 25, 2000, p. 2.

———. "Trail-Blazers in Eastern Europe: Information Technology and the Internet in the Czech Republic." *Financial Times* (London), August 25, 1999, p. 12.

Anthes, Gary H. "IT Walls Come Tumbling Down." *IDG.Net,* November 8, 1999.

Appel, Hilary, and John Gould. "Identity Politics and Economic Reform: Examining Industry-State Relations in the Czech and Slovak Republics."

Europe-Asia Studies, 52:1 (January 2000), pp. 111–132.

Arak, Villu. "Estonia: Government Drafts Legislation for Information Age." *Radio Free Europe/Radio Liberty,* September 16, 1999.

Ariav, G., and Seymour Goodman. "Israel: Of Swords and Software Plow-shares." *Communications of the ACM,* 37:6 (June 1994), pp. 17–21.

"Armenia Calls on Azerbaijan to Stop Internet Warfare." *BBC Monitoring International Reports Series,* February 18, 2000.

Arnold, Wayne. "Hook Up Rural Asia, Some Say, and Poverty Can Be Mitigated." *New York Times,* January 19, 2001.

Arquilla, John, and David Ronfeldt. "The Advent of Netwar: Analytic Background." *Studies in Conflict and Terrorism,* 22:3 (July-September 1999), pp. 193–206.

Ash, Timothy Garten. "Slovenia Update." *West LB Country Profile,* December 2, 1999, pp. 1–4.

Avigad, Doron. "Internet Conquers Israel." *Israel's Business Arena,* December 3, 1999.

"Azerbaijan: Internet Security Council to Be Set Up." *BBC Monitoring International Reports Series,* February 16, 2000.

"Azeri-Armenian Internet War May Lead to Loss of Services." *BBC Monitoring International Reports Series,* February 14, 2000.

Azzam, Henry T. "Globalization.com." *Jordan Times* (Amman), December 2–3, 1999, p. 1 (quoted in "E-Commerce in the Arab World," *World Press Review,* 47:3 [March 2000], p. 15).

Bagnall, James. "Israel's High-Tech Revolution: From Army Intelligence to Internet Warriors." *The Ottawa Citizen,* July 9, 2000, pp. C3–4.

Bahensky, Zybsek. "Czech Mobile Carrier Relaunches IP Service." *IDG News Service,* August 13, 1999.

"Bahrain Cannot Adopt EU or US E-Commerce Laws." *Bahrain Tribune,* December 8, 2000.

Ba-Isa, Molouk Y. "Cyber War Could Be Costly for Arabs." *Middle East Newsfile* (Arab News Service), January 15, 2001.

Bangemann, Martin. *Europe and the Global Information Society: Recommendations to the European Council.* Brussels: European Council, 1994.

Barmé, Geremie R., and Sang Ye. "The Great Firewall of China." *Wired Magazine,* 5:6 (June 1997), pp. 138–150, 174–178.

"Barnes and Noble to Target Internet Users in the Arab World." *DITnet. ITNEWS,* April 16, 2000.

Bart, Aaron. "Israel Online: Changing Perceptions and Relations." *Middle East Insight,* March-April 1999, pp. 47–48.

Beale, Roger. "Developing Under the Net." *Financial Times* (London), February 21, 2000, p. 44.

Begleiter, Ralph. "Syria and the World Wide Web." *Middle East Insight,* special issue on the Internet and Information Technology, July-August 1999, pp. 33–34.

"Belarus: An Ambivalent Couple." *World Press Review,* 47:1 (January 2000), p. 19.

"Belarusian Parliament Leader to Visit Yugoslavia in March." *BBC Monitoring International Reports Series,* February 26, 2000.

Bennahum, David S. "Heart of Darkness: David S. Bennahum Travels to Ground Zero of the Global Epidemic, the Hot Zone That Spawned the Infamous Bulgarian Computer Viruses." *Wired Magazine,* 5:11 (November 1997), pp. 226–230, 266–277.

Beresford, Belinda. "South Africa: Escaping the Information Dirt Track." *Africa News,* June 30, 2000.

Berger, Sharon. "Israel Fourth as Hi-Tech Hub." *Wired News,* June 13, 2000, pp. 1–3, available at www.wired.com/news/topstories.

Best, Keith. "Federalism and International Democracy as a Solution to Global Problems." *Federalist Debate* (Italy), 11:3 (1998), pp. 17–21.

Bichel, Anthony. "Contending Theories of Central Asia: The Virtual Realities of Realism, Critical IR and the Internet." Ph.D. diss., University of Hawaii, 1997.

Bieber, Florian. "Cyberwar or Sideshow? The Internet and the Balkan Wars." *Current History,* 99:635 (March 2000), pp. 124–129.

"B92 Denied Permission to Set up TV Studio Next to Its Radio Station." *BBC Summary of World Broadcasts,* January 23, 2001.

Bogolubov, Leonid N., Galina V. Klokova, Galina S. Kovalyova, and David I. Poltorak. "The Challenge of Civic Education in the New Russia," in *Civic Education Across Countries: Twenty-four National Case Studies from the IEA Civic Education Project,* eds. Judith Torney-Purta, John Schwille, and Jo-Ann Amadeo. Delft, Netherlands: Eburon Publishers for the International Association for the Evaluation of Educational Attainment, 1999, pp. 523–541.

Bojnec, Stefan. "Privatisation, Restructuring and Management in Slovene Enterprises." *Comparative Economic Studies,* 41:4 (winter 1999), pp. 77–78.

Bokhari, Farhan. "Internet City Places Dubai at the Heart of a Regional Hub." *Financial Times* (London), January 5, 2001, p. 11.

Boland, Vincent, and Nicholas Denton. "Record Dollars 1.45bn Bid Secures State in Czech Telecom Group." *Financial Times* (London), June 29, 1995, p. 17.

"Booting up in Andhra Pradesh: The State Election to Watch in India." *The Economist* (London), September 11, 1999, pp. 46–47.

Borrell, Jerry. "Investing in Hope." *Upside,* 12:9 (September 2000), pp. 170–178.

Borzo, Jeanette. "Investors Look to Claim Space on Russian Web." *Wall Street Journal,* April 26, 2000.

———. "Net Start-Ups in Russia Seek Business Smarts—Western Expertise Rivals Cash as Assets Wanted by Fledgling Capitalists." *Wall Street Journal,* June 12, 2000.

———. "Russia Considering Internet Surveillance Policy." *IDG News Service,* July 30, 1998.

———. "Russian E-Commerce Group Formed." *The Standard,* December 2, 1998.

————. "Russian Internet Usage Triples from 1996 to 1998." *IDG News Service,* June 10, 1999.

————. "Russia's Fledgling E-Commerce Sector Is Seeking Its Missing Link: Consumers." *Wall Street Journal,* Eastern edition, June 21, 2000, p. 1.

Braczyk, Hans-Joachim, Philip Cooke, and Martin Heidenreich (eds.). *Regional Innovation Systems: The Role of Governances in a Globalized World.* London: University College of London Press, 1998.

Brandt, Richard L. "It's the Internet, Damn It!" *Upside* (Foster City, CA), 10:9 (October 1998), p. 18.

Brass, Paul R. *Language, Religion and Politics in North India.* New Delhi: Vikas, 1974.

Brauchli, Marcus, Joseph Kahn, and S. Karene Witcher. "Murdoch's Plans Could Aid China in Media Control." *Wall Street Journal,* January 31, 1996, p. 4.

Brewin, Bob. "DOD Boosts Telecom, Computers in Balkans." *Federal Computer Week,* April 12, 1999, pp. 3–5.

Bridis, Ted. "Internet Body Finds Problems Collecting Funds from Nations." *Wall Street Journal,* June 1, 2000, p. B12.

"Briefs: The World." *Christianity Today,* 44:2 (February 7, 2000), pp. 29–30.

Bristow, Damon. "India May Eclipse China in IT." *Far Eastern Economic Review,* 163:31 (August 3, 2000), pp. 29–30.

Bronskill, Jim. "'Big Brother' Gets Free Rein over E-Mail: Report Reveals Russian's Control of Internet Services." *Ottawa Citizen,* May 24, 2000, p. A8.

Brown, Justin. "After More Sanctions, Serbs Fear They'll Be Forced Offline." *Christian Science Monitor,* May 19, 1999, p. 7.

Brunn, Stanley D., and Charles D. Cottle. "Small States and Cyberboosterism." *Geographical Review,* 87:2 (April 1997), pp. 240–258.

Bukowski, Charles. "Slovenia's Transition to Democracy: Theory and Practice." *East European Quarterly,* 33:1 (spring 1999), pp. 69–97.

"Bulgaria: Muddling Through." *Petroleum Economist* (London), 67:12 (December 2000), pp. 36–37.

"Bulgaria Continues to Plough the Reform Furrow." *West LB Investment Review,* February 14, 2000, p. 67.

Burg, Steven L. "Bosnia Herzegovina: A Case of Failed Democratization," in *Politics, Power and the Struggle for Democracy in South-East Europe,* eds. Karen Dawisha and Bruce Parrott. Cambridge: Cambridge University Press, 1997, pp. 122–145.

Burns, Chris. "Walesa: Internet, Computers Helped End Polish Communism." *CNN.com,* October 18, 1999.

Burwell, Frances G., and Ivo H. Daalder (eds.). *The United States and Europe in the Global Arena.* London: Macmillan, 1999.

Bushrod, Lisa. "DBAG Exits Milestone Czech Internet Deal." *European Venture Capital Journal,* May 1, 2000, pp. 1, 5.

"Business China Offers Deal on Name Registration." *Business China,* May 30, 2000, at www.bizcn.com.

"Call for Expert-Led Internet Laws." *Bahrain Tribune,* November 9, 2000.

Campbell, Robert. *Soviet and Post-Soviet Telecommunications: An Industry Under Reform.* Boulder: Westview, 1995.

Canning, Anna. "Privatization and Competition in Hungarian Telecommunications," in *Privatization and Competition in Telecommunications: International Developments,* ed. Daniel J. Ryan. Westport, CT: Praeger, 1997, pp. 103–126.

Carney, Christopher P., and John P. Moran. "Imagining Communities in Central Asia: Nationalism and Interstate Affect in the Post-Soviet Era." *Asian Affairs: An American Review,* 26:4 (winter 2000), pp. 179–199.

Carter, Tom. "Critics See 'Zero' Chance of U.N. Tax." *Washington Times,* February 1, 2001, p. A4.

Caryl, Christian. "Big Brother Covets All the E-Mail." *U.S. News and World Report,* September 14, 1998, pp. 46–47.

———. "Catch a Rising Czar." *U.S. News and World Report,* 128:12 (March 27, 2000), pp. 32–34.

Caspi, Dan, and Yehiel Limor. *The In/Outsiders: Mass Media in Israel.* Cresskill, NJ: Hampton, 1999.

Chadha, Kalyani. "Decontrolling India's Telecommunications Sector: A Case Study from the Developing World." Ph.D. diss., University of Maryland College of Journalism, 1999.

Chamoux, Jean-Pierre. "After Privatization: Neocolonialism?" in *Globalism and Localism in Telecommunications,* eds. E. M. Noam and A. J. Wolfson. Amsterdam: Elsevier Science B.V., 1997, pp. 343–350.

Chandler, Clay. "Putin Makes Strong Bid for Equal Role in G-8." *Washington Post,* July 24, 2000, p. 8.

"Charlemagne: Edward Shevardnadze, Georgia's Foxy President." *The Economist,* July 15, 2000, p. 52.

"Charting a Course with China." *Washington Post,* November 14, 1999, p. B6.

Chatfield, Charles. "The Federalism Papers: Commentary on the History of Federalism." *Peace and Change,* 24:3 (July 1999), pp. 373–379.

Chazan, Guy. "A High-Tech Folk Hero Challenges Russia's Right to Snoop— Internet Service Provider Says No to E-Mail Taps for Security Agencies." *Wall Street Journal,* November 27, 2000, p. A28.

Chendakera, Nair. "AT&T Enters Indian Mobile Phone Market." *Electronic Engineering Times,* March 13, 2000, pp. 43–47.

———. "Korea's LG Group to Put $185 Million into India." *Electronic Engineering Times,* April 3, 2000, pp. 38–41.

———. "New Delhi's Budget Plan Short on Hardware Help." *Electronic Engineering Times,* March 6, 2000, pp. 30–35.

———. "Software-Rich India Starved for Hardware." *Electronic Engineering Times,* February 14, 2000, pp. 1–2.

Chibber, Pradeep, and Samuel Eldersveld. "Local Elites and Popular Support for Economic Reform in China and India." *Comparative Political Studies,* 33:3 (April 2000), pp. 350–374.

"China Channel, CNNIC Disagree over Chinese Character International Domain Names." Trans. and summarized from an article in *Zhongguo Qingnian Bao*

[China Youth Daily], September 30, 2000, in *China Online,* October 10, 2000.

"China Government Creates Draft Ecommerce Policy." Reported in *Wen Wei Po Daily* [Hong Kong], April 29, 2000, trans. and summarized in *China Online,* May 4, 2000.

"China Introduces Chinese Character Web Site Domain Names." Trans. and summarized from an article in *Beijing Qingnian Bao* [Beijing Youth Daily], January 20, 2000, in *China Online,* January 24, 2000.

"China Posts New Business Web Site Regulations." Trans. and analysis of regulations originally published in the *People's Daily,* August 28, 2000, in English in *China Online,* September 12, 2000.

"China Telecom, China Unicom Still the Big Fish in Telephony Pond, Conference Learns." *China Online,* January 17, 2001.

"China Telecom Feeling Increasingly Embattled." *China Online,* January 30, 2001.

"China to Introduce Credit Information Management System." Originally published in *Zhengquan Shibao* [Securities Times], February 24, 2000, trans. and summarized in *China Online,* February 29, 2000.

"China Unveils New Telecom Giant as Nation Prepares for WTO Entry." *Agence France Press,* January 8, 2001.

"China's Beijing Cracks Down on Internet Cafés." Based on trans. and analysis of a March 21 report in *Zhongguo Xinxi Bao* [China Information News], in *China Online,* March 24, 2000.

"Chinese People Can Say (Almost) What They Please on the Net." Based on trans. and analysis of an August 5, 1999, editorial in *Liberation Daily,* the newspaper of the People's Liberation Army, in *Virtual China,* August 11, 1999.

Cohen, Lenard J. "Embattled Democracy: Postcommunist Croatia in Transition," in *Politics, Power and the Struggle for Democracy in South-East Europe,* eds. Karen Dawisha and Bruce Parrott. Cambridge: Cambridge University Press, 1997, pp. 69–121.

Collier, Paul, and Jan Willem Gunning. "Why Has Africa Grown Slowly?" *Journal of Economic Perspectives,* 13:3 (summer 1999), pp. 3–22.

"Comment and Analysis: South Africa." *Barclays Bank International Financial Outlook,* February 1, 2001, p. 29.

Commey, Pusch. "Let the Telkom Games Begin!" *African Business* (London), April 2001, pp. 37–39.

Communication for a Better World. Budapest: MATAV Annual Report, 1995.

"Complete CNNIC Rules for Domain-Name Disputes." *China Online,* November 10, 2000.

"Conditions Not Yet Ripe for B-to-C E-Commerce, Official Explains." Interview with Chen Wenling, in *Zhongguo Jingji Shibao* [China Economic Times], January 20, 2001, trans. in *China Online,* January 25, 2001.

Contreras, Joseph. "Cyber-Savvy in Syria: The Information Age Dawns, Championed by Assad's Son." *Newsweek,* April 26, 1999, p. 54.

Cooper, Caroline. "China and India's IT Connection: Symbiosis or Snafus?" *China Online,* July 4, 2000, pp. 1–5.

————. "Look at India, IT's Where China Wants to Be." *China Online,* June 22, 2000, pp. 1–5.

Cooper, Helene. "Far Cry from Seattle: Tiny Qatar Is Picked as WTO Meeting Site." *Wall Street Journal,* January 24, 2001, p. A8.

"Croatian ISPs to See Fierce Competition." *Russia Extension,* October 2000.

"Croatia's New Beginning." *Euromoney,* iss. 374 (June 2000), pp. 248–249.

Csapo-Sweet, Rita, and Donald C. Shields. "Explicating the Saga Component of Symbolic Convergence Theory: The Case of Serbia's Radio B92." *Critical Studies in Media Communication,* 17:3 (September 2000), pp. 316–334.

Cullison, Alan. "Shareholders Get Short Shrift in Russia—Scandals over Governance of Corporations Keep Foreign Investors at Bay." *Wall Street Journal,* December 5, 2000, p. A22.

Currie, Antony. "E-Lack-of-Commerce." *Euromoney,* iss. 366 (October 1999), pp. 7–15.

"Cyberbill-II: Despite Loopholes a Historic Bill." *Statesman* (India), May 23, 2000.

"Cyberlaw: E-Commerce for Babus, Not Business." *Statesman* (India), May 21, 2000.

"DA Disappointed at Government Telkom Decision." *SAPA* [South African Press Association] *Global News Wire,* March 15, 2001, p. 1.

Daniszewski, John. "A Former Hermit Kingdom, Oman Emerges from Shell." *Los Angeles Times,* December 17, 1999.

David, Stephen. "Infosys City: Technopolis." *India Today,* January 1, 2001, p. 40.

Dean, Katie. "UN Proposes Global Email Tax." *Wired News,* July 13, 1999, pp. 1–3, available at www.wired.com/news/topstories.

de Jonquieres, Guy, and James Kynge. "Beijing's Big Gamble." *Financial Times* (London), November 16, 1999.

Dempsey, Judy. "Adding New States Could Cost $40billion." *Financial Times* (London), May 9, 2001, p. 2.

de Sola Pool, Ithiel. *Technologies of Freedom.* Cambridge: Harvard University Press, 1983.

deBony, Elizabeth. "EU Applicants Slow to Adjust Telecom Rules." *IDG News Service/Brussels,* October 20, 1999.

DeChant, Rick. "U.S. Firm Wades Into International Market: Young Voter Mobilization Slovenian Style." *PR Newswire,* October 10, 2000.

Deibert, Ronald. "Circuits of Power: Security in the Internet Environment," in *Information, Power and Security,* eds. J. P. Singh and James N. Rosenau. Albany: State University of New York Press, 2002.

Demertzis, Nicolas. "Media and Nationalism: The Macedonian Question." *Harvard International Journal of Press/Politics,* 4:3 (summer 1999), pp. 26–51.

Dempsey, Judy. "Israel Opens Telecoms Market to Competition." *Financial Times* (London), September 5, 2000.

Denning, Dorothy. *Information Warfare and Security.* Reading, MA: Addison Wesley Longman, 1999.

Dhume, Sadanand. "India's Awakening: Government Stokes the Interest of Foreign Investors." *Far Eastern Economic Review,* January 20, 2000, pp. 32–33.

Dickie, Mure. "Microsoft Launches China Windows NT 4.0." *Reuter European Business Report,* January 7, 1997.

Dinmore, Guy. "Iran's Ayatollahs Get Ready to Embrace Internet Culture." *Financial Times* (London), June 26, 2000, p. 12.

"DIT's Award of Excellence." *DITnet News Online,* November 1, 1999.

Downs, H. R. "A Quarter of Private Investment to Emerging Markets Will Go to China in '01, Report Says." *China Online,* January 29, 2001.

"Dream On." *The Economist* (London), January 8, 2000, p. 40.

Drummond, James. "Middle East Banking and Finance: Technology Proceeds at Slow Pace." *Financial Times* (London), April 2000, p. 3.

———. "North Africa's Mobile Connections." *Financial Times* (London), February 1, 2001, p. 32.

"Dubai Internet City: The Future of E-Dubai." *Middle East Economic Digest,* November 10, 2000, pp. 6–10.

"An Eastern Promise; Paul Byfield, of the European Bank for Reconstruction and Development, Shares His Insight Into Online Legal Resources for Central and Eastern Europe." *Information World Review,* May 1, 2001, p. 19.

"EBRD in Strategy Talks with Ukraine and Azerbaijan." *European Report,* January 2001, pp. 1–3.

Echikson, William. "Taking Hungary on a High-Tech Ride." *Business Week,* October 23, 2000, pp. 148B–148F.

"E-Commerce at the Grass Roots: Implications of a 'Wired' Citizenry in Developing Nations." Report prepared for the National Intelligence Council by Booz-Allen & Hamilton, June 30, 2000, available at www.cia.gov/nic/nic%5Fpublic...ported%5Fby%5Fnic/grass%5Froots.htm.

"E-Government in Dubai Within 18 Months." *DITnet,* April 5, 2000.

"Egypt: President's Aide Says NGOs Should Not Be Used as 'Pretext to Interfere.'" *BBC Worldwide Monitoring,* February 6, 2000.

"Egyptian Court Says Law on NGOs 'Unconstitutional.'" *BBC Summary of World Broadcasts,* June 6, 2000.

"Egypt's Moslem Authorities to Launch Islamic Web Site." *Agence France Press,* July 15, 1998.

Ein-dor, Phillip, and Seymour E. Goodman. "From Via Maris to Electronic Highway: The Internet in Canaan." *Communications of the ACM,* 43:7 (July 2000), pp. 19–23.

Ein-dor, Phillip, Michael D. Myers, and M. S. Raman. "Information Technology in Three Small Developed Countries." *Journal of Management Information Systems,* 13:4 (spring 1997), pp. 61–90.

Ellis, Frank. *From Glasnost to the Internet: Russia's New Infosphere.* London: Macmillan, 1999.

———. "The Media as Social Engineer: The Failed Experiment, 1953–1991," in *Russian Cultural Studies: An Introduction,* eds. Catriona Kelly and David Shepherd. Oxford: Oxford University Press, 1998, pp. 215–230.

The Emerging Digital Economy. Washington, DC: U.S. Department of Commerce, April 1998.

Emergy, James J., Norman A. Graham, and Michael F. Oppenheimer. *Technology Trade with the Middle East.* Boulder: Westview, 1986.

"Emirates Internet and Multimedia Launches Online Registration Service." *DITnet,* June 6, 2000, pp. 1–2.

Engardio, Pete, Richard S. Dunham, Heidi Dawley, Irene Kunii, and Elisabeth Malkin. "Activists Without Borders." *Business Week,* October 4, 1999, pp. 144–150.

"English Losing Monopoly in Cyberspace." *The Hindu,* July 24, 2000.

Erlanger, Steven. "Croatia Elects a Moderate to Follow the Tudjman Era." *New York Times,* February 8, 2000, p. A12.

———. "Despite Soaring Prosperity, Poland Still Isn't Sure of Itself." *New York Times,* August 25, 2000.

———. "Even Milosevic Foes Criticize Western Media." *New York Times,* March 31, 1999, p. A10.

Erofeev, Sergei V. "Russia," in *The International World of Electronic Media,* ed. Lynne Schafer Gross. New York: McGraw-Hill, 1995, pp. 175–192.

"Estonian Cabinet to Go Digital, Save Paper." *Deutsche Presse-Agentur,* July 6, 2000.

"Estonian E-Sales Take Off." *Retail Week,* January 19, 2001, p. 5.

Estrin, G. "The WEIZAC Years (1954–1963)." *Annals of the History of Computing,* 13:4 (April 1991), pp. 317–339.

Estrin, Saul, and Adam Rosevear. "Enterprise Performance and Corporate Governance in Ukraine." *Journal of Comparative Economics,* 27 (November 1999), pp. 442–458.

Etheredge, Lloyd S. (ed.). *Politics in Wired Nations: Selected Writings of Ithiel de Sola Pool.* London: Transaction, 1998.

"Europe: A Bulgarian Way into the EU." *The Economist* (London), December 9, 2000, p. 56.

"Europe: The Changing Poles." *The Economist* (London), October 14, 2000, pp. 59–60.

"Europe: Fresh Hope for Bulgaria." *The Economist* (London), October 28, 2000, p. 46.

"Europe: Methodical Man." *The Economist* (November 20, 1999), pp. 59–60.

"Experts Group to Study Islamic Television Project." *Moneyclips (GCC),* July 6, 1992.

Fairlamb, David, Dawn Smith, and Christopher Condon. "How Far, How Fast?" *Business Week,* November 8, 1999, pp. 3–7, 64.

"Feeding the Flame: U.S. Firewall Maker Opens Beijing Branch, Introduces First 1,000-MB Firewall." *China Online,* July 20, 2000.

Feuilherade, Peter. "Qatar's Al-Jazeera Livens up Arab TV Scene." *World Mediawatch* (BBC Monitoring International Reports Series), January 7, 1999.

Field, Michael. *Inside the Arab World.* Cambridge: Harvard University Press, 1995.

Finn, Peter. "Czech Communism Returns to Its Roots." *Washington Post,* February 20, 2000, p. A30.

———. "Hungarian East, West Struggling to Connect." *Washington Post,* January 27, 2000, p. A22.

———. "Party Pullout Threatens Polish Government." *Washington Post,* May 29, 2000, p. A17.

"First with the Newest." *Central European,* 9:3 (April 1999), p. E6.

Flusfeder, Helena. "Global Audience for Jewish Studies." *Times Higher Education Supplement* (London), iss. 1423 (February 18, 2000), pp. 12–14.

Fortier, François. "Civil Society Computer Networks: The Perilous Road of Cyber-Politics." Ph.D. diss., York University, 1996.

"42,000 Chinese Domain Names Successfully Registered, 758,000 Rejected." Trans. and summarized from the original article in *Jisuanji Shijie Ribao* [China Computer World], November 29, 2000, in *China Online,* November 30, 2000.

Fossato, Floriana. "Russia: Joining the Cybertimes, But Slowly." *Radio Free Europe/Radio Liberty,* October 20, 1997.

Foster, William. "China and the Internet: Between Control and Prosperity." Unpublished manuscript. Tucson: University of Arizona, May 31, 2000.

"Four to Bid for Stake in Poland's TPSA." *Financial Times* (London), February 9, 2000.

Fox, Robert. "Unwired Iraq." *Communications of the ACM,* 42:3 (March 1999), pp. 11–18.

"France Telecom Increases Its Stake." *TASR* [Slovak News Agency], reported in *BBC Monitoring International Reports Series,* February 4, 2000.

Franda, Marcus. "China and India Online: The Politics of Information Technology in the World's Largest Nations." Unpublished manuscript, 2001.

———. *Governing the Internet: The Emergence of an International Regime.* Boulder: Lynne Rienner, 2001.

———. *Voluntary Associations and Local Development in India.* New Delhi: Young Asia, 1983.

Frank, Steve. "A 'Desert Man' with a Big Portfolio." *CNBC & The Wall Street Journal—Business,* May 15, 2001.

Friedman, Thomas L. "The Fast Eat the Slow." *New York Times,* February 2, 2001, p. A19.

———. "Unfinished Business in Syria." *New York Times,* June 12, 2000, p. 29.

Gall, Carlotta. "A Trail of Misery as Macedonia Fights Albanian Insurgency." *New York Times,* May 18, 2001, p. A8.

———. "What's Ahead in Yugoslavia: Three Men, More Plans, and Many Issues." *New York Times,* January 18, 2001, p. A8.

Gallagher, Nancy. "Middle East and North Africa Human Rights Activism in Cyberspace." *Middle East Studies Association Bulletin,* 31:1 (July 1997), pp. 1–11.

"Germany to Push for Integrating Russia into G8, Cancelling Third World Debt." *DDP News Agency* (Berlin), trans. by *BBC Worldwide Monitoring,* July 20, 2000.

Gerstenfeld, Dan. "Hi-Tech Pioneer Uzia Galil Steps Down." *Jerusalem Post,* August 2, 1999.

Gesteland, Lester J. "China's Business Environment Most Difficult to Navigate: Report." *China Online,* January 29, 2001.

"Getting Organized: China Ready to Create Database of Corporate Credit Records." Originally published in *Zhongguo Xinxi Bao* [China Information News], May 16, 2000, trans. and summarized in *China Online,* May 18, 2000.

Ghareeb, Edmund. "Review of Jon Anderson's *Arabizing the Internet.*" *Middle East Insight,* March-April 1999, p. 65.

Ghneim, Jabra. "Covering Internet Trends in Jordan." *India Line,* November 11, 1997.

"Give Me Back My Name! Foreign Registration of Chinese-Language Domain Name Causing Concern." Trans. and summarized from an article in *Beijing Qingnian Bao* [Beijing Youth Daily], October 23, 2000, in *China Online,* October 24, 2000.

Glain, Stephen J. "New Economy Hits Snag in Israel." *Wall Street Journal,* March 27, 2000, p. A1.

Glasser, Susan B. "Ted Turner Wants Assurance from Putin on Deal for NTV." *Washington Post,* January 20, 2001, p. A24.

Glassman, Elliot. "CyberHate: The Discourse of Intolerance in the New Europe," in *Culture and Technology in the New Europe: Civic Discourse in Transformation in Post-Communist Nations,* ed. Laura Lengel. Stamford, CT: Ablex, 2000, pp. 145–164.

Glater, Jonathan D. "Hemming in the World Wide Web." *New York Times,* January 7, 2001.

"The Global Public Policy Issue: A Discussion of International Governance, Security, Economics, Content, and Conflict Resolution." *On the Internet: An International Publication of the Internet Society,* 6:1 (spring/summer 2000), pp. 9–49.

Goble, Paul. "An Internet Enemies List." *Radio Free Europe/Radio Liberty,* August 13, 1999.

Goh, Debbie. "Global Body for Tamil on the Net." *Straits Times* (Singapore), July 26, 2000, p. 53.

"Goldman Sachs: China's E-Commerce Immature, Won't Grow up Until 2003–2004." *China Online,* July 3, 2000.

Goldstein, Eric. "Cyber-Censorship (and Evasion) in the Middle East." *Middle East Insight,* special issue on the Internet, March-April 1999, p. 53.

Goldstein, Heather R. "Ukraine to Step Up Fight Against Piracy." *Intellectual Property and Technology Law Journal,* 13:4 (April 2001), p. 27.

Gompert, David C. "Right Makes Might: Freedom and Power in the Information Age," in *The Changing Role of Information Warfare,* eds. Zalmay M. Khalilzad and John P. White. Santa Monica: Rand Project Air Force, 1999, pp. 45–73.

Goodman, Seymour E., et al. *The Global Diffusion of the Internet Project: An Initial Inductive Study.* Fairfax, VA: Mosaic Group, 1998.

Gordon, Buzzy. "Experts: Telephone Competition in Israel Hampered." *Jerusalem Post,* June 20, 2000, p. 11.

———. "The New Wireless: Location, Location, Location." *Jerusalem Post,* July 16, 2000, p. 9.

Gray, Stephanie. "Jordan: A Process Set to Inject Much-Needed Revenues: PRIVATISATION." *Financial Times* (London), November 7, 2000, p. 3.

Green, Peter S. "A Czech Internet Venture Will Close." *New York Times,* January 20, 2001, p. C2.

Greenberg, Jonah. "Domain Registrars Scramble to Dominate in China." *Digital PRC,* June 2, 2000.

Guernsey, Lisa. "For Kosovo's Scattered Refugees, the Internet Is a Lifeline." *New York Times,* June 10, 1999, p. G9.

———. "Villanova Effort Sends Computers to Bosnia." *Chronicle of Higher Education,* 43:4 (September 20, 1996), p. A33.

Guldimann, Till M. "How Technology Is Reshaping Finance and Risks." *Business Economics,* 35:1 (January 2000), pp. 41–42.

Guttman, Cynthia. "Kyrgyzstan: Breaking out of the Old Shell, Making the Leap to a Rule of Law." *UNESCO Courier,* November 1999, pp. 21–26.

"Hack Attack: 90% of Chinese Web Sites Not Secure, Report States." Trans. and summarized from an article in *Guangzhou Ribao* [Guangzhou Daily], May 18, 2000, in *China Online,* May 22, 2000.

Hamilton, John. "Balkan Information-Technology Firms Face Exodus of Computer Specialists." *Wall Street Journal,* November 9, 2000.

Hansen, Stephen A. *Getting Online for Human Rights.* Washington, DC: American Association for the Advancement of Science, 1998.

——— (ed.). *AAAS Directory of Human Rights Resources on the Internet.* Washington, DC: American Association for the Advancement of Science, AAAS Science and Human Rights Program, 1998.

"Hard Choices for Croatia." *The Economist* (London), July 25, 2000, pp. 48–49.

Harmon, Amy. "U.S. Gives up Last Vestige of Control over Basic Internet Structure." *New York Times,* June 6, 1998, p. A1.

Harris, Marshall Freeman. "Macedonia: The Next Domino?" *National Interest,* spring 1999, pp. 42–46.

Hasenclever, Andreas, Peter Mayer, and Volker Rittberger (eds.). *Theories of International Regimes.* New York: Cambridge University Press, 1997.

Hazelhurst, Ethel. "Will Privatisations Hit Sweet Spot?" *Financial Mail* (South Africa), January 19, 2001, p. 36.

Headrick, Daniel R. *The Tools of Empire Technology and European Imperialism in the Nineteenth Century.* Oxford: Oxford University Press, 1981.

Heard-Bey, Frauke. "The United Arab Emirates: A Quarter Century of Federation," in *Middle East Dilemma: The Politics and Economics of Arab Integration,* ed. Michael C. Hudson. New York: Columbia University Press, 1999, pp. 128–149.

Hedlund, Stefan. *Russia's "Market" Economy: A Bad Case of Predatory Capi-*

talism. London: University College London Press, 1999.

Held, David, Anthony McGrew, David Goldblatt, and Jonathan Perraton. *Global Transformations: Politics, Economics and Culture.* Stanford: Stanford University Press, 1999.

Helliwell, John F. *How Much Do National Borders Matter?* Washington, DC: Brookings Institution, 1998.

Henderson, Peter. "Russia's Online Enigma: The Internet Boom Is on, But Can Anybody Actually Make Money?" *National Post* (Ottawa), June 23, 2000, p. C12.

Herron, Erik S. "Democratization and the Development of Information Regimes: The Internet in Eurasia and the Baltics." *Problems of Post-Communism,* 46:4 (July-August 1999), pp. 56–69.

Hiebert, Ray. "The Difficult Birth of a Free Press: Entrepreneurs in Hungary Face Severe Obstacles in Establishing Independent Media Companies." *American Journalism Review,* January-February 1994, pp. 34–36.

Higgins, Andrew. "Turner Sets Investment in Russia's Media-Most—Putin's Support of Bid for 25% of NTV Is Thrown into Doubt." *Wall Street Journal,* January 22, 2001, p. A16.

Hilde, Paal Sigurd. "Slovak Nationalism and the Break-up of Czechoslovakia." *Europe–Asia Studies,* 51:4 (June 1, 1999), pp. 647–666.

Hilliard, Robert, and Michael Keith. *Global Broadcasting Systems.* Boston: Focal, 1996.

Hilsum, Lindsey. "No Revolution, Thanks, We're Czech." *New Statesman* (London), 129:4506 (October 2, 2000), pp. 13–15.

Hoelscher, Gregory. "The Next Step: Three Countries Lead the Way." *Business and Management Practices,* 34:4 (April 2000), pp. 76–78, 82.

Hoffman, David. "Itera: Mystery Player in Russia's Natural Gas Market." *Washington Post,* May 21, 2000, pp. H1, 5.

———. "Putin Pits Politics Against Economics." *Washington Post,* July 7, 2000, pp. 1, 20.

———. "Russian Media Fight to Live." *Washington Post,* June 28, 2000, pp. 16, 22.

Holdsworth, Nick. "Czechs 'Losing Internet Race.'" *Times Higher Education Supplement,* iss. 1440 (June 16, 2000), pp. 13–15.

Holman, Otto. "Integrating Eastern Europe." *International Journal of Political Economy,* 28:2 (summer 1998), pp. 12–43.

Horvath, John. "Alone in the Crowd: The Politics of Cybernetic Isolation," in *Culture and Technology in the New Europe: Civic Discourse in Transformation in Post-Communist Nations,* ed. Laura Lengel. Stamford, CT: Ablex, 2000, pp. 77–104.

"How Israeli High-Tech Happened." *Israel's Business Arena,* January 20, 2000.

Hu, Jim. "Is the ICQ Experiment Working?" *New York Times,* May 9, 2001, p. 17.

Hudson, Heather. *Global Connections: International Telecommunications Infrastructure and Policy.* New York: Van Nostrand Reinhold, 1997.

Human Development Report 1999. New York: Oxford University Press for the

United Nations Development Program, 1999.

"Humanitarian Organisations Resist Pact with Sudan People's Liberation Movement." *Al-Ra'y al-Amm* (Sudan daily), March 25, 2000, trans. in *BBC Summary of World Broadcasts,* March 28, 2000.

Hundley, Richard O., and Robert H. Anderson. "Emerging Challenge: Security and Safety in Cyberspace," in *Athena's Camp: Preparing for Conflict in the Information Age,* eds. John Arquilla and David Ronfeldt. Santa Monica: RAND, 1997, pp. 231–252.

Hungary: In Transition to Freedom and Prosperity. Indianapolis: Hudson Institute, 1990.

"Hungary Improving Living Standards." Associated Press report in the *New York Times,* January 1, 2001, p. C12.

Huque, Nadeem U., Nelson Mark, and Donald J. Mathieson. "Risk in Africa: Its Causes and Its Effects on Investment," in *Investment and Risk in Africa,* eds. Paul Collier and Catherine Patillo. London: Macmillan, 1999, pp. 257–288.

Hurwitz, Roger. "Who Needs Politics? Who Needs People? The Ironies of Democracy in Cyberspace." *Contemporary Sociology,* 28:6 (November 1999), pp. 655–662.

"In Southern Africa, Only 20 Percent Have Electricity." *World Reporter,* June 1, 1999.

"India: New Telecom Technology Mooted for Rural Areas." *The Hindu,* December 23, 1999.

"Indian ISP VSNL Ordered to Block Internet Access to Pakistani Site." *India Line,* July 6–11, 1999.

"India's IT Growth Must Take Broadband Route." *Statesman* (India), May 21, 2000.

"Indo-Japan Joint Meeting to Lay Emphasis on IT Sector." *The Hindu,* May 18, 2000.

Ingis, Stuart. "Law Students with Laptops Link Bosnia to the Internet." *Christian Science Monitor,* February 28, 1997, p. 19.

"The Internet: Founding Myths." *The Economist* (London), Review of Books section, June 17, 2000, p. 4.

"Internet Business in an Embryonic Stage in Armenia." *BBC Monitoring International Report Series,* March 8, 2000.

The Internet in the Midcast and North Africa: Free Expression and Censorship. New York: Human Rights Watch Reports, 1999.

"Internet Infrastructure Needed." *Statesman* (India), January 16, 2001.

"Internet Securities Unveils New Services." *Information Today,* 16:9 (October 1999), pp. 29–30.

"Internet Users in Poland." *Russia Xtension,* October 2000.

Iordanova, Dina. "Mediated Concerns: The New Europe in Hypertext," in *Culture and Technology in the New Europe*: *Civic Discourse in Transformation in Post-Communist Nations,* ed. Laura Lengel. Stamford, CT: Ablex, 2000, pp. 107–131.

"Iran to Put Khomeini's Complete Works on Internet." *Agence France Press,* June 1, 1998.

"Iranian Authorities Said to Be 'Jamming' Dissident Ayatollah's Website." *BBC Monitoring Middle East—Political,* December 24, 2000.

"Iranian Cleric Goes to Battle in Cyberspace." *New York Times,* December 17, 2000, sec. 1, p. A1.

"Iran's Telecom and Internet Sector: A Comprehensive Survey." Report of the Open Research Network. Tarzana, CA: Open Research Network, June 15, 1999.

"Iraqi Newspaper, News Agency Launch Web Sites." *India Line,* May 31, 1999.

ISI2001 Information Society Index: Info Revolution Reshaping the Globe. Framingham, MA: IDC/World Times, 2000.

"ISLAMVISION on the Way." *Moneyclips (GCC),* July 8, 1992.

"IT—Superpower Hype." *The Hindu,* December 13, 2000.

"It's a Long Road to E-Commerce, Says SETC Official." Trans. of an article in *Zhonghua Gongshang Shibao* [China Business Times], September 28, 2000, in *China Online,* October 2, 2000.

Ivanov, Ivan. "Kasyanov Discusses with Soros Investment Projects in Russia." *Tass News Agency,* June 9, 2000.

Jalloul, Ghinwa. "Computing in Lebanon." *Communications of the ACM,* 42:2 (February 1999), pp. 25–26.

Jarrah, Fawaz. "Dell Launches Online Business in UAE." *DITnet News Online,* October 28, 1999.

———. "Internet Communication Highlights Need for Arabic Unicode." *DITnet. ITNEWS,* December 20, 1999.

———. "Internet Reaches Layman in Middle East." *DITnet.ITNEWS,* April 25, 2000.

———. "Internet Shoppers in Arab World Spend U.S. $95 Million." *DITnet News Online,* June 13, 1999.

———. "New OS Opens Palm Computing to Millions of Arab Users." *DITnet. ITNEWS,* October 14, 1999.

———. "Organizations Urged to Think eBusiness Before eCommerce." *DITnet News Online,* December 9, 1999.

———. "Practical E-Commerce Conference—'Completing the Electronic Handshake.'" *DITnet News Online,* October 14, 1999.

———. "Private Ventures Lead Arab Migration to E-Commerce." *DITnet News Online,* October 21, 1999.

———. "Saudi Telecom Abolishes Extra Charge Imposed on Internet Use." *DITnet,* June 20, 2000.

———. "Saudi Telecom Criticized for Poor Internet Services." *DITnet.ITNEWS,* November 14, 1999.

———. "Widespread Internet Use Before E-Commerce, Says Expert." *DITnet News Online,* January 20, 2000.

Jasinski, Piotr. "Competition Rules and Regulations in Telecommunications: The Case of Poland's Intent to Join the EU," in *Privatization and Competition in Telecommunications: International Developments,* ed. Daniel J. Ryan. Westport: Praeger, 1997, pp. 127–147.

Jehl, Douglas. "Buffett of Arabia? Well, Maybe." *New York Times,* March 28, 1999, sec. 3, pp. 1, 21.

———. "The Internet's 'Open Sesame' Is Answered Warily." *New York Times,* March 18, 1999, p. A4.

Jensen, Mike. "Algeria/Egypt/Libya/Morocco/Tunisia: North African Internet Round-Up." *Telecommunications,* 33:10 (October 1999), pp. 94–97.

———. "Making the Connection: Africa and the Internet." *Current History,* 99:637 (May 2000), pp. 215–221.

———. "North African Internet Round-Up." *Telecommunications International,* 33:10 (October 1999), pp. 188–189.

Joha, Ghassan. "Iraqi Tragedy Falls on Laps of International NGOs." *Star* (Beirut), March 16, 2000.

Johnston, Kristin. "Romanian President Ion Iliescu's Vision for Technology Modernization." *PR Newswire,* January 22, 2001.

Jordan, Michael J. "Croatians Ready to Leave Cults of Personality Behind." *Christian Science Monitor,* February 7, 2000, p. 8.

———. "New Refugee Aid Worker: The Cell Phone." *Christian Science Monitor,* April 26, 1999, p. 7.

———. "Struggling to Realize Potential, Moldova Faces up to Issues." *Christian Science Monitor,* January 3, 2000, p. 7.

"Jordan Telecom Slashes Fees." *Middle East Economic Digest,* December 22, 2000, p. 16.

"Jordan WTO Membership Approved." *Middle East News Items,* January 5, 2000.

Kaase, Max. "Political Science and the Internet." *International Political Science Review,* 21:3 (July 2000), pp. 265–282.

Kahn, Jeffrey. "Pushing the Cyber-Envelope: Israel as an Incubator." *Middle East Insight,* March-April, 1999, p. 45.

Kalman, Matthew. "Investors Cash in on Israel's Silicon Wadi." *Sunday Times* (London), May 21, 2000, p. C14.

Kaminski, Matthew. "Macedonia Moves to Quell the Albanian Rebels that Threaten Its Diverse Democracy." *Wall Street Journal,* Eastern edition, March 23, 2001, p. A12.

Kaminski, Matthew, and Elizabeth Williamson. "EU Balks at Setting Date for New Members—Instead, Brussels Maps out Plans for Negotitations, Fears of Going Too Fast." *Wall Street Journal,* November 8, 2000, p. A22.

Kamli, Abdul Kader. "ASP Service in the Arab World: The Balancing Act." *DITnet.ITNEWS,* June 26, 2000.

———. "Attracting Foreign Investment." *DITnet.ITNEWS,* April 6, 2000.

———. "Will Dubai Get the Gold Medal for Digital Cities?" *DITnet,* May 6, 2000.

Kanev, Peter. "Bulgaria Tangles with Web." *International Press Institute Report,* 5:3 (third quarter 1999), pp. 14–15.

Kaplow, Larry. "Syria Embraces the Internet Gingerly." *Atlanta Journal and Constitution,* June 25, 2000, p. G6.

Karanja, David. "Expanding the East African Internet Market." *Telecommunications International,* April 1, 2000, p. 22.

Karnitschnig, Matthew. "As Romania Nears Presidential Elections, Foreign Investors Find Few Attractions." *Wall Street Journal,* December 6, 2000, p. B12A.

———. "Romanian Vote Signals Return to the Past." *Wall Street Journal,* November 28, 2000, p. A23.

Karp, Jonathan. "BJP Makes Patriotic Pitch for Investments from Indians Abroad." *Wall Street Journal,* June 4, 1998, p. A10.

———. "India's Finance Minister Calls for Reform—Urgent Need Seen to Open Financial Markets, Lure Investors, Cut Spending." *Wall Street Journal,* February 29, 2000, p. A19.

———. "Reform Raj: India Regains Investors' Confidence." *Wall Street Journal,* February 18, 2000, p. A10.

Kaske, Karlheinz. "Eastern Europe: Opportunities for Development," in *Telecom 91 Global Review,* ed. Hugh Chaloner. London: Kline, 1991, pp. 89–97.

Keohane, Robert O., and Joseph S. Nye Jr. "Globalization: What's New? What's Not? (and So What?)" *Foreign Policy,* iss. 118 (spring 2000), pp. 104–130.

———. *Power and Interdependence: World Politics in Transition.* Boston: Little, Brown, 1977.

———. "Power and Interdependence in the Information Age: The Resilience of States." *Foreign Affairs,* 77:5 (September-October 1998), pp. 81–95.

Keynes, Milton. "Slovenia's Very Own Silicon Valley Challenge." *Corporate Location* (Euromoney Institutional Investor), fourth quarter 2000, p. 22.

Kiarostami, Ahmad. "Could Iran Rival India as a Software Provider?" *Menas Associates Focus Articles,* March 6, 2000, pp. 1–5.

Kiernan, Vincent. "Net Search Could Reunite Refugees." *New Scientist,* 151: 2042 (August 10, 1996), pp. 7–10.

King, David A. "Some Illustrations in Islamic Scientific Manuscripts and Their Secrets," in *The Book in the Islamic World: The Written Word and Communication in the Middle East,* ed. George N. Atiyeh. Albany: State University of New York Press, 1995, pp. 149–178.

Kirchner, Henner. "Internet in the Arab World: A Step Towards 'Information Society'?" in *Mass Media, Politics and Society in the Middle East,* ed. Kai Hafez. Cresskill, NJ: Hampton Press, 2001, pp. 137–158.

Kirillova, Irina. "Prospects of Distance Learning in Kazakhstan and Central Asia." *Bulletin of the American Society for Information Science,* 26:4 (April-May 2000), pp. 14–17.

Kiselyova, Emma, and Manual Castells. "Russia in the Information Age," in *Russia in the New Century: Stability or Disorder?* eds. Victoria E. Bonnell and George W. Breslauer. Boulder: Westview, 2000, pp. 126–157.

Kleinwachter, Wolfgang. "ICANN as the 'United Nations' of the Global Information Society? The Long Road Towards Self-Regulation of the Internet." *Gazette,* 62:6 (December 1, 2000), pp. 451–476.

Knutsen, Torbjorn L. *The Rise and Fall of World Orders.* Manchester: Manchester University Press, 1999.

Kontkiewicz-Chachulska, Hanna, and Denis Phan. "From Path-Dependent Processes of Structural Change to a Diversity of Market Models in Central European Countries' Telecommunications," in *Telecommunications and Socio-Economic Development,* eds. Stuart Macdonald and Gary Madden. Amsterdam: Elsevier Science B.V., 1998, pp. 315–336.

Kramer, Andrew. "Russian Government Approves 'Information Security Doctrine.'" *Associated Press,* June 23, 2000.

Krasner, Stephen (ed.). *International Regimes.* Ithaca: Cornell University Press, 1983.

Kraus, James R. "J. P. Morgan Will Advise Slovakia on Sale of Its Two Biggest Banks." *American Banker,* 169:246 (December 27, 1999), pp. 17–20.

Krishnada, K. C. "India Eyes Foreign Telecom Firm Ownership Proposal." *Electronic Engineering Times,* May 15, 2000, p. 46.

"KSA Online?" *PC Magazine,* April 1998, p. 3.

"La Presse Libre Sur le Web." *El-Watan* (Algiers), October 27, 1998.

"Lack of Net Standards Hampers Reach of Chinese Web Sites." Trans. and summarized from an article in *Zaobao.com,* February 3, 2000, in *China Online,* February 10, 2000.

Lacuna, Gia Marie. "The Future: IT in the Middle and Near East in 2001." *PC Magazine,* summer 1998, p. 6.

LaFraniere, Sharon. "Russian Media Fear for Their Independence." *Washington Post,* February 21, 2000, p. A19.

Laird, Robin F., and Holger H. Mey. *The Revolution in Military Affairs: Allied Perspective.* McNair Paper no. 60. Washington, DC: Institute for National Strategic Studies, National Defense University, 1999.

Lake, David. "Wireless Net: Not Yet." *Industry Standard,* 3:20 (May 29, 2000), p. 202.

Landau, Efie. "Internet Later." *Israel's Business Arena,* January 17, 2000.

Landers, Peter. "G-8 Creates 'Dot Force' to Help Poorer Nations Tap Technology." *Wall Street Journal,* July 24, 2000, p. A21.

Langencamp, Daniel. "Free of Its Iron-Fisted Rule, Croatia Stages a Difficult Comeback." *Christian Science Monitor,* July 25, 2000, p. 8.

———. "High-Tech Hungarians Forge 'Silicon East.'" *Christian Science Monitor,* April 26, 2000, p. 6.

Laris, Michael. "China Presses Anti-Dissent Drive." *Washington Post,* October 26, 1999, p. A20.

Lasica, J. D. "Conveying the War in Human Terms." *American Journalism Review,* June 1999, pp. 76–79.

Leary, Warren E. "U.S. Company Sets Space-Station Venture with Russians." *New York Times,* December 10, 1999, p. A33.

Leggett, Karby. "China Plans Two Stock Markets for Tech Start-Ups to Raise Cash." *Wall Street Journal,* March 10, 2000, p. A13.

Leibowitz, Alissa. "Cover Story: Strong Technology Gives Punch to Israeli Venture Capital Market." *Venture Capital Journal,* July 1, 2000, pp. 1–5.

Leonard, Dick. "Bulgaria Aims for the EU." *Europe,* iss. 392 (December 1999–

January 2000), pp. 4–5.

Lessig, Lawrence. *Code and Other Laws of Cyberspace.* New York: Basic, 1999.

"Lessons from Behind Bars: Did Putin Have a Hand in the Arrest of a Critical Media Mogul?" *Christian Science Monitor,* June 16, 2000, p. 10.

Levander, Michelle. "By Its Bootstraps: The Governor of an Indian State Aims to Lift His People Out of Poverty Through Technological Improvements." *Wall Street Journal,* September 25, 2000, p. R16.

LeVine, Steve. "As Turkmenistan Stalls on Key Reforms, European Bank May Curtail Its Lending." *Wall Street Journal,* May 14, 2000, p. A15.

———. "In Kyrgyzstan, Flawed Election Portends a Shift to Autocracy." *Wall Street Journal,* October 30, 2000, p. A26.

Lewis, John Wilson, and Xue Litai. *China's Strategic Seapower: The Politics of Force Modernization in the Nuclear Age.* Stanford: Stanford University Press, 1994.

Lhabitant, Francois-Serge, and Tetyana Novikova. "Doing Business in . . . Ukraine." *Thunderbird International Business Review,* 42:5 (September-October 2000), pp. 571–595.

Li, Clara. "Great Software Divide." *South China Morning Post,* December 14, 2000, p. 12.

Liberating Cyberspace: Civil Liberties, Human Rights and the Internet. London: Pluto Press for the National Council for Civil Liberties, 1999.

Lincoln, Jonathan B. "Middle East Governments on the World Wide Web." *WINEP Research Notes,* no. 6. Washington, DC: Washington Institute for Near East Policy, February 1999.

Lipman, Masha. "Putin Won. Now What?" *Washington Post,* May 19, 2001, p. A23.

Liu, Sunray. "Motorola Partners on Chinese-Language Version of Linux." *Electronic Engineering Times,* April 24, 2000.

Lovelock, Peter. *E-China: Putting Business on the Internet.* New York: Maverick Research and Virtual China, 1999.

Lubin, Nancy. "Pipe Dreams: Potential Impacts of Energy Exploitation." *Harvard International Review,* 22:1 (winter/spring 2000), pp. 66–71.

Luxner, Larry. "Digital Bridge Spans Deep Rifts: Middle East Nurtures New National Carrier." *tele.com,* 5:10 (May 15, 2000), pp. 20–21.

"Macedonia's Communications Minister Defends Telecom Privatization." *BBC Monitoring Europe Economic,* December 21, 2000.

Machlis, Avi. "Israel's Orthodox Approach the Internet with Trepidation." *Financial Times* (London), January 18, 2000, p. 6.

Machlis, Sharon. "Intranet Project Aims to Heal Bosnia." *Computerworld,* 31:46 (November 17, 1997), pp. 57–58.

Maheshwari, Vijai. "Lithuanian City Guide Provides Surprise Lead: A Canadian Entrepreneur Faces Competition as He Develops an Expansion Plan and Internet Strategy." *Financial Times* (London), October 4, 2000, p. 14.

———. "Small Could Be Profitable in the Baltics." *Financial Times* (London), October 4, 2000, p. 14.

Maltz, Judy. "First of Large Banks to Offer Internet Foreign Currency Trading." *Israel's Business Arena,* January 20, 2000.

"Management Split on Future of China C-Net." Trans. and summarized from an article in *Renmin Ribao* [People's Daily], March 24, 2000, in *China On-line,* March 27, 2000.

Mandelbaum, Michael. *The New European Diasporas: National Minorities and Conflicts in Eastern Europe.* New York: Council on Foreign Relations, 2000.

Manuel, Gren, and Leslie Chang. "Will Language Wars Balkanize the Web? Battle over Chinese Sites Portends an Internet of Isolated Domains." *Wall Street Journal,* November 30, 2000, p. C22.

Marples, David R. "The Demographic Crisis in Belarus." *Problems of Post-Communism,* 47:1 (January–February 2000), pp. 16–28.

Marquand, Robert. "Fast-Rising Leader of a Cyber-State." *Christian Science Monitor,* September 22, 1998, pp. 1 ff.

———. "From Farms to Firms: The Net Casts Its Web on India." *Christian Science Monitor,* February 11, 2000, p. 7.

Marsden, Ken. "Enterprise Networking in Africa—Is Wireless the Way Forward?" *Africa News,* July 6, 2000.

"Matav Purchases 51 Percent of Maktel." *RCR Wireless News,* 20 (January 8, 2001), p. 24.

Matic, Veran, and Drazen Pantic. "War of Words: When the Bombs Came, Serbia's B92 Hit the Net." *Nation,* 269:18 (November 29, 1999), p. 34.

Matloff, Judith. "Bargain Beets, Babushkas, and Russia's Internet." *Christian Science Monitor,* February 3, 2000, pp. 1, 9.

Matthews, Jessica Tuchman. "Power Shift: The Rise of Global Civil Society." *Foreign Affairs,* 76:1 (January-February 1997), pp. 50–67.

Mayhew-Smith, Alex. "Entrepreneurs: Lithuania Needs You." *Electronics Weekly,* October 18, 2000, pp. 18–19.

"Mbeki's Words of Website Wisdom." *The Economist* (London), November 13, 1999, p. 46.

Mbogo, Steve. "Can Africa Exploit the Internet?" *Review of African Political Economy,* 27:83 (March 2000), pp. 127–130.

McCarthy, Jack. "China, Russia Develop Cyber Attack Capability." *The Standard,* February 24, 2000.

McCullagh, Declan. "Mideast Misses the Net." *Wired News,* July 8, 1999, pp. 1–3, available at www.wired.com/news/topstories.

McGrane, Sally. "A Web Site That Came in from the Cold to Unveil Russian Secrets." *New York Times,* December 14, 2000, p. G8.

McMillan, Andrew. "Romania: Wireless Spurs Telecoms Growth." *Business and Management Practices,* 34:4 (April 2000), pp. 92–94.

McNatt, Robert, and Catherine Yang. "Democratic Rule for the Net." *Business Week,* March 6, 2000, pp. 8–9.

McNeil, Donald G., Jr. "Opportunities in a Rusting Romania." *New York Times,* December 25, 1999, Business/Financial section, p. 9.

Mcrae, Hamish. "Only Deregulation and Competition Can Help Close the Digital Divide." *The Independent* (London), January 19, 2001, p. 20.

Mecham, Michael. "India Opens Door for Satellites Services." *Aviation Week and Space Technology,* 152:21 (May 22, 2000), pp. 54–55.

Melody, W. H. "Internet Development and Infrastructure Regulation." *Telecommunications Policy,* 24 (2000), pp. 85–87.

Michalis, Maria, and Lina Takla. "Telecommunications in the Czech Republic: The Privatization of SPT Telecom," in *Privatization and Competition in Telecommunications: International Developments,* ed. Daniel J. Ryan. Westport: Praeger, 1997, pp. 88–102.

"Mikulas Dzurinda, Slovakia's Turn for the Better." *The Economist* (London), December 11, 1999, p. 48.

Miller, Judith. "Belarus Fines Soros Foundation." *New York Times,* May 2, 1997, p. A3.

"MMDS Systems to Provide Russian Customers with High-Speed Internet and Data Transmission Capabilities." *Canada News Wire,* June 29, 2000.

Moffett, Julie. "Armenia: On the Information Superhighway, Despite Daunting Problems." *Radio Free Europe/Radio Liberty,* June 13, 1997.

———. "Baltic States: Internet Connectivity Leads Former Soviet Republics." *Radio Free Europe/Radio Liberty,* April 15, 1997.

———. "Belarus: Government Regulations Strangle Internet Growth." *Radio Free Europe/Radio Liberty,* January 16, 1998.

———. "Big Brother Watches Internet in Belgrade." *Radio Free Europe/Radio Liberty,* January 11, 1999.

———. "Bulgaria: Making Progress on the Information Superhighway." *Radio Free Europe/Radio Liberty,* June 11, 1999.

———. "Georgia: Internet Making Inroads." *Radio Free Europe/Radio Liberty,* July 4, 1997.

———. "Gorbachev, Thatcher Say Internet Powerful Political Tool." *Radio Free Europe/Radio Liberty,* June 25, 1998.

———. "The Internet in Central Asia." *Radio Free Europe/Radio Liberty,* May 21, 1997.

———. "Moldova: Slow, Steady Progress Improves Internet Access." *Radio Free Europe/Radio Liberty,* June 2, 1997.

———. "Russia: Demand for Internet Use Growing, but Restrictions Loom." *Radio Free Europe/Radio Liberty,* February 19, 1997.

———. "Russia: Evolving Internet Policy." *Radio Free Europe/Radio Liberty,* February 19, 1997.

———. "Russia: Secret Policy Lowering Iron Curtain on Internet." *Radio Free Europe/Radio Liberty,* August 20, 1998.

Moschovitis, Christos J.P., Hilary Poole, Tami Schuyler, and Theresa M. Senft. *History of the Internet: A Chronology, 1843 to the Present.* Santa Barbara: ABC-CLIO, 1999.

Moses, Lucia, and Joe Strupp. "Press Mobilizes to Cover Kosovo." *Editor and Publisher,* 132:13 (March 27, 1999), pp. 9–11.

Moudrak, Marina, and Christine Zimmerman. "Newsfront: Keep the Spy Out of ISPs." *Data Communications,* 28:11 (August 1999), pp. 11–14.

Mueller, Milton, and Zixiang Tan. *China in the Information Age.* Washington, DC: Center for International and Strategic Studies, 1996.

Munro, Neil. "Governments Off-Line." *National Journal,* 31:47 (November 20, 1999), pp. 3380–3389.

Mutume, Gumisai. *Africa-Development: More Than Just Internet Connections Required.* Addis Ababa: Communication Team, Economic Commission for Africa, 2000.

Naegele, Jolyon. "Czech Republic: Public Protests Telephone Monopoly's Proposed Rate Hikes." *Radio Free Europe/Radio Liberty,* November 19, 1998.

Naffakh, Mohammed. "Will Syria Embrace the Cell Phone?" *Middle East Insight,* special issue on the Internet and Information Technology, July–August 1999, pp. 35–36.

Napoli, Lisa. "Iraqi Exiles Reach for Home on Web." *New York Times,* February 20, 1997.

Netanel, Neil Weinstock. "Cyberspace Self-Governance: A Skeptical View from Liberal Democratic Theory." *California Law Review,* 88:2 (March 2000), pp. 395–499.

Nevin, Tom. "South Africa: 'Plum' Assets for Sale." *African Business* (London), iss. 258 (October 2000), pp. 35–36.

"New Dabbagh Group Technology Head Announces Internet Initiatives." *DITnet.ITNEWS,* November 1, 1999.

"New eAsia Report Indicates China and India Will Outpace Japan in Internet Growth over the Next Four Years." *eMarketer,* December 28, 2000.

"New Start?" *The Economist* (London), February 12, 2000, pp. 50–51.

New Telecom Policy 1999. New Delhi: Department of Telecommunications, 1999.

Niccolai, James. "Hungary: The Silicon Valley of Eastern Europe?" *IDG.net,* March 17, 2000.

Noam, Eli. *Telecommunications in Africa.* Oxford: Oxford University Press, 1999.

Nolan, Dermot. "Development of Satellite Services in Eastern Europe: Entering the Harsh Reality Phase," in *Telecom 91 Global Review,* ed. Hugh Chaloner. London: Kline, 1991, pp. 98–104.

Nosik, Anton. "How to Ban the Internet." *Moscow News,* June 16, 1999.

"Nowhereland." *The Economist* (London), June 26, 1999, pp. 61–62.

"Number of Internet Users in Armenia Said Higher Than in Georgia and Azerbaijan." *BBC Monitoring International Reports Series,* March 2, 2000.

Oaca, Nicolae. "Romania: The Fixed Line Arena." *Business and Management Practices,* 34:4 (April 2000), p. 94.

Okolicsanyi, Karoly. "Hungarian Telephone's Landmark Privatization Deal." *Radio Free Europe/Radio Liberty Research Report,* 3:6 (1994), pp. 41–43.

O'Neill, Mark. "Beijing Commits on Easing Net Laws." *South China Morning Post,* September 12, 1999.

"Online in Saudi Arabia: How Women Beat the Rules." *The Economist* (London), October 2, 1999, p. 48.

Otorbayeva, Asel. "Entire Kyrgyz Opposition Locked Up." *Current Digest of the Post Soviet Press,* 52:14 (May 3, 2000), p. 15.

Ottaway, David B. "U.S. Considers Slugging It Out with International Terrorism." *Washington Post,* October 17, 1996, p. 25.

"Over-abundance of Rules Repels Technology." *Bahrain Tribune,* November 7, 2000.

Oyama, David I. "China Aims at Its Own Internet Network." *Wall Street Journal,* January 8, 2001, p. A3.

Pai, Uday L. "India's PC Industry Reaches 5 Million Installed Base." *Central Business Information,* January 8, 2001, p. 26.

"Palestinian Refugees Join the Net." *Reuters,* July 26, 1999.

"Palestinian Refugees Online: Virtual Bridges." *The Economist* (London), October 2, 1999, p. 48.

Pan, Philip P. "China Opens a Broad Drive Against Dissenters." *International Herald Tribune,* May 12, 2001, p. 1.

Panfilova, Viktoria. "Opposition Activists Seek Political Asylum." *Current Digest of the Post Soviet Press,* 52:14 (May 3, 2000), pp. 16–17.

Pantic, Drazen. "Internet in Serbia: From Dark Side of the Moon to the Internet Revolution." *First Monday: Peer-Reviewed Journal on the Internet,* iss. 2, January 1997.

Parker, Philip. "Survey—Mastering Management: Developing Study for a Not-So-Global Village." *Financial Times* (London), January 22, 2001, pp. 12, 14.

"Parliament Okays IT Bill." *The Hindu,* May 18, 2000.

Parthasarthy, Rukmini. "'The World Needs a Strong India.'" *Business Today,* February 7, 2000, p. 110.

Patni, Ambika. "Silicon Valley of the East: Bangalore's Boom." *Harvard International Review,* 21:4 (fall 1999), pp. 8–9.

Pecht, Michael, Weifeng Liu, and David Hodges. "Semiconductor Companies in China." *Semiconductor International,* 23:10 (September 2000), pp. 148–154.

Peel, Michael. "From Glasnost to Gazprom: NTV." *Financial Times* (London), April 30, 2001, p. 21.

Peled, Alon. "First-Class Technology—Third-Rate Bureaucracy: The Case of Israel." *Information Technology for Development,* 9:1 (March 1, 2000), pp. 45–58.

Perlmutter, Amos. "Shifting Balance of World Power." *Washington Times,* February 1, 2001, p. A15.

Pipes, Daniel. "Islam and Islamism: Faith and Ideology." *National Interest,* 59 (spring 2000), pp. 87–93.

Pisik, Betsy. "U.N. Panel Now Aims to Banish Private Groups." *Washington Times,* May 17, 2001, p. A1.

Platt, Gordon. "Fund Backed by AID Offers Finance in Russia." *Journal of Commerce,* March 15, 2000, pp. 9–10.

Plaza, Gerry. "Lotus Nears Completion of Dubai Shopping Festival Site." *DIT-net News Online,* December 22, 1999, pp. 1–3.

"Poland: Internet Market Research Findings." *Gazeta Wyborcza* (Warsaw), trans. by the *BBC Monitoring International Reports Series,* February 8, 2000.

Pomfret, John. "China Plans for a Stronger Air Force." *Washington Post,* November 9, 1999, p. A17.

Pond, Elizabeth. "Come Together: Europe's Unexpected New Architecture." *Foreign Affairs,* 79:2 (March-April 2000), pp. 8–12.

Pope, Hugh. "Autocracy Is Spreading in Former Soviet States." *Wall Street Journal,* October 14, 1998, p. A15.

———. "Corruption Stunts Growth in Ex-Soviet States—Fresh Probe Reflects Big Drag on Reforms, Foreign Investment." *Wall Street Journal,* July 5, 2000, p. A17.

———. "Why Is the Tech Set Putting Down Roots in the Desert? Dubai, Of Course." *Wall Street Journal,* January 23, 2001, p. A15.

Popov, Vladimir V. *The Currency Crisis in Russia in a Wider Context.* Ottawa: C. D. Howe Institute Commentary, March 2000.

Post, David. "The New Electronic Federalism." *American Lawyer,* October 1996, pp. 93–94.

Power, Carla. "For Refugees, a Cellular Lifeline." *Newsweek,* April 19, 1999, pp. 34–37.

"A Prelude to Info War." *Reuters,* June 24, 1998.

"Premier 'Moderately Optimistic' About Open Issues with Slovenia." *BBC Summary of World Broadcasts,* January 25, 2001.

Press, Larry, William Foster, and Seymour Goodman. "The Internet in India and China." *INET 99 Conference Proceedings,* pp. 1–16, available at http://www.isoc.org/inet99/proceedings/3a3a_3.htm.

Preston, Lee E., and Duane Windsor. *The Rules of the Game in the Global Economy: Policy Regimes for International Business,* 2d ed. Boston: Kluwer Academic Publishers, 1997.

Prince, Cathryn J. "World's Aid Groups Find Neutrality Badges Tarnished." *Christian Science Monitor,* December 8, 1995, p. 6.

Pufeng, Wang. "The Challenge of Information Warfare," in *Chinese Views of Future Warfare,* ed. Michael Pillsbury. Washington, DC: National Defense University, Institute for National Strategic Studies, 1997, pp. 317–327.

Ramani, S. "Humble Beginnings of the Internet in India." *India Line,* May 13, 1997.

Ramphele, Mamphela. "India: Networking in the War Against Poverty." *Business Line,* July 14, 2000.

Randolph, Eleanor. "Russia's New President Eyes an Unruly Press." *New York Times,* July 16, 2000, sec. 4, p. 14.

Rao, Madanmohan. "First South Asian Internet Workshop Recommends Rural Infrastructure." *India Line,* April 23, 1999.

———. "Indian ISPs Form Alliances to Tackle Market Growth Challenges." *India Line,* March 4, 1999, p. 2.

———. "Indian Portals to Take Off in Year 2000: First Indian-Language Portal Will Be in Tamil." *India Line,* February 1, 1999.

———. "Internet Is Emerging as a Key Component of Telemedicine Infrastructure." *India Line,* July 16, 1999.

————. "ISP Boom in India: Will the User Base Triple by Year 2000?" *India Line,* November 26, 1998, p. 2.

Rashid, Ahmed. *The Resurgence of Central Asia: Islam or Nationalism?* London: Zed Books, 1994.

"Record Dollars 1.45 Billion Bid Secures Stake in Czech Telecom Group." *Financial Times* (London), May 29, 1995.

Reed, John. "Better Late Than Never for TPSA." *Financial Times* (London), April 17, 2000, p. 4.

Rees, Matt. "Where Wired Is a Way of Life: These Ten Towns." *Newsweek International Edition* (November 9, 1998), pp. 23–33.

"Regulating the Internet." *The Hindu,* May 18, 2000.

Reid, Dickson. "IT Craze Favors Poland." *Central European,* 10:3 (April 2000), pp. 46–47.

————. "Web's Tentacles Draw Investors Eastward." *Central European,* 10:3 (April 2000), pp. 39–41.

"Revision of Slovak Programme on EU Entry to Be Completed by End of February." *Financial Times* (London), February 10, 2000, p. 4.

Rittberger, Volker (ed.). *Regime Theory and International Relations.* New York: Oxford University Press, 1993.

Rodger, Will. "Kosovo Project: Free and Safe Speech." *Interactive Week,* April 12, 1999.

Rodrik, Dani. "How Far Will International Economic Integration Go?" *Journal of Economic Perspectives,* 14:1 (winter 2000), pp. 177–186.

Rohozinski, Rafal. "How the Internet Did Not Transform Russia." *Current History,* 99:639 (October 2000), pp. 334–338.

————. *Mapping Russian Cyberspace: A Perspective on Democracy and the Net.* Geneva: United Nations Research Institute for Social Development, 1999.

"Romanian National Bank Inaugurates Internet Home Page." *Mediafax News Agency,* May 9, 2000, available in English in *BBC Worldwide Monitoring,* May 9, 2000.

Rothchild, John. "Protecting the Digital Consumer: The Limits of Cyberspace Utopianism." *Indiana Law Journal,* 74 (summer 1999), pp. 893–989.

Rubin, Joel. "Transitions: A Country-by-Country Review of the Media and Press Freedom in Former Warsaw Pact Nations Since 1989." *Media Studies Journal,* 13:3 (fall 1999), pp. 60–70.

Ruffin, M. Holt, Alyssa Deutschler, Catriona Logan, and Richard Upjohn. *The Post-Soviet Handbook: A Guide to Grassroots Organizations and Internet Resources.* Seattle: University of Washington Press for Civil Society International, 1999.

Russell, Alec. "Romania Places Future in Hands of Past." *Daily Telegraph* (London), December 16, 2000, p. 18.

"Russia Opens First in Series of Internet Training Centres." *Radio Moscow* broadcast trans. by BBC Summary of World Broadcasts, July 6, 2000.

"Russian Firm Makes Landmark Deal to Upgrade Nation's Favorite Web Site." *Wall Street Journal,* Eastern edition, January 31, 2000, p. A26.

"Russian Internet Community Comments on Project for On-Line Trading in Oil." *Interfax Russian News,* July 21, 2000.

"Russians Lose Six Satellites in Rocket-Launch Failure." *Seattle Times,* December 29, 2000, p. A9.

Sachar, Howard M. *A History of Israel: From the Rise of Zionism to Our Time,* 2d ed. New York: Alfred A. Knopf, 1996.

Sadowski, Bert M. "The Myth of Market Dominance: Telecommunications Manufacturing in Poland, Hungary, and the Czech Republic." *Telecommunications Policy,* 24 (2000), pp. 323–345.

"Sakhr Develops First Automatic Indexer for Arabic Text." *DITnet.ITNEWS,* January 13, 2000.

Salem, Amr. "Syria's Cautious Embrace." *Middle East Insight,* special issue on the Internet and Information Technology, March-April 1999, pp. 49–50.

Sander, Gordon F. "A Tale of Two Countries: The Finnish-Estonian Rapprochement." *Scandinavian Review,* 87:2 (autumn 1992), pp. 61–73.

Sandler, Neal, and Robert McNatt. "Israeli High Tech's New Promised Land." *Business Week,* April 26, 1999, p. 8.

"Saparmurad Niyazov." *World Press Review,* 47:4 (April 2000), pp. 43–44.

Sarin, Ritu. "A Caring System." *Asiaweek,* July 28, 2000, p. 37.

Schmitt, Eric. "Military Puts Bosnia on the Web." *New York Times,* December 17, 1995, sec. 4, p. 14.

"Seminar to Focus on IT and Internet Law." *Bahrain Tribune,* November 1, 2000.

Sender, Henny. "China Flirts with Venture Capitalism." *Wall Street Journal,* January 3, 2001, p. A3.

———. "Nations Strengthen Ties in Software, Consumer Electronics." *Asian Wall Street Journal,* August 21, 2000, p. A7.

Sennott, Charles M. "Syria's Leader Wants to Cast Strictures on Internet Use." *Boston Globe,* June 21, 2000, p. A4.

Serban, Rares. "Wired Romania: Making Networks a Way of Life." *Netware Connections* (Bucharest), November 1997, p. 6.

"Serbia: Government to Take over Control of Internet Services." *BBC Summary of World Broadcasts,* July 27, 2000.

"Setting a Fast Pace for Hungary and Europe." *Financial Times* (London), October 8, 1999, p. 31.

Shapiro, Andrew L. *The Control Revolution: How the Internet Is Putting Individuals in Charge and Changing the World We Know.* New York: PublicAffairs, 2000.

Shapley, Deborah. "Rebuilding the Web in Kosovo's Ashes." *New York Times,* April 18, 2001, p. H14.

Shetty, Vineeta. "Crown Jewel: Jordan Is in the Vanguard of Middle East States Moving Towards an Information Economy." *Communications International* (London), March 2001, pp. 13–14.

Siegel, Judy, and Tamar Hausman. "Haredim Abuzz About Halachi Ban on the Internet." *Jerusalem Post,* January 11, 2000, p. 5.

Silver, Victor. "Saudi Prince Goes Shopping." *Gazette* (Montreal), April 7, 2000, p. C2.

Simpson, Eileen. "Internet Providers Tout Bells, Whistles to Beat Competitors." *Warsaw Business Journal,* July-August 1998.

Slakey, Francis. "In Central Asia and Russia, the Educated Learn to Endure." *Chronicle of Higher Education,* 46:9 (October 22, 1999), p. B8.

Slaughter, Anne-Marie. "The Real New World Order." *Foreign Affairs,* 76:5 (September-October 1997), p. 183–198.

"Slipping Backward in Russia? The Raid Against Media-Most Clouds Putin's Image." *Christian Science Monitor,* May 15, 2000, p. 8.

"Slovenia's Government Collapses." *Associated Press,* April 8, 2000.

Smetannikov, Max. "Russian to the Web." *Interactive Week,* 7:15 (April 19, 2000), p. 110.

Smith, Benjamin. "In Drive for EU, Estonia to Shift into Reverse." *Wall Street Journal,* December 12, 2000, p. A18.

Smith, Craig S. "China at Gate of Profound Shift," *New York Times,* December 28, 2000, p. A1.

Smith, Pamela Ann. "The Bridge from East to West." *Telecommunications,* 33:10 (October 1999), pp. 179–182.

Smith, R. Jeffrey. "Belgrade Shuts TV Station and Paper: Independent Media Accused of Sedition." *Washington Post,* May 18, 2000, p. A18.

———. "Croatia Rapidly Abandoning Authoritarian Past." *Washington Post,* February 13, 2000, pp. A23, A28.

Sokolov, Andrei. "Million-Dollar Investments as Internet Euphoria Reaches Russia." *Deutsche Press-Agentur,* May 7, 2000.

Solomons, Mark. "IFPI: Ukraine Top Piracy Spot." *Billboard,* 111:31 (July 31, 1999), pp. 7–11.

"Sonera, Nortel Networks to Bring First Long Haul Optical Network to Finland, Russia." *Canada News Wire,* July 7, 2000.

"South Africa Gets Heavy on the Internet." *International Tax Review,* 11:10 (November 2000), p. 7.

South African Internet Access: Users and Devices. Johannesburg: BMI-TechKnowledge, 2000.

"South African Web Presence Is Growing, But Is It Fast Enough?" *Africa News,* November 17, 2000.

"South Eastern Europe: Digital Divide or Digital Opportunity?" *Romanian Business Journal,* April 30, 2001, pp. 2–6.

Southwick, Karen. "Beating Swords into Boards." *Upside Media,* January 31, 1996, p. 4.

"The State That Would Reform India." *The Economist* (London), September 2, 2000, p. 38.

Steele, Robert David. *On Intelligence: Spies and Secrecy in an Open World.* Fairfax, VA: AFCEA International Press, 2000.

Stein, Arthur A. "Coordination and Collaboration: Regimes in an Anarchic World," in *International Regimes,* ed. Stephen Krasner. Ithaca: Cornell University Press, pp. 115–140.

Stephen, Chris. "Polish Peasant Holds Key to Phone Link." *The Scotsman,* December 20, 2000, p. 13.

Stolyarov, G. K. "Computers in Belarus: Chronology of the Main Events." *IEEE Annals of the History of Computing,* 21:3 (July-September 1999), pp. 61–65.

Stones, Stephen. "Bulgaria: Intrigues on the Mobile Scene." *Business and Management Practices,* 34:4 (April 2000), pp. 95–96.

———. "Slovakia: Incumbent Operator Raises Standards." *Business and Management Practices,* 34:4 (April 2000), pp. 98–100.

Straubhaar, Joseph D. "From PTT to Private: Liberalization and Privatization in Eastern Europe and the Third World," in *Telecommunications Politics: Ownership and Control of the Information Highway in Developing Countries,* eds. Bella Mody, Johannes M. Bauer, and Joseph D. Straubhaar. Mahwah, NJ: Lawrence Erlbaum, 1995, p. 15.

Stremlau, John. "Bangalore: India's Silicon City." *Monthly Labor Review,* 119: 11 (November 1996), pp. 50–51.

"Survey of Obstacles to E-Commerce." *Jisuanji Shijie* [China Computerworld], January 5, 2000, trans. and analyzed in *China Online,* January 6, 2000.

"Syria Online." *The Economist* (London), April 29, 2000, pp. 42–43.

Tan, Zixiang (Alex), William Foster, and Seymour Goodman. "China's State-Coordinated Internet Infrastructure." *Communications of the ACM,* 42:6 (June 1999), pp. 44–52.

Taubman, Geoffry. "A Not-So World Wide Web: The Internet, China, and the Challenges to Nondemocratic Rule." *Political Communication,* 15 (1998), p. 265.

Tavernise, Sabrina. "Dot.Com Deals Come to the Steppes." *Business Week,* April 17, 2000, pp. 188–189.

Tayler, Jeffrey. "Back in the USSR? Eight Years After Independence, Belarus Ponders Reunification." *Harper's Magazine,* 300:1797 (February 2000), pp. 62–72.

"Telecommunications: Cooperation by the Balkan Countries and Cyprus." *Tech Europe,* February 11, 2000, p. 159.

"Telecoms: ANC Government Must Underwrite Competition." *Financial Times* (South Africa), April 20, 2001, p. 14.

"Telkom Sets Out Its Stall." *Corporate Finance* (London), 193:30 (December 2000), pp. 30–32.

"Telkom Welcomes Competition from May 2002." *SAPA* [South African Press Association] *Global News Wire,* March 19, 2001, p. 1.

"Telling the News, as It Is." *The Economist* (London), September 19, 1998, p. 39.

"Thabo Mbeki, Micro-Manager." *The Economist* (London), July 15, 2000, p. 44.

Thomas, Pradip N. "Trading the Nation: Multilateral Negotiations and the Fate of Communications in India." *International Journal for Communication Studies,* 61:3–4 (1999), pp. 275–293.

Thurber, Barton, and Iskra Djonova-Popova. "The Spirit of the Internet in the Balkans and the Enactment of the Macedonian Academic and Research Network." Freiburg: University of Freiburg Working Paper, 1996.

Thurston, Charles W. "Poland: Full Speed Ahead." *Global Finance,* 14:5 (May 2000), pp. 71–72.

"Tight Controls Make 20 Countries Internet Enemies: RSF." *Agence France Presse,* August 9, 1999, p. 1.

Timewell, Stephen. "With Many of the World's Economies Expecting a Rough Ride, *The Banker* Takes a Closer Look at Some of Those Affected." *The Banker* (London), 151:903 (May 1, 2001), pp. 3–6.

"Tirana's Link with the World: Cyberculture." *World Press Review,* 47:3 (March 2000), pp. 9–10.

Tismaneanu, Vladimir. *Fantasies of Salvation: Democracy, Nationalism and Myth in Post-Communist Europe.* Princeton: Princeton University Press, 1998.

"A Toy for Middle Eastern Times." *The Economist* (London), April 10, 1999, p. 45.

Travica, Bob, and Matthew Hogan. *Computer Networking in the XUSSR: Technology, Uses and Social Effects.* Baltimore: Department of History of Science, Johns Hopkins University, 1992.

Triffonova, Elena, and Vanya Kashoukeeva-Nousheva (eds.). *Regional Infrastructure Projects in South-Eastern Europe.* Sofia: Institute for Regional and International Studies, 1999.

Trofimov, Yaroslav. "Mobile-Phone War Erupts on Italian Border—Slovenia's Power Wireless Signal Stokes Nationalist Passions." *Corporate Location,* November 20, 2000, p. B13A.

Tuck, Barbara. "Israel: A Remarkable Hotbed for Hi-Tech." *Computer Designs: Electronic Systems Technology and Design,* 36:7 (July 1997), pp. 16–22.

"Ukraine's Grim Choice." *The Economist* (London), October 23, 1999, p. 55.

"The Ukrainian Question: With Leonid Kuchma Still President, Can the West Do Anything to Make Ukraine Less Awful?" *The Economist* (London), November 20, 1999, pp. 19–20.

Understanding the Digital Divide. Geneva: Organization for Economic Cooperation and Development, 2001.

Ungerer, H., and N. P. Costello. *Telecommunications in Europe.* Brussels: Commission of the European Communities, 1988.

"'Uniquely Chinese Internet' to Be Built Through China C-Net Strategic Alliance." Trans. and summarized from an article in *Xinhua News Agency,* January 6, 2001, appearing in *China Online,* January 9, 2001.

"U.S.-Russia Foundation to Invest in Russia." *Russian Business Monitor,* June 19, 2000.

Useem, Andrea. "Wiring African Universities Proves a Formidable Challenge." *Chronicle of Higher Education,* April 2, 1999, p. A51.

"USTR Says Mexico, Colombia, Taiwan, South Africa Must Open Telecom Markets." *AFX-Asia,* April 2, 2001, pp. 1–2.

"The Value of Mobile." *Communications International* (London), 2:27 (February 2000), pp. 50–53.

Varoli, John. "In Bleak Russia, a Young Man's Thoughts Turn to Hacking." *New York Times,* June 29, 2000, p. G10.

———. "A Wide Open Mobile Phone Market." *New York Times,* November 28, 2000, p. W1.

"Venture Capital in Hungary Amounts to U.S.D. 800m." *MTI Econews* (Budapest), November 30, 2000.

"The Very Long Arms of Its Law." *The Economist* (London), December 16, 2000, pp. 57–58.

Vintar, Mirko, and Mitja Decman. "Telematics in the Service of Democracy: The Slovenian Parliament and Other Slovenian Public Institutions." *Parliamentary Affairs,* 52:3 (July 1999), pp. 451–464.

Voelker, Rebecca. "Bridging the Digital Divide." *JAMA: Journal of the American Medical Association,* 285:2 (January 10, 2001), pp. 156–159.

Vogel, Steven K. *Freer Markets, More Rules: Regulatory Reform in Advanced Industrial Countries.* Ithaca: Cornell University Press, 1996.

Vystavil, Martin. *Internet: Supporting Democratic Changes in the Post-Communist Slovak Republic.* Internet Society Paper, August 7, 1995, available at www.isoc.org/HMP/PAPER/089/abst.html.

———. *Virtual Community: Seeking the Real Influence.* Internet Society Paper, November 28, 1997, available at www.isoc.org/inet97/proceedings/G4G4_3.htm.

Wade, C. M. "China's War Against Internet Cafs." *United Press International,* April 25, 2001, pp. 1–3.

Wagstyl, Stefan. "Eastern and Central Europe: Infrastructure and Politics Hinder the Region's Online Advance." *Financial Times,* October 4, 2000, p. A13.

———. "Survey—Eurozone Economy." *Financial Times* (London), February 25, 2000, p. 5.

Wagstyl, Stefan, and Christopher Bobinski. "Poland Pays High Prices for Delaying Telecoms Selloff." *Financial Times* (London), February 9, 2000, p. 3.

"Waiting for the New India." *The Economist* (London), March 4, 2000, pp. 18–19.

"The War on the Web: A Guide to Following the War in Yugoslavia on the Internet." *The Economist* (London), May 15, 1999, p. 8.

Warkentin, Craig. *Reshaping World Politics: NGOs, the Internet, and Global Civil Society.* Lanham, MD: Rowman and Littlefield, 2001.

Warner, Tom. "Lessons for Foreign Investors in Ukraine." *Wall Street Journal,* August 16, 2000, p. A18.

Watzman, Haim. "A Virtual Jewish-Studies Program Attracts Students of Many Faiths." *Chronicle of Higher Education,* 156:34 (April 28, 2000), pp. A51–52.

"Website Set Up to Promote Romania's Image on Internet." *BBC Summary of World Broadcasts,* July 13, 2001, p. 1.

"'Web-War' Puts Knesset's Internet Site out of Service." *Mideast Mirror* (Israel), 14:207 (October 26, 2000), pp. 1–11.

Weiner, Jed. "Jordan and the Internet: Democracy Online?" *Middle East Insight,* May-June 1998, pp. 49–50.

Weiner, Tim. "U.S. Sees bin-Laden as Ringleader of Terrorist Network." *New York Times,* August 21, 1998.

Weiss, Jeffrey. "Road to Ancient Muslim Hajj Starts on Internet." *The Gazette* (Montreal), March 18, 2000, p. B2.

Weymouth, Lally. "'We Need Massive Assistance.'" *Newsweek,* December 20, 1999, p. 26.

Whalen, Jeanne. "Kyrgyzstan Poll May Cost Democratic Reputation." *Wall Street Journal,* February 22, 2000, p. A26.

———. "Russians Seek Investment with a Telecom Overhaul." *Wall Street Journal,* May 31, 2000, p. A23.

———. "Ukraine President Sees Big Election Win as Mandate for Swift Economic Reform." *Wall Street Journal,* Eastern edition, November 16, 1999, p. A22.

Wharry, Steven. "Sorry, thebest.md Is Gone." *Canadian Medical Association Journal,* 161:1 (July 13, 1999), p. 66.

Wheeler, Deborah. "In Praise of the Virtual Life: New Communications Technologies, Human Rights, Development, and the Defense of Middle Eastern Cultural Space." Available at www.cwrl.utexas.edu/~monitors/1.1/Wheeler/onedocwheeler.html.

Whelan, Carolyn. "Emerging Markets That Live up to the Name." *Fortune,* 142:14 (December 18, 2000), pp. 184–187.

Whitaker, Brian. "Online: War Games on the Net: But This Time It's for Real." *The Guardian* (London), November 30, 2000, p. 17.

———. "Saudis Claim Victory in War for Control of Web." *The Guardian* (London), May 11, 2000, p. 17.

"White and Case Advises on Slovak Telekom Sale." *International Financial Law Review,* 19:9 (September 2000), p. 13.

"Will China Tax the Internet?" Based on an article in *Caijing Shibao* [Financial Daily], May 8, 2000, trans. and summarized in *China Online,* May 11, 2000.

Williams, Karen. "Syria Plods into Net Revolution." *Times Higher Education Supplement,* iss. 1414 (December 10, 1999), pp. 14–16.

Williamson, Elizabeth. "Poland Seizes Insurer, Ejecting Foreign Investors." *Wall Street Journal,* January 10, 2001, p. A19.

———. "Poland to Name Bidder for Stake in Telecom Firm." *Wall Street Journal,* May 22, 2000, p. C11E.

"Windows 2000 to Open New Opportunities for Middle East." *DITnet.ITNEWS,* January 20, 2000.

Winestock, Geoff, and Matthew Kaminski. "Preparing for the Enlargement, EU Agrees to an Overhaul—France Summit Paves Way for Effort to Bring in up to 12 New Members." *Wall Street Journal,* December 12, 2000, p. A23.

"The Wiring of India." *The Economist* (London), May 27, 2000, pp. 63–64.

"Wiring the Wilderness: South African Telecoms." *The Economist* (London), June 10, 2000, pp. 67–69.

Wirsing, Robert G. *Socialist Society and Free Enterprise Politics: A Study of Voluntary Associations in Urban India.* New Delhi: Vikas, 1977.

"With the Death of Hafez Assad, Syria Appears to Have Lost a Dictator and Gained an Ophthalmologist." *The Economist* (London), June 17, 2000, p. 120.

Wolfe, Elizabeth. "Russia Ranks 42nd in E-Readiness. *The Moscow Times,* May 16, 2001, p. 8.

Wolosky, Lee S. "Putin's Plutocrat Problem." *Foreign Affairs,* 79:2 (March-April 2000), pp. 18–31.

"Women NGO Group Pledges Support to Islam and All It Stands For." *Middle East News Items,* July 29, 1999.

Woodard, Colin. "Transylvania Goes On-Line with Internet." *Christian Science Monitor,* April 27, 1995, p. 5.

Woodard, Joe. "No Heroes in This War." *Alberta Report/Newsmagazine,* 26:18 (April 26, 1999), pp. 8–14.

"World: Middle East Khomeini Immortalised Online." *BBC Monitoring Reports,* June 10, 1998.

World Telecommunication Development Report. Geneva: International Telecommunications Union, 1997.

World Telecommunication Development Report. Geneva: International Telecommunications Union, 1998.

Wresch, William. *Disconnected: Haves and Have-Nots in the Information Age.* New Brunswick: Rutgers University Press, 1996.

Wright, Robert. "Croatia: New Government Looks to EU Accession." *Financial Times* (London), February 11, 2000.

———. "Slovenia Looks to Liberalisation." *Financial Times* (London), April 19, 2000, p. 2.

Wu, Timothy. "Cyberspace Sovereignty? The Internet and the International System." *Harvard Journal of Law and Technology,* 10 (summer 1997), pp. 647–666.

———. "When Law and the Internet First Met." *Green Bag2nd,* 3 (winter 2000), pp. 175–178.

Yang, Catherine, and Robert McNatt. "The Net Frenzy Feeds Even Tiny Moldova." *Business Week,* November 22, 1999, pp. 8–9.

Yeomans, Matthew. "Planet Web: The Language Gap." *Standard,* January 20, 2000.

Yevreinov, Alexander. "Encrypt Your Messages." *Moscow News,* June 16, 1999.

Young, Oran R. "Regime Dynamics: The Rise and Fall of International Regimes," in *International Regimes,* ed. Stephen Krasner. Ithaca: Cornell University Press, 1983, pp. 93–113.

Zacher, Mark W., and Brent A. Sutton (eds.). *Governing Global Networks: International Regimes for Transportation and Communications.* Cambridge: Cambridge University Press, 1996.

Zahlan, Antoine B. "The Impact of Technology Change on the Nineteenth Century Arab World," in *Between the State and Islam,* eds. Charles E. Butterworth and I. William Zartman. New York: Cambridge University Press, 2000, pp. 143–187.

———. "Technology: A Disintegrative Factor in the Arab World," in *Middle East Dilemma: The Politics and Economics of Arab Integration,* ed. Michael C. Hudson. New York: Columbia University Press, in association with the Center for Contemporary Arab Studies, Georgetown University, 1999, pp. 259–278.

Zalewski, Tomasz. "Poland: Telecommunications, the Millennium, the Internet and Beyond." *International Financial Law Review* (London), January 2000, pp. 37–39.

Zanini, Michele. "Middle Eastern Terrorism and Netwar." *Studies in Conflict and Terrorism,* 23:3 (July-September 1999), pp. 247–256.

Index

About the Book

L aunching into Cyberspace explores the Internet as an increasingly important variable in the study of comparative politics and international relations in diverse national settings.

Focusing on Africa, the Middle East, Central and Eastern Europe, Eurasia, China, and India, Franda examines the extent to which Internet development has (or has not) taken place and the relationship between that development and the conduct of international relations. His case studies—incorporating an analysis of such wide-ranging variables as language and literacy, cultural values, political parties, leadership, and the availability of capital and technological expertise—also illuminate policy processes in differing political systems.

Franda provides new insights into the diffusion of the international Internet regime from its original moorings in the United States, western Europe, and Japan and, especially, to the understanding of Internet development as a major issue on the global policy agenda.

Marcus Franda is professor of government and politics at the University of Maryland. His numerous publications include *Governing the Internet: The Emergence of an International Regime.*

0043
8632